City of Gold

City of Gold
An Apology for Global Capitalism in a Time of Discontent

David A. Westbrook

Associate Professor of Law
State University of New York
at Buffalo

ROUTLEDGE
NEW YORK AND LONDON

Published in 2004 by
Routledge
29 West 35th Street
New York, NY 10001
www.routledge-ny.com

Published in Great Britain by
Routledge
11 New Fetter Lane
London EC4P 4EE
www.routledge.co.uk

Routledge is an imprint of the Taylor and Francis Group.
Printed in the United States of America on acid-free paper.

10 9 8 7 6 5 4 3 2 1

Library of Congress Cataloging-in-Publication Data

Westbrook, David A.
  City of gold : an apology for global capitalism in a time of discontent / by David A.
Westbrook.
    p. cm.
Includes bibliographical references and index.
  ISBN 0-415-94539-9 (hardcover : alk. paper) — ISBN 0-415-94540-2
(pbk. : alk. paper)
 1. International economic integration—Political aspects. 2. International economic
integration—Social aspects. 3. Capitalism—Political aspects. 4. Capitalism—Social
aspects. 5. Globalization. 6. Economic development. I. Title.
  HF1418.5.W44 2003
  337—dc21

                                                                          2003006596

Contents

v

Acknowledgments

I have been lashed to this fish long enough. By way of cutting the line and starting to make my way home, let me thank some of the many people who have helped me finish this book. As is customary, I will try to thank the most prominent, but this list is far from complete, cannot be complete, and I hope that my sins of omission will be forgiven.

I thank my colleagues and students at the State University of New York at Buffalo Law School for their patience, interest, and unobtrusive support. The willingness of the administration, especially Deans Nils Olsen and Peter Pitegoff, to support such an ambitious project is quite appreciated (it would have been all too easy to ask for more law review articles). I thank my students for the opportunity to teach them much of the substance of this book; my thought has certainly benefited from the rigors of exposition. Intrusive support has been welcomed from fellow villagers in East Aurora ("What chapter?!") and from friends around the world.

Turning to the messy business of producing a text, Henning Gutmann took the safety off by introducing himself to me at a conference where I had been obstreperous, said he liked my comments, and solicited a proposal for this, a primary work by an obscure author. Crossing the endless plains of drafting, and even into the tangled thickets of publishing, Guyora Binder, Barry Boyer, Jim Chen, Mary Ann Glendon, David Kennedy, Phil Halpern, Tom Headrick, Estelle Lau, George Marcus, Frank Michelman, Marc Miller, Susan Silbey, Siva Vaidhyanathan, and Jim Wooten were supportive of me, each in their own way. Pierre d'Argent, Rosa Lastra, Betty Mensch, and Pierre Schlag made especially helpful comments, for which I remain grateful. I also appreciate the hard and often obscure work done by my research assistants, Joseph Barker, Stephen Coolbaugh, Lisa Danish, Jonathan Duncan, Maggie Juliano, and Charles Miller. I have been told that the real editor was an extinct species, but I found one in Dave McBride, who read and even reread the text, and did so very well. His objections were so good they were almost welcome at the time, and are deeply appreciated now. My secretary (a nobler word than "administrative assistant") Barb Kennedy has done a great job of getting this text out, and perhaps as importantly, has made sure the barn did not burn down while my attention was so focused. Angela Chnapko, Nikki Hirschman, and Donna Capato at Routledge have also been very helpful. The mistakes and limitations that remain in the text are my responsibility.

As I have already suggested, I cannot properly thank all those who helped me write this book. I cannot account for, much less clear, what our commercial society misleadingly calls "debts," because thought and influence and expression do not work that way. Suffice it to say that I have come to realize how many people have helped me over the decades with their learning, their conversations, and when necessary (it has been necessary) their indulgence. I have been very well treated, and for that I am deeply grateful.

That said, let me mention three fortuitous encounters that allowed me to write this particular philosophy of money and politics after World War Two. First, the remarkable Brandon Becker (anthropologist, bureaucrat, securities lawyer extraordinaire, brilliant dinner companion) helped me develop a structural approach to our financial markets. Second, my reading of James Buchan's beautiful yet problematic book *Frozen Desire* not only eerily recalled a poem I had just finished writing, but also seemed to point a way for a contemporary humanistic sensibility to address what it means to live together in a world structured by finance. And in my efforts to think and write about money against the grain of the professional meritocracy, to earn my own text, I could not ask for a better colleague, reader, or friend than Jack Schlegel.

A big book perforce feels like something of a summation, and in thus encapsulating a portion of one's life, a book can serve as a reminder of how support and expectation and obligation are intertwined across generations. My mother taught me to think about internationalism as a response to war. My father repeatedly has told me that all I have written, I took from him. This is true enough, but artists steal, and it is a real act of filial piety that I give him this much attribution. My brothers believed in me when doubt was more advisable, indeed, kept me from doubting myself. Finally, my wife Amy—perhaps I would have held the disparate strands of my longing together these many years without her, but quite probably not. However that may be, my life would not have been the deepening joy (and deepening realization that it is a joy) that she and our children Thomas, Sophia, and Peter have made it.

. . . for an essay is not a provisional or incidental expression of a conviction capable of being elevated to a truth under more favorable circumstances or of being exposed as an error (the only ones of that kind are those articles or treatises, chips from the scholar's workbench, with which the learned entertain their special public); an essay is rather the unique and unalterable form assumed by a man's inner life in a decisive thought. Nothing is more foreign to it than the irresponsible and half-baked quality of thought known as subjectivism. Terms like true and false, wise and unwise, are equally inapplicable, and yet the essay is subject to laws that are no less strict for appearing to be delicate and ineffable. There have been more than a few such essayists, masters of the inner hovering life, but there would be no point in naming them. Their domain lies between religion and knowledge, between example and doctrine, between *amor intellectualis* and poetry; they are saints with and without religion, and sometimes they are also simply men on an adventure who have gone astray.

Robert Musil, The Man Without Qualities[1]

Introduction

The supranational capital markets have joined many of the world's various peoples and societies into a new polity, a single virtual metropolis. A trader can sit in Canada and deal in Poland, Thailand, South Africa, and Chile. The communicative space thereby established among Toronto, Warsaw, Bangkok, Johannesburg, and Santiago not only spans the globe, it establishes a cultural context. A seemingly simple order to buy stock in a company rests on a great deal of shared and legally enforceable culture: contracts must be formed; the order must be cleared; payments must be made and accepted; accounts must be settled and agreed to; property rights and hence local control must be conveyed. Language, contractual obligation, institutional relation, money, accounting, property, and hence deeper matters like the past, the future, the individual, and the exercise of the will, must be understood in similar ways. Phenomena traditionally considered local, the stuff of daily life, like housing starts, available medical care, and the price of fuel oil, reflect such activity in the international capital markets. As a result, this communicative space has become the frame of reference for those who care about money or the things money buys, and, more broadly, for those who care about politics, and more broadly still, those who care about the efforts to make sense of our time that we call culture, art, literature, religion and such. For us, the world is a City of Gold, a polity defined by the flow of capital, and that ancient dream, to be a citizen of the world, has become an everyday and not altogether comfortable reality. *This apology attempts to describe the polity created by supranational capitalism, and to provide a defense, albeit partial, for how that polity's inhabitants, we, live.*

The idea that supranational capitalism needs a defense may seem a bit odd to some. In 1989 the Berlin Wall fell, and all the world, except a few bitter professors, acknowledged what conservatives, in the United States especially, had been saying for a century or so: The communists were wrong. After a brief hesitation in the early '90s, the paradigmatic capitalist economy, that of the United States, then commenced to enjoy a most wonderful decade. Real growth was disputed but up substantially; real rates of inflation were disputed but down substantially; unemployment was less disputed but low.[1] What more defense could supranational capitalism, and by extension, the City of Gold, need? Even in the 1990s it was easy enough to point out that other developed countries were not doing so well, and the majority of this world was in poverty, but did that not make the American economy exemplary? Although this may not have been quite the best of all possible worlds, the U.S. economy, the engine of the world economy, generated more wealth for more people than any economy, anywhere, had done. There was serious talk of an economic transformation comparable to the industrial revolution, and widespread consensus that the center of the transformation was the United States. In 2000 the boom, by many measures the largest in U.S. history, came to an end. The stock market indices, and to lesser extent the real economy in the United States, began a downturn that continued as the writing of this book drew to a close. However, the most capitalistic of the developed countries nonetheless remains far and away the most successful, at least in terms of raw economic output. Although the boom has ended, market ideology remains regnant. As countless commentators have remarked, generalized faith in markets is both widespread and deep, not only in the United States but in most quarters of the globe, despite crises ranging from currency failures in Latin America and East Asia, to ongoing chaos in Africa, to the persistent failure of the Japanese economy to recover its traditional vigor, and to accounting scandals in the United States. Since the fall of the Berlin Wall, such problems have been widely understood to be problems, rather than indictments of capitalism itself. More profoundly, the belief that our economy has undergone a deep transformation, generally conceived as a shift from an emphasis on the production of goods to the control of information, has persisted, and it seems undeniable that the new economy is capitalistic in character.

One might be surprised that supranational capitalism needs a defense for reasons quite apart from the system's ability to generate wealth. One might expect that the Cold War decades of ideological struggle would have forged a powerful and generally accepted articulation of the world that we in the West have been trying to construct, and have been willing to defend with nuclear weapons. We appear to have achieved some version of that world, and so should we not be content, if ever a culture were, to rest on our laurels?

Yet these same times have also seen widespread expressions of disfavor with capitalism. Recent meetings of the Bretton Woods Institutions and other symbols of globalization have occasioned massive protests, and a sense of discontent is common even among the affluent classes who have benefited so much from globalization. In response, some establishment commentators (i) have attempted to articulate, however clumsily, arguments they believe express the frustrations that lie at the root of the protests, arguments that the protesters might have made had they been sufficiently coherent, such as globalization hurts the poor, harms the environment, threatens human rights, increases inequality, and so on. Such establishment commentators then tend (ii) to argue that supranational capitalism does not, in fact, do the bad things in question, generally on the basis of a recitation of David Ricardo's comparative advantage mantra (free trade increases the wealth of even poor countries, so long as they do whatever they do best) and the capitalistic intentions of most developing nations.

Like many defenders of the status quo, this book begins with an attempt to articulate the discontent with capitalism, expressed on the streets of cities like Seattle, Washington, Prague, and Nice, and in more thoughtful quarters throughout the G-8 societies. Rather than complaints over specific negative consequences of a definite set of practices called globalization, this book understands the widely if vaguely voiced discontent with globalization to be rather inchoate expressions of frustration with the essential character of contemporary political life. This apology attempts to render such frustrations into arguments on the basis of a theorization of contemporary political life, i.e., a theorization of modern capitalism. The book then attempts to respond to such arguments, that is, asks whether a less frustrated modernity is possible, and whether our frustrations might not have their own justifications. From the beginning, however, it is obvious that one of the things that much, perhaps most all, of the frustration is not about is insufficient material wealth, for the simple reason that wealth has never been so abundant, and many of the discontents (including the vast majority of those who travel great distances to protest, and virtually everyone in a position to read this book) are comfortable by almost any material standard. To respond from Ricardo, then, is profoundly and laughably to miss the point.

Although it is difficult to judge whether the protests against supranational capitalism are more foolish than the defenses for it, the antic quality of political posturing reveals a deeper problem: capitalism (as currently understood by either the left or the right) is an inadequate ideology for the polity created by supranational finance. Contemporary capitalism cannot explain the City of Gold to its inhabitants, and therefore cannot serve as the basis for sensible political discourse. The errors of our communist adversaries once provided justifications for our own society, but now that the adversaries are gone and we can think in peace, our old justifications have come to seem insufficient. Thus the fall of the Berlin Wall and the associated collapse of Marxian thought have perversely revealed the poverty, rather than the strength, of our own ideology.[2] Simply put, communism was indeed wrong, but that does not make us right.

Any number of recent developments highlight the fundamental questions now at issue for which traditional thinking about capitalism provides scant answers. Consider the following examples:

A. The widespread rejection of Marxism inevitably led to practical and specific—as opposed to ideological and abstract—questions regarding what sort of societies should be developed, and how to go about doing so. The United States and others have been quick to provide answers, but it is difficult to gauge the success of such answers. Certainly capitalist solutions have preceded much unhappiness, for example, in Russia, in East Asia, and in much of Latin America. On the other hand, it is not clear whether, or how, such countries could have confronted their histories better. Or, for that matter, whether and how developed market societies, such as the United States, could be better constituted. In each of these cases, one may presume that much of society will be articulated through markets, and still ask whether the situation is being well handled. Such nuanced questions cannot be answered by simple reference to a generic ideal of capitalism.

B. The fabric of civil life in the United States is increasingly permeated with capital. More and more Americans use the financial markets to plan for retirement; compensation of American corporate management is driven by equity incentives rather than wages; even the workforce has begun to understand itself in terms of (human) capital. Can we all be capitalists? Even if we can, are we comfortable with the consequences of making capital so central to our identities?

C. The financial markets are quite dependent on government, despite books claiming that markets have triumphed over government. For example, in January, 1998, Treasury secretary Robert Rubin and Federal Reserve Board chairman Alan Greenspan asked Congress to vote funds for the International Monetary Fund's bailout of various East Asian countries in order to forestall possible economic harm to the United States. For another example from the same year, in September, 1998, the New York Branch of the Federal Reserve Bank of the United States, worried about systemic risk, forced a number of almost unimaginably large financial institutions, including several foreign ones, into what might be called a work-out of Long Term Capital Management, a distressed hedge fund. For a final example, worries about fundamental weaknesses in the capital markets such as the risk of inflation or a stock market bubble continually occasion calls for government action (in these cases, usually tight monetary policy). That is, capitalism seems to require a competing ideology (presumably liberal democracy) to legitimate the regulatory bureaucracy that capitalism seems to require, but it is unclear what the relationships between these ideologies might be.

D. The responsibility of traditional governments, in the context of contemporary finance, remains unclear. For example, in joining the European Economic and Monetary Union (EMU), national governments agreed to give up their currencies, and to cede almost all control over monetary policy to a central bank largely unaccountable to electorates or markets. But central banks have only limited capacity to steer markets, raising the problem with which we began: what sort of governance, national or otherwise, is possible at this point in history?

Such developments suggest why capitalism, as currently understood, inadequately articulates our situation. Whether used by the left or the right, the word "capitalism" denotes a set of positions in the old-fashioned bifurcation between markets and governments, specifically, capitalism is the ideology of market activity as opposed to government activity. This bifurcation between markets and government structures many discussions of globalization, discussions in which globalization is presented as an historic shift from governments to markets.[3] But markets are themselves a system of governance, a mode of social arrangement. Choosing to conduct ourselves through markets as opposed to another mechanism of governance (such as a legislature, court, bureaucracy, and so on) is an essentially political choice. Therefore the common understanding of capitalism as government's antagonist makes it difficult to think clearly about capitalism as government, that is, about the mechanism most fundamental to global politics. Because it clouds contemporary political thought, the bifurcation between markets and government, already present in Adam Smith and mightily encouraged by Marx, needs to be put aside for a while, perhaps to be revived later but only under stringent conditions.

Our political thought should start by understanding that markets do not make government unnecessary; markets are a type of government. Governance is an unavoidable task, an activity that takes place within any group of humans, including the far flung band of people who more or less self-consciously participate in the processes we call globalization. Markets are the institutional devices such people, we, have chosen to govern a wide range of matters. Mechanisms of governance, in this case capital markets, are important because such mechanisms are literally constitutional, they inform the character of the society they govern, and so human lives. Supranational capitalism structures the way we live together, and thus our understanding of politics, and hence our own identities. In order to live together in their world, people around the planet share minutely detailed and fundamental faiths about the nature of communication, property, time, community, self, and so forth. We should ask our global society the usual simple but difficult political questions: Is the government true? Is the society just? Is life here admirable? A capitalism that acknowledges rather than denies its essentially political nature, a serious capitalism, must confront such questions.

This book is about "globalization," the inescapable name for the ill-defined collection of historical processes that have brought us to the current state of affairs, and more specifically, about how supranational capitalism has created a new form of political life, a form that in fact dominates the planet.[4] Apart from the title and this introduction, however, the word "globalization," is used sparingly, because the supranational capital markets are not, and are not soon likely to be, as broad, nor as deep, nor as total, as the term implies. First, the capital markets are only everywhere you want to be, and that is not everywhere—capital flows in many poor countries are negligible. Even truly emerging markets, notably the Asian tigers, remain miniscule compared to the markets of the developed world. The persistence of phrases like "emerging markets" and "developing nations" ought to remind us that modernity has not yet achieved its universal aspirations, and hence it is a bit premature to speak of globalization, except perhaps as an uneven historical current. Second, with regard to the depth of the markets, it is healthy to remember (before we embark on an inquiry into the nature of capitalist politics) that much of the world, even in the United States, is relatively untouched by, and certainly unconscious of, the ebb and flow of finance. Although unprecedented numbers of people are directly and indirectly involved in the capital markets, not all people are affluent. While the concerns of the relatively rich are vital to politics, it is obnoxious for us to forget that we are not the world. Third, capitalism is by its terms an insufficient way of understanding how contemporary societies organize either the public or the private realms, and hence the totalizing ring of "globalization," is misleading. Dominance is not everything. And for all its importance, globalization in practice remains less than the term implies. This book, however, will explore globalization as if it were fully achieved, as a book on democratic theory is likely to take, as a working presumption, the democratic character of its audience and their government.

"Globalization," does suggest a vitally important aspect of our situation—the success of modernity's efforts to conquer space. The trader in Toronto is the product of highly evolved sequences of technologies that make distance less of an obstacle to trade. The trader may communicate electronically, in the medium of his choice, with all of the parts of the world with which he is concerned. At least as a matter of data transmission, such communication is for all practical purposes instant and perfect. Transportation of objects heavier than ideas, though not quite as quick, is almost as amazing. From the steamship to the railroad to the highway to the automobile to the airplane to the interstate to intermodal shipping, the costs of transportation have fallen so far that when the financial economy affects the real economy, the distance separating objects is less important than it has ever been before. The costs of transportation have fallen so far that our hypothetical trader might be involved in one of the current schemes to ship fresh water from the lakes outside his office to deserts on the other side of the world. So the trader, and the economy he has helped build, is hardly constrained by brute geography. And neither are consumers, when they fuel cars or go grocery shopping or engage in other activities that require materials to be moved across thousands of miles and dozens of national borders.[5]

The political significance of the technological conquest of space is commonly misstated. One frequently hears arguments to the effect that the state has become irrelevant in global markets, because the economy recently has grown too big and too interconnected to be the object of politics. Looking across history and cultures, however, we see any number of situations in which the economy was defined on a geographic area greater than the territory of the state. Communication and transportation were indubitably slower, but Homer's horizons extend far beyond the borders of any king's realm. For the Mediterranean world over the millennia, or most of medieval Europe, it makes no sense to talk about economies in terms of principalities. Victorian England was more dependent on foreign trade than the United States currently is, or is likely to become. Sovereignty was hardly irrelevant in such times and places.

The general understanding of the historical significance of globalization reflects the centrality of the nation to our conceptualization of not only political life, but also economic life (the *Wealth of Nations*, the Gross Domestic Product, and so forth). The French and the American Revolutions, and certainly the Russian Revolution and the New Deal, expanded the role of the centralized state in the life of the nation, and in so doing, fostered the tendency to think of the economy in national terms, indeed, as the object of national economic policy. During the Cold War, the very real drama of nuclear confrontation ensured that life, including political economy, would be understood in national categories. (Nuclear weapons, after all, are owned and operated by national governments.) Thus the history and drama of national politics has long made it difficult to think about political economy outside of the conceptual apparatus of the nation state. From this perspective, the main significance of globalization is negative, the end of the nation state. But now that the Cold War is over, we are able to think less nationalistically, and wonder what globalization might mean on its own terms.

A related confusion surrounds the question of when globalization began. Globalization is widely understood to be a very recent turn in world history, largely brought about by the end of the Cold War and the rise of the Internet, and, in at least some accounts, by the social movements (the sexual revolution, feminism, environmentalism, and so forth) associated with the 1960s and '70s. Without denying the relevance of such developments, it is important to recall that the *political* institutions of our globalization are not that new, and all date from at least a generation earlier, the end of the Second World War. Globalization seems so sudden to so many people at least in part because they have abandoned the tacit expectation of the last few generations, that the economy be thought and discussed and perhaps even governed within the bounds of the nation state, and the end of the Cold War, 1989, made the national governments seem so much less important.[6] Once we no longer understood the economy through the lens of the nation state, globalization suddenly appeared to us, as if by magic. But the City of Gold has been under construction for several generations now.

It may be remarked that this book simply misunderstands the international political situation. Rather than living in the City of Gold, a single global context, we live in an environment comprised by competing, often antagonistic, and sometimes openly bellicose interests. With the decline of the Cold War's suppression of violence, we are seeing the reemergence, in different form, of the old particularities of political identity, and the resulting strife. The dissolution of Yugoslavia, the civil war in Indonesia, and the terrorist attacks on the World Trade Center demonstrate that the character of politics—hatred and war—remains essentially unchanged. From this perspective, it matters little whether the particular identities in question have national, ethnic, religious, or some other origin—the salient fact about the contemporary world is faction, not unity. At the beginning of the twenty-first century, one world is no closer than it was at the end of the nineteenth. Indeed, from this basically Hobbesian perspective, in which the natural order of things is the war of all against all, we may say that the salient aspect of any imaginable political world is violence, real or suppressed.

This is an interesting argument, and one I have devoted considerable attention to elsewhere.[7] However, this argument misses the point of the present book. Nowhere does this book claim that nationalism (or ethnic violence or religious fundamentalism) has ceased to exist or to be important. This book does not claim that the City constitutes the only political reality. At the same time, it seems undeniable that we have transformed the political context in which many of us live, a set of transformations commonly called globalization. Global markets are an important way of doing politics, if not the only way to do politics.

At the same time, the prevalence of violence and war cannot be denied, and especially from an American author publishing after September 11th, Afghanistan and Iraq, a word about the relationship between patriotism and critique is appropriate. It makes some sense to understand the resurgence of nationalism, religious zealotry, and similar tribal phenomena, as well as homegrown horrors, such as the Oklahoma City bombing, as symptoms of globalization. We reflect this understanding—of civilization versus its discontents—when we call terrorism an attack on civilization. Understanding our civilization as beleaguered may, and to some extent should, make us impatient with the sorts of critique of-fered in this book, which is filled with discontent felt, if perhaps not ex-clusively, by the privileged.

Critique, however, remains important, even insofar as this is wartime. The fact that some of the people discontent with the City may themselves be sav-age, even evil, hardly constitutes an intellectual defense of our polity. Enemies are a distraction, not an excuse, from political thought. Enmity with Persia or Sparta hardly served to silence Athenian political inquiry. Similarly, the City should be understood—both criticized and defended—in its own right. It may be that the City will fall (perhaps to resurgent nationalism), but if it does, political thinkers will have more pressing responsibilities than understanding how we in the developed world did politics in the generations following World War Two. Until then, however, we owe it to ourselves to understand our politics. It may also be the case—indeed, we must hope—that the City ex-pands its reach, that the wars are won, and the frontiers extended until, as happened in the United States, the frontier ceases to exist. At which point we should confront, if not exactly justify, our history even in our success.

Understanding the City as a way of doing politics turns out to be very hard work. Most of the metastasizing literature on globalization remains dependent on the conceptual apparatus of the nation state. As already sug-gested, such literature tends to present globalization as a pair of historical trends: the increase in human intercourse across national boundaries, and as a result, the decline of the nation as the organizing principle and guardian angel of social life. In probably the most prevalent version of the story, traffic increases across boundaries until the boundaries become meaningless, and the nation exists only as a relatively powerless adminis-trative convenience. Aficionados of large markets think this is a good thing or can easily be made into a good thing. Advocates of the social services provided by the state think this is a bad thing, and may therefore protest at the annual meeting of an international organization. Unsurprisingly, sto-ries that contradict the popular account have arisen among academics, stressing matters like the prevalence of trade at other points in history, or the continued importance of the nation. Both dominant and contrarian accounts of globalization, however, tend to tell stories in which the nation is the protagonist whose existence is challenged, and as a result, the current literature on globalization rehearses political arguments familiar to those trained in the context of the nation state. This book, in contrast, is an effort to think about globalization on its own terms, without relying unduly on the conceptual tools of another era.

This perspective requires reinterpretation of the idea of globalization as the conquest of geographical and hence of much social space. The specific mechanism of globalization that has received the most attention is inter-national trade in goods, and consequently, much of the ire directed against globalization has been addressed to the organization that forms the context for much trade negotiation, the World Trade Organization (WTO). In addition to international trade in goods, increasing attention is being paid to the rise of transnational markets for services, intellectual property (especially associated with the computer, pharmaceutical, and entertainment industries), currency (the foreign exchange markets are the world's largest), and portfolio investment capital (especially after the East Asian, Russian, and several Latin American currency crises).

Even this view of the mechanisms of globalization is too narrow. Most transnational companies compete less through trade than through foreign direct investment, i.e., a company buys or builds an affiliate in another country. Rather than moving goods, modern companies move legal entities.[8] At this point, an understanding of globalization based on motion across (formerly significant) political borders begins to be inadequate. The company that establishes itself in another country need not move much across borders. Presumably, the success of Ford in Europe is reflected on the New York Stock Exchange, even if not much beside the occasional executive or engineer travels between Köln and Dearborn. This is clearly globalization, but it is not trade.[9] To make matters more amorphous still, a market may be defined by potential, as well as actual, market activity. Transactions that might be done in other jurisdictions need not actually be done in order to create a single market. So long as Airbus is known to be able to sell planes to U.S. airlines; Boeing must reckon with the existence of the European company in what it might traditionally regard as its "home" market.[10] The ability to compete, as opposed to actual sales, disciplines prices and thereby creates a single market context, or what in other circumstances would be called a world.

Understanding markets as frames of reference leads to the central concern of this book—globalization is at bottom a process of cultural formation, and so subject to political critique. If, for example, two corporations in the developing world choose to do business under New York contract law, with a side agreement to arbitrate any disputes that might arise in London, and with the transaction to be denominated in yen or some other hard currency, then those actors are globalizing, even if all the players and the substance of the transaction are local. Those actors understand their business in a way that has little or nothing to do with their nationality or local culture. From this perspective, the significance of the globalization of services (diplomatically expressed by the shift of emphasis from the General Agreement on Tariffs and Trade (GATT) to the General Agreement on Trade in Services (GATS) and the Agreement on Trade Related Aspects of Intellectual Property Rights (TRIPS)) is important not so much because of the dollar value of the services and rights traded, but because the widespread acceptance of services and rights shows that societies are, in important respects, homogenizing. Rephrased, globalization entails the emergence of a supranational culture, a context that cannot be reduced to the terms of the nation state, or even of trade understood as movement among discrete states.

If we return to our trader, we see that he shares profound cultural understandings with his counterparties around the planet. He even shares the concrete formalizations of the politics we call law. Nor is metropolitan culture visible only on the trading floors and in the back offices of financial professionals—it is the stuff of daily life in affluent societies everywhere. A new world, a new culture, is emerging. The geographic reach of this new world is unprecedented, surpassing even the Dar al Islam, stretching from the Strait of Gibraltar to Indonesia, or the European empires of Charles V or the British Empire, upon both of which the sun never set. Quite apart from its effects on the once European, now nearly universal, institutions of the nation state, the City of Gold is significant—and needs to be criticized—in its own right. To what extent can the City of Gold fulfill the functions traditionally expected of a polity? Are we living in a time of new politics, as this book argues, or should our circumstances instead be understood as a wasteland of ruined traditions?

And yet serious political criticism seems difficult for reasons quite apart from those mentioned above, namely our antiquated conceptual apparatus and the intrinsic difficulty of reconceptualizing politics. Recent changes have been perceived to be so sweeping that they are characterized in terms of grand historical forces, the action of "the market," or the consequences of "technology," that seem impervious to political critique, with its normative, practical, implications. Globalization is widely understood to be unstoppable, about as responsive to political thought as the weather.[11]

But politics is worth thinking about even if we are helpless to change anything (for that matter, trying to understand the weather, or the life and arrangement of the stars, is a worthwhile pursuit, too). It is a particularly American conceit to treat politics in purely practical terms, to conclude that if we cannot shape history (the traditional American concern), we need not bother thinking. Even if globalization could be shown to be so inevitable as to make all political thought futile, it would behoove us to consider our situation, just as it behooves us to think about our situation in the cosmos.

Moreover, globalization is not like the weather. While grand historical forces may well be at work in our time—they usually are—the City of Gold did not come about altogether by accident, or through the spontaneous unfolding of history, or as the inevitable result of technological progress.

The City of Gold is also the consequence of political decisions in the ordinary sense, the collective efforts of officials of the governments victorious in World War Two to solve a problem, the totalitarian danger posed by the nation state, the problem expressed most perfectly by Hitler. Philosophically phrased, the City of Gold is an answer to Leviathan's claims of hegemony over social and economic life. Substantively, the terms of the answer are economic and particularly financial, that is, the response to the failure of the nation state was to use supranational markets, particularly capital markets, to build a new sort of polity. Procedurally, the answer was made largely through treaties that established the Bretton Woods Institutions and the European institutions, and the actions of national governments that ensured that the peace following this war would be different from the settlement of prior wars. Objectively, the City of Gold, like the European Union and the United States, is a creature of legal texts, which are eminently suited to political critique.

Political forms, such as the nation state, are not immortal. From time to time, the primary form of political life, and with it the grammar of politics, changes. The polis gave way to the empire; the empire gave way to the clan, the feudal principality, and the fortified city. The corporate church and the medieval city arose, only to be supplanted by young republics and centralized monarchies . . . It is significant, perhaps even epochal, but by no means unprecedented, that politics must be rethought in light of a change in the primary form of political life. This book's attempts to understand the way we now live rest therefore, on a restatement of politics as it appears in the context of supranational capital, legitimated through our faith in the institutions of money and property, as opposed to the modern nation state, legitimated through the familiar mechanisms of the liberal republic.

* * *

The structure of this apology is dialectical, and begins from the thesis that political thought has entered a new era. Globalization is assumed, but what does it mean? What this apology terms the City of Gold, the way in which we now live together, conceptually and legally established after World War Two, and realized after the fall of the Berlin Wall, requires us to think anew about politics. The communicative space formed by financial markets is the object of political thought in our time, as the nation state was for most political thought during the time we still regard as modern, the pope, king, or emperor were the protagonists of the medieval political imagination, and the *polis* was the context of classical Greek thought. This book uses urban imagery and self-consciously revives the old Marxian personification, "capitalism," in order to solidify the understanding of financial markets as the grammar through which much contemporary political thought should take place.

Founding the City was the right thing to do. Nationalism had run its course and had become both technologically able and likely to destroy the world. For us now to imagine that a better politics was possible in the wake of World War Two is, therefore, somewhat idle. Our political inheritance is what it is. Much is well settled, and can only be undone with difficulty, probably with violence. Realizing the historical imperatives that drive contemporary politics, however, barely begins the discussion of the substance of such politics. Political thinking starts, rather than stops, with the founding of the polity. Different political forms, constitutions, present different possibilities, and have different limitations. Because the City of Gold is based—as a matter of intention, law, and practice—on finance, its character is imbued with both the possibilities and the limitations of money. Therefore, although criticism of money is not new (generations have inveighed against it), criticism of money is of special political importance to us, who have made money central to political organization in ways that it has never before been. From the perspective of the City, political economy is not a question of the wealth of nations constituted by geography, politics, religion, history, and the like. Instead, for us, money is itself constitutional, and the task for political thought is to understand what this means.

The essays in part 1 undertake to describe the occasion for, and the conceptual architecture of, the City of Gold, a *tour d'horizon* of the new political order. The essays in part 1 in turn define the City historically, synchronically, diachronically, genetically, and juridically. Part 1 concludes, however, by asking whether political life so imagined can satisfy a range of yearnings traditionally addressed by political thought. The City seems impoverished. Although brilliant, the constitutional innovation of structuring politics on the basis of markets, and specifically financial markets, appears to define social life overly narrowly, venally. In other words, even if we concede that it was correct to transform national politics through supranational capitalism, we are left asking whether supranational capitalism is enough.

The remainder of this apology is a dialectical exploration of this problem. The interrogation is loosely structured around three concerns traditional in political thought, broadly speaking, truth, justice, and virtue. So chapters VI, IX, and XII ask what we can know together. What truths does the City of Gold claim? Chapters VII, X, and XIII wonder what the political virtue of our polity is. In what sense, if any, is our social order just? Chapters VIII, XI, and XIV ask how an inhabitant of the City should regard her citizenship. What can identity, virtue, or honor mean in the City of Gold?

Each question is asked three times, because different parts of the book approach the City from different perspectives, perspectives that are compelled by the dialectical structure of the underlying argument. As mentioned, part 1 is descriptive, and the traditional philosophical questions are raised only *en passant*. The essays in part 2, however, explicitly raise such questions, and do so from within the City. The essays in part 2 deepen our understanding of the structural limitations of the City by asking, how, if at all, can supranational capitalism, on its own terms, satisfy very traditional longings: What can we know collectively? How do we think about justice? How do we understand ourselves as citizens? What does it mean to suggest that all of politics—or all the politics that really matter—is to be lived on monetary terms? The answers are hardly pretty. Part 2 charges that the City of Gold is not an achieved polity, that humans yearn for more than the City can possibly provide. If this is so, then the City must be deemed, in important respects, a failure, a polity that dehumanizes.

More specifically, the City's failure to articulate a truth makes contempt the central intellectual attitude (chapter VI). The phoniness of the City makes it unworthy of allegiance, and thus makes thinking about justice difficult if not impossible—and a society that has no sense of justice is a loathsome thing (chapter VII). And an unwillingness to consider oneself a slave—a desire for some human nobility—forces citizens to construct private realms in tacit opposition to the City (chapter VIII). More graphically put, these failures seem to lie near the roots of our contemporary intellectual life, our culture of shallow experience and ruthless politics, and most of all, our violence.

By way of response to these charges, part 3 will turn to familiar intellectual approaches to market societies—economics, progressive social thought, and liberalism. The essays in part 3 argue that these enlightened modes of thought do little to soften the charges spelled out in part 2. Our familiar thoughts tend to be inapt, because they were conceived in other contexts, addressed a different world, and can hardly be applied directly to our present circumstances.

Specifically, the discipline of economics discussed in chapter IX is unable to relieve the sense of alienation discussed in chapter VI. Economists cannot adequately respond to the critiques of globalization because they cannot provide a compelling vision of the truth, in the sense of necessity, of the City's politics. A more sophisticated economics is imaginable, but is likely to be even less definite, and therefore is even less likely to comfort the individual. Conversely and as a result of our lack of faith in economics, the City is founded and articulated in untruth.

In response to chapter VII's discussion of metropolitan social life as a fabric of lies, inauthentic rather than just, chapter X asks whether the labor market could be structured in just fashion. This would require that the price mechanism both reflect the meaning of work to the worker, and organize workers in some defensible collective whole. It quickly emerges that this aspiration is a mistake: the price mechanism simply does not account for the meaning of work. By extension, the labor market—and, we may presume, other aspects of the society constructed by markets—has no genetic relationship to the right order of things. They may be fair in the formal sense of conformity to the rules of trade, but no deeper notion of justice seems available to our markets, and hence to the City.

What does citizenship mean in this polity? Chapter VIII argues that metropolitan citizenship is a very partial affair, in which public life is understood in terms of the near future of financial convention and advertising temptation, terms that constrain human possibility even as we celebrate the freedom of choice. As a defense, we define private realms in which—one may hope—more meaningful existence is possible. In response, chapter XI explores liberal efforts to make such private selves the building blocks of a political ideology, a personal identity, and even a religion. These efforts are uncompelling: though liberalism has become the virtually unchallenged rhetoric of our politics (in which the self is publicly validated, if only as a personification of capitalism), its efforts to fulfill psychic functions, like creating an identity or an account of the meaning of things, have run their courses. Liberalism has not even delivered a substantive political theory; the best that it seems capable of is ceaseless efforts to substitute formality (on the model of property law) for substance. Chapter XI thus suggests that liberalism can no longer provide an ethos in which the thoughtful citizen is truly at home.

The inadequacy of our inherited thoughts does not make these questions go away. We are left with a polity founded on markets. Americans in particular tend to justify the act of thinking—as if thinking needed an excuse—on practical grounds: one provides a political service by thinking about the ever present question, what is to be done? As ever, that is a good question, and one which we cannot really think about from within the financial grammar of contemporary political discourse. But the urgency of the traditional radical formulation is a bit melodramatic. Nothing needs to be understood anytime soon. Politicians and business folk can be expected to take care of themselves and thus our affairs prior to attaining enlightenment. Still, we may hope for a thoughtful politics, and that presumes we think.

It would be disingenuous, however, to claim that the arguments made in this apology are offered in a spirit of republican usefulness, as nice as that might be. This book is written for other purposes. As thinkers, we tend to require normative conclusions to critical arguments, even idle proposals

based upon impotent arguments, for good reason. We must compose ourselves in some relationship to our society, about which we must have some
idea. The need for perspective, for myth, is inescapable, because we require
a stance. How should we feel about our world? while finishing up the Sun-
day morning papers and drinking superfluous coffee. Must we simply concede the criticisms of part 2, and defend the City on the basis of necessity
and the horror of history, or can we say something more positive about
how we live now?

One way to start is by reasking political questions, almost as if for the
first time, not about our texts (as important as they are, especially to academics), but about our world. The fact that we need to think anew does
not mean the world itself is new, young, or unformed. We are everywhere
informed by practice and by history; the raw materials for political
thought are everywhere around us. Precisely because the politics that we
can articulate and justify to ourselves is so different from the way we actually live together, precisely because our words are inapt, formulated for
other ages, we live in a time of opportunity for political thought. The task
is to think about what the life we actually live together means. We should
begin this task by confronting the world anew, by retraversing ground we
thought we had covered long before. We should turn to our history and to
our actual practice in order to begin thinking about our politics. The owl
of Minerva may have gone to sleep for the day, but Socrates washes his face
and goes to the market, starts over, and so should we.

In this spirit, the essays in part 4 explore ways in which the human
yearnings addressed in part 2 may be satisfied, at least partially, within the
context of the City and without undue reliance on the exhausted philosophies discussed in part 3. The City comprises a world (described in part 1)
with shared suppositions about history, space, time, communication, institutions, governance, and so on. There is more here than the logic of
money, for money must be situated, dealt with by humans, and so culture
is inevitable, if perhaps suppressed by the City. We see traces of this culture
even in the caustic criticisms of part 2 and 3. It is true that contempt,
loathing, and the fierce protection of a private realm are part of the story.
(To deny this is to be an ideologue for markets, a dishonest stance understandably popular among the *rentier* class and therefore our politicians,
and a major purpose of the essays in part 2 is to discourage such denial.) At
the same time, however, and as ugly as life in the City can be, these same essays suggest that our society affords efforts at truth and beauty, that markets have their own morality and faint traces of authenticity, and that from
a certain remove, we may philosophize and even laugh about life in market
societies. Similarly, although the essays in part 3 discuss the exhaustion of
our inherited modes of thinking about political life, even here we can find

possibilities: discrediting economics as physics suggests a more worldly philosophy; abandoning the idea that markets automatically generate justice and ought to be left alone might foster a more sympathetic and humble politics; and recognizing the limits of liberalism encourages us to take responsibility for the exercise of power. Such fragments and ruins are a quarry, a source of raw materials we can use to build a more humanistic political economy. The essays in part 4 are preliminary efforts toward accomplishing just that.

This apology concludes with a few words on the extent to which we may ever feel affection for the world we have felt it necessary to construct.

PART **1**
Desire's Constitution

Most wars end with meetings. Such meetings provide not only the terms of the peace, demarcate borders and so forth, but also the rough drafts of the stories we will later tell, in order to know what the war meant, and if the war was an important one, who we are.

Paul Delvaux, *The Congress* (1941)

So the meetings at the end of the Thirty Years' War ended with the Peace of Westphalia (1648), which again committed much of Europe to the nominalist conception of politics announced at Augsburg (1555) and soon afterwards known under the slogan *cuius regio, eius religio,* under which the ruler decides the religion of a territory. More generally ultimate things, even God, are to be decided or, after Westphalia, tolerated, by national sovereigns. The Peace of Westphalia is the traditional marker for the birth of what is still called the modern era of international politics, in which international law and relations were dominated by, even defined as, interactions between nation states, and more deeply, in which the nation was understood as the fundamental unit of our lives together.[1] Conversely, the meetings at the end of World War Two engendered plans for the economic integration of nation states. It has become evident that the processes of economic integration have as fundamentally transformed the grammar of politics as did the historical processes signified by the Treaty of Westphalia. More specifically, at the end of World War Two, supranational capitalism was used to found a new polity, the City of Gold, to supercede the nominalist nation state inaugurated at Westphalia as the fundamental unit of civilized political life. Part One of this apology sketches political life under the new constitution.

CHAPTER I

Conception

Founding of City. Bureaucratic character. Difficulties for modern political thought.
Founders' understanding of history of nationalism. Responses to nationalism. Responses
to communism. Relation between economics and politics in founder's conception.
Emergence of post-enlightenment politics.

Most polities look to a founding, a mythic point in history when the people came into being as a collectivity, from when it made sense to think in terms of "we." As with individual humans, the circumstances of a polity's birth are seen to influence the identity and career of its people. So Rome had Romulus and Remus, suckled by a wolf, and for centuries thereafter the Romans ranged the world. The Russians turned back the Teutons on the ice outside Novgorod, thereby beginning the violent half of the dialectic with Western Europe that would continue at Tannenberg, Moscow, Tannenberg again, and through the Cold War (and that would nurture not just Eisenstein and Solzhenitsyn, who treated these particular battles, but more broadly the Russian tradition of Turgenev, Tolstoy, and Dostoevsky, artists who sought a Russian identity vis-à-vis Europe). Although there has always been an England, the nation appears to have founded and lived its political life on the grass, from the meadows at Runnymede, to the playing fields of Eton, and more recently, Prime Minister Major's evocation of shadows lengthening on village greens. Lawyerly gentlemen of independent means founded the United States through enlightened argument. Such are the myths that have informed lives in other polities.

What follows is the foundational myth of the City of Gold. After World War Two, the mandarins of the victorious North Atlantic powers founded the City by fostering the "economic" integration of "free" peoples (especially those defeated in battle) across national borders. Economic integration was intended to break the identity of geography, government, economics, culture, and emotion that had too often engendered violent nationalism, and to create instead a new cosmopolitan situation, in which geography, government, economics, culture and emotion are polymorphously linked rather than coterminously arrayed. Integration was to be accomplished in three major ways: the Allied reconstruction of the Axis powers, the Bretton Woods Institutions, and, a little later, the European institutions.[1] The mandarin effort was more profoundly successful than could have been imagined by men born into another age. We now plainly see that their efforts amounted to the redesign of Western Europe and Japan, the transformation of North America, the development of great swaths of Latin America, Asia, and even some of Africa, and, through the Bretton Woods Institutions, the establishment of a supranational regime that linked and interconnected what was then called the free world, and what has since come to include most of the planet. In short, this was the birth of our world, a world which has now, in the wake of the Cold War, reached its majority.

The institutions through which the City has been constructed ("the metropolitan institutions") reflect the mandarin character of their founders. Although the reconstructions of the defeated nations were projects of limited duration, the metropolitan institutions have had decades to establish their existence and patterns of operation, their institutional characters and cultures. The metropolitan institutions work through bureaucratic toil in relative obscurity; by paying serious attention to and having involvement with contemporary thinking, that is, by possessing an openness to truths emerging from other sectors of the establishment, notably the university; by the gradual building of consensus; by cooperating with established forces in the political, corporate, and financial worlds; by possessing the ability to alter course, while rarely admitting error; and through the accretion of legal authority. The City has been established under the auspices of bureaucratic meritocracies. It is therefore unsurprising that their personnel display a filmily veiled lack of genuine egalitarian sentiment; exhibit a hubristic estimation of the manageability of facts; seem unashamed of their lack of transparency and palpable disregard for the substance, if not the form, of democracy; and the most damning, if perhaps the most difficult to articulate characteristic of the mandarins, are somehow inauthentic. In the face of perennial and often trenchant criticism along these lines, the metropolitan institutions foster the political skills pejoratively implied by the term "Byzantine": a somewhat hypocritical culture of modesty; a self-effacing desire to facilitate quiet and orderly transactions while denying the existence of institutional power; and an insistence on the necessity of whatever particular choice is under criticism, thereby disclaiming guilt for the inevitable losses. The metropolitan institutions, in short, are bureaucratic, for better and worse.

The mandarin character of our founding institutions poses a problem for our political thought. The modern political imagination remains dominated by the figure of the prince, the national sovereign, ever liable to become a tyrant. We just know that those with power inevitably try to increase the scope and depth of their power; we fear that political success culminates in totalitarianism. If power corrupts, and absolute power corrupts absolutely, then the object of political thought is to devise ways to frustrate power's tendency to tyranny. So we worry about the amorality of the prince; we find it necessary to have checks and balances and perhaps federalism and certainly rights (consider the first ten amendments to the U.S. Constitution) lest Leviathan grow too strong; we fear the tyranny of the majority; and as every administrative lawyer knows, we have a hard time thinking about bureaucracy except in terms of granting and then limiting discretion. The fear of tyranny revealed by such familiar political tropes is sensible enough, and modern political thought has done well to confront tyranny, nobly even though too often unsuccessfully.[2] However, this fear has produced a certain astigmatism, if not outright blindness, with regard to less dramatic forms of political life, in particular, bureaucracy, or more broadly, civil life conducted within a bureaucratic legal frame. The mandarin is not a prince; the bureaucrat tends to seek order and comfort rather than glory. Emphasis on the prince fosters superficial understandings of mandarin politics in general, and in particular obscures the seductiveness of orderly markets. As a result of its focus on restraining the political lust of national sovereigns, the modern political tradition fails to articulate much that is required for an understanding of the City.

Metropolitan political thought, as opposed to political thought oriented to the nation state, could begin by shifting attention from the prince to the mandarins who founded the City and who continue to serve its institutions. Rephrased, we should think less about the will to power, and more about the normative structures that inform bureaucratic policy. Such structures are not drawn on an empty canvas. Mandarins perforce learn from experience. Public policy is informed by the policy community's interpretation of historical events it believes to be relevant. History, in this sense, is a mythic and therefore normative narrative. Such history may or may not be true, but it cannot be ignored. Just as we may learn the wrong lessons from our individual experience, the received interpretation of historical events may be wrong. But the policy community nonetheless can only think, or act, or refuse to act, in terms of the history it believes it knows. Not only is the policy community informed by its understanding of history, when there is a need to act, the policy community literally must tell itself a story in the course of deciding how to act.[3]

Men like John Maynard Keynes and Harry Dexter White, George C. Marshall and Dean Acheson, Jean Monnet and Robert Schuman, members of the class of educated officials that great powers require for administrative purposes, are rarely revolutionaries. Career bureaucrats and military men, along with leading academics and businessmen called to advisory public service, are hardly the sort of men that we, romantics that we remain, might expect to make grand social changes like founding the City of Gold. But the end of World War Two was an epochal moment; the victorious understood world history to demand an epochal response. Winning the war was not enough—it was necessary to "win the peace."[4] The mandarin understanding of their times, and so what was at stake for their policies, was not without reason. By any absolute and most relative measures, World War Two was the largest war that had ever been fought. Millions and millions were dead. Whole countries were devastated. Barbarism—the Holocaust—had broken out at the heart of Europe, calling into question not only European civilization, but the very possibility of history as a progressive narrative, the notion of civilization toward which we still gesture when we speak of development. Old antagonisms between liberalism and communism had reemerged, more virulently than before, feeding war in China and beginning a sequence of violent confrontations throughout the developing world. The United States had developed a new type of weapon, with theoretically limitless power, and proven its efficacy on Japanese people. There was a widespread sense that the world would not survive the next major war, especially if it were fought with such weapons. Confronted with this situation, the history that significant parts of the North Atlantic policy community told itself implied the policies expressed by the founding of the City of Gold.

These mandarins' history may be sketched roughly as follows: The long peace following the Napoleonic Wars withered at the end of the nineteenth century. Germany and Italy united, industrialized, and fought wars in the process of forging various principalities into nation states. Russia struggled to modernize. Seeking markets and sources of raw materials, the nations of Europe entered a dangerous scramble for colonies in the as yet uncolonized parts of Africa and Asia, and competed everywhere. Acquisition of colonies required the building of navies to protect the sea lanes between the colonies and Europe; Germany's navy soon rivaled Britain's. Attempting to defend their nascent industries, the nations of Europe and the United States erected protective tariffs. Aware of the intensifying antagonisms, nations entered military alliances in an effort to ensure their own security, but only succeeded in further heightening tensions. By the time war broke out, the belligerents had industrial economies integrated along national lines, but military obligations and thus vulnerabilities that spanned the globe. As a result, there was both wherewithal and reason to continue the killing until the economies—and so, the nations themselves—imploded. War in Europe had become total.[5]

After what was for a time called the Great War, the victors met and demanded reparations from the vanquished, standard practice. The French, in particular, recalled the German levies after the Franco-Prussian War. German reparations may or may not have contributed to the hyperinflation of 1922–23, but they certainly contributed to the resentment of a large part of the German people toward France and the other Allied powers. Unwilling to enforce the impoverishment of Germany, which might have required colonizing the country, the Allies watched as the German economy was rebuilt, stronger than before, and again on a national basis. Meanwhile, even before World War One had ended in the West, the Russian government's efforts at liberalization failed, and the communists seized control of Russia.

After the armistice, there was a widespread sense that civilization somehow had to organize itself in order to prevent horrors like the Great War. A host of international institutions were founded, most notably the League of Nations. President Wilson was unable to prevent Americans, most of whom had not wanted the war, from retreating to their own shores and their own concerns. American isolationism, among other things, rendered the League, the Kellogg-Briand Pact prohibiting wars of aggression, and other expressions of pacifistic internationalism ineffectual against the rising tide of hostilities. At the same time, economic competition among nations intensified. The Smoot-Hawley Act, raising U.S. tariffs, was passed in 1930 over the protests of the economics profession.[6] Tariffs impoverished domestic consumers and encouraged other nations to erect tariffs of their own. As crossing borders became ever more expensive, contacts, experience, and horizons tended to stop at the border. Life came to be lived within the bounds of individual nations; foreigners became strangers. Nationalism was further aggravated by competitive devaluation, which led to ruinous competition.[7] When the worldwide Great Depression hit, millions of workers lost their jobs and with them their personal security, and it was easy enough to blame others (Jews, foreigners, capitalists, and so on), and to look to strong leaders for salvation. Strong leaders, in turn, sought to consolidate their power base and extend their glory in the most traditional way, warfare, or even more spectacularly, the declaration of empire, a rising sun, the rebirth of Rome, a thousand-year *Reich*. Hitler is thus the dark prince against whom metropolitan politics is organized.

Drawing on such a view of history, the North Atlantic mandarins believed that economic isolationism fostered the development of competitive national societies that were capable of, and indeed had incentives for, warfare. Prevention of future wars required the suppression of nationalism; the vehicle for such suppression was economic integration. More generally, economics came to be seen, not as opposed or ancillary to politics, but as a constitutional mechanism in its own right.[8] Properly deployed, economic interests could prevent the coalescence of the identity that had made Hitler so powerful: mass nationalism, the military power of the state, and modern industrial capacity integrated along national lines. Just as Madison thought that faction based on economic interest was the best security against the mob's seizure of the power concentrated in the new, more centralized, national government, so the North Atlantic mandarins believed that private economic connections spanning national borders could provide a web of financial interest, emotional affinity, and practical difficulties in which larval tyrants would be ensnared, unable to mature and gather their forces.[9]

This vision of an integrated peace after World War Two was established in three major institutional ways: the reconstruction of the defeated Axis powers; the establishment of the Bretton Woods Institutions and exchange rate system; and the establishment of the European Communities and their attendant institutions. Such political organizations are not achieved overnight, and planning for the peace began long before the war was over. In a series of conferences, mandarins from different countries met to discuss how the war was to be won, and what was to be done with the defeated.[10] Germany was almost exclusively the focus of negotiations by the time the war ended, because Italy had in the meantime joined the Allies. Japan was controlled solely by the United States, and so was the subject of less negotiation (mostly involving Soviet commitments to open an Eastern front), but Japan generally was to be treated in the same way as Germany. Although the consensus that emerged from these negotiations was soon to be eroded by the Cold War, the consensus held long enough to establish the institutions that would foster the new world.

The metropolitan institutions could not have been established if the Allies had not reconceived what it meant to win a war. It was agreed that, in contrast to the end of World War One, the Allied victory in World War Two was to be regarded, to the extent possible, as the liberation of people subject to military dictatorship. The dictators would be punished in accordance with the law. New laws, even new constitutions, would be enacted as necessary. Power would be organized along democratic lines, and a thoroughly modern state would be returned to the German and Japanese people as soon as practicable. The Allies, especially the United States, would maintain an extensive presence in Germany and Japan, for geopolitical reasons of their own and to support the stability of the new regime. Economies devastated by the war would be rebuilt. Rather than reparations, the Allies would provide material aid to the impoverished. Rather than salting the earth, the Allies would help to rebuild the industrial economy (with a few limitations on military technology), in part to provide markets (and some reparations), in part to prevent the resurgence of resentments such as those that followed World War One. At Harvard University on June 5, 1947, one-time General, then U.S. Secretary of State George C. Marshall announced that the United States intended to create, in cooperation with the Europeans, a massive program of credits and grants. Although not uncontroversial, such aid was openly understood to be in the interests of the United States as well as Europe. Not only did the United States hope that peace could be put on a more secure footing than it had been after World War One, deepening ideological competition with the Soviet Union, discussed further below, counseled generosity. The fact remains, however, that a program of generosity was chosen in lieu of the traditional prerogatives of the conqueror. And it appears to have worked— Allied generosity, indeed mercy in the face of extreme provocation, continued Allied presence, and the rapid reintegration of the vanquished nations into the fabric of international life ensured that there was no serious resentment, no talk of vengeance, no new belligerency in the conquered lands.

Economic reconstruction and integration was not the only approach to security at the end of the war. The Allies also created a new, global, security regime to ensure the peace, the United Nations. Unlike the old League of Nations, the new security regime was intended to have enforcement powers, and the United States, along with the other great powers, would have permanent representation in a "Security Council" empowered to conduct police actions, to go to war to ensure the peace. The Wilsonian dream would be realized at last. Rather than an alliance organized against past and possible future threats, the United Nations would prevent the outbreak of violence by creating a true community of nations, where violence between nation states was as barely thinkable and completely unfeasible as it is in a well-ordered civil society. Germany and Japan would be recreated, and as reborn, integrated into that dream. Thus the political/military and the social/economic approaches to security complemented one another.

As already suggested, policy is an expression of beliefs about history. The interwar years, to say nothing of the war years themselves, provided a powerful negative object lesson into how the international economic order should function. The metropolitan institutions can be understood as the antithesis of the economic policies leading up to and including World War Two. So, where the victors of the First World War had demanded reparations and sought to prevent the recovery of economic capacity, the mandarins sought to facilitate rebuilding. Where the interwar years had competitive devaluation and the collapse of the gold standard, the mandarins sought to construct a fixed exchange rate system.[11] Pressures on the exchange rate would be addressed by an institution that could extend credit as necessary until the pressure subsided or the currency could be repegged, the International Monetary Fund (IMF). Where the interwar years had been marked by excessive and rising tariffs, the mandarins sought to establish sensible rules for trade, tending to a free trade regime.

Placing the world on a sound economic footing after the war was over was a matter of particular concern to the British government, which had been the dominant creditor nation before the First World War, and the United States government, which was widely expected to become the dominant political, economic, and military presence on the global stage after the war. After considerable efforts on the part of the British government, led intellectually and diplomatically by John Maynard Keynes, and the United States government, led especially by the Treasury Department in the person of Harry Dexter White, two conferences were held, attended by representatives from many countries. The first, held at Atlantic City in the spring of 1944, was mostly technical. The second was held in June of 1944 at the Bretton Woods Hotel, in the shadow of Mount Washington in New Hampshire. It was there decided to establish an International Bank for Reconstruction and Development, to bring those parts of the world damaged by the war, or which had not yet developed, into the modern trading regime. The gold standard—which had in effect been a sterling standard, run by the Bank of England as de facto central banker to the world—would be replaced by an international system of fixed exchange rates, in which currencies would be pegged to the dollar. The dollar itself was pegged to gold, at a price of $35 dollars an ounce, redeemable only by other governments at the U.S. Treasury. An International Monetary Fund would be established; member governments could borrow against the fund, according to a formula, in order to bring their currencies back into line with their par values.

A separate conference, held in Havana in 1947, proposed to establish an International Trade Organization (ITO) under the auspices of the United Nations, and even concluded a charter in 1948. Due to the failure of the United States to join, however, the ITO failed, leaving trade relations to be conducted under the auspices of what had been a series of preparatory conventions, the Generalized Agreement on Tariffs and Trade. While institutionally confusing, the GATT was quite successful in bringing tariff rates down, and in broadening the conception of free trade to include less obvious, but nonetheless politically motivated, barriers to the free flow of goods. In addition, the substantive ambit of the concept of free trade has broadened, to include not only hard goods, but services, including certain capital services, and intellectual property. After decades of fairly successful negotiations and the establishment of a de facto organization, it was decided, as part of the Uruguay round of GATT negotiations, to establish the World Trade Organization, which began its existence on January 1, 1995, and is headquartered in Geneva. Thus, while somewhat newer than the other metropolitan institutions, the WTO is thus a direct descendent of the tripartite—development, trade, and currency stability—understanding of how the world economic system was to be reformed that Keynes and White reached in preparation for the Bretton Woods Conference.

In 1950, French Foreign Minister Robert Schuman, with the aid of his friend Jean Monnet, cognac merchant, banker with the American/French firm of Lazard Freres, and friend to many across Europe and in America, proposed the Schuman Plan. The essence of the plan was that the coal and steel producing capacity of France and Germany—and therewith, much of their capacity to sustain warfare—should be placed under a joint bureaucratic authority. In theory, without the ability to devote production of coal and steel to armament, it would be very difficult to set a course for war. While France and Germany, whose antagonism had been at the center of European politics for most of the past century, were the critical nations, other nations were invited to join, and did. The Schuman Plan led to the Treaty of Paris, signed in 1951. The European Coal and Steel Community went into effect in 1952. The idea of integrating economic relations across national lines—of disconnecting economic and political space—was soon expanded. In his memoirs, Jean Monnet is quite explicit about the transformational nature of such politics. From the draft of what would become Robert Schuman's proposal for the European Coal and Steel Community, he quotes: "This proposal has an essential political objective: to make a breach in the ramparts of national sovereignty which will be narrow enough to secure consent, but deep enough to open the way towards the unity that is essential to peace."[12] The two Treaties of Rome were signed in 1957, and as a result, the European Economic Community (EEC), which integrated trade across Europe, and the European Atomic Energy Commission (EURATOM), which integrated European nuclear capability, were established. The process has continued to grow, and now a bewildering array of "European" treaties, laws, and institutions, generally referred to collectively as the European Union, or more colloquially, "Europe," bind most of the continent's old enemies so tightly that, one hopes, emotional distance, antagonism, and war yet again cannot occur. This hope has been abused by the dissolution of Yugoslavia, but the European solution to the problem posed by Germany—the suppression of political enthusiasm by economic engagement—remains brilliant.

* * *

At the end of World War Two, there was another view of twentieth-century history, and another solution to the problem of fascism, and indeed of social organization, namely communism. From its theoretical beginnings, and afterward as a matter of policy, communism claimed that human identity was determined along economic as opposed to political lines. The proletariat was believed to be independent of the nation; the socialist international called together workers of the world. The dictatorship of the proletariat and the subsequent withering of the state logically entailed the abolition of the violent nationalism embodied by Hitler. From this perspective, the Nazi state was merely a particularly pathological form of industrialized capitalism.

This position had a glorious run as a political ideology. Old Russia became the communist Soviet Union in the wake of defeats at the hands of the Germans in World War One. By the time the Russians finished defeating the Germans in World War Two, the Soviet Union contained or controlled much of Asia and half of Europe, far more territory than any other state. China and much of East Asia also became communist (while remaining intensely nationalist, theory be damned) in the wake of World War Two. Marxism dominated political rhetoric and often informed government policies in much of Latin America, Africa, and Asia, and various flavors of Marxian thought shaped intellectual life worldwide. Thus the City of Gold was founded not only as a solution to the violent nationalism embodied by Hitler, but also as a polity in practical and theoretical competition with another, the communism that Stalin (along with Mao, Ho Chi Minh, Castro, and others) claimed to embody.

Quite apart from the global claims of Marxian theory, it soon became apparent that actual communist states presented threats much like those that fascist states had presented. Militarized governments with expansive ambitions that commanded both an industrialized economy and enthusiastic nationalism raised worries, regardless of the details of their ideology. The Soviet Union and other avowedly Marxist states transcended neither the supposedly bourgeois enthusiasm of nationalism nor the equally bourgeois arrangement of the modern bureaucratic state in command of a large standing army. Russians, Chinese, Vietnamese, and other peoples governed by communist states gave every evidence of thinking in terms of national culture, a reality acknowledged by the Soviet government in World War Two, when it returned to the rhetoric of protecting Mother Russia, again, from the unholy Germans. Moreover, despite theoretical problems with the bourgeois fetishization of the individual, the Soviet Union, as well as other communist nations, tended to be ruled by individual leaders with evidently dictatorial powers. That Stalin and other leaders were in fact tyrants who killed millions eventually became incontestable. The Soviet leaders, and in time the Chinese, had nuclear weapons at their command, making them all the more fearsome. In short, the fascist enemy appeared to be reborn, brown shirts exchanged for red, and a new word, "authoritarianism," was coined to describe the general danger for liberal democracy. If Hitler personified the evil against which metropolitan politics was organized, it was competition with communism that shaped the first half century of the City's ideological existence, its formative years. The willingness of government figures, mandarins, to undermine the sovereignty of nations that had treated them so well, and hence the radical character of the City of Gold, can best be understood in terms of the desperate circumstances, personified by Hitler, in which the City was founded, and the desperate threats, personified by Stalin and then Mao, with which the City was confronted in its first few decades.

Although the competition between the metropolitan and communist views of history was wide ranging, the radicalization of government officials in the West—their willingness to weaken the independence of the nation states on which their own authority rested—may be simplified by thinking about the political character of one centrally important institution, property. For the Marxists, collectivization of the means of production, and the abolition of private economic interest generally, was intended to abolish the alienation of labor, thereby engendering human solidarity. It did not work out that way, of course, but that it would not work was not apparent to many people for many years, that is, it took a long time for the Marxian faith to become unavailable to us. From the perspective of the North Atlantic mandarins, however, abolishing private property through collectivization presented an important political problem. Without private property, the shared economic interests of certain groups (which we tend to call special interests, and Madison called factions) could not be used to block the tendency of the state to become tyrannical. A choice therefore had to be made: a society, and by extension, international society, had to decide whether its constitution would seek peace through Marxian or Madisonian mechanisms, through the abolition of economic interests or the multiplication of economic interests.[13] As a philosophical matter, there was little room for accommodation.[14] Would property be used to increase the number of factions, and so neutralize the power of any one faction, as Madison had suggested? Or would solidarity be used to preclude faction? The answer to this question turned on a still deeper question, which can only be considered a question of faith. To what extent are we, as Aristotle proposed, political animals, who should build their societies upon their longing for community? Or is communal solidarity not possible for us, who live in such large modern societies? Are we condemned to some degree of alienation?[15]

The phrase "possible for us" deserves special attention, because it suggests a problem that haunts this book, the intellectual tension between acknowledging the limitations of our circumstances, on the one hand,

and the freedom of imagination, and perhaps political thought and maybe even better politics, on the other hand. In our attempts to assess our situation, we are unresolved one way or the other, constantly torn between the competing claims of history (respect for the limitations imposed on us by our situation) and social criticism (which appeals to our sense of justice, our imagination, and our hopes). It does not appear that this war can be won, that political thought can proceed very far without both recognition of experience and hope. And yet thoughts determine themselves, political convictions are formed, books are written, regulations are promulgated . . . how do such things happen? As has already been suggested by the discussion of foundational myths, resolving a hope within the context of our circumstances, of what is "possible for us," is the function of myth, understood as a moral and instructive account of history. While circumstances do not determine political thought, neither can we think free of our situation, as if we had no place and no past. Political thought is constrained, or more positively, informed, by the stories within which such thought takes place.

While many myths are durable, they are not unchanging, and from time to time there is news. Religions wither; gods fail; concentration camps are discovered; walls fall. On such bases do allegiances shift and fundamental constitutional questions get decided. So, for example, over ten years since the reunification of Germany, it is difficult if not impossible to see markets as a stage to be overcome in the course of political history.[16] From this perspective, political thought and hence argument turns on the prior configuration of deep myths that are difficult to name, much less contest. Perhaps the most important function of intellectual history is that it allows us to isolate the times and places when our structures of meaning were revised, thereby helping us to understand what we already, if inchoately, think.

The postwar era is our founding because it was then that the mythic structures on which contemporary political life is founded were substantially transformed. The mechanisms for that transformation were a set of explicitly political decisions (mostly memorialized in formal treaties among states) to integrate economies across national lines. At least vis-à-vis the constitutional politics of the earth's masses, the billions of humans who must somehow live together, Marx lost and Madison won, that is, we gave up on universal solidarity and founded the City of Gold. Our political world therefore, is just over fifty years old, not just over ten, as many commentaries on globalization assert.

The postwar developments—the founding of new institutions, the expansion of international law, the rebuilding of nations—were understood at the time to be of profound significance. Dean Acheson, Assistant Secretary of State and a participant in many of these developments (particularly the Marshall Plan), called his memoir *Present at the Creation.*[17] In the aftermath of World War Two, however, it cannot have been particularly obvious that the new economic structures would pose serious difficulties, as well as opportunities, for constitutional political thought. The structures were presented as new, quite different from anything that had been tried before, and in some important sense, apart from the familiar institutions of politics. Business and politics (narrowly understood) traditionally were seen as quite different activities, and the institutions that comprised the City of Gold have often exploited that tradition by stressing their economic natures, and downplaying their political ones. Germany would remain Germany, France would remain France, even if the European Coal and Steel Community was intended to mean that neither could effectively establish a national war-making capability. So for some period of time, many people seem to have thought that the economic arrangements made after World War Two would somehow prevent the chain of events that led to war from ever getting started, but would not transform political life in doing so.

In hindsight and stated in the abstract, the idea that the policies which founded the City of Gold were "just" economic may sound so ludicrous as to suggest bad faith. Perhaps, but in context the distinction between economics and politics seems hardly surprising, much less a sign of bad faith. Markets are easily distinguishable from other sorts of political activity such as elections, or trials, and even today, we tend to consider markets different from politics. The distinction is on display any time we speak of letting the market decide, or of the triumph of markets over government, or worry about the lack of public interest lawyers.[18] So, whatever its theoretical inadequacies, the distinction between economics and politics is still alive and well, and powerfully, if usually subconsciously, shapes how we think about our situation. Nor is this surprising. The exaggerated bifurcations of two generations, especially the Cold War bifurcation between free markets and planned economies, are likely to continue to influence our thinking for some time to come.

The idea that economics would literally become politics, would need to be considered in explicitly political terms, even while old political virtues (liberty, equality, fraternity, and others) retained a claim on our allegiance, cannot have been too clear, if for no other reason than the fact that the idea had not yet been lived. We have had centuries to think about political life in terms of the nation, and as any glance at the raft of books on globalization will confirm, old habits die hard. Certainly the vast majority of thinking in the postwar era—which was also the beginning of the Cold War—was done in profoundly national terms. No other terms were available. Since the end of the Cold War, however, the idea of a polity founded through markets has become much more obvious, easier to consider.

The political, indeed constitutional, character of the metropolitan institutions was further obscured by a great deal of important, but less profoundly new, political activity at the end of World War Two, in particular, the revival of international legalism, the flowering of international institutions, and the birth of international human rights. In view of the horror of the war, idealism seemed to be a moral imperative rather than a mere pious hope, and the international community articulated its laws more fully than ever before. War criminals were punished at Nuremberg and Tokyo. Out of the ashes of the League of Nations arose the new, more powerful, more realistic, and ultimately much more elaborate United Nations. The Permanent Court of International Justice was succeeded by the International Court of Justice. International conventions meant to secure fundamental human rights were drawn up, acceded to, and entered into force. The old idea of self-determination was reborn and conflated with the idea of anticolonialism, and the colonial empires were dismantled. While the significance of these political developments should not be minimized, it is now clear that such developments did not constitute the break between our world and that which had gone before—they were reiterations and extensions of enlightened political thought, most of which was envisaged prior to World War Two, and much of which had already been institutionalized. The League of Nations, the Permanent Court of International Justice, decolonization, and even the self-determination of peoples and human rights were not new ideas during the late 1940s, were indeed copies of earlier efforts, themselves realizations of Enlightenment dreams.

The City, however, was constituted by treaties that reflect fundamentally darker political visions. Presumably many of the founding mandarins had little understanding of the deeper significances of their actions. In general, there is no reason to assume that the participants in a historical process intend, or even understand, what they actually accomplished. So, for example, we look to Twain and Faulkner to tell us what the Civil War meant. Similarly, at the end of World War Two it may have seemed to many mandarins that restructuring international economic life was at least but not much more than a sensible complement to other important political developments, such as the founding of the United Nations. A sound international economic order might have been considered merely one of several improvements to the international environment required for long-term peace.

It is difficult not to suspect, however, that the more thoughtful minds at the City's founding were animated by a dark suspicion that politics, development, and civilization itself were limited enterprises, that beyond a certain point of sophistication, the mind becomes alien and unstable, prone to violent enthusiasms. This doubt is suggested by Keynes' remark that in the long run, we are all dead, but finds its full expression in the anxiety that pervades high German culture from Nietzsche to Mann and that came to seem prophetic after the Holocaust.[19] Behind postwar international liberalism, whether more economic or political in expression, yawns Auschwitz, and farther back, German breadlines and American soup kitchens, and farther still, Verdun, Passendale and the Battle of the Somme, the fear that civilization has limits, beyond which lie savagery: "We resort to violence because, after much long and futile talk, the simplicity of violence is an immense relief."[20]

Violence had its own demands. So many had died, but what had their deaths redeemed? In their not fully articulate answer to this question, we begin to understand why mandarins, bureaucrats, would become radicals and transform the world. Since World War One, this question—what justified the killing—had been understood in the United States to be a struggle between isolationists (who believed that American exceptionalism required distance from the corruption of the world), and internationalists, who believed that the time had come for America to fulfill its own prophecies and so reform the world. Campaigning for the League of Nations, not long before his collapse, Woodrow Wilson spoke more candidly and horrifically than perhaps any other President, not excepting Lincoln at Gettysburg:

> Again and again, my fellow citizens, mothers who lost their sons in France have come to me, and taking my hand, have shed tears upon it not only, but they have added, "God bless you, Mr. President!" Why, my fellow citizens, should they pray God to bless me? I advised the Congress of the United States to create the situation that led to the death of their sons, I ordered their sons oversea, I consented to their sons being put in the most difficult parts of the battle line, where death was certain, as in the impenetrable difficulties of the forest of Argonne. Why should they weep upon my hand and call down the blessings of God upon me? Because they believe that their boys died for something that vastly transcends any of the immediate and palpable objects of the war. They believe, and they rightly believe, that their sons saved the liberty of the world. They believe that wrapped up with the liberty of the world is the continuous protection of that liberty by the concerted powers of all civilized people. They believe that this sacrifice was made in order that other sons should not be called upon for a similar gift, the gift of life, the gift of all that died—and if we do not see this thing through, if we fulfilled the dearest present wish of Germany and now dissociated ourselves from those alongside whom we fought in the war, would not something of the halo go away from the gun over the mantelpiece, or the sword? Would not the old uniform lose something of its significance? These men were crusaders. They were not going forth to prove the might of the United States, they were going forth to prove the might of justice and right, and all the world accepted them as crusaders, and their transcendent

achievement has made all the world believe in America as it believes in no other nation organized in the modern world. There seems to me to stand between us and the rejection or qualification of this treaty the serried ranks of those boys in khaki, not only these boys who came home, but those dear ghosts that still deploy upon the fields of France.[21]

A generation and a world war later, campaigning for the United Nations, and, more generally, for the entire program of political and economic internationalism, after millions more were dead and shortly before his own death, the Wilsonian President Roosevelt said that "Never again, after cooperating with other Nations in world war to save our way of life, can we wash our hands of maintaining the peace for which we fought." The dead—those "dear ghosts"—had their own demands. "For this generation must act not only for itself, but as a trustee for all those who fell in the last war—a part of their mission unfulfilled." World War Two required nothing less than the transformation of politics. Indeed, World War One had required such a historical transformation, and the failure of the victorious allies to win that peace had not gone unpunished. The mandarins in power after World War Two determined that they would not make the same mistakes as their predecessors.

Roosevelt appears to have thought, as a great man of his generation would, that the trust owed to the fallen would be fulfilled through the politics of great men like himself and Churchill, who would set themselves and their collective institutions—the Nations United first to win the war and then to keep the peace—against those of evil men like Hitler. The sacrifices that would be demanded by the times were familiar: commitment, effort, courage. We only gradually have come to see that the sacrifice demanded of us was our belief in the sort of politics that made national crusades possible, a belief that had proven too much to bear without cracking.

* * *

The mandarins' problem was how to create a viable international order out of the ruins of the order in which they had grown up. This required a delicate balance. On the one hand, modern society needed rational, literate, educated citizens, that is, citizens with a relatively developed intellectual life. On the other hand, such minds had to be sane. Minds that could schedule trains were needed, but such minds could not be allowed to become inflamed, so that they scheduled trains to deliver, promptly, the cargo required for the Final Solution. The new politics therefore had to be rational, orderly, but at the same time, not too spirited. The petty rationality of bourgeois life, the nation of shopkeepers ridiculed by Napoleon, seemed to strike the right balance.[22] In founding the City of Gold, and regardless of their actual understanding of the limitations imposed by the human condition on politics, principled and cultured men established a polity constituted by orderly markets, that is, the cycle of arousal and satisfaction of banal desires, rather than one constituted by ideas. The victorious West bet that insanity (the rebellion against excessive consciousness, whether understood as government's demands upon the people to fulfill the dictates of History in spite of circumstances, or the superego's repression of the ego) could be avoided if the mind were to be denied, distracted by pleasantry. As philosophy, this idea was neither new nor enlightened; Plato ridiculed a similar proposal as a City of Pigs.[23] As a way of actually doing politics, however, the substitution of economic integration for ideological enthusiasm, of personal satisfaction for political passion, was the most important development of the twentieth century.[24]

The tension between the enlightened edifice of public international law and institutions (which require a certain degree of ideological enthusiasm in the form of idealism) and the City of Gold (which requires no such selfless enthusiasm) would not become evident for some time. A political understanding, the "free world," hoped that the "three legged stool" of reconstruction/development (World Bank), trade (the ITO, GATT, and now WTO), and monetary stability (the Bretton Woods currency arrangement, buttressed by the IMF) would secure the bourgeois conditions under which liberal democracy had been developed and seemed to do best. Thus, for quite a while, political liberalism coexisted rather unproblematically with economic liberalism, unified by the idea of freedom.

If the Italian High Renaissance may be defined as the brief period when the beautiful and the true were not understood to be different, we might call the years after World War Two the North Atlantic Renaissance, when the politics of desire and of principle were unselfconsciously understood to be the same thing, the politics of a free society.[25] The High Renaissance ended when it became obvious that each artist painted in his own manner, that the work of different artists would not converge on the truth (at least, no truth visible in the world), and yet art might remain beautiful. And, likewise, our Renaissance, too, has wandered into its mannerism. It has become clear that the freedom to exercise our desires, satisfied through market mechanisms, has little to do with whatever truth, freedom or otherwise, we may hope to find through the principled exercise of traditional political processes.

Certainly it has remained true that societies tend to demand both the forms of political liberalism and the forms of liberal economic life. Although political liberalism may fail (and has in Russia, Germany, and various South American countries), it appears to be more durable than any other system on offer. While liberal regimes are capable of horrors, liberalism remains, to paraphrase Churchill, the worst system except for all the others.[26] Or one may still talk like Isaiah Berlin or Karl Popper, about the dissemination of information in an open society, and conclude that political liberalism of a relatively familiar sort is necessary to secure the flow of information, technological innovation, and other good things. These are fine and orthodox arguments, particularly with regard to the alternatives presented by totalitarian regimes. And so there is scant reason to argue with such positions, so long as their fundamental limitation is understood: these arguments are concerned with the proper relationship between civil society and its prince, in a republican democracy, the collectivity of formally representational institutions that we usually and simplistically think of as "the government." However, political liberalism is less successful addressing the politics of the City of Gold, which is constituted not by the will of the prince but instead by the aggregation of desires regardless of political boundaries.

Like so much else, the deeper meaning of the City of Gold was obscured by the Cold War. The West talked about the head—the individual's liberty to think, speak, and act—and bet the constitution on the gut, the individual's ability to shop in a society organized by appetite. The East talked about the gut, the right to work and to a decent level of material wealth, but bet on the head, the individual's solidarity with a society organized by bureaucratic planning.[27] After the mostly velvet revolutions that ended the Cold War, it is clear that we were right and they were wrong as a matter of constitutional practice, but now we in the City of Gold should ask to what extent we can conceive of a politics of the head.

CHAPTER II

Money as Communication

Functional understandings of markets. Modern, not Greek, idea that market is political. Understanding market as political requires understanding of money. Definitions. Money as limited mode of communication. Money and words compared. Interrelationship among traditional definitions and money. Money's lack of normative authority. Objections. Metropolitan politics and the rejection of Enlightenment political aspiration.

The word *market* can refer to physical or functional situations of buyers and sellers. Physically, markets are the places where buyers and sellers meet, whether that be the corner grocery or the floor of the New York Stock Exchange. These days, however, the word less often denotes a place. The telephone order from a catalogue at midnight, to say nothing of the internet securities trade, do not occur in any single place, or even in any readily identifiable group of places.[1] Where we used to experience a physical place, for example a store or an office, we now often experience only a communication, a phone call or an e-mail. Even the communications we experience may be very partial. Through the use of agents (consider retail insurance and equity markets), we may not even be aware of most of the transactions conducted on our behalf. Markets are dematerializing; the physical character of economic transactions is on the wane.

We therefore increasingly employ a functional understanding of markets, as the collective activity of buying and/or selling and selling and/or buying something else with little or no specific physical location.[2] To be "in the market" is less and less a statement about where one is, but has become a statement about one's attitude towards one's fellows (a desire to buy from, an interest in selling to). To consider society in terms of counterparties is a matter of considerable political significance.

By way of contrast, it is worth noting that even though the ancient Greeks were traders, and the agora was the marketplace before it was Socrates' forum, the idea that buying and selling might be central to political life was anathema to the Athenians. Political life, the public life of the free citizen, was understood to be distinct from and ultimately at odds with economic life, the private life of the household.[3] Simply put, the condition of desire (more graphically, the state of arousal) is not admirable. The desirous man is not free, but is in thrall to his desire, and to the circumstances of its satisfaction. Such a man is instead a slave, and therefore an object of ridicule rather than a political subject. ("People look ridiculous when they're in ecstasy."[4]) A man who is not in command of himself is not fit to exercise political power, to lead. Phrased more positively, in the Greek view, command over the self, autonomy, is a prerequisite for political life. Autonomy in turn requires that lusts and other forms of servitude be mastered, or at least limited to their proper sphere, such as private life or festival time, thereby leaving public life to the realm of men who were masters of themselves, and so could be asked to lead others. Consonantly, the supreme political virtue for the Greeks was courage (freedom from fear in the face of physical danger), because it is the courageous man who is most clearly in command of himself, that is, able to face down the instinct for self-preservation, and hence most likely to be worthy of commanding others. The courageous man best embodies the aesthetic to which the polis aspires. That, at any rate, is a rather Apollonian statement of an Athenian view.

But the City of Gold does not harbor such Athenian aspirations. Our citizenship is exercised through, not after, trade. In the City, money and property are the institutional devices by which relations of desire and satisfaction are objectified, so that they may be aggregated, manipulated, postponed, or otherwise handled. Without such reification, the constellation of relations now handled through markets would be no more manageable than sex without marriage (and associated laws, rules of inheritance, prohibitions on employment discrimination and rape, and the like) or dominion over things without property (and the associated prohibitions on theft, laws against nuisance, and so forth).[5] Thus a political understanding of the City of Gold hinges on an understanding of our institutions of money and property.

While property has its mysteries (which will be discussed as necessary), a political understanding of money is especially difficult to come by, and is the concern of this essay. Money is uncanny, hard to talk about clearly. Money, like language and even law, is so fundamental to our world, so prior to our understandings of so much else of vital importance, that despite being what Aristotle calls a conventional thing, money continually represents itself to us as a condition of nature, akin to gravity.[6] (Indeed, an entire science, economics, is based on just this illusion.) So the first difficulty to be overcome, if we are to have a serious political economy, is the tendency to understand money as a condition imposed on us by the fact of our humanity. But this is not the place to talk about cowry shells and buckskins, warrants for internet start-ups and derivatives based on fuel costs or weather patterns, and the collapse of the Bretton Woods currency regime.[7] This book restricts itself to those aspects of money that seem to be of political—in the special sense intrinsic to the City—importance.

We all know, at some very basic and empirical level, what money is: it is a thing. Money often appears as rectangles of green and white paper, with complex printing, or an assortment of metal disks. We know what money is in ways akin to which a child announces that a black thing with something green around its neck is a dog, that is, her dog, wearing a collar. But this is merely the all-too-human tendency to mistake our particular impressions for general experience. We see the embodiments of money that we use, or what monetary aficionados call specie (coins containing precious metal), really no more than crude fetishes that locate the complexities of money in something tangible, and think we understand the nature of money itself. A bit of history or comparative discourse soon cures us of the idea that our money is "real," that is, would function as money independently of its particular cultural situation. To make matters worse, in today's economy, people use money—make payments—with much besides coin or paper, things which some people call money and some do not. Consider the ubiquitous plastic cards with black strips magnetically encoded to carry data. Such cards work in various legally distinguishable (for those so inclined) ways. Which, if any, should be considered money? What about automatic deductions from payroll accounts or automatic roll-overs in other accounts, that is, money that does not even pretend to embody itself in anything other than accounting conventions? Credit extended by banks in making loans is generally considered to be money, but what about credit extended by broker dealers who allow their customers to buy on margin? None of which begins to resolve the extent to which other talismans of desire and thus of control, such as stock ownership, should be considered money, as Chairman of the Federal Reserve Alan Greenspan obliquely has suggested.[8] So what is money? The Federal Reserve does not know, and admitted as much when it stopped using measures of money supply, such as $M(1)$, $M(2)$, and $M(3)$, to set interest rates.

The concepts surrounding money interpenetrate one another, and are subtle, shifting, and generally difficult to keep sorted. In the interest of clarity, therefore, and so far as euphony allows, this book will endeavor to distinguish between tokens, cash, currency, and money as follows. (1)

"Token" denotes a physical representation, a coin or bill or other physical thing that serves as money. (2) "Cash" is used in the accounting and hence corporate sense of tokens and highly liquid legal claims to a sum certain of such tokens, such as bank accounts. Money in the bank is cash, but not a token. (3) "Currency" denotes the set of all claims, real or potential, to a given class of tokens, without regard to the holder. Examples of currency are the dollar, the yen, and so forth. Currency implies an issuer, generally a government, and more deeply, a community that uses the currency. (4) "Money" refers to all of the above, but more generally to a complex of ideas which may be discussed in the abstract, as when we discuss money vis-à-vis natural language, or money's relation with its inverse, property.

For present purposes, it suffices to note that money has not been (indeed, cannot be) defined by some set of inherent characteristics. Money is instituted, defined, by a given society; money does not exist independently of a society that uses it. Consequently, rather than some set of characteristics that would distinguish money from other objects like tulips or gold or representations of political leaders or the promises of financial institutions to one another, traditional definitions of money such as medium of exchange, method of payment, store of value, and unit of account, refer to the uses of money, its functions in society. Closer examination reveals that the social functions of money are all communicative in nature. The traditional functional understandings of money thus presume a social, and hence political, act of communication.

This idea that money is in essence a form of communication is rarely stated explicitly, yet is entailed in ordinary talk about money among the citizenry, financial professionals, academics, and government. We view the rise and fall of various indices (in the United States, usually equity indices, for reasons not entirely clear but probably largely historical) as oracular pronouncements of national health, and even the wisdom of specific policies. Financial theory tacitly affirms the communicative nature of money in its emphasis on information. Markets in derivative instruments, which trade opinions—bets—on price movements are justified as price discovery, as if being told the future price of an item were in and of itself a good thing.[9] The phenomenal growth and increasing attention paid to transactions in the financial markets (the financial economy dwarfs the real economy), the electronic mediation of such markets (almost nothing is certificated), and the conflation of finance, news, and entertainment (caused and required by the democratization of capitalism) each mean that capital is now understood in the context of, and ultimately as a form of, news, information, communication. As former Chairman of Citicorp Walter Wriston remarked, "information about money has become almost as important as money itself."[10] He should have gone further, and admitted that money is an especially concrete form of communication, our society's way of talking to itself. To begin to understand political discourse in the City of Gold, a polity founded on monetary communication, we must understand how monetary communication works.[11]

*   *   *

While money must be understood in terms of communication, money can say very little. Money differs structurally from the form of communication that would seem to be closest to it, writing. Writing is different from money because words in a language, for example American English, are different from units of currency, such as U.S. dollars. Although the relationship between a word and its referent is highly problematic, as every poet knows and the poststructuralists never tire of reminding us, a more or less specific set of relationships is claimed by the user of words, who expects to be understood to mean something in spite of the play of language, the vagaries of history, and the folly of interpretation. In contrast, money has no specific referent. A dollar received is simply the capability of future payment, the satisfaction of some future desire. Nothing about the dollar establishes a specific relationship between the dollar and that for which it is payment. A dollar bill "represents" anything for which a dollar bill may be paid, that is, nothing in particular.

In certain circles, sometimes identified by reference to Jacques Lacan or Ferdinand de Saussure, it is common to note that money is a floating signifier. Money represents nothing in particular, but receives content from its context, the will of its users. A currency is thus complicitous in the power relations of the society in which it is useful. While true enough, this line of thinking tends to miss something more profound: money *never* receives much content. A dollar paid has no relationship to the property bought. Although the dollar may momentarily be associated with the purchase (these dollars are "the payment"), once the transaction is complete the dollar has left the control of the buyer and passed to the seller, for whom the dollar is, again and as ever, potential. Money is not just a floating signifier, it is a perpetually floating signifier. Money forms no associations; its promise to represent anything in particular is never fulfilled.

In contrast, words represent relationships, actual at least in language. Like relationships, words are distinguishable from one another. Their referents are different; when spoken, they sound different; when written, they look different; they function differently in the language and in society; and so they are understood differently.[12] Without taking a position on the nature of language, it suffices for present purposes to note that there are no such differences among dollars. Dollars are fungible. Each dollar is exactly as good, is exactly as sensitive to events, is exactly the same, as the next. We can all think of thousands of different words in American English, but only of one kind of dollar. Because nothing about the dollar limits the purposes to which a dollar may be put, one kind of dollar—or, more precisely, a set of institutions which are collectively considered "dollars," ranging from the cash one leaves as a tip to the credit card debt with which one pays the bill for lunch while discussing the underwriter's pricing of an initial public offering (IPO) and hence one's "worth" some months hence—suits almost every purpose.[13]

The supply of words is potentially infinite, but the supply of dollars or any other currency must be considered limited. The characteristics and context of a word secures (determines, limits, restricts) its relationships and so its role in society. This situation may be replicated indefinitely without affecting the word's functionality as a word—few if any words become literally meaningless so long as their communities survive. No matter how often the word "car" has been or will be used, we have a pretty good idea what Henry Ford meant when he said you could buy a car from him in any color, so long as it was black. The meaning of an oft-used word may change over time, as role, context, and so forth evolve—without prodding, we do not imagine a Model T when we think of a car—but the word can still function as a word regardless of how often it is used. Thus a word tends toward determinacy, limitation, if not certainty, in how it can be used, but is almost completely unrestricted in how often it can be used.

Again, money is different. The supply of a currency must be believed to be finite for the currency to retain its worth. As the supply of currency increases, its worth decreases, and the price of goods goes up (this is a classic inflation). A limitless supply of instruments claiming to be money would be worthless—recall the famous pictures of the Weimar hyperinflation, in which wheelbarrows of bank notes were used to make trivial purchases, or, more recently, the hyperinflation in Ecuador, resulting in the abandonment of the sucre and the adoption of the U.S. dollar.[14] Currency thus has worth only insofar as it is widely believed that the currency will be acceptable for future payment, which entails another wide belief, that the supply of the currency will not outstrip demand for the currency. Though a dollar may be put to an infinite number of purposes, there cannot be an infinite number of dollars.

Words and money are thus not merely different, they are in some important ways reciprocals, mirror images, of one another. A language requires many words but a currency requires only one unit of account. The scope of a word's use is relatively limited, but a unit of currency may be used for any purpose, that is, the scope of its use is indeterminate, unlimited. A given word may be used by anyone and everyone almost (if not completely) without effect on the meaning of existing instantiations of the word, that is, the supply of any given word is infinite. Changes in the supply of a unit of currency affect the worth of similar units of currency already in circulation; the supply of currency must be finite in order for the currency to function. We may write this relation so: fungibility: limited supply: : particularity: unlimited supply.

This reciprocal relationship between money and language may seem surprising—after all, we set out to discuss money as a form of communication, which it is. But if money is a form of communication, then why is it also structurally opposed to language? And what does it mean to found a polity based on markets, to understand citizenship as the condition of buying and selling, the cycle of satisfaction and arousal and satisfaction of desire? A bit of history and a simple example may help us make some sense of these questions.

*　*　*

Intuitively, we consider money to be a thing—a gold coin, traditionally—rather than a message. And both individuals and nations have thought, as a general matter, that it was better to have more money rather than less. But how much better has long been unclear. Since Spain was awash with American gold and the Dutch were rich, the relationship between a nation's money supply and its real wealth—how, in some deep sense, the nation was making out—has been a puzzle that has received a great deal of attention. But to speak of "money supply" is to skip the beginning of the story, to assume its outcome, and so to miss much.

The Spanish who conquered much of the Americas appear to have thought that gold itself was wealth. Although we still have some mystical attachment to gold, from our vantage point it is difficult to understand a feeling for gold so powerful that desire for it would set the course of nations, construct empires, destroy cultures. The usual imagery for this passion is sexual desire, as in "lust for gold," implying a powerful urge, irrational, barely articulable, and difficult to control. While trenchant in some ways, understanding the desire for gold in sexual terms renders inexplicable the magnitude of the Spanish achievement. Mere lust hardly accounts for the awesome fortitude, the meticulous organization, and the collective commitment it takes to begin an expedition of years with substantial risk of not returning. Discovery and conquest require more than physical passion, they require a sense of history. The Spanish had to win—it was their destiny—and the talisman of that destiny was the gold that Marco Polo and others promised was to be found in the Far East. Gold, in this account, is like the grail.[15] Although Columbus himself found little gold, later Spaniards found a lot of gold, and even more silver. Their national quest was outrageously successful.

But acquisition of enormous amounts of precious metal did not make the Spanish rich, or not as rich as they expected. Spain seemed to get poor as fast as it got gold. The intellectual significance of the decline of Spain is comparable to that of the Soviet Union—both declines discredited certain faiths. The decline of Spain and the rise of Holland conclusively demonstrated that those who thought that a country's wealth consisted in its stores of gold (conveniently called bullionists) were wrong. But if the bullionists were wrong that gold was wealth, then what was wealth? More precisely, what was the source of value, what quality was shared among those things recognized to be valuable, or rephrased, what was the objective reason for prices? And, for that matter, what was gold? In trying to answer these questions, modern economics was born.

While the effort to put value upon some objective basis has not been very successful, the worldly philosophers have had somewhat more luck with the second question, what is gold, or more generally, what is money? Gold, it emerged in the work of Adam Smith and others, is not equivalent to wealth, but instead represented wealth. Gold is merely a symbol of wealth. Money, to put the matter in modern terms, is a medium of exchange, an institutional device for facilitating trade; Adam Smith called it "an instrument of commerce." It was trade that created wealth, both by allowing goods to be purchased by those who wanted them most badly, and by allowing producers to specialize, producing only what they did best, and trading for their other needs.

The policy ramifications of the antibullionist position seemed to be clear. The Spanish had made a category mistake: they had confused a representation for the thing itself. So long as a country had enough gold to facilitate the exchange of goods, it did not matter how much gold a country had. Moreover, since gold had no intrinsic value, a government could in theory declare that any given amount of gold represented a certain value. In due course, it became obvious to governments that it was far easier to work with paper, backed by gold, or ultimately, paper that was not backed by gold, that is, without a link between the representational—and hence exchange—function of money and the actual gold supply. Instead of expending great effort in the hunt for gold, like the Spanish, a nation should focus on developing industries in which it enjoyed a comparative advantage, and trading such things for products which it could not make easily. In short, a nation should be like the Dutch: concentrate on domestic strengths, trade freely, grow wealthy, and the money takes care of itself. The Spanish debacle in the Netherlands, culminating in the victory of William of Orange, was taken to demonstrate the superiority of Dutch economic policy, a sort of trial of

ideas by battle, much like the superiority of markets over planned economies was understood to have been demonstrated by the end of the Cold
War and the fall of communism. To overstate the case, the stolid Dutch de-
mystified gold. The realization, by Smith and others, of what happened was
the invention of modern economic policy, and for that matter, the creed of
the WTO and a central belief in the City of Gold itself.[16]

And yet this demystification of money can be taken too far. Money is not
just a medium of exchange, or, to put it differently, a medium of exchange is
no simple thing. Money in fact functions as a mysterious agent, as any number of Dutch artists were aware. Some of the uncanniness of money—and
much of the now orthodox modern understanding of what money is—can
be teased out of the traditional definitions of money and a simple example.
Imagine some marketplace actor, A, who sells some chattel, X, for some sum
of cash, say $1000, and some time later uses that sum to buy some other chat-
tel, Y. Money functions here as a medium of exchange. A begins with property X, which she really does not want, and later acquires property, Y, which
she does want. Money is the middle term which allows A to trade X for Y.

Because it can function as a medium of exchange, money can serve as a
unit of account. Assuming that both transactions take place at book value,
A's net worth (her equity in herself) does not change in the course of these
two transactions. At first, A owns a thing, X, worth $1000; then she owns
$1000 in cash; then she owns another thing, Y, also worth $1000. Absent
transaction costs, A's worth is unchanged.[17] We may therefore say that the
currency in which the cash at issue is denominated, U.S. dollars, serves as
the unit of account for A's assets.

In order for money to function as a medium of exchange, it must be acceptable to the parties. The person who accepts money as payment presumes that the money is "good," which means that the same money can be
used in the future to pay somebody else. A accepts $1000 in exchange for
her property X in the belief that the money can be exchanged later for
something else that A wants, or may come to want, in this case Y, currently
owned by B. Because there is a time difference between the two transactions, A must hope that the currency retains its value over the time she
holds the cash, or she will lose. That is, in order to function as a "medium
of exchange," and hence a "unit of account," money must also be a "store of
value."[18]

To elaborate: suppose that, for some reason, there soon would be many
more dollars in circulation (relative to the economy's growth). Such an increase in the supply of dollars would tend to lead to inflation, that is, a rise
in the nominal prices of goods, because more dollars would be available to
spend on a finite number of goods. Knowing this, A would be wise to demand a higher price for her X, in order to have a chance to buy Y, the price

of which may be expected to be rising in the interim. Such money would no longer be "good" or "sound." Suppose, however, that the increase would be huge, that U.S. dollars would be printed day and night in an orgy of hyperinflation, for which the usual image, already mentioned, is Weimar Germany. Then A would be well-advised not to accept the money at all, because it might collapse altogether, and become worthless, in which case it would not function as a store of value. As discussed above, to function as a store of value, the supply of money must be believed to be finite, that is, the party that accepts money does so in the belief that all demand for the money has not been satisfied, and will not be satisfied. If, however, the money becomes so common as to be believed to be worthless, then A will not be able to exchange $1000 for a pack of cigarettes, much less Y. Because A has refused to do the transaction, the currency has ceased to be a medium of exchange, at least in A's case. Should such refusal become widespread, the currency would become mere paper printed with images of U.S. presidents. At that point, it would make no sense to calculate A's net worth in terms of U.S. dollars, no more sensible than calculating her worth in *Reichsmarks* or Confederate dollars. Again, the functions of money depend on one another: for money to function as a medium of exchange, and hence a unit of account, it must also function as a store of value. But to function as a store of value, the money supply must be believed to be finite.

If finite, money is a commodity in the technical sense that oil and grain are commodities—a finite resource of fungible units that can be priced (and that even can support a futures and options exchange). The charge for possessing money for a length of time, rent for the use of money, we call interest. The antibullionist position that money is a medium of exchange, and currency is merely a technical device used to facilitate trade, is easy to overstate: money is not, and cannot be, viewed purely as a conduit. Money can only serve as a medium of exchange insofar as money is, itself, believed to be valuable, worth holding, that is, so long as there can be a market in money. So the Spanish were not entirely wrong—for monetary exchange to work there must be a belief that wealth is somehow locked within money, and that possession of that wealth requires possession of the money.

But we do not accept money in the abstract; we accept some token as payment. The Spanish were wrong—as goldbugs today are wrong—to think that all tokens must ultimately be backed by a scarce physical substance, such as gold or silver. As suggested above, a currency functions so long as a community exists in which it is believed that the currency will continue to be acceptable. She who accepts a token as payment must believe that the currency is sound now and will be in the future, so that the token will remain good for making payments, that is, that other people will want her token when she decides to spend it. Accepting money is thus an act of political faith, the acceptance of a community's promise to take the money back, at some later date, in the course of some other transaction. While such faith is sensibly and often sustained by the common and ancient love of scarce and shiny metals, it need not be. Such faith may also be sustained by belief in the ongoing vitality of the state issuing the money, coupled with the belief that the state in question will not devalue the currency within the time horizon for which the currency is likely to be held. But whether gold or fiat currency, acceptance of payment reflects belief in the continued existence of a community in which such money is acceptable.

If money works only when it is believed that its future supply will be limited (if it is believed that there will be continued demand), the question arises: What limits the supply of money? The answer is not obvious. If money is a form of communication, talk, then what prevents people from doing more of it, thereby making more money? This question will be considered in more detail in chapter XIII, but for present purposes monetary relations depend on a social, often explicit, political constraint on the members of a community. For money to function, a society's supply of money must be limited by society itself. This limitation can be accomplished in a number of ways, by the reserve requirements of a central bank, or by laws that constrain the lending abilities of banks, or, most traditionally, by social conventions such as the old custom that an instrument would be deemed money only insofar as it was backed by gold, which is naturally of limited supply.

Thus money supply, and indeed virtually every aspect of money, takes place within a framework of law, regulation, or custom, what Aristotle collectively called convention. Money only exists in terms of such conventions, laws. Money can only be sent, or received, or stored, or spent, in accordance with countless rules for manipulating funds. The spectrum of risk and return stretching from banking to risk management to securities do not represent money in paper, much less gold, but only as a quantity kept "on the books," that is, electronically, and communicated according to various protocols.[19] Money's evolution from specie to contract to fiat has culminated in accounting—the system of accounts that underlies the modern financial industries. Should such money be lost, that is, should there be an error in the data management of a financial institution, one could sue. Thus, if one owns money, that is, claims property rights to a sum of money, the only thing one actually holds as a matter of right is a potential cause of action against a financial intermediary with whom one enjoys a relationship of privity. In short, we have defined money in terms of accounting conventions backed by legal conventions and the power of the sovereign.

*   *   *

In chapter I, we discussed the City as a polity founded on markets. In this chapter, we have examined the nature of money, and found it to be a set of interlocked communicative functions, enabled by the conventions of a community. With this understanding of money in hand, what does it mean to say that our polity is based on monetary communication? Rephrased, what does it mean to say that markets are authoritative—which we say every time we claim that the market has, or should, replace the government. One familiar response is to argue that markets are a form of democracy, that marketplace governance is consumer sovereignty, and that since consumers are people, markets must be government by and for the people. From this perspective, and conveniently enough, outcomes of market transactions (the status quo) can be justified as the collective decision of the people, or at least of the monied interests, on questions of general importance. So our journalists unselfconsciously evaluate the importance of events by reporting the "reaction" of the market indices, that, like the priestess at Delphi, are expected to judge such things. We take markets to be authoritative mechanisms of public choice. Americans in particular are loathe to disturb what they understand to be the judgment of the marketplace; the disfavor of the stock market (rarely: "the interests of those who can lend money") is widely understood to be a powerful argument. When they think they hear the markets speaking, Americans in particular listen and obey.

Americans sometimes even understand participation in the market as a form of political expression. It is darkly funny that the markets resolutions are understood to constitute a free society. It is almost unbearable, even if entirely understandable, that the opening of the financial markets on the Monday following the bombing of the World Trade Center and the Pentagon was thought to be a response to evil, and that Americans were urged to express their patriotism by buying.

There are, of course, politely received objections to the idea that market outcomes are, or should be, normative: market outcomes under conditions of free choice will not be rational; various sorts of market failure abound; initial distributions are unjust; the utility of a dollar is inversely proportional to the wealth of its holder; and so forth. But at least when we are prosperous, the faith in markets is so great, and the alternatives presented by the traditional institutions of government have over the last generation seemed so paltry, that objections to the normative authority of markets are generally ignored, or brushed aside as necessary difficulties for a second-best world.

Such objections, however, mask a more fundamental claim: the nature of monetary reference makes money a more indeterminate mode of communication than eavesdropping on a private communication in a natural language, and that therefore marketplace outcomes should not be presumed to have normative import. Simply put, money does not transmit much information, and therefore one should not grant markets much authority. We only have one unit of account, in contrast to the thousands of words we need to get our meaning almost across. Money is structurally incapable of transferring much information, as a language composed of a single word would be.

The inability to transmit information is not accidental, some technical shortcoming in our monetary institutions, but is instead intrinsic to those relations we understand as monetary. As discussed above, tokens are ciphers. Tokens of a given currency are fungible because the token represents nothing specific about the world, merely the capability to make a future payment, priced among the parties to a transaction vis-à-vis some other good. Since a token means nothing in particular, perpetually floats, it can be used as a placeholder for anything that is desired. More specifically, its very lack of a referent, literally, its meaninglessness, enables money to be used to make things that are entirely different equivalent to one another. Money makes things commensurable. Money's other functions, its ability to serve as a medium of exchange, a store of value, or a unit of account, all hinge on commensurability, which in turn hinges on its meaninglessness. As a social institution, money may be almost as pervasive as language, but it is important to remember that tokens are not words. The financial markets do not speak much because they have no language. In claiming "the judgment of the market" we confuse collective action phenomena with messages.[20]

Which is not to say that we cannot speak about the markets. We continually tell ourselves stories about the ebb and flow of money, either in particular transactions or in and out of entire markets. Marketplace stories are efforts to amplify, refine, and interpret events in the market, to understand the market as if it were talking to us, as if it were an oracle. The financial press consists of little besides post-hoc articulations of a rationale for marketplace events. There is no reason not to believe that many of these stories are actually true; financial journalists often live in the same world as players. By all accounts, the oracle at Delphi was often right, too, which is not too surprising—one would assume the high priests of Apollo who served the oracle (a woman) would be pretty sharp. The point is not that the markets are meaningless—they have a great deal of meaning for us, as do our other social practices—but that it is raw superstition to believe financial transactions "say" anything specific about the world, only a little more sensible than asserting the authority of bird entrails, smoke patterns, or the flight of geese, all of which both convey (scant) information and (easily) serve as the object of (often fanciful) interpretation. Marketplace stories may be told by words in a culture; they cannot be inscribed on money itself. To overstate slightly for emphasis: markets provide no rational authority for political thought.

* * *

Three objections to the proposition that the price mechanism does not communicate help to specify how we may begin to understand the political meanings entailed by our participation in markets, drawing on (i) economics, (ii) poststructuralist thought, and (iii) this text so far. The first objection springs from the perspective of the economic disciplines, particularly finance. Within such disciplines, the financial markets are constantly discussed in terms of information; the market itself is understood to be a device for the dissemination of information and the formation of consensus. This sort of thinking attains its perfection in discussion of the efficient capital markets hypothesis, in which the market price always and already reflects the collective balancing of all available information regarding the asset in question—that is, the communication of the markets, and hence the truth revealed by price, is the most to which humans can aspire.

Despite all the lip service paid to information, thinking about information, the actual substance, structure, and transmission of meaning in the marketplace, remains strikingly naive.[21] Financial theory is cluttered by immensely important sounding and fundamentally difficult words like "information," "efficiency," and "technology." Even more difficult words, such as "wealth," "value" (sometimes eschewed by finance types, but beloved by practitioners of law and economics), "property," and "progress," are implicit and hardly considered. Perhaps most strikingly, and as mentioned above, the ways in which money can and cannot serve as a carrier of meaning are almost completely unexamined. With so much assumed, it is not surprising that we have not deeply considered what sort of truth price or brand or goodwill represent. But once we understand markets to be communicative spaces, we should expect to find the truths within the marketplace to be at least as complex and contestable as the truths we attempt to discuss in other contexts. Why should we expect markets, alone among human institutions, to be lucid[22]?

Twentieth century intellectual history is dominated by the implications of the problematic status of meaning in our culture, referred to by tags like "the turn to interpretation," the "turn to language," "postmodernism," and so forth. While much of this, particularly in the American academy in the last few decades, has been overdone, one cannot speak as if the critique of Enlightenment claims about the possibility of knowledge, a tradition stretching from Kant through Nietzsche to today's college students and even law professors, has not happened. Although many still speak as if Truth were readily apparent on the electronic tickers our computers all have, it is not too soon to ask how a poststructural political economy would consider the communication entailed in the financial markets.[23] The question is how should we understand—think—within the interpretive communities structured by financial markets, once we concede that the central medium of interaction within such communities, the price mechanism, is radically underdetermined?

Recognition of the problematic nature of truth in the marketplace—bringing market ideology into the twentieth century, epistemologically speaking—raises the second, and antithetical, response to the proposition that markets do not say very much. To a poststructural mind, other forms of communication, for example painting or even ordinary speech, may seem just as problematic as price mechanisms. Why, one might ask, should one language game be more difficult than another? Or, if meaning is only possible within an interpretive community, why should we think it any more difficult to interpret within one community, rather than another? Markets do not say very much, but neither does language—so what?

Three responses to this poststructural objection suggest themselves. First, while the poststructuralist perspective may have become orthodox with regard to many other forms of communication, it is not orthodox with regard to financial markets. Few intellectuals would maintain that a painting meant "X," in the same unproblematic sense that market outcomes are routinely presented as simply meaning one thing or another. Although from certain intellectual perspectives it is old hat, the idea that markets, like all other objects of culture, have no simple, objective, much less easily discernible meaning and must be interpreted, read, in order to be understood as meaningful, is so far outside the economic disciplines as to sound heretical. Second, and practically, nobody treats paintings or other systems of communication as oracular—politically authoritative—in the same way that the financial markets are treated regularly. Third, as already discussed, the ways in which money signifies are different in kind from the way in which language, or for that matter painting, signifies. Even language, powerful practice and wonderful metaphor that it is, does not exhaust the possibilities of communication: there is no reason to think that different media communicate in the same way. Because money refers to nothing specific, the transmission and availability of meaning through the medium of money is even more problematic than the transmission and availability of meaning—the sense in which we can talk about Truth—in writing.

The third objection to the proposition that the price mechanism does not communicate much is drawn from this apology itself. On the one hand, the preceding section of this very essay denies the possibility that the price mechanism can communicate truth, and consequently denies that markets should be politically authoritative. But, judging from the first chapter, the entire book is premised on the idea that markets are the foundation of modern politics, and therefore meaningful, indeed authoritative. The text thus seems self-contradictory.

Intellectual ideals are not quite social realities. This book oscillates between money and currency, between ideas and their institutional realizations, between exploring the abstract logic of supranational capitalism and our actual economic practices. So, for example, only in principle is money universally acceptable, and hence represents nothing, and therefore is perfectly fungible. In an actual transaction, money must be embodied, even if only notationally, and that embodiment limits the ways in which that instantiation of money can be used for payment. A beer cannot be paid for by wire transfer; a company cannot be bought with coin.[24] Conversely, insofar as money is embodied and thus representational, we may say such money has weight, communicates. Receipt of a wire transfer strongly suggests, besides the sum transferred, that one is sufficiently part of the establishment to be recognized by a bank, itself probably complicitous in the activities of a state, and so forth. Nonetheless, money does not transmit much information. Most obviously, the wire transfer does not say anything about what the recipient of the funds is going to do next. Money is like light, almost but not entirely impervious to gravity.[25]

The politically important distinction here is between message and culture. Money should not be understood to transmit messages; prices do not tell us anything in any definite way. Markets do not speak truth, and therefore should not be regarded as politically authoritative. To regard markets as authoritative is irresponsible, a way to avoid politics. But the fact that price does not transmit messages does not mean that capitalism, as a system, does not constitute a culture, with its own grammar and in that sense, logic—the point of this book is to explicate that logic in political terms. Only if we understand how markets work can we assess the choice to conduct a given area of politics through markets.

We might steer between the Scylla of efficient markets (in which the oracle must be obeyed) and the Charybdis of lazy postmodernism (in which truth is not worth considering amidst the general chaos) and make a start by considering the context that exchanges comprise. The conventional character of money is not a new discovery—as mentioned, Aristotle made the point—but it can be strangely hard to consider money as a social practice in the hurly burly of economic life, or even academic thought, that presumes the practice. However, now that we have abandoned the physical token of money for all but the most trivial purchases, money's ancient tendency to present itself as an aspect of nature is fading somewhat. Electronic money (indeed, more conventional credit cards) are merely retail embodiments, reminders, of our awareness that money payment is a binding communication that collective fictions, such as dollars, or representations of dollars, or representations of legal rights priced in dollars like shares, have been transferred from one party to another. Money is nothing besides a particularly fixed, even if oftentimes physically ephemeral, form of political commitment. The monetary system has become self-evidently social—conventional—to its bones.

The differences between tokens and words as signifiers means that the politics of the City of Gold cannot be understood in modern terms. Both Machiavelli and Hobbes sought to construct a politics based not on morality, but instead on psychological reality. Modern political thought loudly distinguished itself from its classical and medieval forebears by its claim to be based not on men as they ought to be, but on men as they are. That is, both Machiavelli and Hobbes claimed to be political scientists, and to suggest a political order that would mirror the most important aspects of what it was to be human. This sense that the aspiration of political thought is to create institutions that mirror society is explicit in the phrase representative democracy. We still speak of politics in terms of truth, and condemn regimes that are untruthful. We still hope for reasoned political discourse. But speaking in terms of truth requires faith in one's language. So George Orwell, in worrying about totalitarianism, correctly worried about totalitarianism's ability to subvert the language, and make truthful communication impossible. Indeed, Orwell thought that even nontotalitarian societies like Britain needed to attend to their language, a matter which this book takes up in a later essay.[26] Orwell's fears for the health of language now seem almost quaint, because for so many political purposes we have abandoned words in favor of money. Our politics does not reduce to truth, at least not a truth of rationality. The City's turn to money, and therefore away from meaning, means that its politics has broken decisively with the modern tradition.

Many of those responsible for rebuilding after World War Two understood the conventional nature of money, and therefore could understand the financial system in constitutional terms, as a mechanism through which a polity could be constructed. Most pressingly, Germany and Japan had to be reconstituted along new lines. The idea that the economic structure lay near the core of the polity was not entirely new: the New Deal was both an economic reform and a constitutional moment. Going further back, the founders of the United States, for example, were concerned with national money and national banks (or concerned to avoid the same) precisely because they understood that the choice of economic institutions informed our lives together. What was new after World War Two, however, was the idea that such community could be formed across (or above or beneath) the traditional identities expressed by the nation. The City of Gold thus came to be defined as the communicative space in which the legal conventions surrounding our instantiations of money hold sway.[27] A contemporary political economy should think about how such conventions inform social life.

CHAPTER III

Finance and the War Against Time

Structure of finance. Finance and progress. Conservative character of finance. Homogenization. Finance as collectivization of risk/opportunity. Finance and fear.

As the legal profession dominated the founding of the United States, banking dominated the founding of the City of Gold. Financial institutions played lead roles in establishing the City: the Marshall Fund, the International Bank for Reconstruction and Development, the Bretton Woods currency arrangement, stabilized by the International Monetary Fund. The very names of these institutions proclaim their lending; our polity is quite literally based upon such debt. One might therefore expect the citizens of the City of Gold to have a sense of what the shape of a financial polity is, in the same way that we have a sense of what the shape of the state is. We "know" that a state is composed of legislative, executive, and judicial elements, discussed in the U.S. Constitution and elsewhere in that order; and we "know" what representative democracy is; and we are quite comfortable endeavoring to establish or reestablish such institutions when states around the planet fail, and to recapitulate such architecture within international institutions. But the citizens of the City of Gold do not have a comparable image of finance. Perhaps it is too soon. Though finance is quite old, we have long organized political thought in terms of the nation or its ideological exaggeration, the Cold War, and have rarely thought of finance as a constitutive process. Now that national categories no longer suffice to organize political thought, however, we really ought to ask what it means to organize a polity, our polity, through finance.[1]

An image of the polity founded on finance requires some understanding of what finance is. In brief, finance is an enterprise's effort to overcome constraints by using an investor's money, with a promise to repay.[2] This can be schematized:

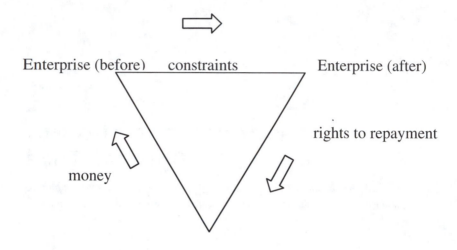

The use of a third party's money, coupled with the promise to repay at some point in the future, defines a monetary transaction as a financing. In contrast, a simple purchase in which an enterprise spends its own money is not a financing; spending a grant or other gift of money is not a financing. The fundamental structure of finance is the same regardless of whether the enterprise in question is an individual (consider student debt), an aggregate of individuals (consider the initial public offering of a start-up company), or a national government (consider sovereign debt or World Bank assistance). Nor, at this level of generality, does it matter whether the investor is legally defined as a shareholder, a bank, or some other entity, or whether the rights received by the investor are structured as debt or equity—the fundamental geometry remains the same. A financing is a transaction in which an enterprise acquires money from an investor, and hopes to repay it; an investor provides money, and hopes to be repaid at a profit. Both enterprise and investor live in the near future, each hoping that the enterprise will make money and the investment will pay off, and fearing that it cannot and it will not. This anxious business is the social contract in the City of Gold.

Consider, by way of contrast, the world without finance. In such a world, accrued assets (generally from surplus income) limit the scope of transactions in which an economic actor can engage. Most actors feel constrained; the world limits their ability to realize their aspirations. For example, because few law students have or could save enough money to go to law school, many students require student loans. If they were for some reason unable to borrow, many students, perhaps most, would work at low paying jobs, life would get in the way, and they would never retain sufficient earnings—save enough out of their paychecks from a job at the mall—to pay for an education at even an inexpensive law school in an inexpensive city. So, for most lower and even middle class students, the ability to transform oneself from retail clerk into legal professional depends on the opportunity to convince third parties (usually student loan programs, many guaranteed or otherwise subsidized by the government) to lend the money to pay for education.

It is easy to forget, especially here in the land of credit cards, student loans, and day traders operating out of their bedrooms, that financing has not always been widely available in the United States, and that access to finance remains unevenly distributed here and is largely unavailable in many other societies. In many developing countries it is difficult for all but the wealthy to borrow money, which makes it difficult for even the not so wealthy to undertake large projects. In order to build a house, for example, people buy what they can, when they can. So one year, a foundation gets laid. The next year, maybe, the house gets framed. As the years go by, it becomes difficult, often impossible, to complete the house. The day job is insecure, concrete is lost to moisture, lumber is stolen, the children need money for education—the builder becomes discouraged. All the while, the need for the house remains unfulfilled, pending construction. In the jargon, finance provides leverage, that is, multiplies the strength of an economic actor in the same way that a lever mechanically multiplies the strength of a physical laborer.[3] With the leverage of borrowed funds, the actor can accomplish a task that would have been slow or impossible. Thus, for those without a sufficient surplus, the hope of progress—the idea that we can get ahead of our present circumstances, and become something different from what we are today—is dependent on the ability to borrow, or to wait. But waiting is hard and risky. Enterprises, whether they be individuals or entire societies, without access to finance are doomed to operate out of retained earnings, and will therefore progress slowly, if at all. Finance accelerates time; finance is progressive.[4]

The international organizations charged with "development" have only gradually come to understand the progressive nature of finance. For several decades following World War Two, the development institutions of the City of Gold and others thought that grants and loans made on a concessionary basis would provide poor societies with leverage sufficient to engender progress. Development thinking has evolved. It now appears that it is not enough to provide money—grants—because gifts are undisciplined and soon spent. Government loans are seen as inefficient at best, badly planned and corrupt at worst. Progress appears to require not just the leverage that money affords, but the selection, discipline, and know-how that only financial markets, preferably relatively local financial markets, can provide. Development, it now appears, requires that people have access to capital markets, so that they can help themselves. So, if we believe in progress, access to capital markets needs to be made available.[5]

If we desire progress to improve local conditions, and if progress requires finance, a fundamental question of practical political economy arises: How to create capital markets? The answer is not obvious. One cannot create a market by fiat. A market, by definition, requires voluntary agreement among autonomous actors. Government cannot order people to trade in a market; that would not be a market. But if markets cannot be created directly, they can be fostered, that is, conditions can be established in which trade is likely to flourish.[6] The question, how can capital markets be created, must therefore be rephrased: What can be done to foster the development of capital markets? How can we make it easier for individuals and collective enterprises in underdeveloped nations to acquire financing? To build a house? To open a small retail operation, or even a manufacturing facility?

An obvious place to begin is with the people who supply finance, investors. What can society do to encourage investors to put their money at risk? Generally speaking, investors expect to be repaid with interest in the broad sense of cash or other benefit that serves as a rent payment in exchange for the use of their money. Take, for important example, banks: if we wish to increase the availability of bank finance in a given society, we should ensure that the society provides the institutional requirements, the environment, for banking to be successful. Specifically, banks require legal assurance that their contracts will be enforced, and banks often require collateral. That is, in order to be "induced to make the loan," a bank is likely to insist that the rights obtained by the bank through the loan documents are enforceable. Moreover and especially, in the event that the borrower defaults, the bank is likely to insist that it gets something else of value in lieu of repayment, the collateral.

Even superficial examination of just these two ubiquitous requirements—enforceability of contracts and security of collateral—suggests some of the complexity on which banks rely. Banks count on a set of stable legal concepts, including, *inter alia*, a doctrine of contract; an understanding of the legal personality of the parties (often defined by corporation law); a relatively hard currency (and attendant financial institutions, particularly arrangements with the treasury and the central bank, and back of that, a relatively responsible fiscal policy); and a doctrine of property, particular with regard to security interests and bankruptcy. Banks further rely on workable judicial and other government systems such as a land registry to make these legal concepts concrete (enforceable), reliance that presumes political, cultural, and linguistic conventions that underlie both legal concepts and their institutional realization. "Loans are made" (the traditional passive language seems entirely appropriate) on presumptions most vertiginous, epistemologically dizzying, even dazzling.

This is worth a pause. Development policy, if development requires access to finance, appears to need solutions to some profound intellectual problems. Quite apart from the likelihood of default, bankers must be unsure what contract, corporations, money, property, or law are, if for no other reason than these are fundamental and probably indeterminable questions in jurisprudence. As a rational matter, in order to devise an effective development policy, one would want to know not only how to define such institutions, but what the cultural requirements for such institutions are. So, for example, is a legal culture of contract law dependent on some broader societal notion of bargained-for, and binding, exchange? Nor is it easy to think about the direction(s) in which a given society should, or is likely to, develop . . . one could go on, but the point is that development institutions cannot be expected to resolve such questions in any particularly rational fashion, and so the hope of development must persist without the comfort of reason. In the absence of reason, we turn to habit. More slowly: due to the indeterminability of issues that finance would have to resolve logically if it were to proceed on a rational basis, habit must substitute for logic. The question of progress and autonomy with which we began—how do we encourage the growth of financial markets and so progress?—is answered by a need to extend the status quo, because while present arrangements may be a mystery, we know nothing else.[7]

For their part, bankers do not rely on logic. Despite its importance to progress (here understood to be the furtherance of private interests), finance is at the same time deeply conservative and social.[8] Bankers are conservative for good reason: they have no way to be certain that their world is secure, and they are personally and institutionally committed to the uncertain proposition that the medium-term future will be like the present in all relevant respects. Retail banks recapitulate this uncertainty in their very structure. Retail banks take deposits, payable on demand, and invest that money in relatively illiquid investments, particularly loans. Depositors, therefore, can respond to newly adverse circumstances faster than banks can. If the depositors demand their money back faster than the bank can liquidate its investments, and no injection of liquidity is forthcoming from some other source, the bank fails.[9] Retail bankers therefore must hope that the future plays according to plan, so that depositors will not all simultaneously demand their money (so that there will be no run on the bank) and deposits and loans can be cycled in orderly fashion. If the future proves to be as expected, bankers will be happy.

With regard to their fundamentally conservative character, retail banks may be different in degree, but are not different in kind, from other providers of capital. Equity investors are generally regarded as less conservative, willing to accept more volatility in individual investments and even in their entire portfolios. But just like bankers, equity investors must make presumptions about the continuity of the institutions upon which they rely. Similarly, options traders and hedge fund managers and others derided as gamblers may actually welcome risk, but here again, this zest for volatility takes place within presumptions about the continuity of institutions and culture, that is, the culture in which a deal made to the trader's advantage is honored when payment is due. Regardless of the character of the investor or the particular risks at issue (and such traditional distinctions make less and less sense in a world of financial conglomeration), the point remains the same: because of its commitment to securing repayment in the future, the activity of finance is institutionally and legally conservative.

It may sound odd to call options traders, some of whom have a great and demonstrable stomach for risk, conservative. To resolve this seeming difficulty, a practical—and from a political and business point of view, crucial—distinction must be made between risk and uncertainty.[10] "Risk" is here used in the sense of academic finance, as a quantifiable probability of a deviation from expected return; "uncertainty" is used in the ordinary sense of awareness of one's ignorance. At bottom, the distinction between risk and uncertainty is a practical one. Risk is a form of information; knowledge of risk informs a decision. Uncertainty is the awareness that information is insufficient to make a reasonable decision. A mildly uncertain investor may take a flyer on a good intuition; a sufficiently uncertain investor will not place any bet at all.[11]

Many in academic finance do not like the concept of uncertainty, and argue, in essence, that uncertainty is merely imprecise risk, which nonetheless can be quantified. For academic purposes, we can always assign a number that will account for our ignorance of a situation. However, the desire to conflate risk and uncertainty misses the practical point: risk presumes a context in which probability can be calculated. To know a situation is comprised of heads, tails, and a fair coin is to know much more than most decision makers know about the context of their decisions. When uncertainty extends to the context of decision, that is, the uncertain situation is no longer well defined, the model is broken, probability is incalculable. In such circumstances, "quantification" no longer serves to inform decision, and may even provide a veneer of knowledge, masking ignorance.[12] As mere placeholders for ignorance, the numbers lose their credibility.

Risk, properly understood, is no barrier to investment. Investors do not expect a guarantee of a profit. On the contrary, investment may be understood as the shouldering of risk in exchange for a payment. Investors do require, however, that they be able to reach an investment decision with which they are comfortable, that is, a decision in which the probability of different outcomes may be assessed, and priced accordingly. Knowledge of risk is real knowledge. Such knowledge can be the foundation for entire industries, for example, the insurance industry, or slightly less explicitly, the market for Internet start-ups or the junk bond market. More generally, however, all investments are full of (more or less well-calculated) risks.[13] Uncertainty, in contrast, is not information, but is instead a psychological barrier to investment—by definition, an uncertain situation is one in which the investor is aware of his ignorance, and so feels uncomfortable, uncertain of his pricing. If the uncertainty of an investment cannot be reduced sufficiently, the investment will not be made. Thus, assuming that investors are rational enough to evaluate the quality of their information and act accordingly, the distinction between risk and uncertainty is important in assessing investment decisions, to buy or not to buy, and hence the flow of capital. If investments are made only where providers of capital believe they have assessed risk properly, and if development requires finance which in turn requires investment, then development will be fostered in situations where uncertainty is reduced, that is, where investors think they understand. The distinction between risk and uncertainty thus deepens our appreciation of certain conservative tendencies of finance, a matter not without academic interest.

Investors do not have to demand, explicitly, that investments conform with their view of the world. An investment opportunity is only viable, can only attract capital and become an actual investment, if its risk can be assessed, if it fits within some investor's view of the world and can be priced accordingly. This is obvious in hindsight: the investor who has spent money presumably believed he understood the risks, and priced them appropriately. To acquire capital is therefore to have conformed to the worldview whence that capital came, or, at least, to have convinced the investor of conformity. Herein lies the conservative tendency of investment: an investor is likely to prefer what has worked, because presumably it will continue to work. Repetition, habit, minimizes uncertainty. Reassured by familiarity, the investor need not have a deep understanding of the culture in which the investment is made, any more than a habitual user of a given technology, a personal computer or a cellular phone, for examples, needs to have a deep understanding of how such technology works.

In this light, the affection that investors such as banks have for their own legal documents makes some sense. Bank counsel are famously unwilling to alter the bank's legal documents. Even when they are good lawyers, who have no articulable objection to a suggested change, bank counsel typically will refuse to rewrite documents, deviate from habit, and expose themselves to uncertainty (and worse, personal responsibility). Banks usually win such negotiations, not because they are right, but because, to be blunt, they have the money. Those who seek money from a bank are thus encouraged by the financing process itself to fit themselves within molds that are familiar and thus reassuring to the lender: patterns of business culture and etiquette, backed by a system of contract law that in turn rests on a system of property rights, as modified by a system of secured interests and a bankruptcy regime, in a regulatory, particularly tax, environment that is neither particularly onerous nor unpredictable, all of which is enforceable within a reasonable amount of time and expense, either through binding arbitration or an impartial judiciary or, more realistically, a legal system that structures negotiations in the shadow of such mechanisms of conflict resolution . . . all of which, and more (for which we have no time to pay attention), comprises the environment of business that already exists. More generally, in order to reduce the uncertainty confronted by investors, finance remakes the world in its own image—like God, man.

In fulfilling the requirements of the investor (becoming more godlike), enterprises are forced to choose between doing without money (freedom from their constraints, leverage, and hence progress) and transforming whatever part of themselves is not in conformity with the culture from which they seek capital. The desire for financing fosters conformity and so tends to destroy the borrower's old self in at least three ways: first, the borrower agrees to the requirements of the loan (almost never phrased as "submits to the dictates of the lender"); second, the good faith borrower in fact endeavors to govern itself accordingly; third, in the event of default, the lender almost certainly has recourse, that is, the financing will multiply rather than reduce the constraints upon the borrower. The situation is fundamentally the same for equity investments: enterprises must make themselves understandable, must facilitate their pricing, by late stage capital, underwriters, professional analysts, and ultimately the market itself. Is it any wonder that IMF conditionality raises hackles in the developing world?

Except at the margins, however, requiring conformity is hardly understood as a moral issue for investors, who tend to insist that enterprises provide security, at least some sort of comfort, for the financing.[14] Investors understand themselves to be vulnerable by virtue of their positions. Lenders must worry about what borrowers will do with their money, and whether borrowers will be available and able to pay back the loan when it falls due. Similarly, shareholders must worry about what management does with their capital.[15] More generally, and regardless of the particular legal relationship at issue, the investor must try to eliminate uncertainty whenever possible, and price risk as accurately as possible, or the investor is likely to become insolvent and cease to be an investor. Eliminating uncertainty and pricing risk, in turn, requires that investments be made in as familiar an environment as possible, in light of expected returns. Lured into an unfamiliar environment—if opportunities for great returns present themselves in East Asia or Latin America or Eastern Europe—an investor based in the United States or Japan (with regard to Asia) or Western Europe (with regard to Eastern Europe) will have incentives to make the environment as familiar as possible as soon as possible. It is therefore unsurprising that experts from the United States and elsewhere in the developed economies advise that capital markets be fostered by the adoption of institutions familiar in the developed world, perhaps a bankruptcy code that would reassure potential lenders of their ability to realize some value from underlying assets, or a system of land tenure and repossession that would allow homes to be used as collateral. The homogenization that "globalization" is often correctly accused of is no accident. Homogenization stems, in great part, from the structure of finance, specifically, capital's antipathy towards uncertainty and fondness for the familiar.

The conservative tendency of finance constrains the possibilities of a polity built on finance. When the Berlin Wall came down and most developing countries renounced Marxian prescriptions for development, there was much debate over a renewed possibility of realizing the old socialist dream of a "third way" to constitute society. This third way, it was proposed by those on the left, would lie somewhere between the ideological pole once occupied by the Soviet Union and the antipode still occupied by the United States, and would avoid the excesses of either. Those on the right responded by asserting the impossibility of any sort of capitalism materially different from that which ought to exist in the United States (tending to ignore the details of actual U.S. practice, which are often a far cry from neoliberal ideals, and any differences between the United States and other viable market societies). Nations that wished to liberalize needed to undergo "shock treatment," presumably some sort of political lobotomy from which a country would emerge deeply committed to a libertarian world view practiced nowhere, at least not among those countries not yet lobotomized. This rather sterile debate has recently resurfaced in muted form, as political parties with progressive traditions have tried to distance themselves from the enthusiasms of the Reagan/Thatcher and other center-right regimes without jeopardizing more recent economic successes.

The usual arguments for one capitalism—No Third Way!—do not bear scrutiny. Different economic arrangements function in different times and places. Particular institutional arrangements—land and water tenure in the American West, for example—are products of the particular sequence of events, policies, prejudices, happenstance that go to make up the history of the society in question. Our economic arrangements were and are subject to debate, some of it significant; our economic institutions are no more necessary, in their particulars, than our other laws. Indeed, the United States has had this very debate at length and in detail before. In the nineteenth century it was argued, with great seriousness, that the legal structure of the United States was logically necessary, and the particular doctrines of contract, tort, and property—the private law on which business generally depends—were thought to be especially necessary. Academics and judges maintained that the edifice of U.S. law had worked itself to its present state of near purity over a long and glorious historical process that was nearing its completion, at which point the law would be perfect, a geometry of formal social arrangements. Then the edifice fell apart, as several generations of legal critics, both judges and academics, successfully argued that U.S. private law was far from perfect, was in fact and appropriately subject to ongoing revision through democratic political processes, and was indeed in substantial need of reform. There is no reason to believe that contemporary economic arrangements, and the laws that sustain them, are any more theoretically necessary, any more likely to be the unfolding of some rational historical process, than the legal classicism of the late nineteenth century.[16]

The proponents of a truly distinctive third way, however, have also missed something very important. The City of Gold is defined by economic integration, a form of communication. Communication, whether conducted via natural language, money, or data stream, requires a *lingua franca*, a common currency, a shared protocol. Translation is a poor second best, and even translation assumes that the translators can operate in both worlds. The act of economic integration, specifically, the ability to make investments across borders, tends to homogenize the relevant aspects of the societies involved. If money is the blood of this body politic, then it is unsurprising that massive infusions of the cosmopolitan money of the supranational capital markets have homogenized much. When they sought to enter the City, no third way was possible for the East Germans, or the Poles, or the Mexicans, or the Indonesians, or many others, because the capital markets to which they turned comprised a communicative space defined by its *lingua franca*. The City already had a business culture, a way of doing things. It is not that the arrangements reached by the City were somehow inevitable; the City is itself an almost miraculous appearance on the world stage. But the answers to a wide range of institutional questions were already well settled, and were not going to be asked by, or on account of, a country seeking to borrow money in order to develop. Tersely put, the City of Gold provides the terms on which the City's investors are willing to invest.

Financial markets thus give us, as individuals and as states, some hope for the future and some assurance against disaster, but at the cost of anxiety and conformity. That, one might add (as defenders of the Bretton Woods Institutions and other liberals often do), is our choice. Students choose to borrow in order to go to law school, and states choose to borrow in order to develop. Indeed. It is not clear that there is a real alternative, that the choice is more than illusory. There are few places to go, and the City's true claims are based upon notions, collective fictions, of great power and of which we are hardly conscious. Social contracts are signed on our behalf, and are not open for renegotiation. But whether our choices are real or illusory, it must be conceded that progress, moving towards the land in one's dreams, is a temptation, as tempting perhaps as the possibility of living off the interest. When we succumb to this temptation, we should understand what we do: extend the dominion of the City of Gold as powerfully as any army ever extended the boundaries of the empire it served.

* * *

And when all are converted and the universal aspirations of the City have been achieved, what then? Up until this point the discussion has focused on the structure of a financing. From this perspective, finance accelerates the passage of time, hurrying an enterprise, whether an individual, a business association, or an entire nation, into the future, or helps the enterprise attain a future it would otherwise be unable to reach. An enterprise begins constrained, here and now, and finance liberates it, there and later. That, at any rate, is the hope. For their part, investors trade in interests whose value depends on a particular future. Consider again the triangle: the investor provides money (along the left hand side), and in exchange receives a bundle of rights, including some expectation of repayment with a profit (along the right hand side). But that repayment is not immediate—it is planned for some point in the future, and such plans may not come to pass. In any given financing, the investor's profit (or loss) lies in the future. The fascinating question for both enterprises and investors is, which future will come to pass? Financial markets are expectant, for enterprises, because they facilitate but do not guarantee the realization of hopes, and financial markets are expectant, for investors, because their investments have yet to be repaid. In its focus on finance, the City of Gold is a polity of the future, and has no genuine present, is perpetually becoming but is incapable of simply being.

The expectant character of the City of Gold is reiterated if we shift attention from financings to markets in such transactions, from the acquisition of capital used to overcome constraints in the real economy, to the capital markets themselves. To do a financing is to make a contractual arrangement among the parties. Once done, however, contractual obligations become property, which may be bought and sold. In the capital markets, investors think in terms of the bundles of rights—properties, in the plural—received in exchange for their money, such as shares in funds or companies, government or corporate bonds, options, warrants, futures, and so forth, in a word, securities. In a case called *Securities and Exchange Commission v. W.J. Howey Co.*, the U.S. Supreme Court noted that the open-ended definition of security for purposes of the Securities Act of 1933 included an "investment contract," a term that was itself undefined by the act. The Supreme Court went on to define "an investment contract for purposes of the Securities Act as "a contract, transaction, or scheme whereby a person invests his money in a common enterprise and is led to expect profits solely from the efforts of a promoter or a third party . . ."[17] This definition is insufficiently precise for certain lawyerly purposes—it does not, by itself, make it clear enough which instruments are governed by the regulatory regime for "securities"—but it does provide a conceptual framework for thinking about securities. With a minimum of violence to the *Howey* definition, securities can be understood in terms of expectation ("led to expect profits"); fungibility (implicit in "*investment* contracts"); and collectivity ("common enterprise").

Expectation is a fundamental aspect of a security. Let us assume, plausibly and for the sake of convenience, an institutional investor that is able to buy the common stock of a for-profit corporation at an initial public offering, that is, the first sale of such stock to the general public. In doing so, the investor provides the offering company with the purchase price of the stock, and receives in exchange the rights associated with a common share, such as the right to vote in corporate elections, dividends if distributed, and a residual claim on the assets of the corporation, as well as the right to resell the stock on the open market, subject to the existence of a market in the stock at the time the investor wishes to sell, and subject to certain regulatory restrictions. Ordinarily and within broad parameters, the investor, now a shareholder, will not be interested in corporate governance nor in the residual claims to the assets of the shareholder that may exist in the event of a bankruptcy after all debt has been discharged. Such a shareholder perhaps expects dividends (increasingly, shareholders do not expect dividends, particularly in new economy companies), but expects to make the bulk of its profits from the eventual sale of the stock. Therefore, what the investor really cares about is the ease with which the shares can be sold, and the price the shares will bring at sale, when that time comes. The investor has made a bet that the company, its business carried on by "the efforts of others," will achieve a share price higher than the purchase price.

The price of a share of common stock may rise like the sun, or the company may go bankrupt and its stock become worthless, that is, not exchangeable for money.[18] The structure of finance itself, the lag between money provided and money repaid, makes investing inherently uncertain. Various things might happen. Excitement over a new technology may cause the price of an equity to be bid up a hundredfold, or maybe not. Even if a technology is truly significant, investors may not be able to ascertain whether a given company can profit accordingly, for shares are in companies and not directly in "the future." Or the beliefs driving bidding may be substantively correct, but in the wrong timeframe. One of the first market bubbles was the Dutch tulip mania that burst in 1637. But it bears remembering that tulips in fact have colonized the world. In the long view, the Dutch were no more wrong about the tulip than those Americans in the late twenties who invested in a great new technology, radio, only to watch the Great Depression destroy their profits (and ownership interests take decades to recover) or those countless investors who lost money betting on another, ultimately critical, technology, the railroad. Investment awaits reality.[19]

But investors need not wait for reality in order to trade. Within certain legal restrictions, investors have the right to sell their securities at any time. Practically speaking and in the usual circumstances, selling securities is very easy, perhaps the easiest sort of sale. A deep secondary market exists for securities listed on exchanges (most famously the New York Stock Exchange) and even for many technically unlisted securities (such as those traded with NASDAQ). A pool of buyers stands ready and willing to exchange money for such securities, at a price set by auction. (Securities are, to varying degrees, "liquid," that is, they may easily be converted into money.) Securities thus allow investors to price future outcomes, and trade rights that embody those beliefs, on a continuous basis. Put slightly differently, securities provide a way of doing business now, with the future, or, the next best thing, with bundles of property rights that embody claims to be redeemed in the future. Securities markets make the future a present interest. Conversely, in the financial economy, we attend to, live in, the future.[20]

The second aspect of the *Howey* definition of investment contract—and hence gloss on the meaning of "security"—is a "transaction, scheme or contract." The contract entailed in a security, however, is not the memorialization of a particular relationship between specific parties. Instead, securities are invariably issued severally, and usually *en masse* (an offering may consist of millions of shares). Each security bundles together a set of discrete rights, but each bundle, every contract, is identical to every other bundle in its class, and can be resold (traded) countless times. Insofar as securities are acceptable as payment (such as in exchange for management services or for an entire company), then securities may serve as a form of money. But even in those situations in which we feel it appropriate to characterize securities as property rather than money, the liquidity of the securities markets means that securities are comparable, not merely within their class (where they are legally identical), but with investments across industries, and even across the capital markets. This point is usually made with regard to the cost of capital to a firm. Firms issue securities in order to finance growth (whether through the issuance of debt or equity); firms with a lower cost of capital have a substantial competitive advantage. Firms therefore necessarily compete with other firms in their industry (other firms bearing similar risk) to raise money as cheaply as possible. Securities markets thus not only facilitate, they require, the comparison of the prospects of different enterprises.

The third important part of the *Howey* definition of investment contract is "common enterprise" and the investor's reliance on "the efforts of others." Securities allow the creation of enterprises too large for individuals to fund. Railroad, and now airline companies, for example, which have high start-up costs, would be unimaginable without the pooling of private capital, that is, without the exchange of diffuse surplus cash for securities. Perhaps of greater importance, however, a securities market takes the activity of a private firm, and makes it public. The buying and selling of a company's shares, which we usually think of as the interplay of quintessentially private interests, becomes a matter for public price discovery, that is, the pricing of the capital structure of the enterprise. As any die-off of recently public technology companies or any wave of mergers demonstrates, the fate of public companies depends on public perception. The situation is only slightly more complicated for "private" equity or other nonpublic forms of finance. Investors, especially investors in private equity markets, have options. Their money spends in many places, including the market for publicly held companies, so a decision to make one investment is simultaneously a decision to forego other opportunities. A decision to invest is therefore implicitly a valuation across a range of options. Finance thus subjects companies, even privately held companies, to collective judgment.

So, to bring together these three aspects of the *Howey* definition of investment contracts understood to be securities, namely, expectation, fungibility, and collectivity, we can think of securities as legal instruments through which the financial markets collectivize, even socialize, beliefs about the future of firms, and because securities are liquid, convertible into money and hence into each other, the economic future writ large. Securities markets are thus comprised by present beliefs about our collective future, the center of gravity among the *rentier* class, the position of which is assiduously if rather witlessly reported by the press. Securities markets may even serve, like gothic cathedrals or epic poems, as collective summations of the belief structure of an age—or so our incessant reporting of the movement of market indices would suggest.[21]

Humans tend to be at least as worried about future losses as we may be greedy for future profits. Insurance policies appeared at about the same time as securities, and markets for insurance such as Lloyd's appeared alongside stock markets.[22] With the hindsight afforded by modern financial theory, this makes perfect sense. Risk and return are aspects of any financial transaction; there is no investment opportunity without risk. This banality has a rather counterintuitive result: for all its apparent significance, the distinction between a good and a bad event is unimportant to the structure of finance. Returning to eighteenth-century London, we see this symmetrical structure at the beginning of the modern financial markets. The joint stock holder must discount his expectation of profits from a voyage to the West Indies by the possibility that the ship does not return or the voyage is for some other reason unprofitable. The name at Lloyd's (individual insurers are called "names") might be more certain of the maximum return on his investment—the insurance fee having been fixed by contract—but he too must discount his anticipation by the risk that the ship will be lost, and he will be liable for a share of the losses. The venturer has bet that the voyage will end profitably, but has a side bet with the insurer that the ship will sink. The insurer is equally an investor, betting that the voyage will end safely. To insure a voyage is thus to trade in risks: the venturers are willing to give up a certain sum in exchange for protection against catastrophic losses, while the insurers are willing to bear the risk of such catastrophic losses in exchange for a certain sum.

More generally, one may bet on a win (be "long") just as easily as one may bet on a loss (hold a "short" position). A purchaser of a share in a publicly traded company hopes that the price of a share increases, but is exposed to the possibility that the price declines. Conversely, the short seller of the same security hopes that the price of the share decreases, and is exposed to the possibility that the price of the share increases. Or, for another example, consider a call option, the right to buy at a certain price, as opposed to a put option, the right to sell at a certain price. To abstract, and generalize these developments: finance has become the art of creating an array of legal instruments that anticipate the future's vagaries, whether positive or negative, and pricing such instruments appropriately.

Devising such an array of legal instruments has required centuries. The proliferation of securities instruments began with the seventeenth century, and has continued up to the present. Securities have been issued by, in rough order, individuals, government, quasi-public chartered institutions (such as the Bank of England, the South Seas Company, or the Virginia Company), an increasing number of limited liability companies (still somewhat protected by the state), and now financial companies, such as mutual funds, whose only "products" are themselves financial instruments, conveying beneficial interests in still other instruments.[23] In the twentieth century, in America and throughout the City of Gold, we are "securitizing" a host of things besides entities that, we hope, have incomes.[24] Debt is now, generally speaking, securitized: income streams from sources like mortgage loans, car loans, student loans, or consumer debt, particularly credit cards, are assigned to special purpose vehicles (SPVs).[25] Shares in such SPVs are floated on the public capital market. Similarly, commercial real estate is increasingly owned by real estate investment trusts (REITs), which often issue shares that are publicly traded. Small to medium-size businesses are "rolled-up" by companies often formed for the sole purpose of buying such businesses. The money for such purchases is raised on the stock market; the acquired businesses (and their earnings sheets) are assets of the acquirer, allegedly reassuring to stockholders. Commodities unproduced are traded through the futures markets . . . one could go on.[26] The economy, in short, has become securitized.

As a result of the realization that financial instruments may differ in their particulars, but are fundamentally alike, that is, different packages of risk and return, the distinctions among the various financial industries (particularly banking, capital markets, and insurance) have come to be recognized as cultural and institutional rather than logically necessary. In the last few decades, the practical differences among the industries have diminished, and the cultures have begun to converge. With advances in mathematical modeling, it has become possible to design securities ("derivatives") that in theory account for any risk.[27] At the same time, and to some extent as a result, insurance, banking, and securities firms began doing business that had traditionally been part of other segments of the financial services industry. A wave of cross industry mergers has followed.

But the consolidation of the financial industries is hardly the most significant aspect of the securitization of the economy, the increasingly nuanced trading of risk and return. Marx famously said that "all that is solid melts into air," by which he meant that the profoundly felt human relations of earlier times was, in his time, being replaced by the abstract and formal relations of property law and cash payment.[28] This process has accelerated: much of property as once understood—rights held by individual people to control specific things in the real world, paradigmatically land—has melted, too, replaced by financial obligations. Society moved its economic activity from natural persons to legal persons, corporations, and then began to trade interests in the corporations and their activities, and then interests defined in relation to such corporations, and lately interests defined in relation to such derivative interests.[29] In an economy so dominated by finance among legal persons, the real economy begins to serve primarily as security—in the old sense of collateral—for the financial economy.[30] As the economy has grown ever more abstract, ethereal, even vertiginous, we look to private law as if the right letter from our broker would make our circumstances feel any less surreal. But our City appears as Amsterdam did to the rest of seventeenth-century Europe. Amsterdam's fabulous wealth was to all appearances the product of little conquest and less manufacture, but instead the accumulation of countless contracts, expectations. In the City of Gold, as the financial market has increased its share of the total economy, the near future has been substituted for the present, and because it is the substance of our trades, the future is with us already.

The preceding chapter closed by characterizing the City of Gold as a communicative space, the space in which our monetary conventions held sway. The present chapter has turned from monetary transactions generally to the structure of finance, which revealed that the City of Gold is defined temporally as well as spatially. Understood as individual transactions, contractual arrangements, finance forces both enterprises and investors to attend to the near future. At the aggregate level of the financial markets, where contractual obligations are understood as property, the translation of the real economy into the terms of the financial economy may be understood as the effort to price the near- to medium-term future. That which is priced can be bought: the City of Gold is thus defined temporally as the Sisyphean effort to control the near future.

The City's emphasis on the near future is not without consequences for how we live. Most of us think of the world of finance as a far country, and we are cautious when we go there. We try to keep our personal finances somewhat separate from the tooth and claw of competition on the financial plane. We do not want to put ourselves, to use the corporate warrior term, in play. At the same time, we do go to the land of finance, and often. If there is security to be found in market societies, it is found through prudent use of the markets themselves. So we tell individuals to incorporate, extol the virtues of investing, hold property, never venture our entire capital, get an education, take out insurance, and plan for retirement. The idea is that we can use the financial economy to shift the acute risks of individual error, the slings and arrows of outrageous fortune, and even inescapable human maladies, onto the broad back of society. With luck and smarts, we may be able to ameliorate the harms we will inevitably suffer, and to conserve and perhaps increase our personal wealth. In short, prudent use of the financial markets holds out the promise that we can secure a prosperous life, the bourgeois dream.

Still, one can be ruined in the financial economy just like one can be destroyed in the real one. Many of the same legal vehicles that allow an individual to participate in the financial economy pose substantial risks to the individual. So, for example, even in the eighteenth and nineteenth centuries overdraft privileges might cause a young nobleman to lose the family manse, an abiding concern of both the law of trusts and certain class of novels. Being a name at Lloyd's was (and is) immensely profitable, except when it is not, at which point one had (and has) unlimited liability.[31] Although these pitfalls and their ilk are real, most of them can be avoided. Life in the developed countries is, in historical terms, amazingly certain. With a little work, a little talent, and a little luck, we are fairly justified in expecting that we and our loved ones will live long healthy lives, full of fun things to do and good things to eat. Securing this "good life," without undue exposure, comprises middle-class life. The temptation—the promise of personal security so long as our bodies last—is powerful. For all the talk about progressive and conservative aspects of metropolitan politics in the first part of this chapter, the City's seductiveness finally unfolds from this rather private promise, which can be only partially fulfilled, to free us not just from history and its wars, but from time itself, to relieve even our own very human fears.

CHAPTER IV

Urban Renewal

New enterprises and the problem of valuation. Bubbles and new economies. Relations among conventions. Exclusion, permission, and status. Erotics of the market. Dialectic between liberty and dominion. Political capital. Historical capital. Waste. Inflation and betrayal. Temptation.

Chapter I discussed the founding of the City; chapter II described the City in spatial terms; and chapter III explored the concept of time that informs the City. The present essay asks a more organic question: How does the City grow? In order to do this, this essay starts relatively small and considers the so-called valuation of start-up companies, the art of assessing the possibilities of a company, represented by its common stock, which has in recent years financed the construction of the wave of new businesses collectively referred to (with varying degrees of enthusiasm or irony) as the "new economy."[1] The inquiry is undertaken, not so much with a view to its answer, but as an object and occasion for critical reflection on the deeper structures of our economy, the grammar through which our desires are combined and our future constructed.

There has arisen a typical way in which internet, software, biotechnology, or other high technology businesses ("tech companies") come into being.[2] Entrepreneurs have an idea. The entrepreneurs attempt to articulate their idea in a business plan. The business plan is then sold to investors, of which there are various types, who are alike in their basic function: they contribute a certain amount of money in exchange for a percentage of ownership in the company. So, for example, a $1 million investment in a company valued at $2 million (typical numbers for a so-called "angel" investment) would be worth ⅓ of the company, because $1 million is ⅓ of the three million that the $2 million company with a $1 million cash infusion is deemed to be worth. The entrepreneurs use the money thus acquired to attempt to realize the ideas expressed in the business plan—they develop technologies that have been promised, they hire employees to fill functions merely budgeted, they lease space and cease using their homes as business addresses, and so forth. As the company begins to take shape, and gets closer to beginning business operations, it consumes more and more money, and the entrepreneurs have to seek more and more financing. Each financing, a sale of a percentage ownership of the company, requires the company to be valued again. The closer the business gets to being a real business, however, the larger and less riskier it is, and thus the less equity a given investment dollar buys.[3] If all goes well, the business begins operations ("roll out"), and attempts to dominate its market. It may even earn revenues. At some point, generally after operations have begun but often before any revenues have been earned, the business is likely to offer common stock to the general public in an initial public offering.

After the IPO, shares in the company will be traded continuously on the secondary market at a price that is constantly renegotiated. This price, multiplied by the number of shares outstanding, provides real-time valuation for the company as a whole (the "market capitalization"). At some point, often shortly after the IPO, the entrepreneurs usually lose control of the company—throughout the financing process, the entrepreneurs have sold control off piecemeal to investors in order to raise the cash without which the business could not have been built. Well-mannered entrepreneurs are supposed to anticipate losing operational control to professional managers. This is called having an "exit strategy," and its implementation brings the start-up phase of a company's existence to a close. Thus, throughout the start-up phase of a tech company's life, the valuation question is asked and reasked: How much is a share in this company, with all its risks and opportunities, now worth? Thus estimation of the desirability of shares in companies en route from idea to reality is at the heart of the construction of the new economy.

When this chapter was first drafted, the equity prices for high-tech companies were at historically high levels. On Friday, March 10, 2000, the NASDAQ index closed at 5048.61. This proved to be a peak. On Friday, March 9, 2001, the same index stood at 2052.78. At the time of NASDAQ's peak, all agreed that the rise in equity prices had been historic. There was widespread disagreement, however, over what such increases in share prices might mean. There were two common but diametrically opposed accounts of the valuation of such companies, which may be caricatured as the "bubble" theory, held by bears, and the "new economy" theory, held by bulls.[4] While this text was edited, bulls were chagrined and bears felt vindicated, but for years both positions were held. As this text goes to press stubborn bulls are regrouping, arguing that, despite its excesses, a profoundly new economy is here to stay, and bargains are now available. We are not interested in determining who was or is right. Instead, let us look at how such diametrically opposed views of the market could coexist for so long.

The bubble theory was rooted in the frustration felt by many people (well, traditional capitalists) with the market capitalization of many tech companies. The bubble theory maintained that the valuations of tech stocks are too high, that the stocks are overpriced. Many of these companies had no earnings. To make matters worse, such companies did not pay dividends.[5] Therefore, a shareholder could realize the "value" of such stock only by selling the stock, that is, the stock only had value because a sucker is born every minute. The prices for tech stocks, traditional capitalists argued, were negotiated upon the floating surface of a bubble, rather than the solid ground of fundamental value. More rudely, the market for tech stocks was seen as a form of ponzi scheme, in which prices were supported by the enthusiasm (Greenspan called it irrational exuberance) of the market's participants, and liquidity was provided by a steady stream of new entrants.

The new economy theory held by the bulls was a countervailing story of stock market valuation. In this story, new technology, particularly the Internet, would transform the economy. Productivity would grow, the business cycle would be largely eliminated due to perfect information, and most established companies would either be transformed or would cease to exist. Old ideas about valuation, particularly the ratio of a stock's price to the company's current earnings (P/E), were irrelevant. Current earnings could not be expected to predict future earnings; the status quo meant almost nothing in the world after the revolution.

Adherents of the bubble theory started from the assumption that a company's value, and hence the value of its stock, must be a function, or at least limited by, the company's ability to earn money. As a general proposition, a company is valuable because it already earns or will soon begin earning money, and the more money over time, the more valuable it is. Consequently, the worth of the company must be some discounted present value of the earning stream the company will generate, and therefore, companies should trade at some reasonable multiple of their present, or reasonably foreseeable, earnings. A P/E of, say, 20 seemed to be fine, but a P/E of 75 was ridiculous, and must be "corrected," that is, the price of the stock will fall as soon as a sufficient number of actors in the market realize the price for it is too high. And most young tech companies had, mathematically speaking, undefined P/Es, because they had no earnings.[6]

Advocates of the new economy theory responded that what mattered was *future* earnings. Because new technology would change everything, tech companies would make unheard of amounts of money. Proponents of the bubble theory retorted that future earnings must be discounted to account for the time value of money, and for the likelihood that the company in question would not, for whatever reason, generate high earnings—a chance of even spectacular earnings in the distant future could not explain many current valuations. Adherents of the bubble theory maintained that bullish investors lost sight not only of the "fundamentals," the business realities that constrained a company's potential to earn money, but the basic principle that a company could not be worth more than the net present value of the money the company was likely to make in the future.

Another group of traditionalists, traditional economists, are skeptical of the existence of bubbles. Market participants, they argue, process information efficiently. Therefore bubbles cannot exist or cannot exist for long. This is called the efficient capital markets hypothesis, and is the stuff of endless discussion in finance theory. Although the argument is elegant, it commands limited assent, because it appears to fly in the face of history. There are simply too many examples of prices being bid up to stratospheric levels. Eventually, the mania subsides, the bubble pops, and prices are corrected. Conversely, the price at the height of the mania must have been wrong. So, for example, since this essay was drafted, the price of shares in technology companies, particularly those without earnings, has fallen dramatically. At the instant of this revision, it is difficult to deny that the peak of the NASDAQ index at over 5,000 points in March 2000, which was driven largely by tech stocks, represented something of a bubble. Whether tech stocks are now correctly priced—the same index stands at around 1200 points as this essay is revised—necessarily remains disputed.[7] The argument becomes exciting, and seems new again, in times of boom or bust. But the structure of the argument is quite stable over the years.[8]

Again, rather than take sides in the argument over whether tech stocks are now well priced, let us ask what it means to have such an argument at all. What does it mean to talk about whether or not something, here a share in a tech company, is well priced? Money is, after all, a conventional thing, as are stocks. The language of both the bubble theory and the new economy theory suggests that we expect the relationship between these conventions to follow some set of rules, to be reasonable in some way. The bubble theory claims that tech stocks are not following the rules, and therefore are not well priced, and therefore, there will be a "correction," or worse, a "break," or even a "crash," as prices fall, bringing the rate of exchange between common stock and fiat currency to a more reasonable level. The new economy theory stated, at bottom, that the old assumptions of what was "reasonable" did not apply, and tech stocks were, in fact, following new rules. Under the new rules, tech stocks were priced correctly, or were even bargains, and therefore no correction was necessary. While the subsequent repricing makes it hard to repeat this argument verbatim, it was very plausible for a few years, and even now it is difficult to be sure that tech stocks are correctly priced.

But why should we expect social conventions to have a principled relationship? Why should the exchange rate between fiat currency and common stock—the price of stock—be stable, or even reasonable, however we
may choose to define reasonable? In an era which is self-consciously rela-
tivistic ("postmodern") in many respects, the idea that social conventions
are not very rational, and so there is little reason to think the relationship
between conventions would be rational, seems self-evident. This point is
not obvious, however, at least in part because not all conventions are created equal. There is a hierarchy of conventions, even if we are generally unaware of this hierarchy. Consider: fiat currency feels more concrete than
common stock. For many people all the time, and almost all people in
times of crisis, gold feels more concrete than money issued by governments. Conversely, the conventional nature of common stocks is more
readily apparent than the conventional nature of paper money, which is
more evidently the product of political commitments than the esteem in
which gold has so long been held. Adherents of the bubble theory proclaim
their hierarchy of belief when they maintain that the true value of tech
stocks—as distinguished from their price, which is inflated by the mania
for such stocks—rests on "the fundamentals," on the stock's pro rata share
of the company's appropriately discounted ability to earn fiat currency.
Such a proposition relies on money as an antecedent, base, reality. Similarly, the convention of paper money long rested on the antecedent, somehow more concrete, convention of gold, even when coins contained less
gold than their face value, even when bills were not redeemable for gold.
We simply do not hold all beliefs with the same tenacity, and a strong belief
can serve as a foundation for a weaker one. We may not even perceive the
strong belief to be a belief. A strong belief may be a fact of our lives, an aspect of our world not in question. We seek to relate stock (price) to fiat
currency (earnings), because we believe in the government's money in
ways we traditionally have not believed in a company's stock.

This may be true as far as it goes, but it does not go far enough. Stocks
and fiat currency are not mere gradations of the same rather mysterious
set of conventions, chips of different colors at a casino. Stocks and fiat
currency are different in kind, not just degree. Articulating that difference and why it matters is the task of criticism (aided and abetted by law,
which relies on just such distinctions). Understanding the set of conventions—markers—known as fiat currency and the set of conventions—
markers—known as stock presents us with the possibility of understanding
the stock market as an economy of culture, in which tokens of different
relationships are traded, and relationships are thereby altered. Thinking
about the valuation of high-tech start-ups presents the opportunity to
think about a *literally political* economy, a market of things defined by
political life and without other foundation.

The relationships among people with regard to things, the politics of things, are the stuff of property law. Through property law, we can begin to understand the exchange of conventions (stock exchanged for cash) that we have chosen to exemplify the mechanism of the City's economy. Stocks are a kind of property, ownership interests in the company in question. In buying a share in a company, the shareholder receives certain rights.[9] That is, a share is the token (in an age of certificateless stock, the notational token) of a set of particular relationships between a company and the holder of a share. These particular relationships are defined by law, the public law of corporations, and the private law of the corporation's documents.

In contrast, fiat currency is a species of those conventions called money, and money is anything but particular. Money is an absolutely fungible token of value "stored" (if we think of accounting as storage), a payment instrument, a medium of exchange, a unit of account, a commodity, certainly, but one that is useless in itself. In fulfilling each of its functions, money is money with almost no regard to the specifics of any situation whatsoever. The owner of money holds title not to some thing or other, but to an amount, which will only become a thing if she buys something. The owner of money can use it to fulfill any wish that can be granted in exchange for payment, without regard to some characteristic of the money—money can realize desire from among an indefinite range of possibilities, but until such choice is made, the money remains unspecified, open.

Understanding the differences among the conventions that comprise property and money is critical to understanding how enterprise is organized, that is, the maneuvers through which citizens of the City of Gold come to together to construct the City's future. To flesh out these abstractions in the context of valuing tech companies: the cash provided in a private sale in exchange for equity helps entrepreneurs to realize their desires for legal representation and documentation, commercial space, employees, and the other things establishing their business requires, and without which operations cannot begin. In exchange, private investors receive common stock, the opportunity to get richer,[10] a chance for a modicum of power (be a director of a company that may be important), a hedge against inflation, and tax advantages (deferred income if all goes well or a loss if it does not), and, truth be known, a fashionable pastime. Different parties bring different things to the table, and hope to take different things away—otherwise, trade would be impossible. For entrepreneurs, cash provides the freedom to realize their idea, while investors give up cash in exchange for a share of control in a company that may become more desirable. By way of illustration, just suppose, for some reason, that our entrepreneurs had to try to proceed with debt financing. They have only an idea, that is, no readily marketable assets and no revenue. In such circumstances, it is difficult to provide security for, or service, a loan. Our entrepreneurs would not qualify for a loan; Silicon Valley was not built on debt financing. Thus, different tokens of value—debt and equity—are all worth money, all confer status in a market society, but they have important differences from one another, and fit different parties in different situations.[11] The existence of trade thus reveals the mutual willingness to exchange one sort of property (embodied in a legal instrument, conveying property rights and hence a certain standing) for another.

As mentioned above, conventions are not held with the same level of self-consciousness. In particular, fiat currency, both specie and accounting done in its name, such as bank accounts, is often unselfconsciously treated with little regard for its conventional nature. Because currency can be used to realize such a wide range of desires, we tend to equate currency with no particular thing of value, but with value itself, the attitude toward a thing that presents itself as objectively true and that seems to justify our desire. This equation of currency and value underlies the insistence, by adherents of both the bubble theory and the new economy theory, that the "true value" of a share be related in some reasonable fashion to the fiat currency issued by a government. From the perspective of both theories, currency is value, the general standard against which particular properties, shares in individual companies, can be measured, and by extension, compared.

Many illusions work by drawing the audience's attention to a particular object, a diversion, and the audience wrongly assumes that nothing is happening elsewhere on the stage. Similarly, discussion of the nettlesome problem of valuing stocks tends to distract attention from the nettlesome problem of the valuation of money. Blinded by the effort to divine the future, even financially astute people forget all the reasons that currency is not value, such as history, deflation, inflation, currency risk, reinvestment risk, and so forth. Instead, currency begins as an assumption for convenience, but soon becomes a foundation for thought. But there is no nonpolitical foundation here: again, currency, like stock, is a convention. Rather than asking what is the value of one convention, stock, the question instead should be, what relationship, if any, exists between the two conventions?

Both property and money have an essentially triadic structure, that is, both institutions are ultimately defined in reference to third parties. Property rights are claims that can be validated in court, before a judge or other decision maker, and enforced by the state. A currency is sound if it is accepted in the faith that it is good—that it will be acceptable to another party in the future. Both share certificates and specie are thus inherently public tokens, that is, both receive their meaning from indeterminate third parties who embody society. Both ultimately rest on, and so signify, social relations—partially define the social status of their holders—despite their private appearance.

If we understand both property and money politically, in terms of the status they entail, then it is perhaps unsurprising that in many situations stock is a form of money. (That is, shares simultaneously are to be understood as property, as discussed above, and as money, as discussed below.) At least in certain circumstances in this society, shares fulfill the functions of the fiat currency of the national government. Shares are the currently preferred form of payment for the acquisition of companies and for compensating executives, and the preferred store of value for retirement and other long term accounts. Shares are a medium of exchange (for labor or companies); shares are a store of value (such as, for retirement); shares are a unit of account (particularly useful for deferred compensation, or allocating the interests within a conglomerate).

If both the fiat currency issued by the U.S. government and shares in technology companies are money, at least in some situations, then the question posed by the problem of valuing technology stocks is: To what extent should we assume that there is a fixed exchange rate between them? We do not expect the yen to be fixed against the dollar—at least, not without enormous political will to make it so. Why should tokens of status be translatable, from one to the other, in any stable fashion? In other words, to what extent are our fictions constant, fixed in their courses like Shakespeare's stars? The questions answer themselves. We do not even assume that paper money can be translated into gold, that is, a signifier of value prior to any existing government, perhaps prior to government itself, at a fixed rate. Obviously, more cash should buy more gold. But that relationship may well fluctuate, and we do not have to understand dollars in terms of gold, and indeed we do not. And so it is with tech stocks—there is no reason to believe their price is somehow functionally derived from the ability to earn another token of value, the dollar, any more than we think the tech stock should be priced in some fixed relationship to the company's ability to obtain gold.

Tech stocks have been prized in part because of the relationship they signify to new technology itself (whatever that might mean). Such stock is in effect a currency issued by the company, particularly during the start-up phase, to pay for most things needed by a young company, particularly labor. This currency is increasingly widely accepted. So, for example, law firms often wish to be paid partly in stock. For situations in which stock will not serve as payment—and there are legal restrictions on the dissemination of stock—private equity is willing to provide start-up companies with conventional fiat currency. At least in a long peacetime bull market, there is no reason to assume that dollars, or other currency backed by the state, will be of higher prestige than tokens of control over a firm believed, for a season anyway, to be on the vanguard of history. If people do not believe the U.S. government is on the vanguard of history, they may give up many tokens containing explicit reference to a value system instantiated by the state, for tokens making similarly explicit reference to the right to cast irrelevant votes, receive dividends were they to be declared, and residual assets upon dissolution, should any exist, in a company that earns no money.

Three points are worth making in passing and by way of clarification. First, none of the foregoing implies that tech stocks are now priced "correctly." The fact that there is nothing fundamental about a given P/E implies that current pricing may shift too. Since this was drafted, people have stopped wanting tech stocks so much, relative to other desirable things (and dollars are still quite desirable), and that reassessment has entailed radical shifts in P/E ratios. Unsurprisingly and as already mentioned, the bursting of the tech bubble has not ended the argument between the new economy bulls and the bubble bears. Their argument continues, as it must, because regardless of the day's price, investors must still decide whether or not to buy or sell. So the bulls argue that prices have bottomed, and this therefore is time to buy, while the bears maintain that P/E returns are still high, especially if one figures earnings in accordance with generally accepted accounting principles as opposed to reporting earnings on a pro forma basis.[12]

Second, it is interesting that a de facto currency, the common stock, recently has been considered sexier than our society's explicit currency, the dollar. This state of affairs is hardly unique. For example, in Russia, promissory notes have been widely used in lieu of debased rubles, and throughout the eighteenth and nineteenth centuries, promissory notes were widely used as currency in the United States, and an elaborate law governed their transfer. Also, in times and places when money has been conceived in terms of gold, monetary functions rely on political agreement (belief in the widespread desire for gold) that is beneath the articulations that we recognize as the state or government. But even if we realize that the state's monopoly on the creation of money has never been absolute or secure, it remains interesting that, in the late 1990s in many of the most sophisticated transactions in the United States, the government did not issue the medium of exchange.

Third, no doubt many will find the prominence of the stock market, and the seeming unimportance of the fiat currency, to be further evidence of the historical decline of the state as an institution. Business, in effect, makes much of its own money. It may even seem that the economy barely needs the state. This would be the incorrect lesson to draw: as a legal instrument, the share is not imaginable without a great deal of law made and administered by the same state that issues the fiat currency.[13] Government's ultimate triumph may be to become invisible: the City supercedes the nation even while municipal officials deny the importance of their actions.

Returning to our principal topic, can anything be said about the relationship of the two conventions, fiat currency and common stock? Although shares sometimes may be money, a form of capital, so is the cash used to buy shares. The purchase of shares is a sale of capital, raising the question that the bubble theory proponents have been insisting on all along—what sort of return on capital can be expected? Once we have dispensed with the easy equation, capital = money = value, we are left with a good question: what do we expect from this investment? At least in the heady days of the late '90s, proponents of the new economy theory tended to snort, "'Expect'? Why, son, let me tell you, nothing like this has been seen in the history of the world, and so we're talking about something beyond anything you might have imagined back in the East." With their talk of "getting it," proselytizers for the new economy seemed to believe (and draw a strange sense of election from the belief) that historical change of sufficient scope is inherently profitable. The nature of historical change is an issue, but not here: let us stipulate that technology, specifically the Internet and other electronic communications technology, has transformed the economy. The City of Gold is now, even at the retail level, a largely wired market. But great changes do not mean that the return on investment capital is necessarily high. Capital is invested in companies, legal entities in which one may hold property rights. One cannot invest in "an industry," much less "an historical process," however important such industries or processes may be. Companies often fail, or do not prosper, even—particularly—on a frontier. Railroads transformed the world, but most went through at least one bankruptcy before they became stable entities.

In the aggregate, however, one might think that historical change should generate a positive return on capital. Frontiers are settled; money will be made. Environmental pieties aside, farms and mines are worth more money than wilderness, which has no return on capital.[14] But even considered as an aggregate, it is not clear what historical change means for the return on private investment. If—and it is a huge if—the new industries are competitive, then their profits should converge on their marginal cost, and they should not be any better able to return profits than anybody else. The desktop computer industry, and perhaps the chip industry, appear to be good recent examples of this. Chip speed has doubled every eighteen months for years, in a phenomenon known as Moore's law. Due to the resulting decline in computing costs, chip usage has exploded. While money has been made, due to competition in the chip industry, the returns on capital have not kept pace.

Competition among capital providers is also likely to lower the return on investments. If an industry is sexy, it should draw willing investors, who should compete with one another, thereby lowering the cost of capital to companies, who must sell off proportionately less of the company in order to finance their expansion. As a result, fewer of the benefits of that expansion, if any, are captured by investors. This, of course, is exactly what happened for tech companies, which have at least until recently raised astounding amounts of money by printing shares, bringing their cost of capital very low. Given the amount of money looking to invest in tech companies (to say nothing of the busts), it would be good to know what the average return on capital across the industry over the last few years has been.

Even bubbles often have rational elements, indeed every mania has a rationale, a logic almost irresistible in its time. Sir Isaac Newton invested in the South Seas bubble—twice, the second time at the top of the market. The rational element of bubbles is suggested by the frontier imagery of the new economy. While investments are made in companies, shares, property interests—not industries and not the future—the emergence of new industries, a future that looks different, comprised of relations spawned by new technology, presents opportunity, unclaimed territory for investment. Who will claim dominion over this new territory? Or, more blandly, who has the property rights? The return on capital question, which sounds in money, can only be answered by reference to the idea of property.[15]

The frontier imagery of the Internet is quite apt, not just because it expresses the excitement of the unknown, but because it expresses the opportunity for subjugation, and the status acquired thereby. Like settlers racing across the border into new lands, Internet investing is about staking claims, hoping that the claims will prove to be valuable later, when they are exploited. In the American West, a few farms, a few mines, proved rich, and most operations at best earned a living. On the Internet, a few brands, products, and technologies will prove indispensable, whether protected by patent, trademark, copyright, or other property law, and companies who have successfully staked claims will become gatekeepers, able to extract tolls.[16] The price of Internet companies is determined not by the revolutionary character of the service provided, but how that particular service stands in relation to consumers' desires, either directly (a business to consumer, or "b to c play") or through other services (a business to business, or "b to b play"), in short, by the property the business claims. And the cold heart of property is the right to exclude.

But if property is exclusion, the right to frustrate the desire of others, money is access, the incentive for permission. Prostitution is thus not only the oldest profession, it is also the graphic embodiment of the mechanics, indeed the erotics, of all markets. In all markets, the desire for access is frustrated by the property right to exclude, but the right to exclude is waived or transferred in exchange for money payment. Unsurprisingly, for those of us who are affluent and not overly ambitious, the frustration at the heart of metropolitan life is muted. If we can pay the gatekeeper, we may overlook the fact that we have no right to enter, that unless we pay, we will be excluded, and it is the threat of our exclusion that induces us to pay. It is not too difficult to shut up about such unpleasantries, however, so long as we can afford to put up. We in the affluent classes are mostly merely threatened; we are seldom frustrated in fact.

Frustration is an awkward topic in the United States because the contrast between the nation's high and rising inequality, and simple, if somewhat dishonest, egalitarian political philosophy is becoming too obvious. Other boroughs of the City of Gold are somewhat better off in this regard, but in polite society here in the United States, property is regarded as necessary but somewhat embarrassing. Aside from discrete references to gated communities, even the political right makes little of the exclusive nature of property, except perhaps as a bulwark against an overweening state. But our silence does not avail us against the ugly truth that property is exclusive by nature, and because the City of Gold is defined by markets, the reciprocal exchange of money for property and back again, exclusion lies at the heart of the City's charter. To take a not insignificant example, the digital divide between those with computer technology and those without it is not only the result of policy failings and prior inequalities and the usual devils and backstabbers that have hindered progressives from reaching the promised land, but also from the fact that new technology arises from a process of exclusion—trading property, common stock in companies with intellectual property, for cash. Government (in the traditional sense) may (and should) redistribute technology, but that does not change the fact that technology arises from exclusion.

As discussed in the preceding essay, Marx was right to focus on property law, as old economy as that sounds, and to focus on how property rights establish the character, the feel, of an economy.[17] Even for Marx, property was not what it had long been: "All that is solid melts into air," the human, if exploitative, relationships that constituted the ancien regime were being replaced by property most impersonal, easily converted into money, and to which no trace of an actual, authentic human appeared to attach. By translating human relations into property relations, Marx correctly argued, Western men lost much of their sense of connection with one another, for rights holders are pale shadows of people. A right to a thing is not the thing itself: being able to call on the state to evict one's tenants is importantly different from being strong enough to force a family, with known names and history, to move.

Again, Marx's argument must be extended. A tenancy, while a form of property, is still fairly specific. Now, as discussed in the previous chapter, property, in the usual sense of specific rights to specific things, control of places, is itself melting into the ether inhabited by certificateless securities and other vaporous legal instruments. Since Marx, the melting of property has meant that ordinary citizens in the City of Gold are losing much of their sense of connection. Property was once conceived analogously to sovereignty, and so ownership was a private analogue to kingship as imagined by the bourgeoisie. "A man's home is his castle" is a statement not of law, but of sensibility, the joy of control, exercisable in spite of—to spite!—others. In contrast, property rights to a fund with holdings in commercial office space in Jakarta, whether or not subsequently devalued due to a currency crisis, convey only a pallid sense of election and no sense of domination. Contemporary property ownership affords little of the *joie de moi* that traditionally has made ruling such fun.[18] The exclusive character of our property, and so the power exercisable through property rights nominally ours, is hidden from us, in part, by the fact that our property is itself hidden from us.[19]

As a result, although something like the political sensibility associated with real property into the nineteenth century remains to citizens of the City of Gold (it is still fun to be rich), that sensibility is losing its association with parcels of land or specific things controlled. The activities associated with ownership have changed. Rather than the exercise of power on the ground, contemporary property protects a far more abstract role, choices among a set of exercisable preferences. The set of choices with which we are confronted, perennially about to be exercised, is who we think we are. But our choices are somewhat abstract, open-ended. As already suggested, much of our property is in financial instruments, legal rights, essentially invisible to us. Even the tangible things to which we have property rights, for instance mere mass-produced chattels, or land in a new location or one recently developed and consequently without history for us, tend to be almost indistinguishable from one another and therefore are not important in themselves. Moreover, quite apart from their lack of intrinsic interest, things purchased are choices made already, and as discussed in the last chapter, financial societies define themselves in terms of the future rather than the past. Our purchases require little from us in the way of ongoing commitment, but do not satisfy for long, either. The shift in the character of property suggests a parallel shift in the idea of the property holder, from sovereign to shopper.

Yet even this view of the modern property holder as the owner of a set of rather abstract preferences cannot altogether dispense with property rights in things. Choice must be exercised on something, or else it is mere appreciation, available to any spectator, and therefore hardly prestigious.[20] Choice actually exercised, property acquired, demonstrates not only capability, but also leaves one with a thing which may serve as an object of envy, perhaps a several-hundred-acre ranch with a view of the Tetons, visited for a few days a year over the course of a decade, and then sold via an advertisement in the Friday edition of *The Wall Street Journal*. Property may have lost much of its sense of sovereignty, direct rule, but the capability of acquiring property, coupled with its occasional exercise, retains a central role in our politics: it is the mechanism through which the individual ("who demands, and deserves, only the very best" as the *Journal* copy often reads) defines his place in market society, and hence both himself and his polity. Consequently, in the City of Gold, price is a relative measure of the intensity of a local struggle for social status, the quantity of money (a unit of account) one is willing to exchange for the right to exclude others from a given position. A struggle for social status, by definition, is a form of political ordering. Markets constitute political relations in a way that is the antithesis of classical or Christian ideas of community, or Marxian hopes for solidarity, which understand relationships in terms of something shared. In contrast, the City of Gold is constructed through exclusion (property), and its reciprocal, access (money payment), and not sharing is the point of politics.

The political significance of this desire for status should not be denied, least of all by those who live in institutions as hierarchical as the academy.[21] The desire for status in the community is, after all, the insight with which Aristotelian political thought begins. While modern political thought is different—more focused on the individual, less willing to countenance the reality of groups, and often suspicious of the idea of community, to say nothing of hierarchy—even moderns would concede that money and property are mechanisms through which market societies define individuals, relate them one to another, aggregate them, and thereby define the polity as a whole, if not exactly as a community. In defining status by reference to property, understood not as an attribute of political station and therefore obligation, but instead as the right to exclude without further connection, the City of Gold inverts political traditions that assert that politics rests on the longing for community. The City, in contrast to such traditions, is founded on envy.

Three points that follow from the recognition of this inversion seem important here. First, much of political thought remains true in the context of metropolitan politics, if perhaps sounding in a different key. So, for example, one might understand the City's constitutive institutions of money and property in Hobbesian terms, as compensation for the liberties sacrificed upon entry into society. More precisely, security in one's property is compensation for the liberty sacrificed upon quitting the state of nature, where one is ever fearful that one's property will be taken by a strong or stealthy enemy. Money, on the other hand, is the token of the liberty that remains to man in civil society, namely the liberty to buy and sell property.[22] For another example, recognition of one's claims to property, or desire for one's money, reaffirms the owner's sense of self, relieving the owner of the need for the desperate affirmation of violence that Hegel placed at the root of social life. Similarly, in Freudian terms, both money and property can be understood as ways that the I (*das ich*, the ego) asserts itself in a socially constricted world. Money liberates one from circumstances, and property allows one to exercise dominion over things in the world, both in compensation for the repression that social life requires. In this view, the citizen despairs of true happiness, but instead may be compensated by the great feelings of being rich. The Christians, for their part, have things to say about feelings such as the empowerment of having money, the fun of spending money on things, the envy of neighbors, and perhaps the sense of justification that an earlier age would understand as a faint memory of the time before the Fall, or maybe a premonition of election (as Weber, thinking about Calvin, might have said). These examples are a playful way of making a serious point about what is perhaps an impossible task. Recognition of the newness of our situation suggests that we must reinvent (or lose) our intellectual traditions.

A second and unpleasant result of the City's transformation of political assumptions is that the idea of equality cannot be taken seriously from within the ethos of the City. While a certain formal equality is to be expected (and is discussed in chapter XI), a politics of exclusion—of status defined on the pillars of dominion and liberty—is not egalitarian by nature. Both dominion and liberty are relative concepts; the point is to own more, to be free to do more. Nor can such striving for inequality be overlooked as private, as somehow partisan or self-interested or just plain greedy. The City itself urges its members to increase the distance between themselves and others. In the City, market activity (hitherto understood as private) is explicitly defined as public. Inequality, perhaps relabeled efficiency, is understood to be a virtue, rather than an unfortunate accident.

A third point, equally unpleasant: scarcity is created by, and intrinsic to, market societies, not some preexisting condition addressed by markets, because property, the frustration of the excluded who wish to belong, makes purchase necessary. It is therefore profoundly misleading to say that scarcity—the frustrated desire for things in the world—is the aspect of the human condition addressed by markets, according to rules discovered and articulated by the scientific discipline of economics. The problem is not simply that satisfaction of pressing desires allows humans to dream up new desires, that our possession by Malthusian demons overwhelms the best efforts of a cybernetic Ricardo. The City creates scarcity by making desire, appetites, politically central. Self-mastery, then, is not enough. As a result, defenses of globalization based on the idea that globalization will increase material wealth (which it will, since it is efficient), are internally flawed, because globalization has made it more important than ever before to be wealthy.

*   *   *

Property and money define a spectrum along which political conventions (such as real estate, common stock, or fiat currency) can be located. A number of notions clusters at each end of the spectrum. Property is: particular, usually defined in reference to a named thing (paradigmatically, an address); it is associated with an individual (the owner) who has control, dominion, the right to exclude others; it is conceived in terms of space (land, but even a patent is defined by "metes and bounds"); it is unique, not fungible; and it is immobile and politically responsible.[23] Money is essentially the antithesis of property. Money is generally accepted, defined in reference to a currency rather than anything in particular; it is anonymous and impersonal rather than personal; it is a vehicle of liberty rather than dominion; it is fungible; it is conceived in terms of quantity; and it is without location and hence apolitical. As already suggested, in the erotics of the market, property is female and money is male. Property and money are understood reciprocally, and so are endlessly if not effortlessly convertible into one another. The speed with which one can travel along this spectrum from property to money depends on the "liquidity" of one's property; the ease with which one can travel from money to property depends on the "soundness" of one's money.[24]

Real institutions, as opposed to philosophical conceptions of them, do not exist at either end of the spectrum. There is no pure property, no pure money. Any property right can be priced, has an exchange value, and hence can be thought of in terms of money. Conversely, even the most ephemeral form of money holding requires that one hold property of a sort, at least a cause of action against a financial intermediary. Different legal conventions are located at different points along the spectrum. So, for example, real property is quite close to the ideal of property, and has few of the attributes of money. Cash, on the other hand, is quite close to the ideal of money, and has few of the attributes of property. Common stock in a publicly traded company lies somewhere in the middle of the continuum defined by property and money, with some of the attributes of each. Some of the difficulty in understanding real institutions, and tech stocks in particular, stems from the difficulty of knowing which pole of the spectrum one should be facing.

As with any erotics, the satisfaction of conversion from money to property or vice versa cannot last. As discussed in the last chapter, the City is defined in the near future, and anticipation is encouraged. Humans convert change into context, reinvent their worlds on a rolling basis, and dream new dreams. Consider, by way of example, a simple purchase. The new toy is quickly forgotten; the new house becomes a place to live. Once accomplished, the purchase merely serves to exclude others (including the seller), which is nice but insufficiently so. The purchaser is immediately reminded of other possibilities, tempted to sell, and perhaps does, only to discover that dreams are insignificant unless realized, that capability has little meaning until it is exercised. And so the seller must purchase again, in an incessant cycle. Market society is not founded once and for all, but continually reconstituted by the exchange between property and money.

Imagination assures us that our worlds could be better, that we could be more powerful—if we had more money, or free—if we had more property. In order to realize such dreams, money and property must turn themselves into one another through purchase and sale, and in so doing, articulate society. Each purchase and sale builds upon the last, and when superceded, leaves its trace. The reciprocity of money and property is enormously accelerated through the process of finance: if only ___ could be done over the Internet; if only I owned a fraction of the next ___, and through such wishes are enterprises, much of our future, constructed. Once we disaggregate the idea of capital and understand capital to be a spectrum of conventions that determine the individual's status in a market society, we see that the dialectic is internal to capitalism, indeed springs from the temptation, the Faustian discontent, central to modernity itself.

To recapitulate, the argument of the present chapter thus far is this: Shares and currency are both conventionally defined tokens of value. The relationships between shares and fiat currency are continually being renegotiated; conventions are continually repositioned within the polity. We therefore should not expect a fixed relationship between these two, or any other, conventions. That said, relationships can be understood in structural terms. Fiat currency is an expression of the idea of money. While common stock may be used as money, it is also an expression of the idea of property. Money and property are both different stances toward the community. In accepting money as a form of payment for a wide range of goods, the polity grants the holder of money the right to realize his will across a similarly broad range of possibilities. Money is the token of liberty. In recognizing the right to property, the polity secures and limits the individual's control over a portion of the world, and in particular, enforces the individual's desire to exclude others, and thereby to secure their acknowledgment of his own existence. Property is the token of dominion. Unlike polities in which political identity is founded on the desire for a good place within a community, role and solidarity, the City of Gold is founded on fundamentally different relations: the citizen aspires to be free from constraint, to have money; and to be able to exclude others, to have property. But neither liberty nor dominion is sufficient unto itself, particularly in a financial culture that understands existence as perpetually unfulfilled aspiration. Consequently liberty is continually exchanged for dominion (money is paid for property), and dominion is continually exchanged for liberty (property is sold for money). The City renews itself, grows, through the commercial intercourse of its citizens. Phrased in language more familiar to political economy, the reciprocal exchange of money and property is itself the dialectic of metropolitan history.

* * *

Understanding the interplay between money and property as an erotics or a dialectic begs for a theory of evolution or history. This essay offers no such theory, at least not in the classical sense of "theory." However, a few words about the effects of trade over time, what the financial industries call "wealth," are warranted. In 2000, after a particularly bad week for Internet stocks, "The markets shed over 2 trln usd this week in their declines, according to Miller Tabak Hirsch economist Tony Crescenzi, who noted that this exceeds all of the 1.7 trln of wealth gained at the household level last year, citing data from the Federal Reserve." Although the amounts were noteworthy, the form of this quote is typical. Wealth, the analyst implied, is a thing. Last year, a lot of it was manufactured, but this week, a lot of it was destroyed, by terrorists or a hurricane or something. But clearly nothing happened—no terrorists' truck bomb slammed into a factory, no hurricane destroyed the sugar cane crop—to destroy a thing treasured by somebody. Instead, a range of items (mostly tech stocks) were repriced by the market. That is, society marked down equity in certain companies vis-à-vis the U.S. dollar.

From an Olympian height, this sell-off is of merely passing interest. It had scant effect on the real economy. Society is constantly shifting the relative demand for tokens of status, repricing, which means there will be winners and losers. As Gertrude Stein might have said, the money's the same, only the pockets (and the exchange rates) change.[25] From the perspective of the participants, however, it matters a great deal whose pockets are being lined and whose are being emptied. The repricing of conventions represents a success for some people and a setback for others. In this view wealth, whether money or property, is a relational concept, a statement about who has power within a given society.[26] It is important to remember that, in any given society at any given moment, there are always winners and losers, that somebody is always on top, in Stein's image, the money must be in somebody's pockets. Because this idea of wealth is internal to a society, we may speak of political capital.

Understanding capital within the context of a polity allows us to discern, if perhaps only dimly, another, quite different, way to think about capital. Work, as it accretes over time, creates capital. We need not reinvent the wheel, or the operating system, because we can understand that which has already been done. All else being equal, such capital grows. We humans create order, and we tend to leave behind a bit more structure than we found. Capital in this second sense is a residuum of history, often expressed as a text. Such capital is not relative but cumulative, albeit in the nonlinear sense that snow accumulates, that is, there may be more or less of it. It is probably impossible to quantify such capital, but it may be thought of as the sum of a society's intentions, meanings, texts that have been amassed and incorporated into social life. This cumulative idea of wealth may be called historical capital, the meanings that a society produces over time.[27]

The difference between political and historical capital grows somewhat more clear when we think of war and of waste. Political capital is a question of who is in power; somebody always is. War can only transfer political capital: before, during, and after World War One, somebody was in power in Germany. War may, however, destroy historical capital outright, waste lives and their accomplished works. Texts can be obliterated, stories forgotten, wisdom lost—those fragments that we have shored against our ruins can be scattered into the mud.[28] What was mourned by T.S. Eliot and others after the trenches of World War One was high European culture, the collective effort of millions of lives over hundreds of years. But worse was yet to come. Eliot lived to confront the awful possibility of intentional book burning, the effort not simply to kill—ordinary evil, hurrying nature—but to render works nothing, *vernichten*, as if the people had never been, denying culture. Historical capital tends to grow, but we can waste it—something we intellectual heirs of the Germans who style ourselves as Romans ought to remember.

From the perspective of historical capital, inflation is a profound problem, even a pathology.[29] To begin with the easy case, consider hyperinflation. A society with hyperinflation may collapse, at the very least cannot build—there is simply too much uncertainty to mobilize the present in the service of the future. If one cannot build, then the store of historical capital does not grow, and begins to shrink, diminished by the wear and tear of time. There is a sense in which real wealth was destroyed in the German hyperinflation of the twenties, or the Ecuadorian hyperinflation of the past couple of years. Even ordinary inflation challenges our confidence in the equity markets. If money inflates, then it fails as a store of value, fails to make past values available to present investors. In such circumstances, we might expect to see (and often do) a concomitant loss of confidence that equity and debt instruments can make the future tradable.[30] Confronted with inflation, we doubt our ability to capture, take property rights in, the future. So, insofar as shares are understood as tokens of a particular future, inflation shakes the faith in the future, or at least our faith that we have seen the future and can buy some. This anxiety can quickly become self-fulfilling. If the future cannot be bought, finance cannot be done, and if there is no finance, we are restricted to operating incomes and can hardly grow. Thus inflation tends to hinder the formation of historical capital through economic growth.[31]

Inflation sufficient to retard finance prevents the formation of historical capital—the writing of society's texts—in another way: deals are not done, contracts are not signed, relationships are not cemented. Quite apart from actual things not made, inflation can prevent society's ability to build upon the articulations, a house of cards, perhaps, but nonetheless historical capital. If we understand historical wealth as the sum of society's articulations, then the ability to do deals—regardless of whether the deals are in any other way good—adds to the store of historical capital and so thickens metropolitan life.[32] Conversely, inflation plus a stock market correction simplifies commercial society, and so destroys historical capital.

Perversely enough, even a hint of inflation, the weakness of a currency, often inspires equity investors to sell, that is, to invest in the currency.[33] Although we need not rehearse the rationales, some of which may be sensible under some circumstances, perhaps something of a more general answer lies, again, in the reciprocal nature of property and money. A stock is a commitment not just to an industry, but to a specific company. Although the stock markets are usually considered perfectly liquid, that is a tribute to their organization and an academic convenience. In a falling market, a stock may not be liquid, and an investor may have to ride the stock down. (For dramatic examples that had nothing to do with inflation, consider Enron or Worldcom, in which markets dried so quickly that investors were unable to sell.) From this perspective, it makes no sense to stay invested in stocks that may become vulnerable. Money is flexible, mobile, presents options. Therefore, in light of the uncertainty presented by even a substantial rumor of inflation, it might be better to buy even a somewhat devalued but nonetheless sound currency, so that one's affairs may be reordered as circumstances dictate. Again, war provides a more dramatic version of common reality: as the rebels win victory after victory and people realize they might have to leave the capital suddenly, they begin to buy gold, move their money into foreign accounts, and many sell their houses at substantial losses. The local money is devalued. Inflation thus occasions and reflects a betrayal of sorts, a cashing out, and devil take the hindmost.

If inflation reflects a willingness to flee, a betrayal, the visceral antipathy to inflation felt by many conservatives reflects the converse, the commitment to a society as it is, and the desire that things continue as before. From this perspective, the fear of inflation that has dominated monetary policy in recent years makes some sense. Inflation is not merely against the interest of the *rentier* class, and not merely a mechanism through which democracy antagonizes oligarchy, although it is both of these things. Conservatives correctly intuit something deeper: Inflation is subversive. Inflation undermines allegiance to the status quo achieved by the interplay of contract and property, more fundamentally, to the binding connections, the processes of repression, that are the fasteners of civilization itself. As discussed in chapter III, finance may permit a borrower to realize a dream, but at the cost of incurring a repayment obligation to the lender. Inflation allows the borrower to fulfill this obligation in form—to repay the nominal amount of the debt—but in debased dollars. The fundamental agreement, the promise to repay, is nominally kept but substantively eviscerated. Inflation seems antisocial.

But the conservative anxiety over wealth lost to inflation, more broadly, concern for the connections that bind society together, connections that inflation threatens to undo, is only half the story in any economy. The other half is desire, the dreams that fuel not only the financing of tech start-ups, but also the incessant exchange of money for property for money, and even temptations like inflation, fraud, and theft. Without desire, there would be no intercourse, and the City would not renew itself. In suggesting that the social order is not that solid, inflation is unseemly, tempting, like young bodies that promise vast freedoms, the freedom of young Nicholas Leeson fleeing across a sun drenched Pacific, a national financial institution in tatters and millions upon millions missing, every office drone's daydreams of escape to a horizon pool overlooking an impossibly green sea.[34] When economics seems most dismal, and our complicity in globalization strikes us as at best conflicted, perhaps even tragic, we should remember that the City, like any polity, contains an erotics, the stuff of comedy, voices of happy children rising from the beach below.

CHAPTER V

Governance

Placelessness of City. City rather than empire or republic. Governance through finance.
Examples. Implications of shift to finance rather than direct competition as governance
mechanism. Belief structure of finance. Accidental quality of governance through finance.

The "City" of this book's title has social, political, and cultural meanings, but carries none of the customary physical/spatial sense of a traditional city, a specific, densely populated locality, one of the places that have defined commerce, politics, and much of culture for several thousand years and that may be experienced individually. One may, for instance, speak of Washington in August or Brussels in February, and be understood to mean something specific, a physical situation, with its own feel, but the City of Gold is no place, has no season. How do we locate ourselves in a situation without specific time or place?

Although the City of Gold is in historical terms new, the experience of life in the City is not entirely foreign to us. Much of metropolitan life is similar to traditional urban life, the political experience of those who live in the matrix of economic interests that have long comprised cities. The idea of the city at work in the phrase "City of Gold" is an extension of the idea of the market: people come together to trade, to deal with others in order to secure their own needs and those of their dependents. Trade requires shared conventions. Conventions of language must be shared so that one can haggle; conventions of money so that one can pay; conventions of law so that trade has terms; conventions of government so that disputes can be resolved and to provide for the general welfare. The immediate coming together we call the market. The dense and permanent disposition of such people, continuously engaged in or dependent upon market activity, whose understanding of the world is largely shaped by the requirements of their commerce, we call a city.

Cities can be and have been understood in other ways. In the Middle Ages, whence we get our legal understanding of the city as a corporate entity, the city was often conceived in terms of a communal covenant. Sometimes this covenant was explicit: people held hands, prayed, and founded communities. The Roman empire and others understood their capital to be the focal point of their empire, and other cities to be the images, projections, and practically speaking, administrative outposts, of the capital, and hence to participate in the empire. Such ideas of the city require a shared purpose, a shared sense that the city has its own reason for being, its own *telos*, even, quite apart from the diverse ends held by the participants. But the idea of the city used here is political in a more rudimentary sense: the modus vivendi that arises when people find themselves successfully living among one another. This understanding of the city, apt for both the City of Gold and the city as traditionally conceived, are names for polities that are comprised among discrete and often antithetical interests. The city is thus a concept like an ecosystem, or a solar system, or especially a market—a way of talking about a whole comprised of the contradictions among its parts.

Why is the polity constructed by supranational capital best imagined as a city? Our situation could also be described in terms familiar from other political entities. The empire and the republic might seem to be particularly apt ways to describe, and so understand, contemporary politics. "Empire" captures both the push to hegemony characteristic of our time, and the tolerance, even "celebration" of a certain degree of diversity among the subject peoples, so long as they don't get too big for their britches.[1] And yet the City of Gold is not an empire; the imagery is not quite apt. Empires are about glory, about wresting a place in the sun, about *being* the sun, as various Egyptian pharaohs and France's Louis XIV would have it. Empires require the world to pay spiritual homage, to acknowledge the empire as the center of things. Holy Roman Emperor Frederick IV was called *stupor mundi*, the astonishment of the world. Germany and Japan, sophisticated countries late to modernize, seem to have been the last nations to think that they could win glory by founding an empire, and to have the wherewithal to threaten bringing it off. But empires were going out of fashion even before World War Two, and that process has accelerated.[2]

After World War Two, the United States and the Soviet Union seemed to some critics to offer a variation on the idea of empire, the empire disguised as historical inevitability, or ideological certainty, or some such thing which only indirectly just happened to benefit the country at the cutting edge. So when Ronald Reagan denounced the Soviet Union as an evil empire, he sought to unmask a disguise: if the Soviet leaders were not engaged in the same old imperial politics of subjugation in the name of glory, why did they need the Berlin Wall?[3] And so Reagan urged Gorbachev to "tear down this wall."[4] Astonishingly enough, the "empire" in question demonstrated that it was not in fact an empire, and though Gorbachev did not order the demolition, the Wall did come down.

Similarly, U.S. actions abroad have long been criticized as quests for national glory, expressions of the old lust for empire, rather than, as the United States incessantly has claimed in other words, geopolitically entailed by the unfolding of liberty across the world. But Americans have long combined a very real nationalism with a deep belief that America's claims are not particularly or peculiarly American, that if there were no America, it, like God, would have to be invented. America has always understood itself as a necessary instantiation of timeless truths, easily replicable elsewhere and in other circumstances, rather than as a contingent product of its peculiar situation. Consequently, American ideology does not present itself—to Americans, at least—as ideology.[5] Americans so profoundly believe they are right that they generally do not have the equipment to think other thoughts, to understand their position as willful, an effort to make the world after one ideal among others. Merely obeying their manifest destiny—manifest, at any rate, to them—Americans do not even understand themselves to be imposing their will in any personally gratifying sense. Americans have never had much "true passion to rule spice kingdoms," even though, from time to time and for one reason or another, such places must be controlled.[6] So exercises of American power appear to Americans as necessary if perhaps regrettable, and to other peoples may seem astoundingly callous. Whatever the appearances, however, the old idea of empire is not part of the American psyche, and the idea is useful today primarily for certain evocative purposes.[7] Despite unparalleled military hegemony, and a surfeit of various forms of power, the United States could not now revive a serious idea of empire if it tried.[8]

Although the idea of empire neither animates the City of Gold nor describes the national aspirations of the United States, the idea is not entirely dead. There are imperial aspects to a number of governments that rule large nations comprised of diverse and alienated peoples, and that are willing to enforce rule by force, in accordance with some sense of historical legitimacy. Consider in this regard whether China, Russia, India, Indonesia, or Nigeria, and perhaps others, ought to be characterized as imperial powers. But even if such nations ought to be considered in imperial terms, as the United States has been considered above, that does not mean that such nations can actually achieve the status of an empire. The difficulty is not practical—each of these countries is already quite as large as many of history's empires—but intellectual and spiritual. Contemporary nations can no longer win glory by imperial success. It may be necessary for the capital to subdue provincials who wish to secede, as Russia is doing to the Chechens—it is difficult for an American to argue otherwise—but it cannot be other than a messy business, hardly the glory of Caesar marching into Gaul.[9]

Nor is the City of Gold well described in terms of the paradigm that dominates the political imagination of this and recent eras, the national republic. As discussed in the last chapter, the City of Gold is constructed through exclusion. The City appears to have no public thing, no object of communal concern, no *res publica*, although it has many and complex processes through which the needs of various people—in that loose sense, the public—are met. Ideologically, at least, the market is not the object of common concern by market participants, it is the collection of participants and their transactions, no more.[10] In contrast, the republic presumes inclusion—*égalité* and especially *fraternité*—shared objects of concern, a sense of belonging together as opposed to being held in check. Furthermore, citizens of the republic are supposed to worry about the state of the republic; such concern is part and parcel of being a republican citizen. In contrast, citizens of the City of Gold worry about the extent of their wealth, the quantum of envy at their command.

Each of the foregoing chapters characterized metropolitan political life in a way that may be easily distinguished from republican political life. Chapter I, "Conception," discussed the foundation of the City as a rejection of the politics of the nation, and in particular, of the idea that the nation relied on a shared public sphere coterminous with its geographic boundaries. While the founders of the City retained the idea of the public in the deracinated sense of "public official," they rejected the idea and sought to abolish the institutional expressions of the public in the sense expressed by the Nuremberg rallies, the fusion of individual anomie into a collective, intentional, emotional body. Chapter II, "Money as Communication," understood the City as a polity constructed by capital. Because the lexicon of money is so limited, in comparison to that of language, the City is incapable of articulating a public vision, and so cannot engage in constitutive political discourse, the lifeblood of republican thought. Chapter III, "Finance and the War with Time," discussed how the metropolitan focus on the near future resulted in anxiety and a tendency to conformity, the homogeneity often associated with globalization. Such homogeneity is incompatible with a serious local identity, the life of the citizen in the republic valorized by Rousseau. Chapter IV, "Urban Renewal," discussed the City as the product of the dialectic between dominion over things and liberty. Rather than community, dominion and liberty bespeak exclusion of one's fellows and freedom from the constraints of living together. The genetic mechanism of the City is thus anticommunal, and hence profoundly at odds with republican thought.[11] In sum, the City's politics are metropolitan, as opposed to imperial or republican, in character.

Although comprised by the interests of traders, even cities have government. Indeed, to speak of a polity implies a form of government in the traditional sense of a sovereign; polities are traditionally categorized by the form and legitimation of their sovereignty. As the U.S. Supreme Court said in *U.S. v. Curtiss-Wright,* "A political society cannot endure without a supreme will somewhere."[12] Despite the fact that the City, by definition, is no place, and so can have no capital, if we are to understand the City of Gold as a polity, then we must be able to show how it is governed.[13]

Although there is no short answer to this puzzle, we can begin by dispensing with two attractive but unfruitful approaches to the problem of governing the City. One approach would be to understand metropolitan government and politics in mainstream fashion, as the traditional activities of the avowedly political institutions. From this perspective, the state, at least since the Russian Revolution, understands itself to be responsible for both "politics" and "economics," not only in more or less socialist countries, but even in that purported bastion of laissez-faire economics, the White House. In this view, the City of Gold has no distinct government structure, but is governed by the political mechanisms familiar to the enlightened imagination—national governments composed of legislative, executive, and judicial branches—with two important and historically recent additions: a large standing bureaucracy, and a web of international agreements, including the shifting of a number of governmental roles onto the shoulders of international institutions architecturally similar to national institutions. The second approach to the problem of governing the City, not incompatible with the first, is to argue simply that the City does not exist, and so needs no government to continue its (non)existence. While the idea of a governing will in history, here called the City of Gold, may be a psychological necessity or a metaphorical convenience, there is no such entity in fact. The City of Gold needs no mechanism of governance, need not resist the forces of dissolution, because the City is merely an overly clever riff on the fiction of globalization, itself merely a way of conceptualizing the present situation.

Both approaches are underinclusive. Many aspects of metropolitan culture are more authoritative than other fictions that structure political debate, for example, the nation state. Even contemporary national government cannot be understood outside of the context formed by the City. In an interdependent world, sovereignty cannot even be imagined to be the exercise of national autonomy in a political vacuum, but instead must be reconceptualized as a continuous process of political recognition within a cultural web of supranational scope.[14] It is simply too late in the day to understand international relations as the expression of national interests autonomously conceived, or, more generally, metropolitan political culture as an extension of political forms prevalent before World War Two. To claim that global culture does not exist, in high nominalist fashion, is useless for all but academic debate and certain populist political rhetorics. Such nominalism cannot be maintained in the face of history. Nietzsche welcomed the coming age that would "carry heroism into knowledge and wage war for the sake of ideas and their consequences."[15] This turned out to be more than imagery; the wars of ideology followed. And to deny the reality of the ideas that led to war, and the mandarin efforts to prevent such wars by making those ideas unthinkable, in the face of all that blood and how we live and think now, is not available to us. So we are committed to the City of Gold, and left to ask, again, how the City is governed.

The first answer (first because it will prove to be insufficient, requiring more answers, which part 4 attempts) is that the City governs itself automatically, that there is no political will, and in that sense, no sovereign. *The Wealth of Nations* articulated the hope that, in a properly constituted market economy, individual morality, social mores, and political will could be made superfluous—or as the English like to say regarding their unemployed, "redundant." Get the incentives right, and substantively good policies will follow. In this view, all political efforts are at bottom constitutional, are efforts to set the ground rules by which society's games will be played.

For Smith, competition was the mechanism through which markets governed themselves. Enterprises that produced good products at good prices would be rewarded with business—people would buy their products. Both the producers and the consumers would be happy, each having made trades favorable to themselves. Over time, bad businesses would fail for want of custom, good businesses would devise ways to offer better products at lower cost to consumers, and the wealth of the nation would increase—as if an invisible hand were pushing the nation gently but inexorably forward. Shortly after Smith proposed how self-interest, no matter how venal, could be combined so as to lead to the public good, even in the absence of good people, Madison urged that faction could be used for the betterment of democracy. To overstate for emphasis, Madison thus reinforced Smith's view that the perfection of political economy would be the elimination of politics, in the sense of communal feeling, altogether.[16] It would be a bit of a stretch to claim that the City of Gold has altogether achieved this happy state. But the City of Gold works so well—does so much business with only minimal attention from the institutions we recognize as government—that many people imagine the City perfected, like an ecosystem in a Godless world, running without human oversight or interference whatsoever.

The self-regulatory mechanisms of our economy, however, are different in critical ways from the mechanisms on which Smith focused. In brief, the real economy is governed by the cost of capital provided to it by the financial economy, presumably based upon the best information available to the financial markets. Imagine two companies, A and B, that compete with each other, and with a handful of similar companies. Imagine that for some reason—cheaper land, a new product, better labor relations, it does not matter why—Company A has a discernible advantage over Company B. Company A and B both seek to raise money to expand. Company A should be able to raise money on terms more favorable than Company B can negotiate. Company A should be rewarded, and B punished, for their relative competitive positions. Either Company B cannot expand at all, or its cost of capital for the expansion will be higher. Company A, on the other hand, will reap the benefits from its expansion. In either case, Company B will *eventually* have to charge more than Company A, or produce products inferior to those of Company A. Finance has thus magnified the competitive imbalance between the companies. This need not be immediately obvious to consumers in the marketplace. Company B may keep its costs down, and its products competitive with those of Company A, by cutting corners. Perhaps Company B does not upgrade its equipment, or does not raise its employees' pay, as fast as Company A does. However, such tactics cannot be sustained indefinitely. Long before consumers need be aware of the situation, the management of both companies, and others in the financial industry, are likely to know how matters stand. Suppose Company B seeks to develop a new product; its efforts are likely to be met with skepticism from investors. Suppose, in contrast, company A seeks to raise money to buy Company B, is successful, and goes on to acquire Company B. In fact, seeing the writing on the wall, the management of Company B may have sought the takeover, that is, put their company "in play." Regardless of how negotiations begin, however, the point here is that Company A's acquisition of Company B, and Company B's dissolution, requires no real change in the products offered to the consumer marketplace. The fate of the companies may be decided in the financial economy, not by actual competition in the real economy.[17]

The classical economic paradigm is immediate. The economy is regulated by consumer decisions (is this product a good deal relative to the competition?), which collectively generate revenue and so determine the success or failure of companies. The economy of the City, however, is highly mediated. As discussed above, the City of Gold is governed by access to finance, the result of investor beliefs about future prospects (will this investment make money sooner than other available investments?). Rather than immediately available supply and actual demand that controls operating revenue, the fate of companies in the City turns on the flow of information about the future, including future supply and future demand. This is the deeper meaning of the cliché that ours is an information economy: we are uncomfortably aware that economic decisions are made not on the basis of truths directly known to the actors (I need the following), but on the basis of information and belief (projected earnings). The City thus recapitulates the dynamics of classical economics, but does so in far more ethereal fashion. In this view, financial capitalism is a cybernetic loop that abstracts from, replicates, and ultimately governs the mechanisms of the market. Financial capitalism—it is tempting to call it virtual capitalism—is thus the "mind" that directs Smith's "invisible hand," and the City, like the market in goods that came before, governs itself automatically.

* * *

Finance existed in the world of Adam Smith, and the old philosopher knew a lot about the matter. But while finance is hardly new, since the eighteenth century we nonetheless can perceive a series of shifts in social life and hence thought: from operations to finance; from supply and demand to information about likely supply and demand; from present to future; from immediate "fact" to intermediated "information;" from an economy dominated by competition for actual business to one in which competition for business is preempted by competition for future business, expressed through the cost of capital; from what the financial industry nonchalantly (thoughtlessly?) refers to as "the real economy" to the (fictional? well, yes) financial economy. Taking such shifts seriously and understanding our economy as two economies, a real economy and a financial economy (in which the latter governs the former), has profound implications.

The real economy traditionally has been considered prior to the financial economy. For example, we often consider the stock market primarily as a device for firms to raise capital by issuing shares to the public. The vast majority of activity in the equity markets, however, is on the secondary market, and the company that originally issued the shares is not a party to the trade. Similarly, we conceptualize markets by abstracting from worlds that we believe to be real: scarcity, supply, demand, marginal utility, marginal cost, and the like are all understood to be very real, even urgent, aspects of the world. Finance, in this view, is secondary. Finance serves needs in the real economy; Wall Street exists for Main Street. We thus unself-consciously privilege the real economy over the financial economy.

The growth of the financial economy puts this traditional view under great pressure. Today, financial transactions arising out of real-world needs, a mortgage to buy a house for a prosaic example, are pooled and traded (as an asset-backed security), alongside markets for government debt and wheat unharvested and companies that hope to sell products, or at least be merged, sometime, and markets for delivery of money itself, for currency considered purely as a commodity like pork bellies. The financial economy, the incessant commerce on which the City is built, dwarfs the real economy by orders of magnitude, and there is little reason to believe that the details of real life receive serious attention in the aggregation of financial market preferences. There is certainly no legal reason.[18] As the last essay discussed, Main Street serves Wall Street as a collection of underlying assets, objects of contracts. It is important to remember, however, that the relationship between a financial transaction and an underlying asset need not be more than notional. As just mentioned, most equity trades do not involve the issuing company as a party. More directly on point, a derivative transaction need not involve a property right, even a contingent right, to the underlying. Nor is there any reason to believe that trade in a currency indicates any real knowledge about the government issuing the currency, to say nothing of the people attempting to conduct their own transactions (including those required for daily life) in that currency. Wall Street does not serve Main Street; Wall Street has only heard rumors about where Main Street is.

As mention of the currency markets reminds us, however, the fact that actors in the financial economy have scant knowledge of the real economy does not mean that financial markets do not affect arrangements in the real economy. Financial markets are the central mechanism through which the City determines what jobs get paid or lost, what houses get built, what food costs—in short, what happens to children, women and men, actual jobs, things people need or believe they do, beautiful environments destroyed or not—that is what it means to say financial markets are the mechanism through which resources are allocated. And as recent currency crises have convincingly demonstrated, marketplace governance is likely to be capricious.[19] The City of Gold, the collective, reflexive, self-conscious space in which we bid on tokens of future profitability, is the arena in which our real economy—and so a great deal of where we live and who we are—is somewhat *incidentally* determined. This is cause for mordant laughter.

The shift from a real economy toward a financial economy has helped articulate the fundamental assumptions in a market society. Once articulated, such matters of faith are open to philosophical critique, and hence less easily believed. We begin to understand our circumstances as artificial rather than natural, as the product of lies, perhaps noble but maybe not.

No doubt all polities have noble lies, beliefs which cannot be proven but on which the coherence of the polity depends. One of our noble lies is that prices in the financial markets reflect value that ineffably exists in the real economy, if not right now, then soon. This lie is becoming more and more difficult to sustain as the economy becomes more and more financial, more and more mediated, so that the connections between the financial economy and the real economy are becoming more and more attenuated. Money lost (or made) on paper does not necessarily mean that actual people perceive their material situation to be worsening (or improving) in any proportional fashion. For famous example, on October 19, 1987 the New York Stock Exchange had a day that by many measures was the worst in its history. The Dow Jones Industrial Average fell from 2246 to 1738, losing 22.6 percent of its value. No news seems to have justified the sell-off; the market recovered soon after; the market's gyrations appear to have had little impact on the real economy in the United States. Not only are price shifts difficult if not impossible to explain in terms of the real economy, volatility in the financial markets need not be, and often is not, translated into disruption of the real economy. From this realization it is but a short step to a loss of faith in the idea that financial markets are sensible institutions for the governance of human relations, the things that matter, within a market society. Our noble lie—that much of life should be governed by financial markets, because finanicial markets give the public conceptual purchase on a complex reality—needs buttressing. Or, to put the matter in classic regulatory terms, policy makers should be concerned, very concerned, about confidence.

Such talk, in either its Platonic ("noble lie") or even Keynesian ("confidence") phrasing, may seem unduly mystical, but governance is impossible without religion. Quite apart from the possibility that religion may be necessary in order to ensure the good behavior of the citizenry, governance entails higher-order commitments about the nature of things. Nietzsche's comment that every people hangs the table of its virtues, that is, transcendental values, over itself is not intended as a truth of comparative anthropology, but as a consequence of political life, of forming and ruling a people.[20] Moderns, for historical reasons of their own, have tended to deny that politics requires religion—Jefferson's wall of separation between church and state has its roots in the Westphalian hope that transcendent commitments could be subordinated to mundane political considerations (that we could stop fighting over religion and make treaties with one another). Moderns have therefore tended to treat politics as if it were a "rational" or at least "reasonable" undertaking, about which one should attempt to be "realistic," an attitude that a cursory knowledge of history or mere acquaintance with men of affairs renders ludicrous. Since modern thinkers generally have had more than sufficient knowledge of history, and many have experience in affairs, the modern position cannot be the result of ignorance of the psychology of political life, and must be the result of naiveté or hypocrisy, if perhaps well intentioned. In this light one suspects that Jefferson's antipathy to *The Republic* was not really based, as Jefferson claimed, on Plato's mysticism, but on its opposite: Plato's candor in thinking about the multiplicity of truth, and about the political functions of lies in particular.[21] Jefferson was at least unwilling to countenance publicly, and may not have been able conceive of, the possibility that the truth was complex and politics depended on lies.[22] The political age inaugurated at Westphalia, however, is over, and so we might ask the question suppressed by that age: What religion does our politics require? We may ask, what values orient and legitimate the government's exercise of power? Or, as has already nihilistically been suggested, are we mere incidents to capitalism's arrangements?

The authority of the market is commonly understood in two familiar, complementary, and erroneous ways. Markets are a collective mechanism through which a society can, first, objectively address the parameters constraining a given resource and, second, subjectively choose among the possibilities open to that resource. Markets make decisions that are both true and good. The structure of this claim is familiar, and is presumably borrowed, from the legitimation of liberal democracy. Elections, it is claimed in liberal democracies, make decisions that are both true (the successful presidential candidate is clearly the best man for the job) and good (the people have spoken). Similarly, markets (particularly in America) are understood to be information-processing institutions, capable of ascertaining the truth. Markets aggregate information to answer questions such as what the best run company is, what technologies are possible, and the like—we even speak of "price discovery," in which the market discovers the truth about itself. At the same time, markets are believed to reflect the choice of the consuming public, and so, to determine what is best or at least most popular, and so presumptively legitimate.

The first claim, that markets represent the truth about the world, depends on the price mechanism to process information. Price is widely thought to be the collective assignment of value—represented by a sum of some currency—to an asset. In an efficient market, one in which new information affects prices quickly, the price reflects the consensus view as to the future of the assets in question. We therefore often speak of the judgment of the market, and treat such judgment as if it were a judgment on some aspect of the world. By choosing to submit an area of social life to the judgment of the market, what the Europeans unabashedly call market sovereignty, we admit that we believe no better mechanism of public choice is available to us.

But not only do we believe that the market truthfully values assets, through belief in the allied idea of consumer sovereignty, we also tell ourselves that the market represents our own desires, and in doing so, constitutes the world we demand: market outcomes represent the will of the people and reflect the public's idea of what is good. Crudely put, if people do not want an item, it will not sell, and so conversely, success in the marketplace must be grounded in satisfying people. Enterprises that do not fulfill the desires of the people either change or atrophy and die. Because supply and demand are aggregations across a market, and because we believe that our markets are fundamentally free, which means in part that producers and consumers can enter and exit a particular market at will, we may tell ourselves that particular prices, a $500,000 house, for example, represents the value judgment of society. If $500,000 dollar houses are profitable in a local market, it is easy enough to understand the decision to raze an old farm and build such houses as a collective choice.

Powerful, but here unworthy, metaphors run through the preceding two paragraphs. The market is understood in terms of language, itself unself-consciously understood to be the mirror of nature. Additionally, the market is understood in terms of liberal political aspirations. The pull of such deeply established ideas is understandably hard to resist. It is difficult to think about the social ramifications of price (to write this apology), without understanding price to be an approximation of the truth, at the very least, a consensus belief about the world as it is. And because prices indubitably reflect aggregations of desire, it is difficult to disagree with economic success—for local example, to oppose the transformation of American retail by suburban sprawl—without feeling antidemocratic. That is, the City of Gold diverts attention from its authority by claiming, first, that the price mechanism describes the real world, and, second, that the price mechanism is authoritative insofar as we believe in democracy. Both claims are sufficiently true to be good lies, but they obscure the actual character of the City's transcendental commitments.

With regard to the claim that the market describes the real world, part 1 of this apology has at every turn shown otherwise. As discussed in chapter II, money and writing are different. Money is incapable of being particular, and is therefore incapable of description. Money—by its very nature—does not have the representational capacity required to describe the world. As discussed in chapters II and III, the perpetually undetermined nature of money, as a floating signifier, and of finance, as an expectation, means that the market cannot describe the world as it is, but can only grunt about a world that may come to be. Chapter IV discussed the interplay between money and property, the dialectic between the longing for liberty and the desire to control. Neither desire describes an objective truth about a situation. To want to control, or to be free of, a situation is not the same thing as to describe the situation truly. To want is not to think; an appetite is not an idea. Finally, this chapter has explored how the move from a real understanding of the economy toward a financial one has made the noble lie that price reflects fundamental value—more dramatically, that the traders in places like New York know anything about business in places like Indonesia or even Houston—increasingly difficult to sustain.

Specific prices and entire markets can, of course, be interpreted with lots and lots of words (this is called financial analysis) but the truth of analysis, the interpretation by market observers of the aggregate activity in the market, is and can only be a truth of interpretation, is understandable only within the context of the market. Market analysis provides, at the end of the day, political truth. This is not a bad thing; it is simply human. Nor does it mean markets cannot be understood or are somehow random. Our markets are understandable along with the rest of our culture. Even a cussed contrarian shares any number of beliefs not refuted by price and believes in any number of things for which there can be no foundation. Thus, when we speak of markets we speak of our beliefs rather than its facts, human interpretations rather than Olympian truths. Information in the market is no more or less than a belief about the world that informs action. Marketplace information, for all its air of objective necessity, is a practical rather than an objective concept.

If price does not represent the truth about the world—if a market's resolutions have no strong claim to truth—then we should not expect price to represent the will of the people, and a market's resolutions need not be good, either. The foregoing argument that price does not capture objective truths (in Kantian terms, to which pure reason applies) would seem to mean that price does not express conceptions of the will (to which practical reason applies). Put more simply, if we do not expect a series of grunts to describe the objective world, we should not understand the same series of grunts as ethical argument. Second, price does not represent the will of the people because the *rentier* class, who unsurprisingly speak loudest in financial discourse, are only some of the people. Many people are not in a position to lend money, but remain people nonetheless, with situations that ought to be considered. Third, and more generally, in honoring the people, democracy assumes equality among citizens (who may be a citizen has been contested), that is, those who comprise "the people" are equal among themselves. But capitalism is not only unequal in practice, it is unequal in intention. Making more money—achieving inequality—is the purpose of the game, is what it means to be a success. To put the point in terms of slogans, "One man, one vote" makes no sense in a world in which "he who finishes with the most toys wins."[23]

Perhaps most fundamentally, however, price cannot represent the will of the people because it does not express consensus of any kind. Consider a simple sale, one hundred shares of XYZ Corp. at ten dollars a share. The seller must believe that a share of XYZ Corp is worth less than ten dollars; the buyer must believe that XYZ Corp is worth more than ten dollars. Ten dollars, then, does not represent any agreement whatsoever between seller and buyer.[24] Price is the current level of disagreement. Rather than describe the world, or the will of the parties, price simply situates those with a given asset (potential sellers) vis-à-vis those without a given asset (potential buyers). Price does not describe a thing, is not a measurement, but instead describes a set of relationships, like a ratio, a center of gravity, or an average. Price is a derivative number. Because the relationships are relationships among humans who interact, we may understand price as a description of a social relationship. But it is important for present purposes to remember that the relationship described is inherently adversarial, the current position of those who are attempting to buy low as opposed to those who are attempting to sell high. The day's closing price reflects consensus to the same degree that we might say that the opposing trenches in a war define the border between two nations.[25]

The borders defined by trenches need not be the same as those declared by international law or presumably wished for by the armies. Viewed from within the conflict, however, the line of opposing trenches may be the most important thing imaginable, may define the soldier's reality. Similarly, from within the context of the market, there is nothing more important than price—prices determine market action and are therefore authoritative.[26] From within the market, we are compelled to reify the relationships represented by price, to speak of "the price" as if it were an entity, or collectively, to speak of "the market." Seminal finance theorist Benjamin Graham was candid about this and discussed finance in terms of "Mr. Market," the collectivity of marketplace actors. The point of finance is to bet, successfully, on what Mr. Market is likely to do. For Graham, Mr. Market was a bit like Zeus, whimsical and prone to fancy, and therefore unpredictable in the short term, but wise over the long run. Consequently, he taught investors (most notably Warren Buffett) to take long term positions on things the investor believed had fundamental value but were being ignored by Mr. Market, and then wait for Mr. Market to come round.[27]

If we move from the practice of investment to that of political economy, then this apology's proposition that the market constitutes the City would seem to mean that authority within the marketplace, price, is our political authority. Participation in the City, then, entails submission to the principle that some set of oppositions—prices—should constitute and rule our polity, determine the contours of society, and inform how we as individuals live. We need not fall down and worship money, as Mark Twain said of late-nineteenth-century Americans, but in order to live in the City of Gold we are forced to acknowledge that price creates our reality, and so price is a god, if not necessarily our own.

*   *   *

The purpose of part 1 has been to suggest the political contours of the City of Gold. Successive chapters have described the City as a matter of political history, structurally, as a culture comprised of particular relationships in space and in time, genetically, as a community that reconstitutes itself through history, and finally, as an entity that regulates itself in accordance with its understanding of authority.

It may with considerable force be objected that this is not enough to support the apology's contention that the City of Gold is a polity. Even assuming that establishing the City in historical context, and granting (at least for argument's sake) that the City functions along the lines set out in part 1, and even conceding that it is possible to make a political apology for supranational capitalism so understood, one might nonetheless argue that this apology has not shown that the far flung reaches of the City of Gold comprise a polity. The objection is important to the rest of the book—indeed, the rest of the book may be understood as an exploration and defense of the extent to which we can understand the City as a polity—and so the charge should be stated explicitly and with some care.

A polity is classically defined by certain characteristics that the City does not have. First, a polity is a political expression. A polity represents an affirmative bond among the citizens. Aristotle therefore begins the *Politics* by defining man as a political animal, as one who forms associations with his fellows. Augustine, reading Cicero, therefore understood the republic to be a place of concord, and justice to be the supreme political virtue, for without justice there would be no concord, and consequently the social structure would fall apart.[28] The City, in contrast, is defined in terms of property (dominion, the right to exclude) and money (the liberty to be free from circumstances, especially the hell of other people), and amity or justice seem at best accidental. The City cannot be a polity because its inhabitants are not politically motivated, and even if they were, their connections are too cold.

A second objection might be that a polity is traditionally understood to organize or legitimate *all* that is appropriate to being human. This is done through institutions. Humans have appetites, and a polity must have institutions that both satisfy and constrain those appetites. Many appetites are satisfied through the institution of the marketplace; but many appetites are satisfied through nonmarket institutions. For example, a polity may respond to visceral desires, such as that for sex or the protection of one's own children, through institutions such as marriage and the laws of inheritance. Moreover, there is more to being human than mere appetites—yearnings for truth and justice and beauty, for examples—and a polity must also respond to such yearnings, perhaps through science, the courts, and the arts. While scientists, judges, and artists must be paid, one cannot understand their activity completely in terms of the marketplace. Indeed, each of these activities understands itself to be at considerable variance with, and sometimes in outright opposition to, the mores of the marketplace. Because it seems to have no place for whatever is appropriate to being human but outside the marketplace, this book's assertion that supranational capitalism in itself constitutes a polity is an overstatement.

A third, more specific, objection is that the City cannot be a polity because it is not purposive: it embodies no meaning that unifies the people. Traditionally, polities promulgate and enforce transcendent values, visions of God, history, justice. Such values orient the polity as a whole, and inform the virtues that citizens attempt to embody. Citizens know what, in their own lives, is right and wrong, not as a private matter, but as a matter of their community's morality. In this traditional view, the individuals who best embody the polity's virtues are called heroes.

The City, in contrast, was founded as a rejection of politics understood as the creation of a meaningful purpose, particularly the sort of meaningful purpose for which one might take up arms. The virtues—honor—of the traditional polity are close to enthusiasm, which is dangerous (reconsider Nuremberg). In the City, enthusiasm therefore should be dissipated through sports and other entertainments. More generally, in the City, the experience of transcendent value is not denied outright, but is instead exiled to private life. As for government decisions—market outcomes—they may be meaningful in the sense of efficacious (markets automatically produce resolutions), but they do not produce decisions, that is, articulated expressions of sovereign will in which the citizen may participate. Markets are not the will of the people; they are not even the will of the *rentier* class. Market outcomes carry no guarantee of either procedural logic or substantive truth, serve no god worthy of worship.

If the idea of a polity has traditionally been considered on the metaphor of the body, with government at the head, the City appears to be governed from the gut. To put the charge in Freudian terms: the idea of the polity has always included a law-giving function, a superego. Although the discipline of the law entails frustration, such frustration is more than bearable, is actively sought, because it is the mechanism and assurance of meaning. Only through frustration could the higher values of the society be achieved or even known. But in contrast to other polities, the City is founded as an arrangement of competing individualists, a constellation of egos. The law imposed by the City is therefore experienced as an imposition, alien, not meaningful. The City is not a polity because its inhabitants do not support its laws; the City's inhabitants are not really citizens.

It is true but insufficient to respond to this charge by stating the obvious, that the inhabitants of the City should not be considered citizens of an ancient *polis* or even Rousseau's Geneva. The fundamental issue raised by the claim that the City is not a polity is whether a serious reimagination of politics is possible, or whether we must continue to make do with the now somewhat inapposite political grammar we have inherited. Must we continue to think in terms of the nation state, or the impoverished terms in which we now consider political economy, no other terms being available to us? In order to confront this issue, we need a critical understanding of the limitations imposed by markets considerably more profound than anything developed thus far. Part 2 begins that critique.

PART 2
Constitutional Critique

The protest against alienation and the longing for authenticity have been so central to the spiritual life of the last two centuries that we cannot understand the situation of modern thought—and hence not only the sensibility of our contemporaries, but the quality of life in our self-consciousness, our peculiar lack of happiness—without explicit reference to such protest and such longing. When we question our hearts, we find money is trouble, often simply money, but if we persist, we find our unease is with a society constructed around monetary convention, with people educated by that society to think in terms like "quality of life," and we have an inchoate sense that more is to be hoped. Nor can we who nonetheless insist on building a market society honorably avoid confronting the ancient suspicion that life in markets cannot be considered truly admirable, is at best support for a life well lived elsewhere. Part 2 of this apology relates critiques grounded in the experience of living in the City of Gold, in feelings of alienation, of inauthenticity, and of loathing for our lives as consumers, to the constitution of the City articulated in part 1. What can such criticisms mean in a society founded in hope and out of fear, constituted by the exchange of property for money, and money for property, and little else?

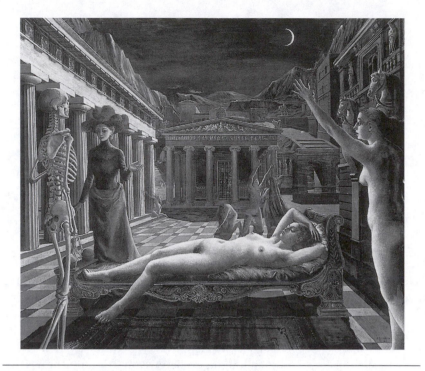

Paul Delvaux, *The Sleeping Venus* (1944)

CHAPTER VI

Alienation

Monetary relations should be defended in terms of the polity in which they are found. Money civilizes, but is nonetheless widely hated. Why good minds hate money. The prevalence of alienation. Contempt.

Apologists often respond to criticisms of monetary aspects of the City with some version of the argument from nature. It is said that venality is natural, that humans are by nature self-interested or rational. At a more sophisticated level, it is said that property, and its exchange value, money (and so venality) are natural to life in society, which is comprised by such relations. These defenses contain an ontological hierarchy: nature (description of facts) trumps politics (normative argument about the present, or for some future society). In the face of nature, as the apologist rarely needs to spell out, political criticism is a waste of time. From the perspective of the defense, the facts about human nature preclude normative criticism of the monetary aspects of our society. The "is" constrains the "ought": because venality undeniably exists, the status quo is as justified as it possibly could be.

Such an apology is wrong in several ways. Monetary relations are not entailed by the human condition, or even by life in society. Not all societies have monetary relations; societies have existed without money at all. Some societies have used money only for certain functions, often ceremonial, such as the payment of fines or religious contributions, but not for mundane economic intercourse. Even within our very commercial society, much culture endeavors to set itself apart from monetary discourse: consider the ideals of equal justice, democratic representation, professional responsibility, or education. Although one can generalize about money, as one can about language, monetary relations are specific to particular cultures, as are languages. Monetary relations are in fact more culturally specific than are linguistic relations. We know of no human groups, past or present, without language; money is a later and more specific and limited thing than is language. Money and language are alike, however, in how they are understood. Understanding how either a currency or a language works, doing it, requires learning the culture, participating in that culture, even if only imaginatively. Other societies do money in other ways, and still other societies do money hardly at all. The mere fact that our society handles certain matters in a certain way at this point in time hardly precludes us from imagining other possibilities. In sum, human nature, monetary relations in a particular society, and political possibility are not synonyms.

Since human nature, the arrangements of a particular culture, and political possibility are distinct concepts, analysis must be careful. The apologist who seeks to defend our present monetary arrangements against critique, or who seeks to deny the possibility of a proposal, on the basis of human nature generally commits a non sequitur. Human nature requires neither money nor even property (at least in anything like our sense of the institution), so perhaps our monetary society is wrong, and perhaps our society could be changed. In short, we who endeavor to believe in the City of Gold must confront our critics without taking refuge in a false necessity.

None of which is to say that one cannot defend the monetary relations of the City of Gold, but only that an apology—this apology—for such relations requires a defense of our politics. As discussed in part 1, we have used money to create a specific regime, the City of Gold, in response to the violent impositions of Western Europe and its progeny. Moreover, as discussed in chapter III, this regime offers its inhabitants a reasonable hope of not just peace, but personal security. For most people and almost all parents security alone provides a sufficient justification for financial society. We have used money not only to tame public and private fortune, however, but also to build the sparkling edifice of modernity. This is the civilization we have used money to build. Do we feel our arrangements can be defended? Do we feel that this is the best of all possible worlds? If not, to what extent is our money the root of our evils?

While it is true that monetary relations can only be understood in the context of their cultures, the reverse is also true: institutions inform their cultures. We can ask what it means for a society to handle an aspect of life through one sort of institution as opposed to some other. We can ask constitutional questions, and the answers to such questions will refer to the institutions central to a given polity. While monetary relations are central to the City of Gold, not all of life need be arranged by the price mechanism. For example, feudalism, monasticism, and many other social relations we think of as medieval are explicitly nonmonetary. Even today, and as already suggested, many relations are not organized along monetary lines. Consider civil rights: poor people too have the right to speak, though perhaps little opportunity to be heard. Nor is the loyalty of members of a national military, for another example, understood to be for sale. To say that such relations are not monetary in nature does not imply that such relations are angelic, but instead means only that the institutional structure of such relations, and hence their grammar, are not monetary. The grammar in which a relationship is conducted informs, shapes, the contours of that relationship, so it matters if we consider a social organization to be organized through price or in some other way. As detailed throughout part 1, the grammars of the institutions that constitute the City of Gold are monetary. Therefore this apology has tried to consider how, at a very basic level, money has built our global culture.

Although, as noted, not all cultures have money, and money plays different roles in different times and places, the cultures without money are, at least in material terms, relatively simple. Money literally civilizes, allows the city (*cives*) to be built, because it makes collective action possible on a large scale. Barter is so difficult: one party, A, must find another party, B, who not only has the desired item, but who also has a reciprocal desire that A can satisfy, all at the same time and place. Money substitutes for the immediate presence of people with specific desires, allowing societies to establish connections among people scattered by time or space. As a medium of exchange, money relaxes the requirement that we please another. So long as we have something of value to someone, we may trade. As a store of value, money affords some respite from the urgency of need (if little respite from the urgency of desire). Money thus allows societies to become bigger, increases the spatial and temporal scope of their interactions, and in that sense, allows societies to become more complex, to generate and store surpluses, which can be used to afford civilization—payment for great architecture, beautiful music, whatever makes us proud.[1]

Despite this civilizing function of money, any number of civilized minds, minds of which we are indeed very proud, have regarded money with suspicion or outright hostility. Entire intellectual traditions, movements of the spirit, have been informed by their antagonism to monetary relations. In lieu of detailed intellectual history, perhaps mentioning a number of such minds will convey some sense of the scope of the trouble, like Homer's catalogue of ships provided some sense of the scale of the war against Troy. From the perspective of classical philosophy, which flowered in a society founded in large part on trade, money was necessary and perhaps even respectable in the way needful things are. Money might be used well, but it was a means to an end, rather than an end in itself. As a means, money could not be honorable. Only ends could be honorable. Money might buy leisure, which could be used for thinking, philosophy, which was an honorable end.[2] But money also had its dangers. Plato worried about sophistry—teaching in exchange for money—because of the likelihood that truth would be exchanged for pleasing one's clients, exchanged for money. Aristotle understood money as the substitution of a conventional representation of a thing for an understanding of the thing's true nature, its *telos*. Money was therefore antithetical to truth, all money has the same end, the satisfaction of desire. A life devoted to money, fervidly thought (if not deeply understood) in terms of money, is thus a life in error, divorced from truth.

The philosophers' problems with money pale beside those of the priests. To start with my own religion, the Christian tradition's obsession with, and often extravagant hatred for, money—Christ's low estate from birth to death, presaged by John and adopted by followers since, like Francis of Assisi—and hence, it would seem, the antagonism between Christianity and much of the world that Christ loved, is one of the more difficult, and inescapable, things about the tradition. Money is everywhere in the Bible, but perhaps nobody has made more trouble over it than Christ, which has been a continual embarrassment to the Christian church precisely insofar as it became a church in the world, a world in which money had its place and uses and authority and had to be recognized. As a part of the world, the church has always been vulnerable to charges of mendacity, and has felt itself to be vulnerable.

At least to an outsider, Judaism and Islam seem to be relatively comfortable with money, but one must tread gently here. These other desert faiths may appear comfortable with money only in contrast to the vehemence of the Christian attack on money. Yet even on their own terms, neither Judaism nor Islam seem completely comfortable with money. Both Islam and Judaism have long traditions of asceticism and communal ownership, and while hostility to money is not precisely the same thing as asceticism or communal ownership, these things are not completely divorced, either. So the Moslems are comfortable with the idea of commerce, but uncomfortable with the idea of money earning money, *riba*, roughly speaking but probably not exactly "interest"—a concern not unlike the traditional Christian concern for usury. The longstanding Jewish banking tradition might seem to indicate comfort with money, but at the same time, Jewish banking must be understood in relation to the political facts of exile (learning and gold travel, land does not) and to the Christian and Moslem hesitancy to lend money at interest. More subtly, one might note that Judaism and Islam have tended toward complicated sets of rules for daily life; behavior is not just intensely circumscribed but also valued by specific rules. Perhaps money represents less of a threat to such traditions. It is tempting to generalize (and support such generalization with a facile observation or two about an Eastern religion or three) that money and the experience of the holy are antithetical. Although religion can make use of the world, even the flesh—can understand money as sacrifice or good works, and physical pain or sex as a holy passage—religion cannot transubstantiate monetary experience. One cannot feel religious and mercenary at the same time.

Romantics have sought meaning in the arts, a view attractive to those who understand modernity as God's terminal illness. And if the arts speak to the longing for meaning, fill a religious function in a secularized world, it is unsurprising that the arts are in tension with the monetary society they serve. Although art generally requires money, often considerable sums of money, to create, we nonetheless prefer to imagine the artist in opposition to monetary society, proudly alienated from it. This is increasingly true across the spectrum from entertainment to the fine arts. Even rock musicians are inevitably chided for selling out if they become too successful. Painters, including would-be millionaires exhibiting to financiers and hangers-on in Manhattan galleries, often present themselves as, and are widely expected to be, somehow opposed to the financial world whose paladins they court.[3] Energetically pursuing money while simultaneously maintaining a rebellious independence from the financial establishment puts the artist in the position of incessantly risking and often succumbing to hypocrisy. But our willingness to tolerate such hypocrisy, or more kindly put, the fact that we expect artists to adopt poses deeply at odds with their actual lives, only underscores the point that we understand art in opposition to money. Regardless of the fact that art and money go way back, we are embarrassed when we see art and money commingling too intimately: we still have many hopes for art and few for money.

When it comes to keeping pure, novelists have it a bit easier than painters, because publication does not require an individual's money, and poets and essayists have it easier still, because they make no money, and so can rant against mammon with some hope of looking honest. Much great writing, even by men who were gentlemen or became gentlemen by dint of their success, takes a dim view of money: think of Shakespeare and Donne; Twain and James; Dostoevsky and Tolstoy; Goethe and Büchner; anybody we might agree was Romantic and anybody we might call Realist; those generally considered on the left (perhaps Brecht?) and those on the right (try T. S. Eliot).[4]

We might even understand what is philosophically referred to as modernity—the same period that begins in literature with Cervantes or Shakespeare or Rabelais and which we feel to have just ended—as a period in which literary minds deeply felt, identified with, both the past and the future. One of the differences between the past and the future was money, which seemed to corrode the values of the past even as it constructed the relationships of the future. Money, these artists all knew, carried its own peculiar temptations and dangers. Even those writers we now understand to be the great modernists (now using that word in its usual literary sense) seem notable not so much for their engagement with the future, but for their equipoise between the future and a past sufficiently different and vibrant to serve as an antagonist, to be contended against. Proust, Eliot, Mann, Musil, Joyce, Faulkner are all writing of a world that they understand to be gone, destroyed by the course of history, most dramatically by World War One. For such writers, modernity was a question, a challenge to tradition, and there was dramatic tension, art, to be made out of the contest. But the contest is over. The intellectual promises of modernity have been widely achieved, even if we may still be waiting for certain technological goodies, flying cars and what not. Now that most of our relations are monetary relations, the future has arrived, and it is difficult to imagine a struggle between money and tradition. Insofar as that struggle defined modernity, we are now postmodern. Insofar as our artists remain suspicious of money, they are left to survey the culture with a generalized discontent, but without being able to base their art upon a struggle between contending historically or politically significant allegiances. Modernity's promises may seem hollow, but that does not mean that other systems of meaning are easily available to us, or are sufficiently public to warrant the name tradition and so serve as communicative terrain that a writer may cultivate.

Not even all the economists—those who have tried to understand monetary relations on the model of physics—are terribly fond of money. In fact, economists as a whole seem to be fonder of their ideas of money, of its putative roles in their elegant worlds, than they are with the messy business of acquiring or protecting a present fortune. It is true that in recent years the development of markets in complex financial instruments (derivatives) has made numerous fortunes, and many people who do such finance were trained as economists.[5] Most economists, however, choose to be smart rather than rich, despite what classical economics has to say about the universality of wealth-maximizing behavior. Turning from the mill run to the great economists, we see that few of the giants were very wealthy.[6] Moreover, even as a matter of theory, a number of important economists decried rather than celebrated markets: Marx discusses the dehumanization of monetary relations long before he develops the theory of communism, and Veblen catalogues the depravities that money works upon the personality, and upon our lives together. An entire tradition of social economic thought—Proudhon, Fourier, Simmel, Weber, and a host of other people who are today identified with the sociologists rather than the economists—is deeply suspicious of capitalism. More surprisingly, perhaps, even staunch liberals like Adam Smith and founder of the City of Gold Keynes, who at least appear quite enamored of capitalism, were nonetheless somewhat ill at ease with money.[7]

We could go on, but we already have plenty of ships. Despite the fact that money is vital to the construction of complex civilizations, philosophers, priests, artists, even many economists (presumably in spite of themselves), in sum, what appears to be the entire party of the spirit, is offended, bothered, troubled by money. This is puzzling for at least two reasons. First, such minds are generally understood to be glories of civilization, and such minds are certainly unimaginable without a civilization to support them. Other developments basic to the construction of civilization, language, or for that matter agriculture or the wheel, are not held in such contempt. More practically phrased, many of these men had money, and hence leisure, and so were able to do the work for which they are remembered. Money was a condition of their being; one would think that they would be downright grateful for the institution. The second reason it is difficult to understand why such a range of minds were troubled by money is that it is difficult to imagine what these people, from different times and places and intellectual traditions, with entirely different concerns, could have in common—and yet money offends them all. How can one thing, money, offend such diverse minds?

Good minds are appalled by the implications of pricing. Price has traditionally been symbolized as an equivalence: some commodity, C, is held to be equivalent to some quantity of money, M, which may in turn be exchanged for another commodity.[8] We may write this $C = M = C$, or, to emphasize specific prices rather than money in general, $C = P = C$. Understood as a sentence representing an objective reality, this is a lie, actually, a tissue of lies. A thing is not its price. For example, an orange may cost one dollar, but the orange is not the same thing as a dollar, which is not the same thing as whatever else it may be spent on, gasoline, perhaps. Objects do not have prices in the same way they have mass or other physical qualities. Prices are assigned by people who have a monetary system. So we have a host of social transactions: a piece of fruit is called an orange and then generalized to a commodity, which is priced in a given currency, which may or may not be exchanged for some second commodity. People with different monetary systems will assign different numerical prices to an object. The price in yen is not the same as the price in drachma, though insofar as arbitrage is possible, prices are likely to be roughly congruent across cultures. Even people within the same monetary system will assign somewhat different prices to an object, just as they will describe the same object in somewhat different terms. So pricing offends good minds by being primitive, asserting simple objective relations in lieu of complex social reality. Money alienates us by distancing us from the truth.[9]

Yet this seems to be an insufficient reason to find money so offensive. Representations vary, but all fail in some ways. Money is hardly unique in failing to represent the truth. Ordinary speech fails to represent the truth, too, and the party of spirit cannot be said to be offended by the existence of ordinary speech. Of course the financial classes are not as expressive as the prophets and poets, but that would hardly explain the anger of so many prophets and poets. There must be more to the party of spirit's hostility than the paltry expressive capabilities of money.

Price does not merely communicate little; price deceives. As an intellectual matter, we know that the price can only be understood within a social context. Pricing is a social act, if a less expressive act than speaking. But while words obviously have a speaker (who can be challenged or contradicted), price presents itself as objective, as a characteristic of the item in question, no more human than mass or volume. The assertion of objectivity is therefore a denial of human agency. Price thus embodies the fallacious argument from nature with which this essay began. In claiming to be self-sufficient, objective, and true enough for the moment, money hides its truly political character. Money lies, the sort of lie implied by the marketplace comment that it ("it" is usually some form of ruin) was nothing personal, merely necessitated by business considerations. Movieland gangsters often say such things to their victims.

The lie works by collapsing the distance between property rights over things and the things themselves. The difference between the legal institution of a consumer's property rights in our exemplary orange and the particular orange in question is so slight as to be irrelevant for most practical purposes, and we often use the same word, "property" to represent both the institution and its object. The difference, however, is crucial and so merits a pause. In the contemplation of property law and hence the economy, our orange is a chattel, a species of property, a bundle of rights, a zone of legally enforceable control, but is *not* a thing in the world, a thing that can be held. Legal representations, the rights to things, are different from things themselves. There is no way, however, for people to talk about control over things themselves, to discuss the ability to buy, sell, or otherwise dispose of things among one another, and for such talk not to involve a political representation of the thing (what we call property). We speak of property because for many purposes we must. There is no transaction without the context of a society, even if only a society formed to conduct the transaction. Property, in the broadest sense of the social representation of a thing, is thus fundamental to a range of important human activities. This necessity makes property feel natural, like nature, a circumstance of particular activities. Because it is comprised by properties, constellations of rights and money, an economy is a vast simulacrum, not the world but its image. Because society cannot avoid socializing things (cannot avoid property of some sort), society must treat property as a fundamental reality. Money makes the world go 'round, people say. What such people forget, but good minds (who by definition have a truth) know, is that what money spins is not the world. In sum, not only do prices fail to constitute authority, as maintained in chapter II, prices present themselves as nature, and thereby lie.

The lying society is antagonistic to the pursuit of truth. The critique suggested in chapter IV—property excludes; money permits—can be deepened to show how the dialectic through which the City reproduces itself threatens those who wish to express a truth. To reprise: without the right to exclude, pricing is superfluous. Buyers will not pay money for something that they can get for free. Many important and valuable things are not priced—air, democracy, sunshine, transit on the high seas—because no property regime gives some owner the right to exclude others. The price, then, is the sum of money in exchange for which some set of property rights, always including the right to exclude, is transferred. The price system is the continual renegotiation of a single political question: Who has the right to exclude whom from what? Expressing and recognizing a truth, however, presumes a degree of community (hence "community of scholars") within which proposed truths can be expressed and evaluated (or art can be appreciated, or religion believed). To try and speak a truth presumes that someone will listen, presumes inclusion rather than exclusion. Nor does the transformation of property into money help matters much; the interplay of the desire to control and the desire to be free, dominion and liberty, property and money, hardly bespeaks a community of truth.[10]

The suspicion that the City neither provides the mechanisms through which a truth can be expressed, nor the context in which a truth can be heard, is deepened still further by chapter V's insistence on the antagonistic character of price. The City, chapter V maintained along with mainstream economics, was governed by the disagreements among those who wished to buy low and those who wished to sell high. At the heart of metropolitan discourse is struggle. The City's laws actively discourage the creation of associations that would ameliorate such antagonisms. In order for there to be a market in a given property, the property must be alienable— there must be an enforceable way for the seller to transfer rights to the buyer. Once transferred, such rights must be good even against the seller, that is, society must extinguish the seller's rights. Buyer and seller paradigmatically come together as strangers, and commercial law ensures that, at least as a matter of property law, they remain strangers after the sale.

Although in commercial societies law recognizes many durable relationships (consider long term contracts or various forms of business association), in the fundamental sales transactions the law acts to curtail relationships, to limit associations. Otherwise, there would be a cloud upon the title of assets, a cloud that would hinder (and if allowed to accumulate, would eventually prevent) subsequent transactions. Thus the reproduction of market societies requires the destruction of past associations. Alienation, then, in both the sense of declaring who is to be excluded (who is a foreigner) and the sense of the right to convey is entailed in the price mechanism, and therefore in market societies. Alienation is not just a response to, it is a requirement of, life in the marketplace.[11]

Life in societies founded on the right to exclude others from property that one may alienate at will in exchange for anonymous cash, thereby severing past associations, is atomistic. Markets are atomistic because the market's constitutive dialectic, the interchange between property and money, oscillates around the individual who owns, and so exercises dominion, or who can choose to own, who has money to spend and may buy. Markets answer the terrible problem of the self indirectly: the exercise of dominion presumes a ruler, and the exercise of liberty presumes an autonomous being, free to choose. I own, or I could buy, therefore I am. Or, if one prefers politics to epistemology, the market is a machine for reassuring the actor of its own existence, of answering the fundamental need for recognition, perversely enough by rejection.[12]

The claim that the market actor is atomistic is ultimately a statement about the structure of markets, rather than an anthropological proposition about the nature of humanity. Much political thought, in a tradition stretching back to Hobbes and Machiavelli, and virtually all political economy, founds itself on the individual, generally presumed to be self-interested. The question was whether a justifiable political order could be constructed among such humans. But this may be putting the cart before the horse: whatever the fundamental nature of humans, life in markets is atomistic not simply because market actors tend to understand selfishness as rationality, or because venality has been glorified since at least the days of Adam Smith, but because atomism is entailed in the functioning of markets. To make markets the central form of human interaction, then, is to accept that most human interactions will be cold and hard, that the self will have to look to its own resources.

The reassurance provided to the self by the autonomy of participation in the market is also something of a lie. Money is fungible, that is, indistinguishable. Insofar as priced, and considered in terms of their price, commodities are fungible, too. One may be the (more or less temporary) owner of any number of things, but it is difficult to see how a serious person could draw an identity from such dominion, from such choices. Money is fungible, and so are the people who spend it. Money's insistence on equality, entailed in liquidity, haunts us with a vengeance, undercutting whatever claim we might have had to exist as individuals. Indeed, our society's insistence on individuality comes to seem a pathetic and cruel self-mockery.

At this point it should be possible to suggest how money both constructs civilization and seems antithetical to civilized impulse. The party of spirit might be thought to hold a variety of concerns dear, to have constructed their lives and their work as efforts toward, variously, the wise, the holy, the beautiful, the true—one might suggest other noble words for other noble ends, and admire lives so lived. No such end, however, can be represented by price. Money is impious. Indeed, money by its very self-sufficiency tends to deny the reality of other meanings, meanings that price does not communicate and around which great minds structure not just their own work and lives, but their judgment of the world. To the contrary, concern for the relative quantity of a venal desire for a set of legal rights over something, in order to provide a thin and even so false sense of identity, hardly impels us to philosophy, or religion, or art, or indeed economics. Money distracts us from communicating the wonders of creation by substituting its own world, a simulacrum formed by a very petty species of social interaction. Money is downright idolatrous, and what could be more offensive to the party of spirit, regardless of the spirit that imbues them?

Money can neither express nor receive truth, and so cannot answer the need for meaning, for the external something upon which the mind operates, for relations that might give the self real content. A polity that suggests its citizens might do without meaning cannot be loved, for the simple reason that there is nothing to love, to be the object of affection. Therefore good minds in monetary societies will tend to consider themselves alone, alienated, a status that such societies, gallingly enough, are unable to understand and often convert into poses—the absentminded professor, the rebellious artist, the effete intellectual. Money civilizes, and then exiles its best children.[13]

*　*　*

Why is the fact of alienation so disappointing? Is some higher meaning necessary to the City of Gold? Should we be surprised that political life, in markets or otherwise, is unsatisfying? To put the matter in more sympathetic terms, the City's founders abjured glory and settled for peace, and is not peace enough? What more can be hoped on a global scale? Perhaps our longings for substantive politics can and should be addressed on some lower level of political organization, as suggested by the European conception of subsidiarity, or the American idea of federalism?

Maybe it must be so. If we have no other possibility, then this peace will have to suffice—there are children (Nietzsche had no children)—but the problem with alienation is even more serious, general, and finally political than this discussion of great minds, with their wounded sensitivities, might have suggested. The sorts of deeper meanings precluded by money are necessary for life, even in the City of Gold, because we all live in a fallen state, or to use another language, because we cannot otherwise justify the repression that makes us discontent with our civilization.

Writing about colonialism, specifically the Belgian administration of the Congo (we may think "global capitalism") shortly before the outbreak of World War One, Conrad required an "idea," something to justify the horror not just of greed, not just of colonialization, but of imposing civilization on others, and finally, of living in civilization at all:

> They grabbed what they could get for the sake of what was to be got. It was just robbery with violence, aggravated murder on a great scale, and men going at it blind—as is very proper for those who tackle a darkness. The conquest of the earth, which mostly means the taking it away from those who have a different complexion or slightly flatter noses than ourselves, is not a pretty thing when you look into it too much. What redeems it is the idea only. An idea at the back of it; not a sentimental pretence but an idea; and an unselfish belief in the idea—something you can set up, and bow down before, and offer a sacrifice to . . . [14]

But the City of Gold, as we have seen, can neither express nor receive such an idea. An idea that would serve as the basis of community must by definition be shared, and therefore such an idea cannot constitute property, and so cannot be priced. Insofar as we live in a world made by the dance between money and property, insofar as we take markets seriously—and who does not?—we are separated from the world that might provide us with collective meaning, that might justify our situation among one another. As it is, in our world, with its limited resources, we have no way to account for the exercise of power. We act in the market, complicitous in all that our society does, but we can have no confidence that our actions are for something, that the things we do are done in the name of something, that the violence (against children, including those quickening in the womb, peoples, ordinary folk, the environment, animals) is sacrificial. The act of pricing, of substituting a symbol of desire for a thing, alienates us from the world of things, from our world, and hence ultimately from the possibility of justification, and we are left to contemplate our loss of innocence in isolation and horror. Is it any wonder that so many civilized minds recoil from money, despite its being a mainspring of civilization? Is it surprising that metropolitan life has a nihilistic odor? That contempt is expected from the educated?

CHAPTER **VII**
Inauthenticity

The cliché of the midlife crisis as the confession of a society that believes itself unworthy of allegiance. Sincerity and authenticity. Why the City of Gold is inauthentic. Relations between truth, alienation, and inauthenticity. Authenticity, allegiance, and injustice. Efforts to save the truth. Coping with inauthenticity. Note on method. Finding traces of authenticity in the City. Loathing and the search for justice.

For a successful man of a certain age to divorce his wife, marry a firm young woman with an evident willingness, buy a fast car in a loud color, and perhaps even establish a more or less manageable drug habit, all within the space of a few years, is perhaps disturbing but also seems so normal that we have a cliché to describe the situation, the so-called midlife crisis. But what is it, exactly, that is in crisis? Obviously, a midlife crisis may damage or even destroy many things—a marriage, relationships between fathers and children, jobs, health—but such destruction is seen as symptomatic of the crisis, not the crisis itself. The clichéd understanding is that the mid-life crisis is a psychological disturbance caused by a man's sudden and profound realization of his own mortality. In this view, what is in crisis, indeed sick unto death, is a man's sense of himself as immortal, or at least unbounded. The foolishness—the babe, the car—are the visible symptoms of a desperate psychological effort to deny that at least half of life is over.

Although there is truth here (after all, these are clichés), this understanding is a bit too primitive (after all, these are clichés). Midlife crises are more than volatile efforts men make to deny an existential realization of their own mortality. First, long before any plausible age for a midlife crisis, most men must have repeatedly acknowledged their own mortality—men do not suddenly become thoughtful one evening and realize that their lives are running out. Second, carrots or religion, neither of which is likely to shorten life, would seem to be a more sensible response to one's awareness of death than, say, cocaine. Finally, even if one thinks that some men are likely to respond to thoughts of their own mortality by acting young in a superstitious effort to deny the possibility of dying, such denial says nothing about the specifics of what men do in their midlife crises. The midlife crisis is diagnosed by a set of behaviors consistent enough to have entered the language collectively and become a cliché, but why these behaviors, and not others? (Nobody ever says, "Rob's taken up gardening. You know, midlife crisis.") What do the specific behaviors we associate with midlife crises actually say about the denial of death, or anything else, for that matter?

If we turn to what men are traditionally alleged to do while in the throes of a midlife crisis, we see the exchange of sizeable amounts of money for experience. Divorces, young women, fast cars, and recreational chemicals all cost considerable sums of money. Such purchases can hardly be resold and consequently cannot be considered investments. Therefore, only the experience gained can justify the expenditure. Rephrased, such purchases do not appreciate, but can only be appreciated. In paying money for fast machines and for women that arouse primitive jealousy, one might even say that a man in the throes of his midlife crisis buys the chance to be surrounded by what is fine and exciting about life, *joie de vivre* as conceived by a guy's guy. In this light, the midlife crisis appears not just negatively, as a denial of mortality, but affirmatively, as an effort to buy experience, the sensation of living.

This is quite strange. One cannot say that our man—let's keep calling him "Rob"—was, until his crisis, without experience. He and Sharon had apparently been married happily for years; Josh and Ellen were just in high school, and doing well; the forest green Volvo wagon needed to be replaced, but it got him to work; Sharon had a new red minivan that she jokingly called an SMV (stretch mark vehicle); the family vacationed for a week every summer at Hilton Head or some other nice Southern resort where they could play golf and tennis and go to the beach. Sharon and Rob gave good dinner parties. If we give names to the abstractions (the man, the (old) wife, and so forth), we see that Rob's life up until the crisis was full of experiences, specific and real but evidently insufficient. So we might further imagine that Rob was hired away by his old company's competitor, which made him COO, where he started working and then sleeping with Lisa, who had children of her own. When that affair ended, Rob began indulging himself . . . none of this is new. These are experiences, too, but indulging in them meant that Rob's old life would unravel. For present purposes, the question is: Can we generalize about the difference between the old and the new sets of experiences? Why did the new experiences seem to Rob worth the cost to people for whom he cares? Why did the old life no longer satisfy?

The answer to these questions, on a thematic level, has also become a cliché, the stuff of middlebrow education. Ordinary bourgeois life, we long have been taught, is just that, ordinary and bourgeois, hardly terms of praise. Rob lived in a suburb. He and his wife owned a minivan. He played golf. How crushingly boring, how banal! Rob simply realized that his life could be something else, more intense, passionate, real, authentic, and that now was the time to make the change, before it was too late. This was not a midlife crisis, it was a midlife awakening. Can we blame Rob for fantasizing, for looking for something young and exciting? Can we blame him for trying to realize his fantasies?

We might have a hard time forgiving Rob's behavior because we like Sharon (we might find ourselves mumbling something about how hard it is for a woman in this supposedly modern society to be over thirty-five), and because a man ought to take care of his children, but certainly Rob's impulses are understandable, even familiar. To make our society's fundamental comfort with Rob's behavior still more clear, imagine that our exemplar were gay, like Oscar Wilde, and the question was the extent to which he should hide his sexuality, should remain in the closet. We have no trouble asserting that Oscar made the choices he did because he had to be true to himself, that to do anything else would be dishonest, even inauthentic. So our ideology is not without support for Rob as he reconfigures his bourgeois life, liquidates a substantial portion of his assets and then spends the proceeds in search of . . .

What? The tendency, reflexive among middlebrow intellectuals, to criticize the middle class in general, and suburbia in particular, implies a different sort of life. As already suggested, there seems to be considerable consensus on what such a life would *feel* like: it would be more intense, passionate, real, authentic. It has long been common to maintain that, if we are middle class, we should find our days numb, unfeeling, phony, inauthentic. And yet while criticism of bourgeois banality combined with some gesture towards the authentic life has been a staple of literature over the last hundred years—perhaps the most important theme in the literature of the developed countries—the actual shape of the authentic life, and what might be done to achieve it, remains astonishingly vague. It appears to be difficult to state what makes an experience authentic, and we are back to where we started. Rob evidently believes that some set of experiences are more authentic than the experiences that comprised his old life, but why? What is it about sex with one woman that is more authentic than sex with another? What does authentic mean?

It is tempting to claim that men like Rob do not think seriously, they simply want a younger woman, act on their inclinations, and consequences flow. But insofar as this is true, we have a case of infidelity leading to divorce, not a midlife crisis. To have a midlife crisis is to have an existential moment reflected by changes in cash flow. For years, Rob appears to have thought he should pay down the mortgage, sock a little money away for the children's college, and so forth. Suddenly, he stops doing such things, and rides a motorcycle from somewhere in suburban Virginia to Austin, Texas, for a music festival. However (in)articulate he may be about the matter, Rob's structure of meaning has evidently changed: he auctioned off his stored wealth and used the proceeds to search for a new life that was substantially different from, in some way we might call more authentic than, his old life. Whether Rob's search will be successful—whether Rob will secure authentic experience, female or otherwise, is a separate point. Even whether men like Rob exist, much less whether their divorces stem from singular acts of infidelity or an existential moment known as a midlife crisis, is beside the point. We are trafficking in cliché here, and the argument is the same whether we speak of actual men with real midlife crises, or a social fantasy of such crises. Either a substantial number of men reach such a point in their lives, or, the more interesting possibility, we appear to believe that men *should* reach such a pass, that is, we long to see the town fathers as Don Quixote. We long to throw off our petty cluttered lives, in search of something more true. Even rich middle-aged white guys appear to believe, at some fundamental level, that our society is not worthy of allegiance.

*　*　*

We should expect a revolt against a monetary society to be hostile to money. And at some level it is: our paladin Rob sold assets in exchange for experience; he did not invest. His divorce, remarriage, and even drugs were antagonistic to his old world, based upon saving and investing, based upon securing that enviable combination of liberty and dominion that we call status or prestige.[1] In liquidating his assets and throwing his money away, Rob abolished his status, that is, he destroyed his life as a husband, a father, a neighbor, and so forth, even as he lost ownership of substantial money and property. A midlife crisis exchanges stability for adventure, investments for consumption, commitment for pleasure. Rob wasted those things that are defined in common and at least superficially honored by his community, in order to seek something vaguely referred to as authentic experience. Our man Rob's midlife crisis is an enormous expenditure of political capital, a willingness to give up presumably hard-earned positions in society, in exchange for the chance to appreciate the curve of a fender or a thigh.[2] In trading money for transitory experience, Rob appears to have escaped the dialectic between property and money, the interminable exchange between dominion and liberty. In a word, Rob left the City of Gold.

Just as money and authenticity seem to be antagonistic, so that the desire for authenticity requires at least the willingness to liquidate one's investments, money and inauthenticity seem to be intimately related. Lionel Trilling (on the young Marx reading Shakespeare's imagination of Athens) quite rightly if obscurely says that "money, in short, is the principle of the inauthentic in human existence." Trilling quotes Marx: "If I have a vocation for study but no money for it, then I have no vocation, that is, no *effective, genuine* vocation. Conversely, if I really have no vocation for study but have money and the urge for it, then I have an *effective* vocation." Trilling closes with the famous passage in which the young Marx sets forth the possibility of a nonmonetary view of existence: "Let us assume *man* to be *man*, and his relation to the world a human one. Then love can only be exchanged for love, trust for trust, etc. If you wish to enjoy art you must be an artistically cultivated person; if you wish to influence other people you must be a person who really has a stimulating and encouraging effect upon others. Every one of your relations to man and to nature must be *a specific expression* corresponding to the object of your will, of your *real individual* life."[3]

We have never recovered from the confusion rooted in this passage, and even articulating what is at stake requires considerable work. Our discussion of the midlife crisis has already raised a set of oppositions: money/experience; politically or socially accepted/real; inauthenticity/authenticity; entering the City/leaving the City. Such oppositions are familiar enough in the abstract, as social criticism. Indeed, cognate oppositions could be added to the list without thinking: suburbia/city; entertainment/art; franchise/sole proprietorship; artificially flavored processed foods/organic vegetables, and so on. Such oppositions, however, do not immediately help us understand the particulars of what actually happened to Rob and his family. What about Sharon and the kids, a sunlit morning in the minivan on the way to Hilton Head—exactly what is inauthentic about that? Having children in a house in the suburbs is a comic struggle to order nature; what makes that inherently less authentic than urban life? Does the fact that the house and the minivan and even the vacation need to be purchased, and therefore are tainted with the same sort of monetary relations that comprise the City, somehow automatically make the object of such purchases inauthentic? Surely the more juvenile pleasures that Rob began to enjoy after his crisis also needed to be purchased? And what do such particular questions have to do with Trilling's grand statement that money is the *principle* of inauthenticity? We clearly need more.

Trilling contrasts authenticity with sincerity, which he understands as an ethical attribute, akin to honesty: the sincere action reflects the actor's effort to speak or act truthfully, to present an exact correspondence between her seeming and her actual being. The sincere woman's persona is the same as her actual personality. Sincerity is the virtue pitted against the evil possibility that one lives in the society of frauds, cheats, and thieves, in which people are other than they seem, insincere, and by extension, society is undermined by mistrust. Sincerity is not only moral, it is ethical in the social and political sense of furthering the credibility of the social code. The sincere person wishes to be sincere, actually to embody the role that society provides and expects. Conversely, the person who so sincerely presents herself is a deeply social being.

Like sincerity, authenticity is a quality of correspondence. While sincerity is a correspondence between social presentation (persona) and underlying reality (personality), authenticity is a correspondence between achieved reality and ideal reality. Something is authentic in the degree to which the thing as it actually exists in the world, as it is achieved, successfully expresses its real, inward existence. Just because a thing exists does not mean it has achieved its ideal reality. Many things are inauthentic, phony, rather than genuine. Something that is phony and inauthentic may even comport to social expectations. Marx therefore speaks of relations corresponding to real individual life, presumably as opposed to the sham relations that comprise the life actually achieved in his society or ours.

As already mentioned, sincerity is a political concept. One must be sincere to somebody. One cannot be sincere alone, just as one cannot be truthful alone. In order to be sincere, one must have the opportunity to be insincere, just as one must have the opportunity to lie in order to tell the truth. Sincerity is thus a political relation: a person's truthful and candid presentation of herself to another. The desire to be sincere, then, reflects a longing for a certain kind of community.

Although they often seem synonymous, both somehow relating to "honesty," the idea of authenticity is in tension, sometimes conflict, with the idea of sincerity.[4] Authenticity is defined regardless of society's judgment. Indeed, society's opposition is often taken to be a demonstration of authenticity. A person or thing that exists in a manner contrary to the prevailing tendency must be reflecting their inward nature rather than society's wishes. The prohibition of Wilde's homosexuality, for example, made his persona—for all of its extravagant artfulness, and for all that he had to say on the topic of artifice—seem somehow more authentic. Similarly, homemade objects in an age of mass production, ethnic food in an age of homogenization, wild animals in a time of extinction, seem authentic precisely because we understand such things to exist in spite of dominant social trends, and therefore, we assume, fulfill the imperatives of their own natures, rather than merely conforming to society's expectations. To be authentic is to be true to oneself, even at the cost of being outcast.[5]

Both people and things may fulfill the imperatives of their natures, that is, be authentic. Only people, however, can present themselves honestly, so that they seem to others as they really are, and so they really are as they seem to others. This effort to be sincere—to present oneself in good faith to society—can only be undertaken by a human. In contrast, at least in modern usage, a thing may be authentic but not, without personification, sincere.[6] Bread can be called authentic but not sincere. Consequently, when one speaks of authenticity there is no morality, in the usual sense, involved. Yet we use "authenticity" in moral fashion, as a term of praise. To call something authentic is to praise it for achieving its ideal reality, for making its inward nature visible. In a broad, aesthetic sense, authenticity is a moral virtue, even a religious stance, from which we exhort the world to have blue skies, aromatic cookies, and otherwise conform to our ideas of what it is to be genuine, but authenticity is not an ethical, social, virtue.

With this much of an understanding of "authenticity" in hand, we may return to the passage from Marx quoted above. Money, as we discussed in chapter II, has no inward nature. Money is a communally recognized token of desire, but nothing about money specifies the nature of the desire or even the exchange value of its fulfillment. As Schopenhauer phrased it, money is happiness in the abstract.[7] But because it has no inward nature, money cannot be authentic. Money is all social function; there is no inward reality for money to achieve. As a result and by extension, a monetary relation cannot be "*a specific expression* corresponding to the object of your will, of your *real individual* life," as Marx has it, simply because such a relation could be replaced by a different relation, negotiated for the same price. Yet despite their unavoidable inauthenticity, monetary relations are ubiquitous in, indeed constitute, commercial societies, to say nothing of cultures founded on commerce in money itself, financial capitalism. If money is the mechanism through which social relations in the City are constructed, then the City is inescapably inauthentic.

*　*　*

Yet the relationship between money and authenticity is not simple opposition. Consider what it might mean to insist that the sky conform to our expectation of what the sky should be. The sky is what it is, even if we have warmed it. Similarly, what does it mean to praise the food served by a certain ethnic restaurant as authentic? Food prepared in a less authentic restaurant, perhaps in an effort to conform to a perception of local tastes, would no less be food, and might even more closely conform to the emigrant experience of cultural distinction combined with assimilation. Why does Rob consider sex with Sharon to be inauthentic, and sex with his newly acquired companion to be authentic? Surely Sharon, suburban mother of two, is not only what she appears to be, but is also living a life that responds to its own inner imperatives? Surely Sharon is not only sincere, but also authentic? Despite the fact that generations of critics have claimed that life in the suburbs is inauthentic, does not the fact that most Americans choose to live in such settings suggest that at least some of them are being true to themselves?

Marx speaks of the individual person, with individual capacities such as artistic cultivation or persuasive power, for whom art or debate are authentic pursuits. The authentic relation is the "specific expression" of the "real individual life." The experience of authenticity requires the satisfaction of the individual vision, in practice often indistinguishable from the individual will. So the babe, the car, the drugs, are authentic because Rob wanted them. They are authentic for Rob, not in and of themselves, not objectively. Authenticity is a quality of correspondence between actual existence and *desired* ideal. Something is authentic to the extent to which it matches the image in the mind's eye, thereby satisfying the self's sense of the world. Authenticity is thus literally selfish; that which is authentic corresponds to the self's vision. So authentic bread corresponds to our ideal of what bread ought to be, the authentically ethnic food corresponds to our desire for the exotic, and Wilde's appeal stems from our fantasies of liberty, especially sexual, whose exercise is forgiven, even celebrated, on account of undisputed talent.

Decisions defended on the grounds of their authenticity are often selfish in the everyday sense, too. Rob's midlife crisis is a set of indulgences that will cause great pain, perhaps even harm, to others. Rob is selfish in the ordinary sense of choosing to fulfill his will as opposed to his obligations to others. While we often wish to see such matters as essentially private—the failure of a marriage, the beginning of new relationships—such choices have serious political implications. Rob's obligations to his children, wife, and broader community are matters of social and even legal concern. Rob's defection, then, among other things represents a political failure. In the terms with which this essay is concerned, Rob's crisis is a choice for the self (the pursuit of authentic experience) as opposed to conformity with his social role (precluding the possibility of sincere performance of that role).

Sex is the obvious issue over which to expect the polity to fail to command allegiance. As in any number of novels (consider *Anna Karenina*) the desire for sexual authenticity often overwhelms the attractions of conformity, respectability, and belonging. Not only is the urge to violate the code (whatever the specifics of the code may be) so widely and keenly felt, the political virtue of sincerity is at its least compelling in matters sexual. A degree of sexual insincerity is universal in politics. To present one's innermost self to the world—to be sexually sincere, always—cannot be a social maxim. Very crudely put, even after all the sexual revolutions, rape remains proscribed. Sex is the issue on which the conflict between the claims of society (elsewhere furthered by the virtue of sincerity but here requiring hypocrisy) and the opposing claims of the individual will (the longing for authenticity) is sharpest. Sex is therefore the issue over which to expect betrayal, like Rob's.

Every society has problems with sex, on which societies depend and yet which must be ordered if the social order is to survive, that is, lust both strains against and requires law. Traditionally, lust was acknowledged—and restrained—by the law of marriage and associated proprieties, which then needed to be enforced. Lust, however, is a literally unruly thing. The theme is familiar: Lancelot and Guinevere, or Romeo and Juliet, or the adultery of a Puritan (whether in New England or Saudi Arabia matters little), are dramas based on the perennial challenge posed by sex for law—as is Rob's breaking of the suburban code. This point is usually made psychologically rather than politically. For the modern consciousness, sex is the most familiar point at which the self is divided against itself, at which urge and discipline are most keenly at odds. (Art is another such point.) In Freudian terms, the ego both struggles against and requires the superego. More generally, the very notion that the authentic human could be honestly expressed in a socially acceptable role, could be sincere, seems either old-fashioned or perhaps naively progressive. We know all too well that the human mind is composed of good and evil, that much that is human must be repressed, and that society is therefore a tissue of lies, but necessary lies. In our longing for and consciousness of authentic experience we repudiate the possibility of making social life completely sincere, which hardly makes social life less necessary.

And so we have a drama, or a litigation, the need to resolve the tensions between sometimes antagonistic sources of meaning. Both lust and propriety are real, encompass aspects of being human, and neither can finally defeat the other. The same can be said of our need to be true to our visions (experience authenticity) and to find meaning in communities we truthfully support (be sincere). On the one hand, Rob's intention, his desire to find his life more meaningful, is surely understandable, and indeed both common and, at least in the abstract, worthy. Even Rob's solution, spending money in exchange for strong, authentic, experience, is common enough. Rob longs for a kind of truth, the sense of meaning associated with the strong experience. In brief, Rob gratifies certain lusts, which he feels to be authentic, as opposed to frustrating those same desires, behavior which he thought both inauthentic (not true to his inner imperatives), and a lie to his fellow citizens, hence insincere.

On the other hand, propriety would seem to have strong claims: Rob's actions are likely to do considerable damage to others, most obviously his family, but quite possibly his colleagues, friends, neighbors, and the people he mistreats in pursuit of experience—hence the social injunctions for keeping marriages, particularly those with children, together. Quite apart from the narrowly moral point that Rob's actions will cause specific harms to others, Rob's justification—his "crisis" constitutes a search for meaning—is weak. Rob found little meaning in his family and other aspects of suburban existence, but only because he is insensitive, not because such things are meaningless. Indeed, suburbia has many meanings, including social and political meanings—life with a degree of community—which Rob's self-indulgence precludes. It takes great arrogance, and conversely, a lack of faith in one's community, to claim that social life is inauthentic, somehow unreal, phony, in spite of its actual existence.

How is this litigation to be resolved? In public, and in the main, we accept the thought that the will must be constrained by some higher authority, embodied by the law. It is true that in fantasy, in secret, in some festivals, and in youth and at other margins, one may skirt or even flout the dictates of the law. But Rob very publicly privileged his selfish demands for authentic experience, private meaning, over propriety's demand for a degree of insincerity. The principle implicitly at issue here is quite broad. The hypocritical law of suburbia, Rob maintains, has no authority over the authentic truths of his new experiences (rebellion is authentic). We might expect society to try and put down such an insurrection, just as the superego disciplines the ego, and just as criminals are punished.

But Rob is not punished. Instead, he appears to be a sort of cultural hero, the subject of clichés and a widely imitated model.[8] This is strange. Rob violates society's mores in search of authentic experience, defined as experience in accordance with his will. Rob has declared his independence from his wife, his family, and even a sensible understanding of his economic role as a prudent investor, and thereby betrayed his membership in the community that relies upon and supports such institutions. Nonetheless, however, Rob's community celebrates authentic experience, and consequently not only allows but even supports (if covertly) his running away from his obligations. That is, in appearing to flout the conventions of his society, Rob finds himself embodying the fantasies of that same society. Why?

How could a truly monetary society do otherwise? As discussed in part 1, money is the institutional expression of the idea of liberty, the embodiment of permission, the liberty to please oneself. Has not Rob seized liberty? All Rob has done is shortened his time horizon, liquidated some assets, and traded up. Certainly no monetary society is in a position to criticize behavior such as Rob's—his is precisely the sort of behavior that is required to be successful in the marketplace. Rob may believe that he has left the City, gotten down to the essential things in his life, but it would be difficult to imagine anything he could do that would be more purely in keeping with money's character than liquidating his property and casting about for something "authentic" to do.

From the metropolitan perspective, Trilling's statement that money is the principle of inauthenticity is inapt. Money is the mechanism of authentic experience. If authenticity is the enjoyment we take in finding a thing that comports with what we desire its true nature to be, that is, authenticity is the experience of finding our dream already realized, then money is the tool of the seeker after authenticity. Nothing allows one to realize dreams more effectively than money; Rob spends lots of money realizing his dreams. More generally, shopping feels authentic for good reason—to make a find, just the thing one had not quite yet envisioned—is to recognize ones desires already for sale in the bazaar. Authenticity thus offers a way to overcome the alienation discussed in the preceding chapter. The midlife crisis, understood as a search for authenticity, is celebrated by the City as an emotionally charged version of a good day in the marketplace. Monetary society can embrace its would-be rebels, celebrate their willful alienation and their egoism, because the City's inhabitants are egoistic by definition.

Trilling's statement that money is the principle of inauthenticity, however, was not made from the perspective of the City of Gold. Trilling, like the Marx he was discussing, was writing as a social critic, trying to discern the truth in social practices. From this perspective, shopping malls often seem inauthentic, even if they are the context for countless authentic purchases. And there seems to be something wrong with Rob's behavior, and further wrong with our society's willingness to countenance the relentless pursuit of the authentic, a pursuit that requires individuals to deny society's own claims. From this perspective, the monetary search for authenticity is limited, because little that we encounter is true to itself, and to the extent that it is true, that truth hardly can be expressed in the logic of the City. Instead, for reasons discussed in the last essay, our activity in the City is true to the simulacrum of monetary politics. Money promises authenticity, but generally delivers mere property, and in continually baiting and switching, money is indeed the principle of inauthenticity. Trilling and Marx had it right.

* * *

Most inhabitants of the City are unaware (presumably blissfully) of the critique afforded by Marx and Trilling, whose analysis was based on so much besides capitalism. There is reason to believe, however, that the City will come to seem inauthentic even to some of its less traveled inhabitants. As discussed in the next chapter, we citizens of the world operate in a context so vast and consequently not home that it affords us no sense that our particular selves belong. We may be masters of our fate—well, careers, anyway—and we desperately celebrate the idea of choice. However, as discussed in the last chapter, we are alienated even from our economic selves. It is impossible to believe that our choices, however made, are uniquely ours and uniquely recognizable as such. The proliferation of choice does nothing to relieve the sense of *anomie*, and may worsen that sense because it demonstrates the irrelevance of our individual action. We are fungible, dimly aware that any number of cosmopolites could do our lives. The individual mind, the self, is incapable of acting in such a way that the City of Gold recognizes its action. The most that can be hoped is that the City will recognize the action of the persona, of the golem, our soulless creature who acts on our behalf in the dangerous world called the market. But it cannot be hoped that the City can know the truth about our true self, just as it is too much to hope that that self can be at home in the City. The self in the City of Gold is perpetually an alien, regardless of choices made, powers exercised. For such selves, an authentic impression of public life is no more plausible than an authentic meal in an airport food court.

But if the City is too vast, it is also too shallow. We ask whether the world constructed by supranational capitalism, the City of Gold, is what it seems to be, that is, corresponds to the truth as we see it, and we inevitably find our truths far richer than the politics of the City, based on property law, can hope to be. An inhabitant's own experience of metropolitan inauthenticity thus turns, not on what the City signifies, but on what it does not. We understand the City of Gold to be inauthentic because we cannot find so many of our truths in it. Young people and academics and organized labor—marginal sorts, with worldviews dependent on things besides capital—frequently rail against global culture, often in spite of personal dependence upon precisely such culture, because the City has so little respect for their deeper convictions.[9] One might consider, as poignant examples, protests organized over the Internet against Bretton Woods Institutions or against well-known hamburger franchises. More generally, the limited nature of the City's political discourse means that the City will never be more than partially responsive to our hopes for collective truth.

The nature of our participation in the City further ensures that the City will strike us as inauthentic. As discussed in chapter IV, by buying and selling in the marketplace, the individual assures himself of his status, his existence in the City. Status is assured, however, venally, by excluding one's fellows from one's property, frustrating their desires, or by appealing to their discontent, taunting them with the liberty that money may provide. The self is thus defined through the rejection of others, who also serve as an audience. Monetary relations entail a willingness to treat one's counterparties, and others in the market, as a means to an end. But to treat people merely as a means to an end is to treat them with a certain contempt, as objects. The City of Gold is thus a polity founded not merely on lies, exclusion, and the harsh necessities of life among strangers, but on outright contempt, a willingness to debase others in order to assure ourselves that we exist in a way the City can recognize.

At some point, concern for the innermost qualities of mere acquisition, in market transactions that reflect only a fraction of the truth, and that require contempt from their participants, can no longer be faked, and the search for authenticity in the City becomes implausible. Tahiti ceases to be Gauguin's island and becomes just a more expensive version of Florida; Mount Everest becomes an adventure vacation; young women and men become designer accessories, "arm candy" or "boy toys." We cannot find our authentic selves in such a world; we are so mercenary that our own environment is unreal for us. If we are honest, we concede that we undertake those activities known as business, or, in the aggregate, view the market, with contempt, even though it is home. We cannot simultaneously be contemptuous of something and find it authentic, worthy of a certain praise. We cannot care much about the authenticity of things we despise.

*   *   *

The longing for truth relates the inseparable but nonetheless distinguishable concepts of alienation and authenticity, flip sides of the same coin. Alienation looks to the world, and regrets the interposition of the middle term, money. Alienation is at bottom an objection to the lies that stem from the act of pricing, to the substitution of money for something else. Alienation is the worry that money obscures the truth, and so, if one is to live in truth, one must live alone in a hated world.

Authenticity, in contrast, is the quality that the world constructed by monetary relations promises but ultimately lacks, groundedness. To long for authenticity is to look to culture and wish it were more substantial, more real. Beneath the desire for authenticity lies a desire for a world more worthy of admiration, rather than a formal, conventional sham. Authenticity is the worry that the polity constructed by money is untruthful, so no reconciliation is possible, and nothing can be hoped from politics.

In particular, in the City of Gold, there seems to be no cause for allegiance and little hope for justice. "It"—presumably meaning social relations—is all about the money, our cynics (including drunk businessfolk and sober economists) like to say, worried that this is the only truth we may have. To be clear about the literally unjust character of metropolitan life, reconsider that Rob's community failed to compel Rob's allegiance. Rob's is hardly an isolated case; betrayals such as his are a cliché. Middle class life, suburban life, often appears uncompelling, often seems inauthentic, to the middle class themselves, especially their chatterers. Rob's infidelity has thus led us to ask whether the City can be espoused. The preceding essay, concerned with the possibility of collective truth, maintained that the answer was no, that because the City could neither hear nor express truth, it made sense to choose alienation, internal exile, rather than allegiance. This essay shifts focus, from truth to social order, and so the question on the table is whether a polity unworthy of allegiance can even begin to speak of justice. Conversely, surely a just City would be worthy of allegiance?

In Rob's story, sex was the occasion for betrayal of society, and for swearing allegiance to one's vision, a trope familiar from the Romantics, who characteristically choose to pursue inner passion rather than maintain social respectability. This opposition, the passionate vs. the political, lies near the root of our sense that authentic experience requires the flaunting of society's demands, and therefore structured the foregoing discussion of authenticity in tension with sincerity. Entailed in such a Romantic view, however, is a condemnation of society: our society is cold and cares little for real passion, has no patience for intense vision or authentic experience. Instead, our society promotes the square virtue of sincerity, exhorts us to be what we are expected to be, urges us to conform. Social life, for the Romantics, is impoverished, inadequately responds to the human condition.

This general constellation of ideas is familiar since Rousseau, who also realized that sex (nature) drove a wedge between allegiance to the self and allegiance to society; that a society which could not account for what it is to be human could be neither just nor worthy of allegiance. But Rousseau also realized that it was just barely possible to imagine a society that did, in fact, respond to the human condition. In such a society, the desire to belong would be authentic, and the Romantic opposition between the demands of authenticity and social propriety would dissolve. In such a world, the political order would reflect the human condition, so that all that was appropriate to being human had a recognized place within that order. Such a world would be just.

If such a society is imaginable, however, it is not the City. Insofar as the City is founded on capitalism, then our politics are based on money and property. The City therefore has the limitations entailed by those institutions, and simply cannot account for much of what it is to be human, much that is very important. The City is perpetually vulnerable to the Romantic critique, precisely because there is so much that is worthy of our allegiance that cannot be spoken within the grammar of the City. Any focus on something that the City cannot say will reveal the impoverishment of the City. The City, however, is never silent; metropolitan life is noisy. And so that which is said will inevitably feel superficial, inauthentic.

The City of Gold stands forth as the first polity to claim inauthenticity as a virtue, the first polity to use inauthenticity for its own sake, even at the cost of justice. Of course, politics in practice has always been more or less untruthful. Plato argued that that political life tended, by its nature, to make philosophical thought impossible, and so the philosopher had no desire to be king. That said, Plato and virtually every political thinker since discussed politics as if it aspired to truth.[10] Certainly American politics has, since the founding, aspired to truth: "We hold these truths to be self-evident," the Declaration of Independence begins, as if our decision to fight Great Britain were the necessary outcome of objective assessment. In elevating monetary relations to constitutional principle, however, the City of Gold has abjured the possibility of a political life in truth. The City is an extended and incredibly successful effort to organize the peoples of the world into a single polity in which truth, in any sense external to the polity, is not only irrelevant, but unimaginable to the political mind, as unimaginable as philosophy is to the pigs.

In part due to the Romantic assault, the anxiety that society was inauthentic, and participation in it was at best hypocrisy, was widespread in the nineteenth century. If one could just understand society on some such principled basis, one could have faith. Throughout the nineteenth century and into the twentieth, great minds struggled to find some principle—scientific materialism, social Darwinism, libidinous cathection, rational self-interest—that could be used to reduce social life to its honest necessity, all surplusage cut away like diseased flesh. While such efforts failed in their intention of putting social life on a sound footing, they succeeded in making politics seem ridiculous. Cultural life came to seem not only dishonest, but downright absurd, and hence unworthy of good faith participation. Once "the best lack all conviction, while the worst are full of passionate intensity," as Yeats has it, political life, even as modestly imagined by modern thinkers, is not far from crisis.

One way of being modern (from Nietzsche forward) is to acknowledge the inevitable failure of and desist from reductionist efforts to put social life on a rational, and hence trustworthy, footing. Instead, we may come to find the culture to be in its own way and on its own terms very true: It is even fashionable to claim that such cultural truths are the only truths available to us.[11] Understanding culture as collective fiction, however, does not solve the problem of authenticity, does not make the culture true in the unproblematic way that one might have hoped. On the contrary, as Nietzsche painfully knew, understanding culture as collective fiction continually raises the question, is the fiction well told, more particularly, is the fiction told in good faith? Is the life so lived well lived, truly and authentically lived, in the respectable sense called for by Havel's phrase, "living in truth"? Do we, who live under the regime of supranational capitalism, live in truth? Or are we, too, worthy of contempt?

We certainly do not live in truth in any simple sense. As a thought experiment, consider some of what a middle-class American like Rob owns. Rob is very unlikely to know if his retirement funds are directly invested in a particular country, perhaps France or New Zealand. It is almost unimaginable that Rob would know where companies in which he is invested are themselves invested or otherwise exposed, or even where such interests are recorded. If Rob perchance knows any such things, his knowledge will in all likelihood be purely abstract, no more concrete than a name or perhaps a billing address. Likewise, presumably Rob's debts have been securitized, and may even be publicly traded. So, were he to fail to pay his debts, Rob has no idea who would be affected, albeit perhaps infinitesimally. Perhaps his default might affect a Japanese pension fund, assuming that Japanese pension funds are allowed to invest in overseas asset-backed securities at the time Rob exists. Rob is not alone or in any way remiss here: it has become difficult to know much more about one's financial situation than a fish does about the bounds of the sea.[12] The City is founded on monetary relations that are conducted impersonally, ethereally, often at great distance and speed. There is no way that one can identify with such transactions; such transactions hardly relate to a citizen's experience. We live in a world that we do not know.

There are a number of ways to respond to this realization. One may, like Rob, attempt to leave the City. Departure from the City of Gold is generally felt anachronistically, as a return, a going back.[13] Just as the young man from the provinces must shed his native ways when he enters the City, our middle-aged rebel must lose the ways of the City in order to find his true self, in a sense, to find his way back home. Authenticity must be reestablished, individual life must be recaptured, that is, reality was once possessed but was lost, and so the task confronting our paladin is to retake his own present. In order to do so, the monetary relationship, pricing, must be undone. Thus, if entry into the City is a commitment to the near future, exit from the City is a rejection of the proposition that we should live for tomorrow. The association of midlife crises with intimations of mortality is not entirely wrong—the effort to exit the City suggests frustration with the endless deferrals, postponements, that mark metropolitan life. Midlife crises are about spending rather than investing, and Rob lives, and more importantly wants, here and now, while the City is about deferred gratification, buying and holding, the accumulation of capital.

Rob need not see matters in terms of such grand abstractions; it would be somewhat surprising if he did. On the ground, somewhere in suburbia, we have a simple case of a man who has lost faith in his way of life, to the extent that he is willing to kick off the traces. Rob seeks a truer life in rebellion, in the exercise of his will with little regard for what had been his community. He has lost faith in the community constructed by price—"four bedroom homes from the low 200's," as the sign outside the development where his children are growing up might say. But real rebellion is difficult. Can we be so sure that the will Rob exercises is not the same will that constructs itself in the dialectic of the market, the same will that excludes through property, or taunts through liberty? Should he himself sense this, Rob may indeed become, like Quixote, a dolorous knight, unable to impress his true self upon his world. While we regard Quixote with affection, what will we think of Rob, whose dreams are perhaps less good-hearted?

If Arcadian flight is one response to the inauthenticity of modern life, surrealist bemusement is another. Financial markets, as we saw in chapter III, are compelling—they play on our fears of the future, promise us our dreams. But such promises perversely make the future a task that must be confronted now, and on the terms determined by capital. In helping us to secure ourselves from, or at least ameliorate, the dangers that lurk in the middle distance, finance robs us of the ability to enjoy the present. The expectation of the near future, the time of finance, is built upon and yet obscures the reality of the present. As a result, we experience the present as quite literally surreal, as something somehow constructed on top of reality. Surrealist art is fascinating for the present time because surrealism can elicit the sensation of living among the inauthentic (almost always referred to as the "unsettling" quality of such paintings), a sensation that typifies life under supranational capitalism.[14] Surrealism portrays us situated among conventions that we understand to have no foundations, to be arbitrary and quite possibly impossible, and that yet stand because no other basis for tomorrow is historically or otherwise imaginable.

Our very awareness that our experience of social life is unbelievable, or at least unconvincing, makes it difficult to have a serious political imagination, difficult to ask how our politics could be made better.[15] To what authority could such a petition be addressed? The City has few mechanisms through which we might claim that our social arrangements are democratically legitimated, or are even legitimated by reference to the mind as opposed to the gut. Conversely, forces that are in fact exercised upon us make scant claim to moral authority. Indeed, much politics is now explicitly handled amorally. As discussed in chapter V, the City governs itself by regulating access to capital, a system that works pretty well. But access to capital in pursuit of private interest is, by its terms, a thoughtless system of governance, as our environment, littered with strip malls, bad architecture, and polluted air, attests. The financial markets explicitly aspire to be fully automatic ("self-regulating"), that is, a system of governance in which our subjugation would be perfected. Moreover, we grant authority to the price mechanism, that is, the current state of disagreement among those with some power. How could we, who live among the accidents (which the economists refer to as "externalities") of such transactions, petition a self-regulating disagreement?

As constitutional myths go, this is not a pretty one. The City provides a terrifyingly limited view of life among humans, subordinated to institutions they hardly know and generally do not understand. Our political situation is sugarcoated by powerful appeals to temptations, usually bodily. (Consider the happiness promised by advertising.) At bottom, however, thoughtful citizens fear that their City, the only home they can have, cannot claim to be more than a bunch of pigs at a trough, and the angry charge of inauthenticity is made in the belief that human life together can be more and better than metropolitan relations.

*   *   *

How are we to regard such arguments? Writing an apology such as this presumes that sense can be made out of life in the City of Gold, that the City itself and the ways of its citizens can be justified in some frame of reference that must, if the foregoing criticism is correct, be outside the grammar of the City of Gold. The critical intentions of this part 2 can only be understood in the context of a presumption—it is tempting to say a faith—that thought and language, the communicability of meaning, are yet more powerful than money's ability to dissolve meaning, or at the very least, that the City of Gold somehow still affords a space in which meaning can be constructed. This apology thus presumes that we do not literally believe, or at least not exclusively believe, that our society is based on contempt for one another, disgust that we abide only by employing complex literary-political delusions about democracy, human rights, autonomy, and the like. For all that we live in a polity constructed by lies, we have a countervailing sense that true things can be said, that, even though human relations in the City of Gold are ignoble, it remains possible for us to talk honestly.

While money is ancient, so is the criticism of money. The first jeremiad must very be old indeed, because Athens and Jerusalem had already well-established versions of the positions that the last two chapters have tried to restate, that money sickens the souls of the citizens and so corrupts polities. Yet if money is the cause of our malaise, one would expect our sickness to have worsened over the millennia, or even over the centuries since the end of the middle ages. Whether our sickness has worsened since the foundation of the City is an open question, but if money is a disease, it is one for which we have considerable resistance. Money indeed corrupts, but the fact that we still recognize and condemn corruption—the fact that we are not completely corrupted—suggests that other forces must also be at work.

Life, even among the propertied classes of the City of Gold, is comprised of much more than the desire to exclude or taunt others. Noble relations are possible; belief is possible. Life, even in the City of Gold, is far different, far richer, than monetary relations convey. Most of life is not property, and things have properties far beyond the legal articulations known as property rights. Little is monetized, and most everything is much else besides its exchange value. One answer to the attack on our way of life made in this part 2 is that the politics of the City of Gold, the political effects of markets, are by their terms partial. Once politics is understood to be a limited enterprise, the failures of our polity may seem less significant. We may look not to what our political arrangements provide directly, but what they allow us to achieve in other areas of our lives. The purpose of politics, in this view, is to provide the security required for civil life, nothing more.

This is a powerful answer, but it gains defensibility from its modesty, and may even be a bit lazy. Insofar as we are attempting to understand a polity explicitly founded on money, the logic of money must be pursued to its bitter end, even if that turns out to be to the point of self-contempt. And insofar as our political thought tries to answer the incessant question of how we are to live together as if it were a philosophical problem, and insofar as we think supranational capitalism is the institutional expression of our answer to this question, we should attempt to address the question in general terms. We should indulge in theory because we believe political life is a proper subject for thought, not because we are under the delusion that political thought fully describes social reality, nor because politics is the sole source of meaning, and certainly not on the vanishingly small hope that theory will make any difference in how people act.

It is wrong to think the diagnosis that money is the root of our evil is incorrect simply because we can still understand jeremiads. (It would be even more wrong simply to dismiss capitalisms' critics as unworldly malcontents.) Money's innocence is not proven by the survival of meaning, because, as suggested above, money is always partial, its scope limited by that of property. Much is not and will never be property; it is no more possible to map life onto a regime of rights than it is to describe it fully. As the Romantics have demonstrated for some two hundred years now, we will always have experiences, and hence meaning, outside the monetary regime, and hence intellectual resources with which to criticize the world of money. It is quite possible that (i) capitalism could be our politics; (ii) capitalism should be condemned; and (iii) we would be in a position to understand the condemnation. It is quite possible that we live in a bad polity. If we are to play this game out and continue to claim the honor of thinking about politics, we are driven to explore such possibilities by undertaking serious political critique, as painful as that process might be.

* * *

It would be unbalanced not to acknowledge that the City of Gold may be experienced as authentic in a number of ways. For the Greeks who gave us the root of the word "authentic," *authentēs,* the issue was the authority of a person, his ability to create a truth. *Authentēs* was a master, a doer, that is, someone able to impose his vision of truth upon the world, we might go so far as to say, able to remake the world in order to be at home, to be able to recognize himself in the world. From this perspective, the further meaning of *authentēs,* a murderer, makes sense—what more complete realization of the will in the world, despite the total opposition of the victim, could there be?[16] It may seem that our better selves cannot want a world in which we are truly powerful, authentic in the sense of able to kill. Yet our entertainment industry suggests that we fantasize quite a lot about being killers, presumably people who matter and are worth admiring. Our predilection for violent crime, at least in America, suggests something darker still, articulated quite explicitly by popular culture's glorification of respect obtained at gunpoint: we use violence to establish an identity because we have no other, the Hegelian state of nature in a neighborhood near you.[17] Consider the books, comic books, songs, electronic games, television, and especially movies about Western gunfighters, urban gangsters/gangstas, private detectives and renegade cops, international spies and even superheroes, who tend to be isolated, without community (travelers, immigrants, drifters, men whose families have been killed, at any rate strangers) and who make an impression because they are so deadly. At the end of the day, however, these are mostly fantasies of rage expressed and poor people, marginal phenomena, or so it might appear, until one remembers that the establishment funds not only a police force but a great deal of private security in your neighborhood. The prevalence of violence in our society, especially when suppressed, lends a sense of authenticity to our political arrangements.

Turning from the neighborhood to the planet, the City of Gold is to some important degree authentic because no other response to Hitler was feasible, that is, the City of Gold draws not only its justification, but a sense of authenticity, from an awareness of history's horror, and most specifically, the Holocaust. Understood as a response to the alternatives presented by the state militant, the City of Gold is comprised by a brilliant set of institutional devices. In this view, the City is the imposition of the will of the mandarin class of the victorious armies, who in the Cold War and since have been willing to do violence when necessary to preserve their idea of the right order of things. The City has been a stunning success, that is, it in fact has achieved its real inward existence, the market with an international bureaucratic frame envisioned, if hazily, by its founders, and is therefore authentic. For the City's inhabitants to find such a world authentic, of course, requires that we identify, at least imaginatively, with the founding mandarins, but that should not be too difficult for members of the educated classes to do (indeed, this apology aims to make that identification easier). So violence, and better still, the necessity of managing violence, provide the first metropolitan experiences of authenticity.

Second, there are myriad ways to experience authenticity even in peaceful City life. Business folk are not simply immoral, and the life of business is not simply self-aggrandizement. Not even an angel, Lucifer, could manage pure evil.[18] We humans, even citizens of the City of Gold, have our virtues, and they are reflected in our institutions. Business requires numerous virtues, perhaps chief among them trustworthiness, and the people who embody commercial virtues, who actually do business, are more than mercenary, even in their business lives.

Third, even economic life strictly construed, by the dialectic between property and money described in chapter IV, gives rise to the sensations of liberty and of dominion. While perhaps not truly admirable, the exercise of liberty and dominion can be great fun, and the primary source of meaning for anybody who understands life in terms of the exercise of autonomy, such as college students, rich people, and liberals.

Fourth, as Aristotle understood, economic life may enable more noble pursuits. For example, while artists have often complained about the difficulties bourgeois life presents for their endeavors, art must be paid for, and much great art has been done under bourgeois conditions.[19] A successful work of art, even if produced within the bounds if not the logic of the City of Gold, achieves its intentions, its real inward self, and is therefore authentic, and such authentic experience is available to inhabitants of the City.

Fifth and finally, this apology has discerned all sorts of truth in market society: truths about politics and the individual, about our culture's ideas of time, about hope and fear, about freedom and domination, and so forth. If we focus on the conventions that inform markets (such as money or property), we see that markets are political institutions, objects fit for political critique. Understanding the alienation and inauthenticity entailed in metropolitan life—understanding what about the structure of our markets engenders these experiences—will lead perhaps to some reform of our markets (Freud's doubt that we can ever be at peace with our constitution notwithstanding), but also an ability to view with some equanimity our lack of peace, our continued experience of alienation and unsettled suspicions that our world is phony. And from this perhaps somewhat Olympian perspective, the City no longer disappoints, no longer lies, is no longer experienced as inauthentic. It is what it is, no more, no less.

Thus, through awareness of violence, appreciation for business virtues and bourgeois sensations, affection for art and other endeavors afforded by our capitalism, and finally, political economy, we may find a modicum of authenticity in the City of Gold. This glass, however, is much less than half full. For those without an imagination of the fragility and horror of history, the City is likely to remain the first polity of the inauthentic. Its citizens will remain foreigners in their home. So we can expect to see efforts to create authentic lives, like Rob's turn to aesthetics, from assets that appreciate to the appreciation of things. Rob kills his golem, the self he has constructed in his own image who does his business in the financial markets, thereby freeing himself to experience life more directly, as an exercise of his own will. Rob will probably fail. We have no reason to believe that his will is much besides the fantasies of the market society whose rules and obligations Rob deludes himself into thinking he has broken. His life as middle-aged bon vivant is unlikely to be more authentic than his life as middle-aged dad. And we must ask what sort of polity would make Rob's choice seem so reasonable, indeed, would perhaps hold Rob up as a sort of fantasy, conversely suggesting how deep our loathing for the City of Gold is. If we are to begin a serious political critique of the City of Gold—and particularly of life in America—there are worse places to start than by asking how we might imagine justice in a world that we loathe.

CHAPTER **VIII**
Identity, Tense

Inadequacy of traditional sources of identity for City of Gold. Living in the future imperfect tense; on being a consumer. Modernism, con and pro. Necessity of the private realm. Intellectual attitudes toward the City: boredom, distraction, bemusement. Turn to the private realm. Oligarchy. How to be an exile: guilt and rebellion. Recapitulation of Part II.

Traditional sources of identity, even though they may remain meaningful, do not resolve the question of where we as individuals stand in this global context, the City of Gold. For example, religion, at least in the ordinary sense, cannot serve as a ground for metropolitan identity. In its refusal to validate one religion over another, the City is classically liberal. Religious identity is irrelevant to status within the City, and so cannot provide cosmopolites with a sense of their place in the polity. Similarly, history might seem to be a likely source of metropolitan identity, but the history that most of us find meaningful—the history of our people, however that may be defined for us—is not the collective history of the various peoples on whom our happiness now depends. World history is a thin, imperial, and so bitter possibility for establishing a metropolitan identity, and is only available at all to people who can identify with the victors. In the same vein, it might be hoped that language, in the broad sense of culture, could provide something of a way to understand the new dispensation—the language of world business, the lingua franca of our modernity, is indubitably a kind of English. But here, again, the language is thin, divided among dialects, and unused by many for serious communication (lovers and children and art and such). To say I speak English, or even several of the world languages, says too little about who I am.

151

Metropolitan identity, such as it is, is rooted in the experience of being a consumer. The reconstitution of the Western economies following World War Two gave rise to what is commonly known as the consumer culture. While consumerism is widely criticized today as spiritually superficial, aesthetically regrettable, and environmentally disastrous, the creation of a consumer culture was once regarded as a major challenge. During World War Two, thoughtful policy minds worried that as soon as the War was over, the manufacturing capacity built up during the war would be idled just as millions of men were demobilized and sought jobs, demand would fall, and the world would return to the conditions of the Depression. From this perspective, the creation of a consumer culture—identity based on shopping, and implicitly, on confidence in the future—may be regarded as a considerable achievement.

Before considering some of what it means to be a consumer, a digression for the sake of clarity might be helpful. Traditional understandings of the relationship between economic situation and identity, the ideas collectively understood in terms of "class," no longer explain the citizen's situation or identity, if they ever did. Class, in the strong sense used by T. S. Eliot, has dissolved. It would be impossibly nostalgic (and very politically incorrect) to reflect on contemporary politics from the perspective of an identifiable group economically privileged in durable ways that afford them the opportunity to have collective experiences, and so an outlook, the time and narrative continuity that forms a tradition. It is not clear that this idea of class was wise when Eliot wrote. It now seems quite clear that the yet stronger idea of class required by Marxian thought was never sensible: class interest was never sufficiently concrete, material enough, to serve as the motor for dialectical materialism and so history writ large. Ideas of class such as espoused by Marx and even Eliot now appear more as a product of historical circumstance than a transhistorical concept with which history, and especially those processes called globalization, can be understood.

The notion of class is actually an obstacle to understanding life in the City of Gold. The historical movements that we understand as modernization undercut the idea of a society built upon orders, classes, like a stream undercuts its bank. Consider, in no particular sequence: the movement from the farm to the city; the economic opportunity, and need for jobs, provided by the great war militarizations, and the rebuilding after the wars; the introduction and obsolescence of various technologies, and the consequent migrations of the workers who operated the machines; various ideologies of equality, including socialism of all kinds; the need to create mass markets; the promise of a better future; the late idea that art is some sort of avant-garde . . . one could go on, but this list should suffice to suggest the hostility between those dynamic processes we associate with modernization and the stable interests, social relations, and traditions bound up in the notion of class. Nor is this hostility accidental. Many of the social movements that we understand to contribute to the modernization of society as a whole were self-consciously modern; their participants understood themselves to be destroying the old order and establishing the new. Similarly, the City of Gold is a fairly intentional effort to replace the nation state with a new form of political life, a new political grammar. Moreover, the City internalizes the idea of modernization. As discussed in chapter III, the City's commitment to the future is facilitated and institutionalized by finance. In consequence of the City's world historical and daily commitment to modernity, the idea of class—the creation of a perspective formed by situation over time—is of limited utility for the establishment of a metropolitan identity.

To claim that the idea of class is of little use for contemporary political economy is not to maintain that economic inequality does not exist in the City. On the contrary: economic inequality is a central purpose of a political system built upon a market. Achieving inequality, making more money than other people, is what it means to be a success. Inequality appears to be growing in the United States, at least since the middle of the century.[1] Without attempting to resolve this important issue any further, for present purposes it suffices to note that inequality is at least the realization of something the republic has always prided itself on, the individual's opportunity to be a success, amass property, and exclude others or become a philanthropist, as the case may be.[2]

*　*　*

As chapter III tried to show, finance, and so metropolitan life, is lived in the future imperfect. The cosmopolite is continually becoming. As Locke almost predicted, the City of Gold aspires to make the world America, not in the sense of a wilderness, nor even in the sense of some specifically American culture, but in the sense of open possibility, which the individual addresses by choosing what to consume, thereby defining itself.[3] We have world entertainment, world media, world music, world cuisines (satay and hamburgers and brie and red wine from South Africa and Chile and Australia), and we locate ourselves vis-à-vis this vast smorgasbord by buying, consuming. We are defined as citizens of the world by our shopping, as any in-flight magazine demonstrates.

The opportunity to realize the self in a consumer society is perpetually defeated not by frustration, as in the old Communist countries, where people were continually in lines, but by success: the item conveyed is no longer the object of desire. As discussed in chapter IV, choice, once exercised, is part of the environment and so no longer an opportunity for the desirous self to define itself. Catalogues are interesting; the delivery man only momentarily so. Market transactions satisfy particular desires, but do little (what could be done?) to satisfy desire itself. The City renews itself in the time it takes to digest a meal or recover the hormonal impulse for sex. The consumer never arrives, but remains always a consumer, en route to the future.

The mythical future in the City of Gold, the destination, is a place of contentment, even the perfection of classical art. This is the world shown to us by advertising, a world in which we are free of desire, because desire is superfluous. The people on the beach, our friends, smiling at us, are beautiful, outside and in, and their promises are true. Where else could we want to be? The same may be said for the casually elegant living room, the authentically rumpled linen shirt, the necklace sparkling on the tawny throat of the champion guzzling the sports drink . . . each moment is so expensive that, as a business matter, it must be deeply thought through, every possibility judged, until everything is just so, and the advertisement achieves some of the burnished perfection of art. Indeed, it is commonly remarked that advertisements are better made than most television productions or even feature films.

The difference between the experience of an advertisement and a work of art is that advertising invites us to participate in such perfection by making a purchase.[4] The invitation is a lie; the consumer can never participate in that perfection. (If the consumer happens to be an artist, too, then she might create perfections of her own, which would be different.) The perfection of advertisement is real—as real as that of art—but as with art, the perfection of advertising is essentially formal. The models and athletes photographed so elegantly may well be wracked and warped by their ambitions and the attendant anxieties. Dust is already gathering on the wine glasses resting on the distressed mahogany steamer trunk used as a coffee table. Perfection is a spectator sport; the opportunity to be perfect and so complete, at rest, is not for sale. What is for sale—property rights in things, even perfect things—cannot satisfy. It is not just that the appetites renew themselves so long as there is breath within the body, it is that the advertising industry will suggest a new and attractive possibility, will whet a new appetite, which the consumer is encouraged to acquire, borrowing if need be.

The consumer's ultimate temptation, which can never be realized, is the purchase to end all purchases, that is, the purchase that would make the consumer content. Advertising presents the especially paradoxical fantasy of becoming someone who ceases becoming and simply is happy with the moment, a world in which our consumer, perhaps while drinking beers after a hard day of fly fishing someplace that looks better than Montana, says "it just doesn't get any better than this." Advertising feeds the consumer's morbid fantasy to reach such a place, soon, when there will be no desire, and the future's omnipresent exigencies will subside. For the consumer, life itself is just a party, or ought to be, without the tensions that inevitably accompany life in financial capitalism, built on a structure of investment, worry.

To put this desire to change the structure of society in more traditional terms, advertising promises life on holiday, in festival time, when the normal rhythms and relations are suspended. Ecstatic festivals undercut privilege explicitly: when everyone is out of station, rich and poor may engage in relations that they would not ordinarily. Even more staid festivals, however, are celebrated with a peculiar timelessness that diminishes the differences in station among the celebrants. Work, and so the honors earned in time, matter little if you are living for this moment. In imagining ourselves within the world of the advertisement, we tend to deny the existence of not only time and privilege, and hence class, but also work, tradition, and the past. In willfully ignoring the possibility of hierarchy, advertising is beyond egalitarian, it promises the life atemporal, an escape from not only the history of work, but also the expectation of finance, and even the dialectic between property and money that constitute the organic principle of the City.

Consumers never learn that the horizon of their dreams is just that, a horizon, and will remain so however far they travel, however much they buy. Even when we are at peace, wealthy, free to do as we please, we are unhappy. Life never becomes an advertisement, and the person defined by the achievement of consumption's promises is doomed to unhappiness or stupidity, more or less willful.

Advertising's claim to normalize festival time, and so to live without hierarchy or time, is, to use an old phrase, false consciousness. We may live to play, but first we have to work in order to pay for whatever fun thing the advertisement was created to sell. In the City of Gold, relative scarcity of whatever is fashionable is continuous, inequality is ubiquitous, and work—the effort to make money and thereby improve one's position vis-à-vis one's competitors—is unrelenting. The consumer is thus caught in a contradiction: desire is aroused by the possibility of losing oneself, but even temporary satisfaction of such desire can only be accomplished by establishing status through the rejection of others in the market, creating and isolating oneself. In order to be happy, party with friends on the beach, citizens find themselves spending years in cubicles. Founded on the quickening of individual appetites, the City may for a while appear to deliver on its promises, but identity in the City of Gold is ultimately schizophrenic.

*   *   *

The City is haunted by the memory of the country, perhaps never real, that still somewhere is what the City has forsaken. Cosmopolites almost visit this country each August when they quit their city, with its private, cloaked, exchanges of things defined by convention, and go to the beach, where they can enjoy public, naked, displays of elemental things. The more energetic climb mountains, canoe wilderness waterways, travel to anyplace where life may appear simple and their relationship to it true, if only temporary and supported by money made elsewhere. This is often called "getting away from it all." Things that are praised for their authenticity, whether art or anything ethnic or commitment to one's sport, are attractive precisely insofar as they enable us to believe that we recognize and take seriously a truth different from our own fabrications, and so have escaped, if merely for a while and in our minds, the constraints of metropolitan life.

Cosmopolites tend to be attracted to traditional societies precisely because they are not modern, that is, so long as the society in question is exotic enough to be interesting, and does not openly offend their own pieties. So, even while we celebrate the diversity of our cities, we are quite excited that the Inuit will comprise 85 percent of the population of the new Canadian province of Nunavut. Tourism to Nunavut is encouraged over the Internet, but tourists are to tell their guides if they do not want to see whales slaughtered. As has been widely remarked, the traditional is often important, not for its own sake, but as a counterpoint to the modern, a stance from which modernity may be criticized safely. After all, traditional societies are authentic, unlike modern societies. And members of traditional societies, unlike cosmopolites, are not alienated (until herded into towns, given alcohol and disease and other things for which they have no resistance, treated badly, and so forth). Sophisticates cherish the exotic not just for being pretty, but for not being modern, and have done so at least since people started reading Rousseau, since long sea voyages carried men and not a few women into the wild, the East, the desert, into adventure contrary to their own civilization.

The distance traveled between traditional and modern worlds is not just a matter of kilometers from the farm to Lagos (where the economy is largely dependent on the spot market for oil, nominally in London), or from the Andean village to Quito (Ecuador has recently abandoned monetary policy altogether, leaving such matters in the hands of the United States Federal Reserve), but the psychic distance from an identity grown in a place, over time, to an identity as a consumer in global markets, whose hopes are pinned on a self to be achieved in the future, and ultimately pinned on the atemporal festival advertised by the global market. In the City of Gold, the village is just a literary device (as in "global village"), but in much of the world, the village remains a reality, actual or at least remembered, a place where people are defined in time, by experience and reputation and community. We destroy much of that when we insist on development. Particularly when historically inevitable, the trip to modernity can be the stuff of tragedy, and the irony of progressive affection for nativism can be almost too much to bear.

Modernity may be better than the ways we call traditional; life in the City may be superior to life in the village; it is likely the die has already been cast. Although modernity has its virtues (consider health care, birth control, speedy travel, imported wine, and recorded music) as well as its failings, cosmopolites literally must insist on the priority of those virtues, not because the failings are not trenchant (cosmopolites do not appear to be particularly happy), but because cosmopolites have no grammar other than modernity with which to address political questions. So well-meaning people hope for the development of indigenous peoples, health care and education and tourism and modernization, in ascending order of troublesomeness, increasingly aware that they are participating in the destruction of that which they thought most attractive.

However, one of the West's glories has been a tradition of skeptical political thought and a sense of articulate homelessness, from which we may ask whether we are doing the right thing when we promote modernization. Your days will be richer, we implicitly argue, if you replace the rhythms of life that you know with the banal festival time for which we long, and the far more exigent, if generally safe, market in which we actually live. Are we so sure we are right? These arguments are usually and conveniently made in the abstract. But what attitude should an actual person—imagine a young woman named Kwayera—take to the world she must join? Should she admire it? Should she find the City of Gold, a communicative space established by the exchange of money and property, something to honor? Does the polity ennoble her, reflect and encourage what is best about her?[5]

Of course not—how can a polity that is explicitly mercenary teach or encourage (to what extent can it even tolerate?) the best that Kwayera might be? The City cannot treat Kwayera in any terms other than those of property, and property most abstract at that. What can nobility of spirit mean in a world devoted to the acquisition of venal status? Kwayera will in time come to recognize the City as her world, an environment if not a home, because she will have no choice—she cannot ignore the fact that so much comes from elsewhere, and travels elsewhere, so that the world she experiences is largely formed beyond her ken. But what allegiance does she owe such an environment? Surely the filial metaphor that has long made political obedience bearable—I have sprung from the loins of this culture, and so am subject, desire to be subject, to its laws—is meaningless to Kwayera as she confronts the City of Gold, a polity of billions of people spread across thousands and thousands of miles, known one to another only through the shallow and anonymous forms of law as electronically mediated.[6] Whatever the substantive merits of the requirements of the City—for obvious example, the International Monetary Fund's austerity measures—such requirements are too distant to be the laws of a father. The City's laws are alien, orders to which she may, and presumably will, submit but is unlikely to adopt. Like any citizen of a large polity, at some point in her thinking Kwayera would have to admit that she views herself as unfree, and that what distinguishes her state from slavery is that nobody else has a personal interest in her.

As a thought experiment, suppose Kwayera refused to be alienated, suppose she determined to make herself feel at home in the City of Gold? In the unlikely event that she seriously began to understand her self, even her bodily self, *only* in the City's dialectic between property and money, would Kwayera not have to admit she is a public woman, a whore? What is a whore except one who rents the pleasure of her body, that is, understands herself to be a commodity? And what relationship can she have with her clients other than a pecuniary one, or, if things go badly, a relationship of fear and violence? Far better for Kwayera to be alienated, to separate private meaning—in which one locates, among other aspects of life, one's physically intimate affections—from the public realm, determined by the market. From this perspective, alienation is a defense, a way of preserving some meaning and a sense of self from a market that has no place for such things. But a cost of such alienation is awareness of one's lack of freedom, obedience to foreign command, and ultimately, a degree of contempt.[7]

Although such criticism is clearly overheated, we are troubled by some of the relationships between eros and property fostered by the City. The fundamentalists (both Islamic and Christian) no doubt understand matters in their own way, but they are quite right to understand sexuality to be central to the City of Gold (the City is built upon desire), and to point out that metropolitan sexuality must be venal (the City is built upon property), and to find that disturbing. The general if still shadowy point is that metropolitan property threatens to make too much of life exchangeable for money, an argument known as the concern for commodification. Demonstrating how much of sex our society understands in terms of the dialectic between property and money is only an instantiation, if a particularly emotive one, of this concern. As suggested above, the general point also could be instantiated in terms of the sanctity of human life—if life is understood in terms of property, it cannot be sacred, and murder may be a rational option—an idea explored by Raskolnikov in *Crime and Punish-*

ment, and continually at issue in the abortion debates. Regardless of the locus of meaning—sex or the sanctity of life or something else—it is not very difficult to show how commodification makes meaning untenable.

But how disturbed should we be by the familiar argument that the commodification of life in the marketplace destroys meaning? Rough words like pig, whore, and murderer are images designed to appeal to a certain sort of mind, both critical and synthetic, that wishes to make shadowy suspicions more concrete. This aggressive expression of the argument against commodification develops and makes explicit the implications of the argument, made in chapter II, that money has scant ability to communicate, but to what end? Why the ugly language? What is at stake here?

One of the abiding problems of this apology is the status of the critique itself. Social critics often claim that they criticize in order to understand, and that they wish to understand in order to contest and perhaps even improve the political life of a society. There is always a chance, of course, that theory will become practical reality. Political imagination informs the education of the young. Moreover, in societies that espouse constitutionalism (the belief that society itself can be created intentionally, constructed on the basis of thought), the effort to make political imagination rational (social theory) is a part of everyday politics, the reason we have think tanks and bureaucracies. Still, political consensus changes slowly (relatively little thinking is influential), and most of the world gets by with little theory. As a result, American-style claims for the likely practical efficacy of extended arguments (such as this one) should be heard with some forbearance. In all likelihood, all that is at issue here is the political imagination of the reader, how it may be possible to be at home, or not, in our polity. But that is enough—thought needs no justification beyond the fact that we are fated to think, and must be at home in our minds.

Assuming that making sense of our lives is a fine reason for political thought, then the question under discussion—what attitude should Kwayera take to the world she must join?—should be reasked in a more self-conscious sense. If Kwayera is or becomes something of a political philosopher, feels herself compelled to be conscious of her responses to her own political imagination, what attitude can we expect her to take to this object of intellection called the City of Gold? Certainly the City of Gold is a suitable subject for philosophical reflection. Indeed, we may need to recapitulate a great deal of thought in our new circumstances. Foregoing paragraphs have suggested ways to critique our situation that echo Freud's idea of the consciousness at war with itself, Plato's contempt for a society that acknowledged only desire, Rousseau's fascination with the natural, and the Romantic concern for private passion as an antidote to public banality. With such tensions in mind, we might ask our immigrant (or prisoner?)

not merely what is it like to live in the City, but what is it like to think here? What are the possibilities for the intellectual life that the City affords?

One possibility is boredom. Most people, even many good minds, think very little about the meaning of politics writ large. Many, many people are "apathetic" about politics in the ordinary sense of the institutions of government. And why not? Few politicians are themselves particularly interesting, although they are usually reasonably intelligent. Their needs (to dissemble, to manage detail, and to cope with personal problems) tend to be distracting to them and tiresome to third parties. Even if they can find the time, the politicians' need to please makes it difficult for them to say anything worth hearing. Rather than unself-conscious efforts to communicate, political remarks are assumed to be, and are analyzed as, moves in a complex game.[8] In spite of political ennui, however, Kwayera may turn to worthy causes, the midlevel policy debates that comprise bureaucracy, which would be an honorable response, if perhaps itself boring.[9] Or she may stop doing politics altogether, and pursue any number of other interests, of a personal or public nature.

Widespread intense boredom with political life may be dangerous. Nietzsche argued that such boredom would engender war, that liberal modernity was so self-evidently meaningless that rebellion was inevitable. Stated in the abstract, this idea seems quite implausible. But it is difficult to live in the academy without the suspicion that much vehemence is an effort to hide vacuity, that much scholarship is an effort at personal moral accreditation, and that administration is a haven—profound boredom may play a far larger role in our lives than we are happy to admit. Perhaps nationalism in its late nineteenth- and early-twentieth-century guises was a response to boredom; perhaps wars are Olympic games by other means. Perhaps Hitler, against whom the City of Gold was founded, is best understood in quintessentially modern terms, as a cipher, a place holder for "a meaning to existence beyond the narrowness of self-interest."[10] Rather than a genius, if by genius we mean a mind from which music or ideas or in Hitler's case evil intentions flows like water from a great spring, Hitler seems to have been a focal point. There need be nothing at a focal point—Hitler's talents cannot explain his success—because a focal point serves only as the location at which diffuse energies are collected, specifically the energies liberated by the Germans' fear that the ordinary course of their lives was meaningless, boring.

Fortunately, two alternatives to war as a cure for boredom suggest themselves, distraction and bemusement. First, the City has developed more and better amusements than Nietzsche may have dreamed possible. Art, drugs, food, music, restaurants, sex, sports, travel—the possibilities, as they say, are limitless (if sometimes a little redundant). One may even choose to be an intellectual, wear black and bemoan the banal inauthenticity of modern life. It is true that such pleasures postpone rather than finally satisfy the desires on which the City is founded, but that is just the point: at least for some people, the City is never boring because its deeper promises are never achieved, while more immediate promises are continually being achieved and requested anew. As a consumer, Kwayera is always about to enter the advertisement, to become part of the festival, to cease being a consumer. But she never does; she is never too thin or too rich. Kwayera may be content to be a better consumer, and thereby cease to be a philosopher, at least a political philosopher. If so, then Nietzsche may have overestimated the love for truth, and hence the risk that the City would be boring.

Second, if Kwayera refuses to be distracted and continues to ask after the meaning of her society, she may end up being amused. We have constructed global webs of communication that communicate little of importance. We have done much to conquer time, but we remain afraid. We achieve autonomy—the gentlemanly state beloved by minds as different as Aristotle and Shakespeare—only to sacrifice it in the impossible and debasing quest for sensation and prestige. We are ruled, perhaps not too badly, by a power we experience as alien, and worse, fictional, a ghost. Kwayera's country has thrown off the yoke of colonialism and joins the community of sovereign nations, only to find itself ruled—if that is the right word—by its participation in capital markets. In place of the politics of the nation state, embodied by a distant but real monarch, our philosopher finds her new world run by the placeless and ineffable politics of the City, hardly embodied at all, unless it be by some young bond trader trying to get a date with a journalist, or a cadre of sophisticated bureaucrats, worried about getting their children into the right private school and such. Our situation is not boring, then, it is hilarious.[11]

To recapitulate the argument of this chapter thus far: traditional sources of identity do not suffice to make the inhabitants of the City feel at home, to construct an identity that could stand vis-à-vis the City. The nearest possibility, consumerism, is riven by contradiction, perpetually unachieved, and is just too shallow to support much of an identity. Consequently, the City's inhabitants attempt to construct a life that makes no effort to be coterminous with the politics that matter. We turn toward the private life as a way to construct meaning, and so a sense of self, within but apart from a public sphere that is not so nurturing. When asked how they feel about the public realm, private citizens tend to give three fundamental responses: boredom, distraction, and ironic bemusement.

*   *   *

Restoration of the public/private distinction may well be necessary for life in the City. An alienated existence in an inauthentic polity appears to be bearable insofar as we can construct other communities of meaning, other ways to be human. We may expect little of politics, and hope to tend to our gardens. Tending to our private affairs, however, hardly seems to be an adequate response to the problem of identity in the City. As suggested by the preceding chapter's refusal to rely, in contemporary fashion, on a vaguely defined "civil society" to remedy the failings of political institutions, the "turn to private life" is something of a dodge, lazy. To claim that there are private spaces within the City where identity *might* form says nothing about how citizens are to go about forming such identities. After all, there is no guarantee that private life will offer sufficient satisfactions. Families are often unhappy; friends may be scarce; we may come to dislike ourselves. Or, and commonly enough, we might not have sufficient funds to construct lives that we regard with warm affection. How are we to expect the ordinary inhabitant of the City to form a perspective from which the City, or anything else, could be judged?

To be unpleasantly practical, what "turn to private life" really means is the hope that money will be used to create a haven from the public realm defined by the market. We are still too democratic to say as much in polite society, for the simple reason that radical inequality means most people have relatively little money. We may even harbor genuine hopes that young love, songbirds, churches and families, and the innate goodness of people and much else besides will mean that "the less privileged" will find their lives to be meaningful. But such things are fortuitous in the City of Gold, not the result of good policy. The terrifying truth is that where money is not spent well, we have come to expect vacuity, what an earlier generation called (with a candor no longer considered to be good manners) lack of background. Without education, broadly understood, one cannot have much basis on which to discriminate, judge, think. And in the City of Gold, acquiring education generally requires spending money well.

The idea that the failings of the public realm may be compensated by a rich private life—that living well is the best revenge—is hardly new: it is philosophy's response to the problem of empire, nascent in Aristotle and explicit in various philosophies thereafter. More importantly for present purposes, the solace of a commodious private life is about all that Hobbes holds out for the possibility of the good life. So it is hardly surprising that the standard liberal answer to communitarian critiques of capitalist society, particularly of supranational capitalism, turns on the good things, including especially private liberties, that markets have brought us. But we should own up to the fact that attempting to define meaning as a private, rather than a public, enterprise is at bottom an oligarchic response to a more egalitarian critique.

And if the readers of this book are honest with themselves, they are likely to find the turn to private life a tempting possibility. How could anyone with any money, and more importantly, sense of taste, think other-wise? The City of Gold has done Anatole France (the law, in its majesty, forbids the rich as well as the poor to sleep under bridges) one better. Cap-italism, in its glory, will provide not only a commodious, but an emotion-ally satisfying, existence, that is, capitalism can silence its critics, can in fact provide a meaningful life—perhaps in a gated community in Arizona, with perfect weather and a Jack Nicklaus golf course and fine views to contem-plate at happier (happier than you!) hour. For those who have achieved a certain station, "high net worth individuals" as the bankers have it, private life alone might satisfy, and is certainly pretty, though as a matter of intel-lectual honesty, if not egalitarian piety, we should admit that much of life in the City is neither satisfying nor pretty.

The oligarchic response is particularly tempting to talented people in a meritocracy, who are likely to earn enough money to protect themselves. At a certain point, it is far better—easier on oneself and one's family, pret-tier, more pleasant, and probably the right thing to do—simply to join up, and put the money to use. Why not indulge in the sort of business/an-glophile vision of the good life that informs so many vacations, so many retirements, among the affluent classes? What is wrong with that?[12] There are far worse things than walking over well-kept lawns, talking to beautiful friends dressed in natural fibers, looking forward to dinner with a view of the water. Does not such beauty justify the political order that makes it possible?

Hardly. While personal wealth has much to recommend it, it must be kept in mind that such an exemplary existence is itself purchased. The golf course is, by and large, private. The community is gated, the perfect expres-sion of the right to exclude. And who is excluded? Only those who have not paid, that is, most of society. Indeed, exclusion on any other (traditional) basis, such as language, ethnicity, religion, history, and especially race—in short, membership in another community—is illegal. The insufficiently wealthy, however, may be excluded with impunity.[13] Thus capitalism, par-ticularly in America, justifies itself by providing the opportunity (for the wealthy) to be insulated. If one does really quite well, does not have to work, and invests soundly, one may even live out one's days secluded from the rigors of capitalism itself. While perhaps pleasant, this is no more a jus-tification for *capitalism*—as a polity—than a lifeboat is a testament to the virtues of a ship, however fondly we may consider a sound lifeboat. The mere ability to afford individuals a commodious existence outside the polity provides scant, only indirect, justification for the polity itself.

At the risk of a degree of repetition, it is worth emphasizing that not only is the turn to private life a form of exile, but that some such exile is necessary—in the logical sense—to life in the City of Gold. Insofar as one hopes for something more from politics (in particular, a sense that the community shares a truth; a sense of living in a just society; a sense of honorable identity), one is necessarily frustrated by life in the City of Gold. Elements of the human condition that cannot be articulated as either property or money are incidental to capitalistic discourse. The market's grammar, the dialectic between property and money, does not express many things important to being human. Capitalism is therefore radically impoverished as a system of politics. Insofar as we long for community, we necessarily experience life in capitalism as a sort of exile. Although we may long for capitalism with a human face, we may rest assured that even the most perfectly functioning markets will require alienation, internal exile. The construction of markets—the creation and alienation of property rights—involves the destruction of meaning, and in longing for that meaning, we complain not only about the market before us, but about the arrangement of social affairs through markets per se. The fundamental experience of exile, while often lived in conjunction with whatever specific ills a particular marketplace may generate, such as fear of unemployment, or oppression of workers, or unsafe working conditions, and so forth, is structural rather than accidental, is in fact incurable.

If we, who understand the structural limitations of markets, nonetheless organize politics through markets, then the question of identity may be reasked negatively: How are we to be exiles? One possibility, explored by both Kafka and Camus, is a kind of acceptance. The self may come to understand itself as radically alone, and even to suspect that such loneliness is in some sense deserved, at least appropriate to the situation, about which it is difficult to think clearly. Internal exiles feel guilty, worry that their abandonment is correct. After all, if they were worthier, they would be more celebrated. Lonely people have only themselves to blame. And do.[14]

Although one response to the alienation entailed in life under capitalism is the guilt, acceptance of society's verdict, that suffuses Kafka's work and in milder forms sets the moral tone of much contemporary political discourse, guilt is not the exile's only response to the sense (perhaps wrong) of being pursued: one might also choose to fight. It has become a commonplace to understand terrorism originating in the developing world as an expression of frustration arising from the conflict between modern and traditional ways of life. Such terrorism from the borderlands of modernity tends to call forth imperial responses.[15] More to the point at issue is domestic terrorism of the sort embodied by figures like Timothy McVeigh or the Red Army Faction,[16] in which violence is understood (or at least declared) to be armed resistance to current trends, and as even as an effort to achieve political ends. Terrorists choose violence over the turn to private life; they force themselves on the world politically.

Such losers (literally, those for whom private life affords insufficient consolation) tend to find politics only gradually, after drifting, living for indeterminate periods of time in various low rent lodgings somewhere, gradually constructing an identity, perhaps joining strange communities devoted to their own persecution.[17] Terrorism, however real, has also become a style choice, a way of combining the Nazi claptrap, the rhetoric of violent freedom, the desire for conspiracy. Mostly, this is fun and games: the paranoia exploited by television and Hollywood; the rantings of talk radio; the weirdness available on the Internet; the joy of gun shows where one can fire a real automatic weapon at an old car; persistent suspicions about various lies told by the government. But sometimes matters get out of hand, and losers live out their fantasies. People are beaten in the street after a soccer game. Day care facilities are bombed. The houses of immigrants are burned. Children are murdered in the school library. Government officials are shot, sometimes killed. The government annihilates the shooters and sometimes their dependents.

Domestic terrorism announces itself as a rebellion against a society and a government that is regarded as tyrannical, as an unwillingness to take it any more.[18] Usually, the loser has committed no specific offense; oftentimes he has not even been officially prosecuted; there is no record of any legal condemnation. It is to be expected that an ordinary person who protests his exile from modernity will claim that the trial was unfair, that he is the victim of tyranny, and hence that he is the enemy of the court and the state of which the court is an organ. It is just as obvious that such claims are not to be taken seriously, particularly if we mandarins have not yet begun the trial. Thus the alienation entailed in capitalism, our politics, engenders its own kind of outcast, criminal, the terrorist.

It is a small step from feeling that one has botched one's execution (as in Kafka's *The Trial*) or exulting in it (as in Camus' *The Stranger*) to understanding one's death—or the death of others—as a constitutive political act. This is Hegel's state of nature story: two strangers without culture meet and fight, in a desperate attempt to assure themselves of their own existence. In acknowledging winners and losers—social hierarchy—culture was born.[19] Precisely because the existence of the self in a world of ephemeral and wildly distributed rights is an increasingly uncertain proposition, losers feel they must fight (again) in order to be recognized in the culture, in order to become somebody.[20] Anarchy, neofascism, various sorts of racism, may be (self-contradictory) efforts to generalize an experience of rebellion with a longing, if not exactly for community, then for recognition, "respect," as is often demanded by popular entertainers who are also thugs. And if this is so, we cannot be surprised by the brazen quality of so much violence. Rather than something to be ashamed of, even a sin, killing lots of people is a way to become celebrated. At the very least, shooters may hope to be the object of one of those television shows that broadcasts the doings of police officers. What matters to modern terrorism is attention; politics more specific is purely optional.

After years of such losers, we may be saddened momentarily but are rarely shocked to hear that somebody has decided to seek fame by killing everybody in their local fast food restaurant, that a child has taken out two teachers and a dozen classmates at a suburban high school. As we drive home, listening to the latest thoughtful essay on National Public Radio or some such, we might wonder who these people are, that think anybody will remember their names, that violence can somehow satisfy their longing for community. And if we are really tough minded, we might ask ourselves who is spending their time in fast food restaurants, post offices, public schools, and other such dangerous places.

* * *

The essays in this part 2 turned on the City of Gold's ability to satisfy the traditional political yearnings for shared truth, a defensible social order (justice), and a sense of identity vis-à-vis the polity as a whole. In chapter VI, "Alienation," we found that the City seems to have no public truth that transcends the requirements of the market. The City appears to be fundamentally impious (it's all about the money), and in response, good minds—who by definition are concerned with something more noble—tend to regard the City as a foreign country. Without a truth that transcends the market, the City provides no sense of community for those who do seek such truth; conducts its politics in exclusively venal terms; and cannot justify the brutality associated with social life. Alienation from the City leads to contempt for the City.

In chapter VII, "Inauthenticity," we explored the idea that the longing for authenticity, and conversely, the sense that metropolitan life is inauthentic, represent failures of the City to provide an adequately meaningful social order, and consequently, the City is often betrayed. Strangely enough, we found the City actually encouraging such betrayal—actively encouraging the violation of its own moral code—because from within the logic of the marketplace, based upon satisfaction of the will, it is difficult if not impossible to gainsay the yearning for authentic experience. More broadly, the City concedes that it cannot articulate what it is to be human, and that compelling claims may be outside the logic of capitalism, and that therefore the City has no real possibility of justice. The City is therefore loathsome.

In chapter VIII, "Identity, Tense," we found that the City's inhabitants constructed their identities through a private realm understood opposed to the public realm. Cosmopolites tend to be bored by, distracted from, or amused at the City itself. Political life, more broadly, social life outside the market, tends to be oligarchical, albeit a patina of democratic manners remains. Yearnings for recognition more substantial than the camaraderie of affluent pleasures tend to be satisfied by guilt, or more dramatically, violent rebellion. In sum, the City—understood seriously as a political idea—seems to have little truth, seems to be unworthy of allegiance, and therefore difficult even to imagine as just, and seems unworthy of being called home. Part 1 set forth prominent features of the City's constitution; part 2 concludes that the constitution in important respects failed.

Life in the City of Gold appears to be both powerfully seductive and yet unlovable, at best a joke. We do not appear, however, to have much choice. The *ancien regime,* nationalism, is gone. In view of current technology, which tends to facilitate intercourse, it is not clear that the political and economic isolation of past days could be reconstructed. But if we are tempted to try, as seems implicit in much contemporary excitement over meetings of the Bretton Woods Institutions, we would do well to remember the horrors of 1914–89. It seems we must be supranational capitalists, with all that entails. So we are left to ask what sort of capitalistic society may we hope for, and can we find something to admire in such arrangements? In short, how happy can we be with our capitalism? It is difficult to think about such questions because many of the ideas with which we have traditionally approached political economy are exhausted, a subject to which we now turn.

Exhausted Philosophies

The ideology of the marketplace has triumphed, but the attitudes with which intellectuals traditionally have approached markets can no longer be sustained. Part 3 attempts to say what it means to speak of the triumph and failure of these beliefs. In general, it does not appear possible to believe that capitalism is a stage in history, destined to be overcome, unless one engages in millenarian speculation. But as yet it is not clear how we are to approach markets, what our intellectual stance vis-à-vis markets ought to be. Three approaches have long seemed fruitful, and now seem less so: economic prescription, progressive critique, and liberal justification. To put matters polemically for the sake of clarity, the discipline that purported to explain markets, economics, has failed in its aspiration to be a science after the model of Newtonian mechanics, and so its prescriptions are uncompelling. Progressive thinking remains committed to a worldview—and in particular, asserts a normative relationship between work and price—that bears little relation to capitalism, and so its critique is irrelevant insofar as capitalism is assumed. Liberalism repackages the conditions of the marketplace as ideals, and so its justification is superfluous. The failure of these approaches presents a problem for politics, and by extension, our personal equanimity: How are we to regard the human arrangements produced through markets?

Paul Delvaux, *Homage to Jules Verne* (1971)

CHAPTER IX

The Reformation
of Economics

Economics as belief system that makes political and scientific claims. Success of economics as science limited. Contemporary economics cannot articulate problem of alienation. The turn from science to politics. Prolegemnon to a revived economics.

As a profession, economists have been quite unified in their responses to the disquiet caused by globalization in general and free trade in particular, a disquiet that has been vociferously expressed in the streets outside several recent meetings of Bretton Woods Institutions and similar ceremonies, but also expressed in circles that economists cannot so lightly dismiss. Within broad outlines, economists just know that globalization is a good thing because, as Adam Smith and especially David Ricardo taught, free trade benefits even countries that are not very good at anything. Most economists also believe that despite the prevalence of inequality, economic growth directly benefits the less fortunate in the global society, if perhaps only in the long run of our sweet reward. At the very least, global economic growth will generate more wealth, making it easier to take care of the less fortunate. The problem with globalization, then, is essentially political: people do not know what is good for them. In such circumstances, a number of prominent economists have maintained that the task for government and enlightened people of good will is to educate the people. (While markets should be used for so much, this particular task should not be left to the market.) Otherwise, it is just possible that the integration of the global economy achieved through such patient effort over the years since World War Two may be undone, as the economic integration achieved in the late nineteenth century was destroyed by World War One. Such, at any rate, appears to be the orthodox position among economists, presented with the confidence of clergy who are sure that they understand what is right.

Yet it is worth considering how deep the political authority of the discipline is, how credible, in the literal sense of believed, economic orthodoxy is. Although formally trained economists are everywhere about government, and never before have so many issues been discussed as if they were to be decided by markets (which would make such discussion practically unnecessary), economists still have difficulty persuading the laity what their interests are. In particular, the establishment of a global free trade regime, incessantly proposed as an indisputably good idea, has taken literally generations of mind-numbingly boring negotiations and still has not been achieved, although substantial progress has been made. As often as comparative advantage has been explained, millions of people evidently are still not getting it. Some people, of course, oppose free trade because they need protection from competition, and are willing to impose the cost of their inefficiency upon local consumers. Economists generally have no more than passing sympathy for such special interests. But even some people who have no such private interests and who do understand Ricardo are dissatisfied with globalization. Succinctly, political affairs continue to be conducted with scant recognition of economic science. Even the greatest political achievement of economists, the creation of the Bretton Woods Institutions, cannot simply be understood as professional consensus made flesh. As discussed in chapter I and too often forgotten by both critics and defenders, the creation of the Bretton Woods regime was a political (indeed idealistic) response to war, and can only in the broadest sense be regarded as economically motivated. Thus, since World War Two, politics has been both conducted in terms of economics, and yet oddly immune from economics. Is the ignorance of the masses, or the narrow self-interest of various special interests, really the sole reason for the partial success of economists in the political realm?

The failure of the economic orthodoxy to be wholly convincing regarding the material benefits of free trade, and hence globalization more generally, reflects the quandary in which the discipline finds itself. Economics, like political science since Machiavelli, makes dual claims: first, to know the world, and therefore, second, to be politically authoritative. The quandary for economics is its inability to resolve the relationship between these two claims without giving up on either. What do the profession's claims to scientific knowledge and hence political authority really mean, how are they related, and can they be sustained, either jointly or severally?

The claim to scientific knowledge and the claim to political authority are different types of claim. As a science, economics is constructed on the model of physics most influentially expressed by Newton. Economics, like mechanics, aspires to provide an objective, nonteleological description of the part of the world with which the discipline is concerned. At the same time, economics, unlike mechanics, aspires to be a normative political discourse, that is, to be defined by its purpose, teleologically. So one task for Adam Smith was to describe the economy in naturalistic and lawlike terms, as Newton had done for mechanics. The second task, to which the first would contribute, was quite different, and political if hardly controversial to his intended audience: how to increase the wealth and thus the power of Great Britain. This presents a problem. On the one hand, economics aspired to be a science after the model of physics. On the other hand, politics is an inherently teleological discourse, and thus cannot be science (as science has been understood since Galileo). Economics thus claims to be objective yet normative, nonteleological yet with an end in view, a science and also a political program. It is not clear that such enterprises have any logical relationship to each other; the tendency since Descartes has been to argue that they are independent of one another.[1]

The tension inherent in the dual ambitions of economics was more explicit (and perhaps better managed) in the eighteenth and nineteenth century, when the phrase "political economy" by its terms raised the question: What was under discussion, politics or economics? For the ancient Greeks and, more to the point, the English and Scots who later admired them, the concepts were both socially and conceptually distinct. Economics, trade, was perhaps necessary and at best respectable, but no more. Politics, in contrast, was a matter for gentlemen who had already gotten their money. To put the matter a bit more philosophically, economics was the realm of necessity, where one might hope to discover law in the sense of physical laws, laws of nature. Politics, in contrast, was the realm of society, in which a certain freedom of action obtained, and where law was complex, organic, and unpredictable, even when it stemmed from God. Economics and politics were thus opposed ways of looking at the world.

Politics, however, was for many years the broader concept: markets were understood to be a part of the larger society, and ultimately to be used by the larger society. Government granted permission to conduct business, often on exclusive (monopolistic) terms, a practice which informed most acts of business incorporation until well into the nineteenth century and which lingers in the contemporary issuance of patents for extracting minerals and exploiting ideas. For centuries, trade with other countries was assumed to be taxed and otherwise regulated. The time and place of trading were often regulated by law; vestiges of this idea that market activity should be concentrated and regulated remain visible in the regulation of contemporary securities markets, with their focus on exchanges, even electronic ones. Economics, then, was long a subset of politics broadly construed; political economy treated the part of society organized through markets.

Around the turn of the twentieth century, however, the term "political economy" was replaced by the term "economics."[2] Economics gradually ceased to be regarded as the study of markets, understood as social institutions, and came to be the study of markets, understood as a priori structures embedded in social life, structures that engendered and regulated observable institutions. (This process accelerated after World War Two; perhaps society's political institutions were no longer felt to be so authoritative.) Because their ideal structure existed independently of any instantiation, markets could be discussed in purely abstract terms. Economics came to understand its truths as ideal truths (the relations that would obtain in an efficient market), as the truths of mathematics are understood to be ideal, without needing to pay attention to the state of things in the sensible world. Unsurprisingly, economists increasingly expressed themselves in mathematical terms. By the middle of the twentieth century, influential quarters had come to consider society to be based on markets, not the other way around. Normatively, the political goal of twentieth-century economics came to be the reformation of social institutions in order to conform to an ideal, perfectly efficient market. The competition between science and markets, on the one side, and politics and society, on the other side, had turned—science and markets took the lead. Politics was ostensibly denied, although the dominant politics was reaffirmed as the order of things.[3]

And yet the victory of economics-as-science over economics-as-politics remains incomplete. Indeed, the victory cannot be won without causing the profession to give up its claims to political authority. Consider, by way of example, a question often asked of economists: How much independence should a nation's central bank have from that nation's legislature?[4] Suppose the question is at bottom scientific, and let us presume the economists know the answer. Then there is no real *political* question: the "is" precludes the "ought." (Physicists have little political authority.) Or let us suppose that the question is clearly political. In that case, the political question, what is to be done, remains open, but the economists have little to offer. Unless we live in a society of economist-kings, economists should receive no special deference. The existence of a question in political economy, in which the economists claim political authority by virtue of expert knowledge, thus depends on the discipline's *partial* ability to deliver on the scientific claim. The question must be scientific enough to give experts authority, but not so well understood that no question exists.

In this meritocracy that entrusts institutional power to people who hold graduate degrees, we have grown comfortable acknowledging and then ignoring the Cartesian fugue that what we know does not logically tell us what to do, that the is and the ought are independent, that the object is not the subject, that value preferences are exogenous, and so forth. Meritocracies ignore such distinctions precisely because they are meritocracies, societies ruled by those with merit, experts. Surely knowing something about the likely ramifications of, for example, different central bank structures, helps democratically legitimated decision makers to take their best guess? And can it be denied that study is worth something? What else are we to found politics on, if not our understanding of scientific truth?

In a world of uncertainty bureaucratically managed, we give power to experts, even if the condition of the experts' political legitimacy is their inability to allay the uncertainty associated with markets; the discipline's very shortcomings deepen society's reliance on those trained in the discipline. There is little need to belabor the duplicities of these rhetorical questions; such duplicities inhere in the use of republican forms to legitimate meritocratic bureaucracy. Nor are such duplicities restricted to economists, who after all are not the only kind of experts. One might hope, however, for economists in positions of making policy to be a bit more forthright about the political—as opposed to scientific—work they were doing.

As a matter of intellectual history, there is every likelihood that economics will continue to model itself after physics.[5] It must be admitted that economics has not been as successful an intellectual enterprise as physics, "queen of the sciences," at least not by the standards that economists and physicists claim they use to judge success (predictive power, falsifiability, and the like), and certainly not by cultural standards (intellectual prestige). But perhaps the stunning cultural successes of physics—in the time of Newton, and again in that of Einstein—should not be regarded as an aspiration for an intellectual discipline. Newtonian mechanics, especially, transformed what it meant to think, to engage in intellectual activity of many sorts. That said, few critics of economics would maintain that economists have nothing to offer. The analogy between physics and life in the marketplace still has its uses. Intellectual endeavors will be pursued as long as the pursuit is believed to be worthwhile, and there are obvious benefits to understanding economic relations as natural facts. That the effort to create a scientific—nonteleological—understanding of markets is fundamentally flawed, like all metaphorical understandings, does not immediately require that the enterprise be abandoned, even as an intellectual matter. There is no obvious or immanent, intellectual or practical, reason for a revolution in the discipline.

At the same time, economics is not without philosophical aspiration, and indeed once went by the name worldly philosophy. Insofar as economists understand themselves philosophically and operate in good faith, philosophical arguments have bite. It remains largely imaginable that economics will reform itself in response to charges that the discipline is internally flawed. Such a challenge would have to come from within the discipline, would require a Luther, against whom it could not be said that "the critic does not understand the discipline." Luther was not only a monk, but also a professor of theology, before he pinned the ninety-five theses to the door in Wittenberg.[6] And the theses were also precisely that, theses, objects of academic disputation, meant to be argued within the confines of the university. The Reformation began as a professional controversy, brought on by an aggressive young scholar who knew intimately, but could no longer abide, various orthodoxies. Perhaps a young professor somewhere is preparing similarly to challenge the fundamental claim that economics is a science, perhaps not.[7]

It may be remarked that few economists baldly make strong claims to scientific knowledge. Even that long-term cheerleader, *The Economist*, has recently thrown in the towel and admitted that economics will never be a proper science.[8] Models, it is said, are a way to clarify thought, as is mathematical expression. Rationality is, after all, the best that can be hoped in an inherently messy world. That is, when pressed, many economists maintain their discipline is a form of rhetoric and a mode of thought. While correct as far as it goes (economics is indeed a way of thinking and talking about the world) this defense is profoundly disingenuous. Economists claim to be right, and further claim that their policy recommendations, regarding central bank independence, free trade, and many other matters, should therefore be followed. That is, economists claim authority, and in a society that still nods in the direction of democracy, their authority is based, at the end of the day, on a claim of superior knowledge. Economists thus maintain, if only covertly, the claim to scientific truth with which we began.

* * *

To mix allusions, our young Luther may not be successful in destroying the economists' graven image of Newton. Old Luther was not successful in reforming Catholicism, at least not in the simple sense he intended. The Catholic Church remained and remains a viable structure of belief.[9] There seems to be no particular reason to believe the professional economist will go the way of the mandarin, the house tutor, or even the public academic anytime soon. We do need a way to think about markets, and we do have a class of intellectuals deeply invested in the idea that economics is a kind of science.[10] In another sense, however, Luther was successful: the Reformation created a new Christianity that existed alongside and often warred with Catholicism, and Catholicism itself was transformed. In the same vein, we might imagine an alternative economics that would exist side by side with the idea of economics as physics. (One may hope that any violence would be confined to ritual if not unimportant ceremonies surrounding tenure.)

We might begin to imagine the contours of an alternative economics by first imagining something contrary to fact, an economics as credible, as prestigious, as mechanics. Imagine that we had, or would soon have, a politically successful economics, one in which globalization was convincingly explained by a theoretically consistent discipline. Imagine an economic consensus that made the currency crises of 1997 and 1998, or the Japanese malaise of roughly the last twenty years, or the stubborn failure of so many efforts at economic development uninteresting. Imagine that the protests against globalization could be dismissed as the result of ignorance or outright stupidity on the part of the protesters, akin to protests against the sun rising. If we had such a convincing discipline, presumably nobody would make the objections discussed under the heading of alienation, the worry that markets obscure the truth. If our economics were literally credible, we would believe that we knew the truth, or where to find it, or at the very least that the truth would be found as knowledge accumulated. If we believed in our economics, the sense that market societies were inauthentic, that the City of Gold was a sham, would be a psychological impossibility. By the same token, if public life in market societies were believed to be true, it would be easier to feel at home in such societies. Under such circumstances, there would be less need for thoughtful residents of the City of Gold to despair of community and understand their lives as such private enterprises.

The sort of economics suggested by this thought experiment, an economics that gives us reason to think we are at home in the City of Gold, is impossible. To recapitulate part 1, the City is the nearly miraculous resolution of unprecedented horrors; monetary transactions are founded on tokens incapable of transmitting much truth; the City is predicated on the future, and so cannot be known; the City engenders itself through a self-referential dialectical process; and the City is fundamentally unconscious of the processes through which it governs itself. If this were not enough, nothing in the intellectual history of the last century or so would lead us to believe that a credible, much less comforting, explication of social life is possible. Even physics and mathematics have come to be understood as terribly human enterprises, as constrained by what it is to know as by what is. Physics is not about nature, said Niels Bohr, but "concerns what we can *say* about nature."[11] But the limitations inherent in physics or mathematics, and so our hopes for scientific rationality, are not just matters of theoretical interest. After the bomb and programs of euthanasia, it has become self-evident that rationalism is not necessarily deserving of our trust. In short, the natural sciences do not provide a good model for the construction of an alternative economics.

Let us therefore consider a different approach to the problem. Instead of continuing to understand economics as a science of society, we should reimagine economics along more modest lines, by seeking a way of thinking that directly addresses economics' other claim, that is to be politically authoritative. More generally, we may imagine an alternative economics as the double, or reverse, of economics as science. Considering worldly philosophy in terms of physics entailed certain philosophical choices; what would an economics that made different philosophical choices be like? If in traditional economics, politics is understood to be like nature (*physis*), and has therefore sought to provide a naturalistic account of political life, what would an economics that understood political life to be essentially *unlike* natural life be like?

An alternative economics could track the mainstream of humanistic thought. An alternative economics would address the critiques offered in part 2, namely, what kind of truths do markets offer, what is the political nature of markets, and how does the individual who lives in a market society compose herself? Philosophically considering alienation, the worry that money obscures the truth, immediately raises ontological and epistemological questions: What is money? What is the nature of the truth we know through money? What is the nature of the truth obscured by money? To use the medieval terminology, economics has traditionally claimed to be nominalist, despite tacit assumptions and practices that are in many ways realist. So, for examples, in its insistence that the individual is the proper object of social thought (celebrated as the principle of methodological individualism), and in its equation of rationality with individual self-interest (more simply, greed), and in its tendency to use utilitarian arguments to reduce social constructions to individual preferences, economics would seem to be perfectly nominalist. However, a bit of reflection presents another picture: economics constantly and unself-consciously traffics in complex collective fictions (at least a thorough nominalist would consider them fictions) like money, property, and the corporation, none of which can be experienced directly. Economists frequently consider ideas like the market, and efficiency, which cannot be known except as collective abstractions.[12] These fictions are generally thought to be the same regardless of the community in which they are found.[13] Thus arguments are made from models, and in positing the entities that inhabit such models, economists share the realist tendencies of mathematicians.

A reformed economics might be more ontologically and epistemologically sophisticated, which would require it to be more rigorous about its nominalism and more forthright about its realism. Although modernity is often taught as the triumph of nominalism, this is probably a radical simplification.[14] The debate lasted for several hundred years because both sides had important points to make. So, here, nominalists could be expected to argue that money, property, and the corporation are not categories found in nature, but instead are constructs of humans in specific times and places. They generally have been different from what they are now; they presumably will be different from what they are now. Our understanding of such things is therefore nominal in the literal sense of dependent on our act of naming, that is, contingent upon our situation. But the realists would have much to add: we have only one history, and it is a collective history. The railroad tracks may have been placed elsewhere in the forest, but they were not. Nor can the railroad—the money, property, and entities involved in the building of it—be understood by reference to individuals. Things such as railroads happen only to groups, are the products of a collective reality with a facticity of its own. And human life may not be constant, but it is sufficiently stable so that it makes sense to speak of human nature. Such are the realities from which an intellectually self-conscious economic thought could begin.

Nowadays (and for the past two hundred years or so) the perpetual anxiety that the truth is not available to us is more often phrased in a language of alienation rather than the medieval debate over whether words, including of course the Word of God, had to be understood on realist or nominalist terms. But it is difficult even to phrase the idea of alienation in terms of traditional economics, in part because alienation is only awkwardly expressed in terms of utilitarian thinking. Utilitarianism (one way to philosophize money) presumes that the various and incommensurable and outright conflicting goods and evils, usually commingled in bewildering ways, that confront us humans can be translated into commensurable units, such as make up a currency or, in the abstract, utils.[15] In the utilitarian view, "good" is merely a relative measure of the quantity of utils at issue. Since all things may be evaluated in terms of the number of utils they represent (that is, their price), it once appeared easy enough to compare anything and everything. At least in theory: actually discussing anything in terms of utils is impossible—the practice is too absurd—and explicitly utilitarian argument has been abandoned in many areas of social thought. In economics and so law, however, one still hears arguments "based on utilitarian grounds," which are considered methodologically more sophisticated than arguments that people should get whatever they want and can afford.

Due to its reliance on utilitarian theory, traditional economics simply cannot understand the concept of alienation. Alienation is a complaint that things are distant, unreal, not present in their unique, specific, intense particularity, that something has been lost. That something, in fact, is just what money (and the util) are structured to throw away. The commensurability at the heart of the institution of money (and hence the philosophical conceit known as the util) is, by its nature, a lack—a lack of everything specific about a thing. Therefore utilitarian thought can hardly express the idea of alienation. The individual in utilitarian thought is a kind of master, who derives satisfaction from the acquisition of a thing. The person wants to acquire; money facilitates the acquisition; the person is happier but otherwise unchanged. Once the world is experienced in terms of utils, however, alienation is literally impossible. The util is a "measure" of the self's satisfaction; it has no existence apart from the self; it is a perfect expression of the self. The assertion that the world may be experienced as a collection of utils entails the statement that alienation is impossible. The alienated thinker, in contrast, longs for a different relationship with the world, longs to be at one with the world, longs for a less exigent experience of the self. Money frustrates such longing, because money expresses and thereby extends the will of the person, who is already alienated, that is, money perpetuates the distance at the heart of the complaint. Is it any wonder that the protests against the Bretton Woods Institutions—against the alienation inherent in the City of Gold established by these founding institutions—have seemed unfathomable to economists? [16]

An alternative economics could address to the phenomenon of alienation, the truths that are longed for and felt to be missing from markets, and in doing so, to things themselves. As discussed in chapter VI, however, things considered for themselves are not traded—property is traded. To move into the marketplace is to move from at least the possibility of particularity and specific truths, as expressed in language, into the simulacrum constituted by the dialectic between money and property, and hence into a form of untruth. An alternative economics would be conscious of the difference between the world as it is traded and the world as it is, the difference between a shadow and that which casts it. Economics would then emerge not only as the logical abstraction of market discourse (its current project), but simultaneously (if inconsistently) as a description of what markets do not express: economics would also be the self-conscious naming of what the act of pricing unselfconsciously throws away.

* * *

Life is more than property, and so an economics that is both phenomenologically pious (aware of the truths that commerce destroys) and descriptively accurate (aware of how commerce is actually conducted) would become a philosophically critical discussion of our effort to trade the world. Such an alternative economics would be "critical" in a sense the word has been used from the Enlightenment: it would understand itself as a discourse that stood apart from, vis-à-vis, the dominant and inchoate practices of the age, in order to discern, articulate, analyze, be able to interrogate and ultimately judge those practices. Contemporary economics, in contrast, tends to deny limitations on the scope of markets, and has little if any way to express that which falls outside of markets. Indeed, when necessary, contemporary economics will invent fictional markets (such as transaction costs), in order to maintain the claim to provide a complete explanation. In contrast, the alternative economics imagined here would not only acknowledge, but would attempt to articulate, the limitations of markets.

Bringing the foregoing argument forward, we have said that an alternative economics would worry about the nature of truth we know through money, about the realist and nominalist aspects of our understanding of the elements of the economy, about the unnaming and renaming that is pricing, and that a critical economics would interrogate such things. Once we understand the world as it is to be irrevocably different from the world as it is to be traded, we might ask after the world in which we trade. We might thus understand economics to recapitulate the historical logic of philosophy: a concern for truth, things as they are, gives rise to a concern for the possibilities of knowledge, which in turn leads to an interest in language. And once we understand the discipline in terms of the language of the marketplace, we might ask into the nature of the polity where that language is spoken and developed. We might understand Athens from its agora. We might even become concerned with the right conduct of an Athenian, that is, alternative economics may end with moral philosophy, where traditional economics began (Adam Smith held a chair in moral philosophy). Economics, in short, could become a critical philosophy, a humanistic evaluation, of that sort of intercourse known as trade.

In its concern for language and thus politics, alternative economics could be expected, at least in the current intellectual climate, to present itself as a discourse without rational foundation, indeed as a form of aesthetics. An alternative economics would not only admit the contemporary truism that a well-founded discourse is impossible, but would understand itself as a commentary on, or exploration of, the contradictions that economic life entails. So, for example, to understand a thing as property, and hence both unnamed and named, or, for another example, to understand money as both the expression and negation of the self, both liberating and alienating, and yet communicable and hence public, even the foundation of society, requires the ability to understand through the adoption of contradiction, an ability developed through aesthetic appreciation.

An aesthetic understanding of economic life—an effort to discern the meanings in our conventions—need not be liberating, is in fact likely to be experienced as confinement. As is familiar from law and other arenas of postmodern argument, the discovery of a lack of ontological foundation (the failure of economics to find its gravity) hardly means that anything is possible. While little is known, surprisingly little of social or even intellectual life is truly open to new possibilities, up for grabs. As suggested in chapter I, possibilities for economic life that are conceivable in the abstract (as fantasies) tend to be eliminated by history, or more precisely, by the fables drawn from (often bitter) experience, by myth. The events experienced by policy makers teach narrow lessons. At least outside the academy, politics presents itself as ineffably constrained, unfree, if not determined by well-articulated rules. Indeed, upon reflection we realize that this sense of constraint amidst apparent possibility is nowhere more intensely felt than in artistic production, and here again we see an affinity between a humanistic approach to political economy and those vague sensibilities we refer to as aesthetics.[17] An aesthetics of our limitations may be just what we need to consider globalization.

What would an aesthetics of globalization mean for politics? Perhaps not much, although we explore the question in more detail in chapter XII. The alternative economics imagined here would address, but could not resolve, the problem of alienation. The destruction of specificity in the name of exchangeability, the translation of things into property, characteristics into rights, involves some violence. This poignancy of the human condition is aggravated, deepened, in these times when we are so aware of the increase in our capability to transmit messages, if not necessarily to communicate. Robert Frost said poetry is what is lost in translation.[18] Frost was right to insist that we attend to *this*, that poetry embodies focus and attention, attitudes that both are respectable in their own right and that can teach us something about how to approach our days. And Frost was sadly correct that in our efforts to make our communications understood elsewhere, we lose something dear, and in sensing that loss, we are alienated. While an alternative economics might be sensitive to the objection of alienation, it is difficult to imagine how any economic learning that treated the global economy, with its incessant translations (and so diminution) of meanings into rights, could lay the objection to rest.

Nor can we expect an alternative economics to dispense with utilitarian argument. Not merely a gaucherie, utilitarian thinking represents the unavoidable comparison of objects which have been priced and so are (with the aid of simple mathematics) perfectly comparable. The City of Gold exists only in translation, as a collection of distant messages whose originalities can only be guessed; within the City messages must be related one to another. Translation, homogenization, fungibility, pricing, utilitarian discussion . . . as a practical matter, a certain amount of utilitarian thinking, thinking in terms of prices, is unavoidable, however primitive it may be. Alternative economics would thus understand traditional economics—economics founded on the model of physics—as a special case, an extended metaphor, a comforting simplification.

Nor is an alternative economics likely to resolve the problems of language and interpretation that have transformed and yet left irresolute so much modern thought. Postmodern critique may have been intellectually necessary, but certainly precious little need flow from such critique. After philosophy, said Lyotard, comes philosophy.[19] And after economics, we can expect to see more, well, economics. An alternative economics could not present itself unself-consciously as the truth, or even the second best, or some n-degree best (where n is an integer, or even a (very) rational number) version of the truth. A more sophisticated stance in such matters will mean no more and no less than our economic thinking will be more civilized, more refined, not that it will be any more final. In other words, an alternative economics might be expected to present its conclusions with a bit more humility. In light of the constitutive role markets play in our society, and the power exercised by some economists, a bit of humility would not be a bad thing.

And so an alternative economics finds itself, along with philosophical thought generally, turning from objective truth to language to politics towards aesthetics. This latest revision of the intellectual life—the turn to aesthetics seems as inevitable in economics as it has been in other areas of thought—is both easy and natural, and fantastically daunting and fraught with very real dangers. To put matters very simply, the fact that we do not believe rationality will get us very far does not mean we wish to hear the poetry written by the professorate. In place of the confident prestige of natural reason, alternative economics apparently leads us to the edgy white wine in plastic cups sensibility of the contemporary humanities, hardly a step up.

But the situation of an alternative economics may be seen in somewhat more inspiring terms. Failure to achieve the status of science leaves economics in a position akin to that of law: an articulation that defines and serves a political elite of uncertain legitimacy. Although inevitably and properly suspect in a polity that bows toward democracy, such articulations need not be in bad faith. To the contrary, awareness of scant knowledge in the face of real need might even inspire great commitment, commitment that is intense precisely because its hold on reality is so precarious. Law gestures toward natural reason, to the will of the sovereign, and to the history of the people. None of these suffices, of course, but other succor is unavailable to those of us who need authority. Similarly, we may alternatively understand economics to be an intellectual tradition in which we consider the history and future of treating one another as objects, specifically as the accidental inhabitants of the terrain on which we satisfy our desires.

CHAPTER X

After Economic Justice

Moralist vision of economic life defined. Related to traditional thinking of left and right, and to new economy. Moralist vision incorrect. Various meanings of work discussed. None can provide a normative theory of the labor market, and hence a theory of justice, adequate for the City. Justice external to the market.

We often personify markets so that they can be criticized, or applauded, in moral terms. We argue that the market ought not have done what the market has in fact done, or claim that a certain situation is correct—and we should be satisfied with it—because it is the outcome of a fair market. Perhaps most commonly and importantly, we often treat labor markets as if they were moral actors. As a result, we quite literally expect that the society configured by marketplace decisions about employment will be just, and regularly are disappointed to discover that it is not so. Let us call this the moralist vision of economic life.

The purpose of this chapter is to discredit the moralist vision, more specifically, to argue that our normative political judgment of markets—metropolitan political thought—cannot be based on the expectation that the human value of labor is, or is likely to be, expressed by its price. The belief that price somehow reflects or should reflect labor is venerable, stretching back from today's rhetoric through the various populist traditions to Marx, Smith, and Locke. This tradition is exhausted. There is little reason to think that the human values associated with particular work, its meaning, are or can be expressed by its price. The translation from work to property to money entails the loss of meaning; the meaning of work cannot be the meaning of the money paid the worker. Insofar as it is foolish to expect agreement between labor's price and its meaning, its moral heft, the idea of economic justice is nonsensical, a category mistake, though perhaps useful for rhetorical purposes.

Let us begin by stating the moralist vision more clearly. Any number of critics on both the political left and right bemoan the tendency of multinational corporations to locate manufacturing facilities in countries that offer the lowest costs, that is, bemoan the movement of manufacturing from rich countries to poor countries, often celebrated as "developing" or even "emerging" markets. Similarly, it is a commonplace of corporate legal scholarship that aspires to be "progressive" to consider ways that corporate law might be reformed to give greater voice to stakeholders, particularly workers, outside the troika of managers, directors, and shareholders, whose internecine warfare is the usual stuff of corporate law. Even conservative candidates for political office feel it necessary to express, early and often, their support for the working people of the polity wherein they aspire to hold office. Such candidates also argue, when the situation demands, that the enormous wealth gained in the last two decades by something less than a twentieth of the U.S. population represents the just rewards for the talent and diligence of that percentage of hardworking citizens. And across the political spectrum one hears complaints about how little money is earned by teachers and nurses and many other folks who really make the City of Gold a fine place to live, and how undeserved is the money paid to ("earned by" is too strong) movie stars, lawyers, and other folks who, while not necessarily pond scum, probably are. Such statements share an attitude if nothing else, namely a tendency to treat markets as moral actors who shape society. The specifics of the moral code that the market is believed to follow are not now important. Presumably the poor should be made rich, the rich should become not only generous but self-effacing, and the lion should lie down with the lamb or something, but none of that is relevant here. The point here is only that a common way to approach markets, particularly labor markets, is righteously: many people understand markets in moral terms.[1]

A moral attitude toward labor markets is not exclusive to the political left. Many on the political right treat markets in explicit moral terms as well. This is somewhat counterintuitive. Conservatism has been defined, at least since Edmund Burke, as an attitude of relative contentment with modes of social ordering other than formal government, that is, contentment with tradition, religion, morality, and the market. At a deeper level, conservatism rests on a suspicion that not much truth is available to the rational mind, and that caution is therefore advisable. In particular, the idea that government, however enlightened, could or would articulate and realize the truth was doomed to failure. Tradition, religion, morality, and the market create and reflect truths very different from the outcomes of arguments by *philosophes* and certainly different from the consensus of legislators. Neither philosophers nor certainly politicians know everything, and therefore the truths of even an enlightened government cannot replace the deeper if perhaps not so conscious wisdom of markets, tradition, religion, and the other processes that constitute civil society. Coming from this tradition, conservatives might be expected to let marketplace outcomes speak for themselves, without benefit of ideology.

But despite the suspicion of mind, and hence moral argument about social conditions (always *en route* to a policy argument and thence a law), that underlies conservatism, the political right often feels the need to justify the status quo, that is, to argue explicitly that how it is also is how it should be. Specifically, the right often feels the need to argue that the dispensations of the labor markets are just. So, as noted above, moralists on the right often maintain that the rich are merely enjoying their hard-earned rewards. Conversely, the real travesty is welfare mothers, federally funded city governments, the National Endowment for the Arts, and other shiftless beneficiaries of government hand-outs. Especially in the United States, the market, not government, often is expected to reward the virtuous and punish the wicked, if government will simply get out of the way. That is, the market exercises a judgment that comports with our moral sense. Or so one sometimes hears from the right.

While left and right agree that price should reflect the moral value of labor, they disagree in their satisfaction with current prices for labor. The left is upset that traditional work does not command a very high price (the right does not mind), and the left finds the literally incredible quantities of money acquired by a few people in the new economy to be obscene (in the view of the right, an appropriate reward for pioneering the future). Putting aside their assessment of the contemporary situation, however, people on the political left and right agree that the price of labor should reflect its moral value. For the left, the reflection is only ideal: capitalism exploits workers; traditional labor is paid less than it is morally worth. Leftist thought has traditionally treated "low" wages as the failure of an unjust market to price such labor in a way that adequately reflects human values. Marxians thought the answer was to abolish markets, but that no longer appears feasible. The problem to which the left has come to devote itself, logically enough, is taming capitalism, organizing the market under a progressive vision, so that price and morality will coincide, and economic justice will be achieved. For the right, the ideal already has been achieved: the price of labor in fact reflects its moral value, at least most of the time. Where the left sees conflict between market reality, on the one hand, and the interests of labor, more broadly justice, on the other, the right sees unity: markets are a technology of justice in society, ensuring that labor is fairly paid. High wages are simply the reward for performing socially valuable activities; low wages are signals that society does not need so much of that work done. Although left and right disagree over whether labor is priced correctly in a given case, both left and right are moralists: their common assumption is that labor should be priced to reflect its human value.

Whatever else it may be, the moralist position, whether delivered from the left or the right, is not a description of the contemporary economy (or any economy). Many deeply meaningful ways of working do not pay well, or even at all. Conversely, many rather formal and unsatisfying, and perhaps bad, tasks pay very well. Consider, for obvious examples, teaching or nursing, on the one hand, and much of the legal or sex or other entertainment industries, on the other. If prices are supposed to be moral, we appear to be living in a world of pervasive market failure.

The moralist stance entails a relationship between two quite different aspects of work. On the one hand, work may be done more or less well; work is more or less meaningful; work is an important context for our moral lives. On the other hand, work can produce property that people want to buy, and so work can be economically significant. The moralist stance asserts that there is, or at least should be, a tight correlation between the moral and the economic aspects of work, so that which is meaningful and so worth doing receives a proportionate monetary sum. Price, the wage, is thus the lynchpin that—in the moralist view—links individual morality with the social order. This tight correlation is one way to understand economic justice.[2]

There is good reason to believe that many people in the youngest generation or so of workers do not understand the labor market in the moral terms traditionally used by left and right, and specifically, have disassociated their (moral) lives from their (economic) jobs. In broad sections of society, wages are not expected to correlate the meaningful and the economic aspects of work. As has by now become a commonplace, the meaning of employment has changed over the last few years. (It has become equally common, and is probably correct, to associate this change in meaning with the consolidation of local economies into a metropolitan economy, the City of Gold.) Many young citizens do not regard a job as a durable arrangement. If a job does last a while, and many still do, its duration is felt to reflect a certain continuity of circumstances and interests, nothing more. The old legalism, "employment at will," has come to be understood literally among many of the young knowledge workers who characterize the new economy: a job is and should be held only so long as it furthers the current ambitions of both employer and employed. For such workers, union membership, the effort to prolong employment relationships after the thrill is gone, increasingly is seen as a waste of time, foolish.

In that playground of creative destruction, the United States, even manu-facturing and older workers are trying to stop taking lay-offs personally. The other big boroughs of the City, Japan and a unified Europe, tradition-ally have prided themselves on providing ordinary workers with more job security than the United States did, but Japan and Europe now appear to be working hard to treat their labor as a commodity, the more liquid the better, that is, to create labor markets in which job security will not even be a public virtue. In the same vein, loyalty between employer and employee can no longer be expected, because once the long-term maintenance of employment relationships is no longer thought to be possible or even de-sirable, loyalty ceases to be a virtue.

From this perspective, a given job represents a paycheck, a benefits package, perhaps a source of social status and professional pride, but it is no longer felt to be an important context for the narration of a human life. For many people, it has come to seem limiting to think of people as "work-ers," economic functions rather than individuals. The American custom of asking, upon being introduced, "what do you do" is increasingly ridicu-lous, because the answer is so likely to be some version of "stare at a com-puter," or perhaps "engage in retail transactions."[3] In sum, the moral context in which one lives—life—is increasingly seen to be distinct from the eco-nomic context in which one is paid to do a given job. Indeed, this devalua-tion of work is to be expected if, as part 2 argued, the public space created by the City is not worth an individual's commitment.

This perspective, however, is far from universal, even within the City. Just as common, and perhaps more common among this book's reader-ship, is the opposite stance, a manic professionalism, life devoted to the doing of a salaried job (usually called "a career"). Anyone who has been a corporate lawyer, for example, cannot deny that some people understand life through their jobs. Even in the depths of corporate legal practice, how-ever, this understanding is widely recognized to be spiritually bankrupt. Such people are commonly if vaguely urged to "get a life." The problem is that getting a life is more difficult than one might initially think; alterna-tive sources of meaning are not easily compatible with careers lived in the higher strata of the City. Maintenance of one's social position, status, re-quires a great deal of attention, and the job can all too easily become life.

Even for those who understand their lives in terms of their jobs, the transformation of the economy means that instead of understanding their lives vis-à-vis the particular job they happen to hold at the moment, young workers increasingly understand their success vis-à-vis markets writ large, and particularly the market in which they compete to offer their services. The microeconomic frame of reference, the job, has been replaced with a macroeconomic frame of reference, the market, which may even be global in scope. This shift in reference is important. Employment, within the context of a job, means the adoption of a specific relationship, with reciprocal duties and obligations, to which the parties are supposed to be loyal. Employment, within the context of a labor market, means the sale of services. Similarly, the word "industry," which once implied manufacturing, the physical making of things, and even the virtue of being hardworking, now implies a market for specific human resources, the use of people. So we speak of the banking industry, the advertising industry, the food service industry, and so forth, and workers understand professional success as advancement in a given industry, as selling their services in return for increasingly larger sums of money. Within the market, the worker offers a commodity, her "skill set," traded like any other commodity. Human capital is quite similar to monetary capital; the distinction between labor and capital is likely to become blurred as the liquidity of labor markets increases. When labor becomes a form of capital, workers begin to think like capitalists, that is, to evaluate the performance of their asset, their skill set, against the broad and impersonal, and in that sense amoral, demands of the market, as opposed to the narrow and personal, and in that sense moral, appreciation of their efforts.

For a society as a whole, this appears to be a marvelous state of affairs. As the United States has discovered to its delight, workers who understand themselves to be in competition with all people most anywhere who might do their jobs are enormously motivated, work like dogs, without expecting life to get better, an expectation that might prompt inflation. The actual rate of unemployment in such circumstances is not very important. What appears to be important, from a macroeconomic perspective, is the widespread perception that one's own unemployment is eminently possible. Young workers look for jobs and distribute resumes over the Internet, but uncomfortably must presume that their current boss receives, either directly or through a headhunter, virtually identical resumes. For such workers, the next job could be right around the corner, but so could the next friendly suggestion that we think you might find a better fit with another company, so it might be foolish to ask for a raise. As a result of this combination of opportunity and anxiety, the United States has been able to enjoy historically low rates of unemployment, coupled with the longest peacetime expansion in history and astoundingly low inflation.[4]

The new dispensation has its advantages for the individual worker, too. Many of today's young workers understand their labor as the exchange of their services for money in vast markets—"Show me the money!" as a popular film exuberantly phrased it[5]—as opposed to more personal narratives of successes and failures in the context of a particular job, itself part of a local market, for which they are paid. In vast markets, what matters is sales, or to put it in another way, young workers understand their employment in the terms of popular culture. What is popular is what sells in the millions and millions; what sells in such large numbers makes a great deal of money. Jobs themselves may or may not be good: professional football player, good; waiter, not so good. But what is good is money, indisputable evidence of success in broad markets, indisputable evidence of popularity, that is, the attention of the marketplace. People who make lots of money are revered simply and honestly, not because of what they do, or even how they do it, but just because they make lots of money. We have seen investment advisers become celebrities, entrepreneurs become stars, small businessmen (renamed entrepreneurs) receive what can only be called a kind of adulation. In the game that we all now seem to be playing, of imprinting ourselves on the vast wildernesses in which we compete, people who make a lot of money are winners, no? Craven, but refreshing.

In such a world, the traditional division of the workplace into orders (capital, management, labor) makes little sense. It is not just, as Thorstein Veblen pointed out some time ago, that labor emulates capital.[6] Today, labor is often paid in capital, usually stock options. While the vast majority of such options are paid to upper-level management, or to anybody with a job in Silicon Valley, it has become quite common to give ordinary workers in heartland companies an equity stake in their employer. Moreover, and even more demographically significant, the privatization of retirement funding (all those IRAs and 401(k)s) has made capitalists out of virtually everyone who holds a job, as they say down South, "with benefits." More profoundly, labor, as discussed above, has come to consider itself capital, the human capital represented by the resume kept updated. The constant training, the effort to keep the skill set current and so marketable, requires that the skill set be viewed much as if it were any other capital resource. And if one has other capital resources to ease transitions, or perhaps even make it possible to exit the working world altogether and live off the interest, so much the better. That is, people calling themselves "labor" can no longer seriously understand themselves in opposition to another group of people representing an opposed economic force called "capital," though one still hears the language.

Once workers begin to view themselves as capital, the significance of money earned as wages changes. Money is openly desired, but for its own sake and for that which it affords, not as a sign of doing a good job, that is, not as a sign of a personal virtue. Again, care is required. Meaningless work is hardly a new development; assembly lines have been around a while. That said, understanding labor as drudgery that makes money for someone else (the owner of the means of production) and is therefore meaningless is quite different from understanding one's labor as producing property that is traded on an anonymous market and is therefore meaningless. For workers who understand their economic selves as capital (rather than as exploited by capital), their wages signify very little about their personal selves. How could it be otherwise? Recent years have seen Internet IPOs in which secretaries at small start-up tech companies became millionaires; public school systems funded by lotteries; companies competing in winner-take-all markets that span continents. In such a context, it is difficult to believe that possession of even unimaginable money—private plane money, as the saying goes—indicates anything specific about the owner. Possession of great wealth suggests the qualities associated with successful investment (namely, a degree of acumen or even foresight, but more importantly some advantage exploited, perhaps inside information, and almost certainly luck) rather than the more personal qualities we associate with hard, or even brilliant, work.

Nor do even fairly successful people believe, to the extent they once did, that their wages will amount to much money. Aggressive young workers seek equity stakes, or found businesses, because they understand that only through capital appreciation can they become wealthy. The mania for early and substantial investment in corporate equity by private individuals that marked, and contributed to, the long bull market of the 1990s similarly reflects a lack of faith that wages will generate wealth even adequate to pay for private education, safe housing, commodious travel, and prosperous retirement, the upper-middle-class lifestyle. At least for the better sort of knowledge worker, the young citizens who are the future of the City, the wage—the work one has done—simply has no particular relation to money and property possessed, and hence to one's position (real estate) in the City.

If the fact that one has money is not presumed to represent the good work one has actually done, there is little reason to suppose the converse, that doing good work, however "good" may be defined, will be paid well. There is no link between the value of labor and one's wealth, between effort and consequences (moral things) and earthly reward (money received). Too much that is worthwhile generates almost no money; too much that is lucky or necessary or just fashionable generates huge amounts of money. The practical and in that sense moral question (what work should I do?) is quite distinguishable from the economic question (what does it pay?), although money is of course always a consideration. One might have opportunities to choose something more or less worthwhile in some public sense, or personally enjoyable, or easy, or remunerative, and a variety of possible combinations might be reasonable. It might be reasonable to be a waiter and a poet; or it might be reasonable to be a bond trader, to buy a fast car and a faster datalink for the Telluride ski house; or to be a paramedic and sail competitively; or to just drop out. In this economy, people who have a certain amount of talent and privilege find themselves making such choices.[7] Although money is relevant to such choices, the value of the work—as indicated by the choices people actually make—is usually not determined solely by its wage. Consequently and conversely, a wage, the price of labor, does not indicate its value to the young worker. That is, the actual choices of today's young workers flatly deny the moralist assertion of a correlation between the meaning of work to the worker and the price paid for the labor.

The young workers are right: there is no correlation between the meaning of work and its price in money, not just in this economy, but in principle. Recent economic developments have only made the flaws in the moralist position more evident. The disconnect between morality and payment is categorical, structural, rather than some failure of accounting, some failure to price time off and other intangible benefits correctly. The moral question, what should the individual do? is inevitably a particular and situated, personal question, even if the individual is merely choosing the sort of capital, human resource, she wants to become. At least among legal occupations, the answer to the question, what do you want to do? is largely an individual decision, grounded in complex and specific terrain. In contrast, the market price of a thing, including labor, is defined by supply and demand in the market, that is, by collective and thus impersonal aggregations. Personal morality plays no part in the question of how much a job pays; the market for human resources is no more personal than the market for Texas sweet crude. There is no fair price for work, if by "fair" we mean a wage that expresses the human meanings attached to the work.

Political outrage or satisfaction at market outcomes—the sense of (in)justice with which moralists approach labor markets, including those of the City of Gold, presumes an idea of justice that accomplishes two things. Economic justice must, first, develop a sense of what justice requires in individual cases, a sense of what is fair, and, second, a broad sense of the right ordering of the polity. The idea of economic justice must somehow relate these two senses, and because the idea is economic, they must be related through the price mechanism. The idea of economic justice, then, is the idea that the price mechanism can, at least under ideal conditions, establish fairness in the individual case, and when aggregated, constitute the just society. But as we have seen, the price mechanism cannot communicate human meaning. In fact, wages have astonishingly little to do with the moral experience of work. Therefore, employment transactions cannot be aggregated by the labor market to create a society that comports with a serious idea of justice. Nor is this surprising. The economy is amoral, not just in the old Darwinian sense—survival of the fittest is thought to improve the breed—but in a more categorical sense. Those of us who are not economists or moralists have lost faith in the idea that the economy, price, tells us much, or can tell us much, about the particulars of the real world, including the moral world in which individuals must make specific choices. Money does not communicate very much, and certainly does not communicate the moral life of the individual. It now seems ludicrous to think that wealth is morally respectable, or even should be made morally respectable, as opposed to a great deal of fun and something to envy. But if the wage cannot reflect the moral system of the worker who earns it, we can have even less reason to believe that the wage reflects a moral system that we would recognize for society as a whole, justice. And if money cannot communicate ideas as complex, particular yet general, as justice, we can have no hope that the market will generate something that looks like justice. In short, talk of economic justice entails a category mistake.

*   *   *

How do we begin thinking about an idea of justice with which we can judge the City of Gold, once we have abandoned the naive hope that the price mechanism itself will produce just outcomes? Similarly, in the last chapter, the question is not whether economics as physics is, or ever could be, simply true. The answer to that is no. The difficult question is, with what sort of gestures towards truth are we to discuss markets, and the chapter endeavors to envisage a better economics. In the next chapter, the question is in what sense may we speak of our freedom to participate in markets. Unsurprisingly, the idea of freedom will emerge as both inadequate and indispensable. Part 4 of the book begins a normative and practical response to the constitutional problems raised in part 2, with little reliance on the ideological apparatus of orthodox economics, progressive thought, or contractarian liberalism, the exhausted ideologies discussed here in part 3.

Although traditional moralism does not seem to offer much, we might prepare for a consideration of justice in the City by analyzing the foundations and intentions of the moralist perspective. Moralist discussion of markets traditionally has proceeded rather quickly to claims that certain workers do not (if this is a leftist discussion) or do (if the remarks are delivered from the right) receive whatever sum of money justice demands as a wage. Even though economic justice is an unworkable concept, we may in pragmatic fashion ask after the impulse that has for so long been expressed in terms of economic justice. What explains this desire to treat labor markets as moral actors? To ask perhaps shocking but important antecedent questions: Why do we care how much *workers* are paid? What specifically are we honoring? If we understand the microcosmic value of a hard day's labor, perhaps we can understand its political significance, that is, the role that work would play if the City of Gold were just.

Perhaps the simplest way of understanding the moralist's solicitude for workers is to equate workers with humans. After the Fall, humanity was condemned to labor, and in our sympathy for labor, we may be thought to sympathize with all our fellows. But in our economy, "the workers" is not at all synonymous with "the people." Workers are only some of the people. Many sorts of people do not work at all, because they are young, or old, or unfit to work, or are simply unemployed. In October of 2002, for example, according the U.S. Department of Labor, the employment to population ratio for the United States was 62.9 percent. Using this number, over a third of the population, presumably deserving of our sympathy, cannot be understood as labor. Many who work do not fit traditional notions of "labor." Obviously, management is not labor, nor is government, including the many government workers supported by the taxing powers of the state. But if we care about people, it is difficult to argue that we should not care about leaders and those who serve. Indeed we should be particularly concerned about such people, for their own sakes and because they have others in their care. Nor, for that matter, have people traditionally considered to be professionals (clerics, lawyers, doctors) customarily been counted among the laboring class.[7] Moreover, in a service economy, a large and increasing share of the workforce considers itself to be either or both "professional" or "managerial." Rephrased, a vast number of people have become part of the knowledge economy, and spend their days looking at screens, or interacting with people, or engaged in other activities that, while clearly work, do not fit within traditional notions of labor. Even such a traditional representative of the idea of labor as a factory worker, may be college educated (with related debt) and may spend time overseeing a computerized assembly line—is this labor? With just a little thought it becomes unclear what we mean by labor; we clearly do not mean all humans. In an economy characterized by the manipulation of knowledge and the provision of services, and depending on our definition of "labor," we may not even mean most people with jobs.

This point should not be overstated: people have often cared about workers because workers are also people. Moreover, as a historical matter, the difference between people and labor may not have been so glaring as it has become. A much larger share of the population once fit under the heading "labor." Children worked; people worked closer to the time of their death; the economy was more dependent on farming and manufacturing and other manual tasks that we easily recognize as labor. Even today, in wanting better working conditions or a minimum working age or retirement benefits or other improvements in the lives of workers, we might have in mind only a view of what humans deserve. We still might speak, if somewhat misleadingly, of labor in an effort to achieve social justice, the idea that wealth should be redistributed to people who are, for one reason or another, poor.

Although the desire to better the lot of humanity cannot be reduced to solicitude for labor, in circles intellectually beholden to Marx it is widely believed that the labor market causes unhappiness to workers. From this perspective, a decent concern for human happiness requires that the labor markets be abolished or at least radically reformed, because only through living in the just society can humans achieve their noble potential. From this perspective, the suggestion, above, that social concerns (justice) might be independent of economic structure is heretical. But why should we equate economic justice with social justice and hence human fruition? The authority of Marxian tradition has seen better days, and here at least we should follow Marx's example of ignoring traditional authority and asking afresh: Why should we care about labor? If labor is not the same thing as humanity, as it appears it cannot be, what is it? What is the object of concern that we call "labor"?

No real answer to the question "why is labor good?" is required in order to deploy the rhetoric; "labor" is first and mostly a placeholder within the ideological superstructure of Marxian thought. Marx did not somehow discover that capitalism was unjust toward workers. He knew that already. The problem he sought to answer was *how* capital exploited labor. The theory of alienated labor is a theory of exploitation, not a theory of affinity. Marx thought that if his sense of injustice could be phrased in terms of Adam Smith's apparatus, if injustice were somehow made scientific, it would be authoritative, and for a long time, it was. The rather impious question, why should those of us who (like Marx) are workers only in the broadest sense care especially about injustice done to workers, does not seem to have been much of a problem for Marx and his heirs, even though class affiliation was supposed to be the single most important determinant of character. It has been widely assumed that we would care for the exploited rather than identify with the strong, cruel, and probably beautiful exploiters, side with the pigs and small deer instead of the tigers.

One might side with the workers if one believed they had been wronged, exploited, and there are classic reasons for thinking along these lines.[9] Assume that the value of a widget, a cell phone perhaps, is defined by the amount of labor that went into its production. The owner of the cell phone factory pays employees a wage that is less per unit than the price the owner, some Finnish corporation perhaps, receives for the sale of each phone. The phone makers therefore do not receive the full value of their labor, that is, a portion of their property (an ownership interest in the full retail price of the phone) has been stolen from them. As it appears in the pockets of the factory owner, this stolen property is called profit. On this view, we should sympathize with workers because they are the victims of a sort of continual theft, that is, we intellectuals side with the workers out of a sort of mental chivalry, a desire to see wrongs righted and justice done.[10] And so, like most Enlightenment thought, the Marxian ideal presumes a world both natural and just in some "self-evident" way; like most Romantic thought, Marxian politics presumes that civilization has corrupted this regime. The thinking is all very elegant, and quite difficult to recapture.

Cataloguing objections to this argument, at this date, would be tedious. For present purposes, the important point is that the argument from alienated labor turns upon a particular, strong, and completely unsupported idea about the nature of, of all things, private property. Marx thought that there was a natural property right in the products of one's labor. If the first reason to care about workers qua workers was a mistaken identification of workers with people, the second reason to care is an odd solicitude for workers as holders of private property in their labor. This idea is not original with Marx, and indeed has a long and influential history. Marx had it from at least Adam Smith, who argued that the division of labor made trade possible, that is, the division of labor made production efficient, but producers then possessed only one or a few types of goods. Trade, markets, were therefore necessary. All of liberal economics, the science of markets, was thus dependent on the idea that labor created property rights. By subverting that bedrock idea to his own ends, Marx endeavored to subvert the discipline of liberal economics, but more importantly to transform the object of inquiry, markets, and the society created by market processes, into something different, warmer, better.

The idea that property rights are derived from labor is not confined to what has come to be regarded as economics: one could trace the idea into political thought, and further back in history. Smith had the idea from John Locke, who argued that the laborer, in transforming an object, made it his own. Locke, in turn, drew on the Hobbesian contention that a man had property in himself, and in the things he made. It is a long way from property as the product of one's transformative efforts to the rents that supported the sorts of aristocratic household where Locke was paid to be a tutor. Nor does the sweat of the brow ensure the endowment for Smith's chair at Glasgow, or the maintenance of the collections in the British Museum on which Marx relied. In other words, the idea that the complex regime of control that sails under the name property is, or could be, simplified to an abstract and ill-defined concept, labor, is no more than a philosophical fantasy. (And it is a very strange fantasy for philosophers;

what philosophers do seems to be work but neither labor nor property in the ordinary senses.) Whatever property is, it is not merely labor; whatever value labor has, it is not expressed by its price; and whatever price property receives, labor will not thereby receive its value.

There are other ways to think about the value of labor quite apart from falsely understanding property to be congealed labor, and property to be priced correctly, and price to be value. Marx also drew, if perhaps not entirely consciously, on a more intuitive understanding of economic justice, the sort of understanding implied by the word "fair," as in "fair price." This understanding is also suggested by the idea of "worth," as in "how much money is it worth?"—a question different from asking after the price of the item. The idea that the monetary equivalent for a thing X *ought* to be some number Y of the currency in question used to be called the just price and is now called the fair price, or the item's worth, or in the language of contemporary financial markets, its fundamental value. The prosperity that marked the end of the twentieth century, with its sudden creation of great wealth, is interesting in part because it presented us with conflicts among people with different ideas of what a fair price was, of what things were worth. So, for example, even quite comfortable people who remembered the Great Depression often had difficulty bringing themselves to pay the going rate for meals or cars, prices that may have seemed quite unremarkable to their professional children. These same middle-aged children, however, if they live in places like Boston or Washington or New York or swathes of California, were often appalled at what the Internet rich were willing to pay for an ordinary but well-situated dwelling at which they received junk mail but spent little time. The collective fiction of money did not tell the same story to the old, the middle aged, and the newly rich people, because each group had its own ideas about worth. The different conceptions of what things were worth reflected differences in economic worldview among generations, thereby suggesting a degree of what used to be called a lack of social solidarity. Even though different generations were living in the same society, they were living in different worlds.

Having a world—for Marx, how one stood in relation to industrialization—made it possible to have a system of values, to have beliefs about what things worth. From within a certain world, it was simply clear that workers *ought* to be paid more, that workers were not receiving a fair price in exchange for their labor, that workers were not being treated fairly. (And what reader of Dickens could quarrel with that sentiment?) Or, in more communal language, Marx understood from the beginning that there was little solidarity among the orders in industrializing Europe, and that this lack of solidarity was the root of the lack of agreement on what a fair wage for a worker's day was.

During the Middle Ages, attempts were made to institutionalize this sense, perennial if inconstant, that a given thing is worth some certain amount of money, that there is some appropriate fit between things and their prices, and that as a result it is wrong, against the order of things and in that sense unjust, to try and extract a higher price for a thing. This is the doctrine of the just price. But the phrase "just price" is a bit misleading. The actual price charged for a given object might be just or unjust, that is, might occupy or not occupy its appropriate place in the scheme of things. In the medieval worldview, it was this scheme, a vision of a just order which is both universal and atemporal, that was important. Certain exchanges were appropriately priced, and because appropriate, just. Other prices were unjust.

In this view of economic justice, ultimately dependent on an atemporal order of things, money was problematic. On the one hand, money was accepted as a mode of facilitating exchange, paying fines, and so forth. On the other hand, the medieval mind noted that money is different from other goods. Money cannot be consumed, and so is not worth anything in itself. Money is fundamentally barren; it produces nothing worth having. Though it produces nothing, money nonetheless reproduces. Money can be lent at interest, that is, money can make more money. But what could the just price for a loan be? It is difficult to talk about a just price for the exchange of money for itself. It would seem that something should be exchanged for itself on a one to one basis (with perhaps a small charge for inconvenience?). Lending money at the going rate of interest, demanding more in return than one gave, appeared immoral to the medieval mind: lending at interest is based only on the lender's ability and desire to take advantage of the need of those less fortunate. Lending at interest quickly shades into usury, exploitation, injustice. Conversely, to borrow at interest was to risk giving rein to one's greed. Lending thus smacked of temptation as well as concupiscence. How could such a practice be just?

Our relative comfort with lending at interest is based on our conception of time.[11] Money has a time value. Money today is worth more than money at some point in the future. Consequently, in order to pay a fair price, in the future, for the use of the lender's money today, the borrower must pay more money in the future, that is, the borrower must promise to pay interest. The modern answer is as circular, however, as the medieval position. Money has a time value under the assumption that money could be put to work during the pendency of the loan, that is, that other investment opportunities exist. Consequently, the borrower must pay enough interest (discounted for risk) to compensate the lender for investment opportunities foregone. The assertion that money has a time-value is merely a reassertion that money can be used productively, that is, can facilitate and profit from the ambitions of those less fortunate—precisely the medieval complaint. The modern mind responds, however, that those ambitions might be achieved, that the borrower may be successful, and may repay the interest. As discussed in chapter III, future success redeems not only the borrower's enterprise, but the entire practice of finance. The modern market economy is therefore morally justified as a promise for a different, better, future. It is quite possible, perhaps likely, that a different future will have different conventions, different prices. Just as the idea of the just price requires an atemporal order of appropriate relationships, modern capitalism, premised on the near future, when relationships will be different, can have no serious idea of a just price.

The tensions between the effort to determine a just price and the practice of moneylending, between old and new ideas of the evils or virtues of finance, between the medieval world and our own, suggest that work may be valued in a third way, religiously. Work may be seen, not as a mere means to an end, a matter of utility, but as itself participation in a higher order. The medieval monk certainly understood work in relation to prayer: Benedict's monks traditionally related the one to the other, *labore et orare*, work and prayer.[12] By establishing an entire day devoted to God, in which a strict and unchanging schedule of worship, work, and sleep created a sense of timelessness, monasticism embodied an ideal of earthly time without motion and so of little significance, an intimation of eternity, but an ideal completely at odds with the ideal of time embodied in finance.[13] In such a world, where earthly time is not taken seriously, work is necessary for temporary maintenance, social advancement is unlikely if not impossible, and finance is a waste of time. The late modern poet Paul Celan quoted the early modern philosopher Malebranche to say that attention is the natural prayer of the soul, and in attending to the offices of their world, the medieval worker may have understood himself to be observant, as well as securing the daily bread of which the Lord's Prayer speaks.[14] Rather than as an effort to transform his circumstances and so realize his worldly dreams (the promise of finance), the medieval worker could have understood his labor as that which he was to do. The stance of such a worker would be worshipful.[15]

Times have changed, and work has taken on other meanings. But labor's strangely durable significance to many of us may stem from roots that can only be called religious. Weber was right to note the asceticism of capitalism, to note that we treat work as in some sense opposed to money, even though we explicitly claim to consider work to be a means by which we gain money. One need not go so far as Weber's assertion that Calvinism treated prosperity as a sign of election, thereby infusing modern capitalism with zealous energy, to acknowledge that hard work has long retained a significance far deeper than the desire for material gain can possibly explain.[16] Indeed, many Americans work harder than is healthy, harder than they can enjoy. It is easy enough to understand the economy in rationalistic terms, but scrutiny of actual people going to work—whether corporate lawyer or janitor—destroys the comforting idea that we work for rational reasons. It is not too excessive to understand the American idea of work as essentially a religious observance, if perhaps one whose deeper meanings have been forgotten.

In this vein, we might understand Marx's famous problems with the Jews, his own background notwithstanding, in terms of this opposition between work and money, in which work is a form of observance, and money seeks to change, and so undermine, that which is respected. Phrased medievally, the worker shoulders Adam's burden and labors. In accepting their station and participating in the just social order, the worker is observant, or, as a vassal to his lord, worshipful. In contrast, the moneylender, often a Jew, makes money without working. Furthermore, the moneylender profits from the ambitions of others, that is, profits from the desire to change the order. Labor, for Marx, held out the promise of authenticity. Certainly the desire for authenticity was explicit in the younger Marx, and in "On the Jewish Question" also written early, in 1843.[17] Even the later, scientific, Marx can be understood in terms of the desire for authenticity, in which the social world was grounded in genuine property, that is, property conferred not by force but by dint of one's own labor, in which everyone had "sweat equity" in what they owned. After the state withers away, the dialectic of history comes to an end. The just social order is atemporal because it is perfect, a very medieval thought. Yet money, as we have discussed, is both profoundly temporal and inauthentic. The Jew as moneylender, that scapegoat of the medieval mind, reappears in the ostensibly atheistic Marx as a "huckster," the figure of inauthenticity, who instantiates and profits from the corruption of contemporary social life, based on financial communication, untruths, and exploitation.

Here again the world has shifted in strange ways. Labor—at least the work most of us do at our jobs—holds out little if any promise for authenticity, and few of us believe that we should imagine our jobs as prayers, even in the subtle sense of attention that Malebranche suggests. While many of us take work far too seriously, most of us recognize this as pathology rather than piety. Paul Celan had not his day job but poetry, "the unremunerated labor of the spirit," in mind when he quoted Malebranche's thought that attention is prayer.[18] It is in attending to activities such as poetry, rather than whatever we may happen to do in the marketplace, that most people today hope to find meaning. Even the symbols have reversed themselves: Celan was a Jew, a suicide, in some sense a Holocaust survivor, and the very figure of authenticity.

Whatever sense it may make for individuals, the idea that we should care about labor because workers are devoted to God (whether God is understood through Christ, history, or the unnamable object of a longing for authenticity) neither puts the idea of economic justice on a firm footing nor, more broadly, has any use for metropolitan political purposes. Certainly the old idea of a just price is unavailable to us, for the simple reason that the City of Gold is founded on moneylending, and more profoundly, on a sense of time different from that of the Thomistic world. Moreover, unfortunately for moralists on the left, the idea that work is religious observance does better at explaining the success of Wall Street law firms than it does in providing a sense of what we mean when we sympathize with men and women who work at humble jobs. And the traditional left, with its "scientific" tendency to atheism, cannot possibly have meant—at least not consciously—that labor should be supported for theological reasons, and their heirs cannot be expected to ground arguments for "economic justice" on a theological vision.[19] Nor, in light of the many religions found within the City, can we imagine political action publicly justified by an explicitly religious valorization of labor. In short, work may have been prayer, and even still, in some dark and convoluted way, may be how members of certain classes confront their voids, but prayer is a private matter in the City of Gold, and cannot sustain the public intentions that talk of economic justice requires.

A fourth way to honor work, besides as proxy for humanity, property, or prayer, is as craft. We might respect the skills of the worker; there is something admirable in being able to do a thing well. Admiration for work is oddly unconnected with the task at hand. We may admire cabinetry, for example, without having the least desire to become a cabinetmaker. We may even admire the skills of workers who are doing something we think is bad. Soldiers often admire their enemies' skills, but presumably do not wish their enemies success.[20] Work thus can be viewed and honored as the exercise of skill, craft, quite apart from its ultimate purpose.

At the same time, a skill must be a skill at some activity—the exercise of a skill is purposive. The activity of making bread defines the craft of baking and the occupation of baking. The activity of surgery defines the craft of surgery, and the occupation of being a surgeon. Traditionally, the ultimate purpose of a craft was to fulfill some need, such as hunger or health, but a craft does not require a need. Consider building or sailing small wooden boats, elegant hobbies. Consider, for that matter, baking bread by hand, especially at home. Clearly these are skilled occupations, and just as clearly they are unnecessary in today's economy. The purpose of exercising a skill simply may be to exercise the skill, that is, we can and do speak of skill in the context of play. Amateur athletes may be skilled, but there is no economic need for their activity. Whether or not the activity produces something that is needful, however, to speak of skill presumes a purposive activity: build the boat, bake the bread, win the game.

Defining work in terms of crafts allows us to speak, in far more specific and coherent fashion, about valuing work. It is not at all clear what is meant by the abstraction "labor," nor is it clear why we should value it. The reasons to cherish labor (whatever kind of labor it is) offered so far—because it is a proxy for humans, or the stolen property of the downtrodden, or one way to pray—are less than completely convincing. If, however, instead of valuing labor in the abstract, we value specific, concrete workings, something rather marvelous happens: we can say quite a lot about who is a good baker, or surgeon, or quarterback, and why. We can talk about skills and good work in ways that we cannot talk about the value of labor.

To recapitulate the point in more philosophical terms: when attempting to make moral judgments about the economy, we should not follow the tendency of economics (utilitarian thought) to treat all good things as good in the same way (priced), and so commensurate with one another. If we are to ask after the value of something, we need to speak about its purpose. Good, we might say, for what? So we speak of a good watch, or a good knife, by reference to the purpose of the item. Watches are for keeping time; a watch that keeps time well is a good watch. Knives are for cutting; a knife that cuts well is a good knife. The goods are specific: the watch makes a lousy cutting instrument, and the knife cannot serve as a timepiece better than a sundial.[21] This is teleology; a thing is defined and judged by its purposiveness. Something is good—at being whatever it is—if it achieves the purpose that defines it. If the thing in question is created, we may say that it is good if it well embodies the use to which it will be put, if it fulfills its maker's intentions. For present purposes, we may think about valuing work in the sense of the English "work of art" (*Werk, oeuvre*), rather than "labor" (*Arbeit, travail*).

The striking problem with this neo-Aristotelian approach to economic justice is practical rather than philosophical. Very little of our economy has anything to do with craft, and so discussions of *arête*, virtue or excellence, do not begin. It is not that such excellence does not exist, it is that such excellence is only occasionally associated with the jobs that most people do every day in exchange for money. In the City of Gold, a communicative space comprised largely by winner-take-all markets, marginal improvements are richly rewarded by broader market share. Moreover, a profound effect of the technology not just of mass production, but of mass communication, is that it lowers the cost of copies. Many things need be done only once; the copies are nearly free. We only need the Hollywood actor to get one take perfectly; we only need the Indian savant to write the elegant code once. The sorts of jobs that a teleological approach to economic justice would require, economically significant jobs that provide a meaningful opportunity to develop and demonstrate a skill worth admiring, are relatively rare.

Perhaps—but only perhaps—the professions could be understood to aspire to some specific excellence, and so could be expected to be both remunerative and virtuous. One can imagine talking in nontrivial ways about the virtues particular to doctors, or lawyers, or clerics, perhaps even to academics. But such talk is difficult to maintain. Doctors are governed by insurance companies. Health care is a matter of economic policy and private profit, and it appears to be difficult for those in the medical profession to think in noneconomic terms. Law is another huge industrial group, and it is easy enough to make similar objections to efforts to view the law in terms of specific virtues. As problematically, at least from an intellectual perspective, people trained in the law (and the clergy) now fill so many roles in our society that it is difficult to specify what being a lawyer or a priest entails, and therefore it is difficult to talk in coherent and broadly applicable fashion about what makes one a good lawyer or a good priest. Which is not to say that there are no good doctors or lawyers or priests—of course there are—it is to question the public availability of some notion of virtue that could make the professions cohere. Nowhere is this more clear than in academe, where the placeholder "excellence" serves to applaud the "diverse," that is, superficially varied yet inclusive, contributions of each member to the well being of a large bureaucracy.

Indeed much of our economy has the superfluous feel of university administration, and talk of craft and certainly *arête* (the *arête* of a diverse *praxis*, no doubt) would be ridiculous. An idea of craft says almost nothing about jobs that are soft, generated by the service economy or even the government itself, justifiable only as a way of providing money to a proportion of the population. Consider much of the civil service, or subsidized production of various sorts, or the notorious burger flipping. Such work is honest, and we may believe that people need to live decently, and we may rebel at simply handing out checks.[22] But our respect for craft has almost nothing to do with such jobs; we have something else in mind. We have few crafts, and so a teleological understanding of work is of little use in helping us to value labor.

If we turn from the craft ideal to the work we in fact do, we find that much work is banal, mundane, well done only in that it is done. Driving trucks, or raking leaves, or changing babies, are all needful things, honest things, if not exactly worth the attention implied by "honorable." This suggests a fifth reason that we may view work as worthy of respect. Doing such work is estimable, even if it is a bit silly to speak about excellence in truck driving, or leaf raking, or baby changing—it is enough if the truck arrives safely, the lawn gets cleared, the baby stays dry. A job, considered in this old-fashioned sense, offers a further opportunity for personal morality, the idea that a worker should do his job right. This idea is still celebrated in commercials for tools, in which a man does a job right, quite apart from his wages, because that is the right thing to do. This is called integrity—it has to do with the worker's understanding of his work, not with the exchange value, if any, of the work. (Not incidentally, many such commercials are aimed at, and depict, people working on their family houses rather than working at their jobs.) The qualities extolled by country music and advertising encomiums to the working man are real qualities, even if we tend to move folks off the farm and we really only care, as a matter of economic policy, about the virtues of the working man so long as we have not figured out how to automate or export his job. Mundane work, banality, is required of most people in order to get through the day. Part of being adult is accepting that banality, and the frustration and, if one is so inclined, sense of mortality that implies. Such acceptance of one's obligation to work is upstanding. We respect the kind of people who work.

At the same time, at least in the United States, most of us conduct ourselves as if we wished to stop working. A comfortable retirement is important in our society. We envy the leisure class; we aspire to win lotteries or game shows. One might think such dreams indicate a lack of affection for work. But in real life there is little contradiction between regarding banal work as upstanding and seeking to avoid such work. Most people do not win lotteries, are not members of the leisure class, and retire uncomfortably. From such folk, who have failed to avoid work, we expect and admire a certain toughness, a lack of whining, an almost Adamic willingness to work, even dumbly, in spite of fate. Such admiration has nothing to do with whether this is a just society, and everything to do with what we expect from an adult.[23]

In a society more traditional than America believes itself to be, one might understand banal work to be upstanding in a more communal way, as the fulfillment of the offices of one's station. So, if a man is a shepherd, he mends fences, trains dogs, herds sheep. These activities are done as well as possible, but can be done well enough even when they cannot be done excellently. Nor are these tasks individually priced—the fences and dog training are not subcontracted out. Instead, the work, in the sense of a set of tasks, and the work, in the sense of being a shepherd, are coterminous. Indeed, the work in a traditional society may be assigned and performed at some remove from the labor market. Consider, for example, the gentlewomen who inhabit nineteenth-century English novels, whose work, the management of not only their individual situations, but domestic and social contexts that inform quite a number of lives, is of sufficient existential moment and complexity to be the stuff of great books. Clearly such work can be done in a manner befitting a gentlewoman, or not. The virtue of work, its worth to a traditional society, thus can be derived from the idea of station, and, conversely, the station is embodied and so defined by people who do its work.

This idea assumes, of course, that one has a station, and that the society believes in stations, and so working to fulfill the obligations incumbent upon those who hold a given station is socially approved. This assumes, in short, a class society, within which labor is both private activity, in the immediate interest of the laborer, and at the same time a social activity that receives public approval, locates the laborer in a station and therefore as a member of a class. As a result of such approval, the good worker feels a certain pride, status, so long as the ancient privileges are not disturbed. Peasants and yeoman show a disconcerting tendency to happiness, even certain American slaves felt not only happiness, but actual pride of status.[24] Work may be meaningful, in traditional and hierarchical societies, if it takes place within a context that provides it meaning, if it is done in solidarity with a community. One may, in short, be proud of one's efforts, and have such pride ratified by the community.

As discussed in chapter VIII, the history of the last few centuries may be understood as a set of developments that make a formal and institutionalized class system impossible for us, and so make a public understanding of the value of work as the fulfillment of the offices of a station unlikely, except perhaps in the special circumstances provided by the military, the university, or some other explicitly hierarchical profession. Such exceptions aside, now that modernity has substantially achieved its rhetoric, it is difficult to understand justice writ large in terms of the idea of class. While modern societies, including the City as a whole, have not abolished hierarchy—even the Cambodians failed, despite intense and unholy efforts—we go to great efforts to justify our hierarchies to ourselves. We tell ourselves that the inequalities produced by markets are tolerable for any number of reasons, for example that property is a bulwark against tyranny, or that the allocative efficiencies of the market requires tolerance for distributional problems, or that (as this apology argues) markets are needful distractions from violent politics. We tell ourselves that the privileges held by others are deserved as recompense for their hard work, or as the outcome of a fair process, paradigmatically a democratic election. We tell ourselves that observed inequalities are temporary rather than entrenched, and are glad to remember that the U.S. Constitution explicitly abolished hereditary titles, to pass redistributive inheritance and income taxes, and to remind ourselves that opportunity is always available to those willing to work for it. Although one may argue over the extent to which such egalitarian stories are true, the important point here is that class, station, does not and cannot be imagined to serve as a normative organizing principle for our society. We are not about to replace our obeisance toward equality with the virtues of class.

There is an enormous exception to such egalitarian pretensions at the root of the City, which after all was founded by mandarins. Professions serve to organize *haut bourgeois* society in the City of Gold in the way that notions of class once did: hierarchies of status justify the rather intense efforts of those who believe in them. The university always created petty nobility—a German peasant became the equivalent of a baronet when he got his doctorate. Moreover, over the centuries and particularly in the last few decades, virtually every human pursuit has been made the object of a university study, that is, professionalized. The old professions, theology, law, and medicine, have been joined by pursuits as various as art, business, advertising, being a woman, being a man, negotiating, sex (including but not restricted to that between men and women), journalism, the construction of weapons, the design of drugs, teaching, and even the administration of universities. As of this writing, no accredited university offers a degree in the administration of university degree programs in university administration, but this exciting new program is expected soon. Once all human endeavor has been made the object of graduate study, it will be possible to restrict all business to those who have the appropriate degree, like theology, law, and medicine are restricted. The university thus in principle could be the basis for an economy of licensed stations that would once again make labor respectable, in the sense of publicly respectable.

The university-based meritocracy of the City of Gold is different, however, from a traditional class system. Status based upon a degree is objective, based upon talent, or perhaps moral, based upon diligence. Really. Or at least it is objective and moral enough to be considered fair in contrast to the advantages of birth, titles of nobility and such, that have been widely felt to be unfair. By and large, accidental hierarchies, and thus class, have been discredited as normative ideals, and nowhere is class more strenuously denied than in the academy, the delivery room of modern hierarchy. Meritocracy cannot serve as an explicit political ideology for the City of Gold, no matter how important it is in fact. We cannot say that we intend to make the world safe for Harvard alumni, however hard we strive to do so—it is just not the done thing. More generally, such distinctions are inimical to the market society; money is indifferent to the person of its owner. Phrased politically, it was just the switch from station, especially national identity, to the anonymity of the consumer that the City of Gold was founded to achieve.[25]

To summarize this section of the chapter: the idea of economic justice, the attempt to ground social concern for labor in economic thought, is exhausted, bankrupt, at best a rhetorical invocation of a number of ideas that do not, individually or collectively, serve as the basis for a contemporary political economy. We may care about labor for a number of reasons, at least including: as proxy for humanity; as an effort to recapture stolen natural property; as a form of prayer, either literally or in the attenuated form of a longing for authenticity; in appreciation of skill; and out of respect for doing what needs to be done. These reasons for caring about labor, however, neither sensibly explain the traditional solicitude for labor nor, more importantly for present purposes, can serve as the intellectual foundation for metropolitan politics. The price mechanism cannot link the microcosmic concern for fairness, however understood, in individual transactions with a macrocosmic vision of a just social order. In short, there is no reason to be progressive, in the old sense of believing that the market can be made to take care of labor. Markets are no more just than they are true.

*   *   *

Why would we have ever believed otherwise? Certainly the tradition of economic thought gives us plenty of reason to believe that labor markets are unlikely to achieve justice for their participants. In different ways, Malthus, Ricardo, Marx, Veblen, and Keynes all taught that markets would not, at least absent radical intervention, adequately recompense workers. Part of the reason appears to be historical. In the United States during the '50s and '60s, at the heart of one sort of capitalism, it appears to have been sensible to talk about economic justice, so sensible that one can speak about a broad postwar "liberal" consensus that included elements of both political parties, and people and ideas that in other contexts are associated with both the left and the right. Such liberals believed that the economy could and ought to offer jobs that paid a fair wage, though they were variously concerned for jobs held by women and minorities, who were paid too little, and rich folks, who were paid too much. Even then, however, the assessment of what was fair, or too little or too much, rested on an unarticulated consensus regarding worth, the expectation of a just price. The substance of this consensus, what constituted a just price, was based on experience of widespread high-wage labor. That experience, at least in the United States after World War Two, in turn was based in no small part on circumstances peculiar to the '50s, notably the way the Great Depression and World War Two came out, and the resulting American economic dominance. That is, the "fair" wages experienced by the expanding middle class were really quite special. Under such circumstances, however, fair wages for meaningful work available to all looked enough like a plausible norm to encourage the theory class, mostly men who worked in universities, and who were paid well for their work, and who in many cases found their work broadly meaningful and important. American liberal intellectuals, lucky, often generous people, found themselves in markets that treated them well. They confused their personal economic good fortune with justice, and hoped that such justice could be extended to all.

The postwar liberal ideal of economic justice entailed more than high wages. Americans traditionally glorify work, so liberals hoped good jobs, both personally rewarding and socially respectable jobs, could be made widely available. But even this is not all. Liberal thinking about justice included variously strong notions of freedom and equality. As suggested above, realizing such notions required the destruction of station. So, sometime after the G.I. Bill of Rights or maybe the War on Poverty, or perhaps come the millennium, American liberals thought that jobs were to be available to all, and yet worthy of respect, both by the worker and by society, and were to pay well. That's all.[26] It was a big, but good hearted, mistake.

To reiterate a point made earlier: the category mistake entailed in hoping markets will be just does not mean that ideas of justice are inapplicable to the people in the marketplace. We may sympathize with our fellow humans, or respect skill or simply working hard, or believe that work addresses ultimate issues of various sorts, or espouse any number of other ideas that might incline us to help poor people, but this is charity, or better still, political power sympathetically deployed, not economic justice, the expression of meanings by price. Economic justice is impossible in a sense more final than the circumstances of birth or other inequality. Contra the left, poor people are mostly unlucky, not oppressed; contra the right, rich people are mostly fortunate, not virtuous. Rich and poor alike, however, are represented in the market only as holders of property rights. Markets are the matrices of our desire, true, but the elements of such matrices are simplifications. A market is not a world. Justice, on the other hand, is an ideal of fit—between our ideal of the world and our experience of the world, or, more precisely, between our variegated and complex sensibilities and similarly complex aspects of experience. Money can make a thing appear commensurate, fungible, and in that sense equal to another thing, but money does so by destroying the particular identities of the things it prices. Money cannot express the fit between the world as it is, about which it says little, and the world as it ought to be, about which it can say nothing.[27] Markets are not just, are not mechanisms for creating a world where we are easy, and cannot be made so.

Contrary to the different hopes of those who still follow Smith or Marx, political thought is necessarily prior to economic thought.[28] The structure of the market cannot convey justice; we cannot derive justice from the market. Our conceptions of justice are therefore external to the functioning of the market. Whether we act or fail to act, we remain inescapably responsible for the justice of our society, more precisely, for the fit between whatever ideal of justice we hold, and the society we in fact achieve. The upstanding thing to do is to confront this problem on its own terms: What sort of markets do we wish to have? That is an essentially political question, a part of the broader question, what sort of civilization do we wish to have, what sort of repression do we choose? The City of Gold is an answer in which markets play a large and vital role, such a vital role that as an intellectual matter our ability to discuss justice may be compromised (because we have difficulty thinking in terms external to the market). But our answer, and hence the substantive answer to the protesters in front of the Bretton Woods Institutions, is essentially political: this is the best constitution possible under the desperate circumstances in which we conduct ourselves.

Such claims are, of course, perennially challengeable. But the possibility of political challenge is cold comfort for both the left as well as the right. On the one hand, the right must give up on the claim that globalization, as it now occurs or even as it may be reformed, is somehow legitimated by the interplay of the market forces with which we contend. On the other hand, the left must come to see that abandoning the idea of economic justice means abandoning the hope that the need for justice can somehow be satisfied through appropriate institutional design. The market cannot be made just in our absence, and even our presence (through law, regulation, private causes of action, or whatever other modes of governance seem to be appropriate supplements) will not suffice. There can be no relief from the work of fitting the world to our ideals; the revolution holds out no hope.

There is a melancholy here. Sympathy with labor, economic justice, was especially attractive to academics and other intellectuals because it promised to give substance to a rather shadowy existence. Association with labor—even if only cheering for the team—long promised something real, solid, a counterweight to endless muttering in the British Museum, to the anxiety of being complicitous in evil. Economic justice long has been attractive to the theory classes despite the real danger of hypocrisy. Academics, like most people, often genuinely love what they themselves are not, and academic solicitude for labor is not necessarily in bad faith. Nor is the obvious alternative, the emotional attachment to capital favored by large swathes of the business community, without its problems. Cheering for capital's inscription of culture, the complexity called wealth, is also unclear and morally risky, and requires great tolerance for inauthenticity, lies of another sort.

But if there is melancholy, there is freedom, too, in abandoning the idea that markets can be just, or can be made just, freedom from the frankly pathological attitudes that often attend a strong belief in economic justice, whether held by those on the left or the right. We might come to see that the world created for us by the markets we have made amongst ourselves is more wondrous and less malign than the world we now inhabit, if also and often very sad. Our attitude towards markets might come to resemble our attitude toward other large matrices with which we imagine our reality, like history more generally, or even nature. We need not be so bitter as the left traditionally has been, even when we confront the sorrows wrought in the market. We need not view ourselves as victims, oppressed in fact, or merely in sympathy with other victims. On the other hand, abandoning the idea that our markets are just may cause the right to view our luck, if we have it, with a bit more gratitude, rather than as recompense for our virtue. After we abandon economic justice, we may go easier on ourselves, and we may be more sympathetic towards others.

CHAPTER XI

The Disenchantment
of Liberalism

A sketch of liberalism. Its practical success and theoretical failure. Its political failure. Inapplicability of liberal morality to marketplace. Liberalism as sport. Identity of economic and political liberalism. Commodification of political discourse. Failure of liberalism as religion. Coping with exile.

So much has been written about liberalism that a thoroughgoing definition would be tedious to attempt, and would be a pedantic way to treat any reader stout enough to journey this far. Nonetheless, a few words of clarification may be useful. The word liberalism here means what it commonly does in political theory: the tradition of thought, customarily begun with Hobbes, that has attempted to address philosophy's failure to reach consensus on the nature of the good (most convincingly demonstrated by the religious wars that followed the Protestant Reformation, including the English Revolution) with a system based on contract. At this level of abstraction, virtually all political discourse in the City of Gold is liberal. Consequently, liberalism as used here indicates no particular partisan bent. Liberal is not here used in the sense of American political discourse, to identify people who suspect the market and therefore support a strong state with redistributive tendencies, although, as discussed below, liberalism entails certain beliefs about the state. Nor is liberal meant in the sense commonly encountered in Europe, to denominate people who believe in a limited state and a strong market.

Liberal politics is political life understood to be an incessant contractual negotiation. Consonantly, liberal political thought is the intellectual effort to devise fair procedures through which such negotiations can take place. Lawyers call it the move from substance to process: liberalism urges us to shift our attention from fruitless argument over whatever substantive good might be at issue, to the fairness of the procedures through which society reaches decision on such matters. A process is fair if one would consent to it in advance. So, for example, a jury trial might not be a consensual process, but one might consent in advance to the idea that criminal cases should be decided by a jury of one's peers. Thus even nonconsensual procedures are legitimated in terms of fairness, and ultimately the consent, contract, on which liberalism is based.

Perhaps the essence of a contract is that it is freely entered into; contracts require freedom of the parties to obligate themselves. Liberal political thought, based upon contract, has therefore been concerned with the freedom of the citizens, often called their autonomy. Conveniently enough, liberal political theories often begin with an imagined state of nature, in which individuals are unconstrained by politics, and hence presumably free to enter into contracts.[1] The problem is that in the state of nature, or more to the point, in war, individuals are too free: they are free to believe whatever they want; to enter into military alliances based on such beliefs; and then to kill one another in organized fashion. So the initial question for liberal politics has been how to restrain individuals through politics, government, and law, while maintaining a level of individual autonomy sufficient to ensure the legitimacy of the government and human fruition more generally. Conversely, and the formulation more familiar to contemporary liberals: politics is the collective effort to provide an order through which humans can flourish by exercising their autonomy, choice. The problem of politics is how to increase autonomy.[2]

The fundamental solution to this problem is to understand government as the product of a contract among individuals, and then to rely on subsequent political life as the continual—and perforce peaceful—renegotiation of that contract. The institutional solutions to the problem, worked out in history and thought over the several centuries since Hobbes, are familiar. Government is constituted through some sort of mechanism designed to ensure popular representation. The sovereign should be divided against itself, into three branches (legislative, executive, judicial), which are "separate," or variously, which have the capacity to "check and balance" one another. Sovereignty may also be divided between central and provincial authority (federalism or subsidiarity). Government as a whole is limited by a system of rights, declared by an independent judiciary. Such a system of rights restrains the government and other individuals, and thereby affords individuals sufficient liberty to make their consent meaningful. Through these and similar institutional mechanisms, liberal thought attempts to create a system of public order that restrains the populace and provides peace, and so fosters freedom, the autonomy that individuals in a liberal order exercise in order to constitute their government, but also to define themselves.

Liberalism is the dominant political discourse in the world today. It has no serious rivals. The vast majority of nations are organized along liberal lines; the system of public international law is a profoundly liberal edifice; the City of Gold is a liberal polity. This is not to imply that political dis-agreements do not exist, but to maintain that such disagreements are rather fine grained. So although the exact relationship between liberal politics in the narrow sense, that is, voting, and liberal markets, that is, trading, is perennially debated, it is a debate within liberalism broadly understood. The intellectual domination of liberal categories is so com-plete—and has been seen to be complete for such a long time—that entire theories of history have been constructed in order to explain how the lib-eral hegemony was achieved, and have even argued that the present hege-mony is a stable equilibrium, the end of history understood as ideological conflict. Without taking a position on whether we have reached the end of history, suffice it to say that there are no contemporary political ideologies that have the reach and authority of liberalism.

In recent years, particularly in the United States, a great deal of atten-tion has been devoted to the "culture wars," the efforts by various interests groups, usually defined on the basis of some quality (racial origin, sexual proclivity, and so on), to secure their interests, and to ratify their identities through ideological expression. These efforts have often been illiberal in two senses: first, membership in many such groups is defined in terms of essential attributes, and second, the efforts are often ungenerous (unsur-prisingly, in light of the fact that these are, after all, efforts to secure iden-tity, not likely to be a generous enterprise). That said, the ideological stances collectively called "multiculturalism," or "political correctness," de-pending on one's partisanship, nonetheless remain fundamentally liberal because they aspire to autonomy, and because they expect the polity to treat their desire for autonomy seriously, as a claim of right.

Turning from partisan claims to the chattering of the theory class, how-ever, liberalism does not want for critics. It is an overstatement, but to the point, to say that liberalism currently seems as theoretically bankrupt as it is ideologically successful. At least in the academy, the critics of liberalism are legion, and discussing the range of contemporary academic criticism of liberalism would be even more tedious than attempting a capacious def-inition of liberal thought. For present purposes, it suffices to limit our dis-cussion of liberalism's failures to suggesting how even the successes of liberal ideology have been disappointing.

Consider the fundamental intention and achievement of liberalism, a set of solutions—involving the proper relationships between the limited state and the autonomous individual—to the problem of conducting politics while disagreeing about fundamental issues. Or, to put the achievement in more fashionable language, liberalism provides solutions to the problem of political order in diverse societies. The problem no longer presses on the mind, in great part because liberalism has gone so far towards solving it. Although, as already noted, the solution remains incomplete—one may argue endlessly over the contour of rights, the relative merits of parliamentary and presidential modes of government, how the powers of coordinate branches should be separated or intertwined, and so on—such arguments take place within a liberal frame. Liberalism provides the armature through which such arguments are conducted. Nowhere is this more evident than in cases of failed states. Precisely because we know, roughly speaking, what the relationship between the state and the individual should be, we know what to do when a state collapses and must be reconstituted. And since the Cold War, we have had ample opportunity, and even some success, realizing our liberal abstractions—the states established by the international community are constituted to be liberal states. Liberalism is indispensable.

But indispensable does not appear to be enough; what about political questions that cannot be answered in terms of the relationship between the citizen and Leviathan? Liberals have traditionally argued that the scope in which individual autonomy could be exercised should be increased. Liberals have defined themselves in opposition to things they perceived as fetters on individual freedom, such as the (tyrannical) state, institutionalized religion, oppressive social codes, market power, and so forth. In response to such institutions, liberals have argued for rights to protect the individual's exercise of freedom. These arguments seem simply inapt, however, in an age in which many conflicts take place with no nonliberals in sight. When medicine and money allow individuals to make choices about matters as fundamental as their personal biology—such as gender and racial appearance, things once thought to be given—it becomes difficult to maintain that the world would be better if only people had a few more options, a bit more liberty. Liberty has reached unheard of heights in the City of Gold, and it simply makes little sense to argue (at least among people with any money) that securing liberty is the key to a society with which we are content.

Old modes of argument, habits that they are, die hard. Much political discourse is conducted in liberal terms for the simple reason that it is so difficult to imagine other terms. For example, Americans discuss the freedom of speech secured by the First Amendment to the U.S. Constitution, as if American democracy were threatened by an oppressive government. To add insult to injury, the U.S. Supreme Court has repeatedly struck down laws attempting to limit political expenditures by corporations, which comprise a very real danger to democracy in America, maintaining that the First Amendment protects the right of corporations to speak freely.[3] Although state legislatures that pass such laws may be well-intentioned, may indeed believe they are helping to preserve a semblance of democracy, such laws in fact stifle the voices of the people/corporations the First Amendment was designed to protect, and in doing so, overreach the bounds the Constitution sets for state legislatures.[4] From within the Court's liberalism, the duty of the Court is to ensure that the sovereign, which we have been worried about since Locke decided Hobbes was a little extreme, does not so overreach. Therefore, state laws that attempt to regulate the ability of corporations to influence local elections are unconstitutional. Liberalism's traditional presumption that the citizen is threatened by the state requires the assumption—and hence the prefiguration—of both state and citizen, thereby making it difficult to address the social processes through which both state and citizen are constituted, that is, liberalism itself makes it difficult to consider absolutely central aspects of political life, even in liberal polities.

Liberalism has traditionally argued for freedom, for open societies and free markets. More freedom, it has been thought, would clearly be better for the individuals involved, who would no longer be oppressed or frustrated by whatever restraint was in question. Plausibly, if often somewhat vaguely, it has also been thought that a society with more freedom would be a better place than a society with less freedom. And there were efforts to show that individual freedom, in the aggregate, produced common benefits, such as Madison's faction, Smith's invisible hand, and the open society variously extolled by John Stuart Mill, Karl Popper, and Isaiah Berlin. The global success of liberal political thought, however, requires us to be more specific when we ask what sort of polities are created by various liberal mechanisms. Once we consider our own situation, as opposed to some tyrant of historical or other imagination, we become bogged down in difficult lawyerly questions. For example, how does the freedom of a citizen governed by laws passed by elected representatives relate to the freedom of the same person, now considered to be a consumer, governed by a price mechanism in which he may participate? Liberalism is too overarching a construct to provide an answer.

Liberalism's failure to provide a way to think about constitutive political choices is structural rather than accidental. Political mechanisms, by definition, create polities, environments. Environments inform and so constrain choice, impose limits on the exercise of freedom. The question is not what sort of freedom are we to have, but what sort of limitations are we to have? Liberalism understands the world as a perpetual conflict between the individual will and the collective will represented by the state. Only when the two are in tension is freedom, autonomy, possible. The total victory of individual wills is civil war, lawlessness. The triumph of the collective will is mob rule, tyranny. But it is easy enough to condemn anarchy and despotism. More difficult problems lie between the poles: Why this configuration of liberty and restraint, institutionalized in this specific fashion, as opposed to that configuration, differently institutionalized? Liberalism has difficulty dealing seriously with such environmental questions.

Even more difficult questions arise when liberal thought turns to issues like nature, or education, or even religion, that can be deeply understood neither as expressions of autonomy, nor in terms of the tension between state and citizen. Now that physical oppression has grown so much less distracting in the rich territories, it has emerged that politics itself—the environment in which we live, the way in which we educate the next generation, the way in which we collectively believe—turns out to be composed of questions that liberalism cannot begin to answer. So, to take a small and local example: a private school in a neighboring community has decided that it wants to cut a forest and drain a wetland, on land it owns, in order to build a soccer field. The land is not particularly ecologically important, but is one of the few remaining unbuilt spaces in its neighborhood. Liberalism provides no help in deciding whether or not this soccer field should be built. This is so by definition: whatever answer one may ultimately arrive at is unlikely to have much to do with the proper relationship between the state and the individual. Instead, the answer to this question (any answer) requires a substantive view of what this particular neighborhood might hope to be, that is, engages in just the sort of substantive discourse, rooted in a specific context, that liberalism was invented in order to avoid.

The best that liberalism can do is devise a fair process through which such decisions—any political decision—can be made. Liberalism can suggest that the board of directors of the school (a not-for-profit corporation) which owns the land should vote; or that the town pass an ordinance restricting the use of the property, presumably after a public hearing; or that state officials, exercising authority delegated by elected representatives, take the property for a park, paying just compensation; or that the federal government restrict the draining of wetlands; or that some combination or other of these be decreed by a judge; or one of any number of other processes designed to be fair. But the substantive question of politics, "what is to be done?" (once we have agreed on the rules of the game), is simply beyond liberal political discourse. Liberals can talk about contracts, the consent of the governed, and fair procedures, but they cannot, *qua* liberals, talk about the outcome of such procedures, beyond stating their personal preferences. As has by now become a cliché, liberal political discourse is merely a ceaseless deferral of substantive political discussion, in which the rules of the game are continually under discussion, but real subjects are beyond discussion, are indeed handled by vote or bid or some other way of

aggregating unarticulated, unargued, and often rather thoughtless preference. In a very real sense, there is no such thing as liberal political thought,
but there is a surplussage of liberal thought about the institutional framework that might be expected to engender a fair politics.

Such thought is not a waste of time; our institutions may always be improved. But lack of fair process (finding the middle road between tyranny
and chaos) might not be our most pressing problem. We have institutionalized liberalism; we have put any number of fair procedures in place.
What now? At some point, the task of governance is unavoidable. Power
must be exercised, and one might hope that it would be exercised thoughtfully. At some point (now?), it makes sense to think about substantive politics. To do that, however, we would have to use a political theory that is
explicitly not liberal, for liberalism appears to be an ideology that positively counsels the thinker to avoid actually thinking through politics, and
thereby exonerates the thinker from responsibility. Instead of admitting
their complicity, liberalism counsels thinkers to try and design institutional mechanisms that make the exercise of power impersonal and im-
peccably fair, that will finally provide a rule of law and not men, that may
provide better government, whatever that might mean, but that will at any
rate spare men (and women) anxiety over their responsibility and hence
possible guilt. More realistically, however, liberalism's ceaseless deferrals
will only result in a regime whose rules have been so thoroughly argued
that nobody would have the temerity to complain.

The world to which fair process is supposed to give rise is therefore never
achieved, perpetually over the horizon, no doubt to be reached after the next
election, when the market settles down, or otherwise in the sweet by and by.
Liberalism's ideological success, indeed hegemony, makes it all the more
clear that liberalism cannot be achieved, even in the mind. There is no liberal utopia. How could there be? What possible scope for the autonomous
will could be satisfactory? And how could a utopian state be described without setting constraints? Any set of specifications would constitute a context,
that is, would limit the will of the autonomous actors who inhabit the liberal
imagination.[5] Liberalism cannot even imagine its end state, the perfection of
its intentions to establish completely fair processes, and so the thoroughgoing liberal need never confront the question of what to do with power.

Liberalism can barely imagine the morally perfect individual, who
through good will and steadfast fidelity to the dictates of moral logic willingly accepts the obligations incumbent on him to treat others in the
fullness of their autonomy. Such individuals obey what Kant called the
"categorical imperative"—the fundamental rule—of moral life. Kant's categorical imperative may be stated in a number of ways, but the simplest is
that we should treat fellow autonomous beings as ends in themselves, not as
a means to some other end (usually some version of our own self-interest).

The categorical imperative is understood to be difficult to fulfill. Even for the individual who strives to be moral, there seems to be little chance for a just political order, and so she will constantly be tempted to place her own self-interest above the interest of her fellow autonomous beings. The Kantian imagination conceives moral obligations, duties, to be heavy burdens, and implies that we must struggle to resist the temptations to self-interest presented by a dark and sinful world. Kantian moral philosophy seeks to teach us how to act under such trying circumstances.

Such circumstances only appear difficult to the uninitiated. From the perspective of Kantian moral thought, the sinfulness of the world is rather convenient. If fulfilling our duty were not felt to be a burden, if moral action did not take place against the temptation to shirk, we would not know that we acted morally. For the Kant of the *Critique of Practical Reason* and related works (known as the moral works or sometimes the Second Critique), the real questions are whether we have the intelligence to know, and the fortitude to do, our duty. So, insofar as we wish to do moral philosophy, we are quite lucky that the world can be relied upon to be a difficult place in which to be good. Kantian moral thought is therefore free to worry serious if essentially sophomoric and distracting questions about dramatic problems—whether one must tell the truth to would-be murderers, and so forth, which the good Kantian answers with a stern Prussian sense of obligation.

There is something fundamentally irresponsible, however, about understanding morality as resistance to temptation, even though temptation can be very real. Temptation presumes the situation, presumes that we must act in one or another relatively defined way. But what if our situation is ill-defined? As Kant himself came to realize in the *Critique of Judgment*, concepts, abstract ideas, do not determine themselves. Therefore, (and despite Kant's claim that moral reason could determine itself), an abstractly defined maxim—for example, act so as not to violate the autonomy of others—simply does not say much about what to do in a given situation, and almost nothing about what sort of situation to create. For all their talk of duty, the moral works are a bit squeamish about responsibility. The real questions of practical reason involve what should be done, right here, right now.[6]

Turning from morality to our politics, the world constructed by markets—that is, the world outside Koenigsburg (a state university, doubly insulated from the market)—is inherently immoral.[7] Life in the marketplace requires that we treat people as means rather than ends. One's boss is the means through which one gets paid; one's waiter is the means through which one is fed. The employee does not care about the autonomy of the boss, the restaurant patron does not care about the liberty of the waiter. Insofar as caring exists between such people, its existence is distinct from the economic relationship. Less immediate but nonetheless important economic relationships—between a person with a 401(k) plan and the staff in the back office of one of the fund managers, for example—exist without any caring, for autonomy or otherwise, at all. Consequently, life in the marketplace is essentially immoral, insofar as we understand morality in terms of the moral works. Despite his brilliance, Kant's morality is radically insufficient for a market society.

None of which is to suggest that there is no morality within the marketplace; indeed markets could not function without moral codes. But the market is more fundamentally the site of transactions in which people are treated as things. Markets require us to view our fellows instrumentally, as the satisfaction of our desires, most graphically, as our slaves or whores. There is no way to square this dynamic with the moral intentions of liberal thought. We now see both the full horror of political economy, and conversely, the reason we need to reassure ourselves that the economy somehow can be made just (Marx) or at least absolved (Smith). Political economy is the effort to delimit the areas in which we lay down our morality and consider one another as objects, specifically as the accidental inhabitants of the terrain on which we satisfy our desires. Liberalism, the moral project, is perpetually unachieved in a market society, as impossible as the possession of the Holy Grail, even while liberalism, the ideological project, has become hegemonic.

The combination of ideological success with intellectual insufficiency, even self-contradiction, has led liberalism to a strange place. On the one hand, as suggested above, we understand contemporary politics almost exclusively in liberal terms; we have little other way to think about politics. On the other hand, it appears to be almost impossible to take liberalism, on its own terms, completely seriously, that is, to engage politics in the same fashion as did the great liberal thinkers. We simply no longer believe that bickering over fairness leads anywhere in particular, except to further bickering over fairness. Liberalism is now both indispensable and uncompelling.

Once liberalism ceased to address our deepest concerns, and so could no longer take itself completely seriously, its substantive account of our political mechanisms lost its force, and we were left with the formal process, the game. Liberal mechanisms, like sports, came to be understood as voluntary competitions among autonomous parties conducted as fairly as possible according to neutral procedures (rules or laws) and may the better (team, candidate, company, whatever) win. Even presidential elections are reported as if they were sporting events. Campaigns are understood, first and last, as competitions. Each statement, position, action is analyzed in terms of its positive or negative effect on the candidacy, rather than in terms of the positive or negative effect such a possibility might, if realized, have upon the common good. Interested citizens have become fans.

Nor do liberal economic institutions retain much gravitas. Business has become entertaining to a wide audience. Legal wars between Hollywood and Silicon Valley over intellectual property; takeover battles among giant corporations that did not exist a few years ago; the gyrations of Wall Street, discussed by uptight plutocrats and beautiful young analysts, who for different reasons are deathly afraid they will look stupid in front of the financial press and so across their world—this is great stuff. Business and finance are more popular than anything else in the newspaper, and nearly as popular as sex on the internet or sports on television, and for good reason. The competition is intense, the action is nonstop, the stakes are high and most of the rules are clear: What else does a great spectator sport need? Winning is not the most important thing, winning is the only thing . . . that is what it means to live for the game. Whatever game that might happen to be.

Liberalism was a great intellectual tradition, and we are now operating at a perceptible, if still slight, remove from this tradition. We can still learn from the liberal thinkers, indeed we should and do. Our most pressing concerns have shifted, however, and so liberal thought no longer provides a deeply compelling account of our political institutions, including the market. The liberal tradition is beginning to become a bit uncanny to us, even as it remains the house ideology. We still may be facile, but we are no longer really adept. Liberalism is no longer enchanting. In watching, we stand a bit apart, conscious of the distance between our political and our personal lives.

* * *

Liberalism institutionalizes distinctions between the personal and the political through the creation of legal rights. From the inside looking out, rights cabin private spaces and declare them inviolable, seed beds for the cultivation of private meanings. Rights stand as the wall between the private (the terrain of meaning) and the public, a wall the public must respect. The public, considered either severally, as other individuals, or jointly, as an association (especially a business association), or collectively, as the state, may not prevent the exercise of rights, interfere with the private cultivation of meanings. Conversely, from the outside looking in, rights define the individual: the authority of the public does not extend within the bounds determined by an individual's rights, and therefore the individual is defined, in the eyes of the public, by the outer bounds of her rights, as we may define a parcel of land by its lot lines, or a house by its exterior walls. Because individuals (and other legal entities) comprise society, liberalism defines the society in the most formalistic and legalistic way imaginable, as the lawful interaction of discrete entities. As a result (so recognized as to have become a cliché), liberal society is fundamentally atomistic, lonely, devoid of a communal sense of meaning.

To play with John Rawls' famous formulation,[8] the liberal individual is to consider *itself* as if it did not know who it was. All liberal individuals are equal in kind, without regard to race, religion, ethnicity, gender, or sexual preference, even if separately situated in the real world, much like fee simple real property interests. Locke explicitly attempted to define property on the basis of the individual, that is, considered property and the individual to entail one another. More generally, liberal discourse, with its emphasis on rights defined by law and in the abstract, is necessarily conducted through the grammar of property. The self, like an interest in land, is seen to be a bundle of rights, legally enforceable and defined, in opposition to its community ("I've got my rights," we say). Both the individual and property are understood as a collection of abstract legal rights, enforced by a sovereign. Although such institutions are often associated with a particular person or parcel, the institutions are legally defined in the abstract, and therefore do not reflect the particular identity of the human or specific characteristics of the land in question.

We are legally equal as citizens, and our souls may indeed be equally beloved by God, as Christians believe, but in actual life in society (political in the broad sense of living in groups) we are unequal. Each of us is differently situated, again in congruence with land, of which no two parcels are the same. That we are wont to think otherwise, consider ourselves equal, is in large part a reflection of our legalistic proclivities, and the quantitative tendencies of a monetary society (in which everything is commensurable, if not exactly equal). Even in the City of Gold, however, actual politics is spatial, a matter of who controls the well, the pass, the trigger finger, and so inherently unequal and incommensurable. The serious effort to create equality may turn violent, as in the Soviet Union or Cambodia, but however zealously conducted, the effort is logically doomed to failure. There is no way to speak of the equality between those in front of and those behind the gun's barrel. Less dramatically, but more to the point for politics in the decent neighborhoods of the City, we may all be legally competent to sign a contract, but very few of us are in a position to buy companies.

As discussed in chapters II and IV, property aspires to the condition of money, and vice versa. As property is to money, so individual rights are to autonomy. The autonomous will, like money, is defined without content, as the abstract potential to choose. Money of course facilitates the realization of the will, that is, while all people may, as a matter of civil rights, have the right to choose, only people with money have the power to choose much. Even more importantly for present purposes, however, money symbolizes the capability to choose among possibilities, to choose properties to dominate, as the idea of autonomy celebrates the potential to choose a self, to "be all that you can be."[9] We are thus left with a neat

analogy between economic and political liberalism—property: money::
rights: autonomy.

If liberal economics and liberal politics are mirror images of one another,
then the logics of markets and politics are substantially identical. The ability
of one aspect of liberal life to complement the other is therefore severely limited. So it is true, but radically insufficient, to note that for Hobbes, economic freedom was a counterweight to the lack of political freedom properly
allowed by Leviathan. It is also true, but insufficient, to note that for later liberals such as Locke and Madison, economic life existed as the terrain over
which happiness, that is, property, was to be pursued, once government had
been constructed in order to protect property. It is even true, but still insufficient, to realize that the freedom of the West presumes that one has the
money to avoid sleeping under bridges.[10] In each of these liberal expressions,
economics and politics were understood to exist in a complementary, perhaps even supportive, relationship with one another. But as liberalism has
worked itself pure, the distinctions between rights and autonomy, on the one
hand, and property and money, on the other, have come to seem distinctions
without much difference, not much more than a convenient way to sort institutions, to tell markets from elections.

The congruence of liberal economics with liberal politics rests on a
shared image of what it is to be human. The liberal citizen is the political
personification—in the poetic sense—of the economic actor, the autonomous self who must exist in order to exercise dominion (property) or liberty (money).[11] The economic structure of liberal politics makes efforts to
secure the recognition of specific identities, so-called identity politics, profoundly self-contradictory.[12] On the one hand, the proponents of such
projects are invested, often deeply, in their transformation of their status
within the polity. On the other hand, and by definition, liberal political
projects establish rights and liberties, which are homologous to property
or money, and similarly rather meaningless. To assert an individual right is
to demand that the issue in question be acknowledged as within the right
holder's dominion, protected by a legal regime analogous to property law.
Conversely, to claim a liberty is to maintain that the owner has the freedom
to dispose of a matter, a liberty whose trace or residue is money (the liquidity of the asset). But deep meanings, such as one's identity, cannot be
communicated or even understood through the arid formality of legal
rights. To be regarded as property is also to be estranged, politically isolated; to have the freedom of money is to be free from obligation, human
connection. As a result, much "progressive" politics consists of a sort of
psychic suicide, a desire to trade specific meaning for legal form, often
combined with a pathetic insistence that the rest of the polity honor the
corpse, as if more than formal civility were possible.

We may have serious doubts as to whether we wish to view certain matters in terms of property and its double, money. Take, for example, sex, specifically the gay rights movement. James Buchan is right—in a truly monetary society, homosexuality must lose all conviction as a social posture.[13] In a world understood strictly in terms of rights, homosexuality ("between consenting adults," or at least adolescents) cannot matter, and we are already seeing social arrangements being modified to recognize homosexual unions, such as through the provision of spousal benefits to same-sex couples.[14] Yet for the present, at least, not even in the United States is the world understood strictly in terms of rights, and to some people, the substantive sexual proclivity, homosexuality, still matters. Some people still hate gays: gay bashing—sometimes horrific, even fatal—still exists. Other people, homosexual and not, "celebrate" gay politics. Gay is still cool, in Hollywood and elsewhere. In the academy, it is virtually impossible to be anything but wholeheartedly supportive of the "gay and lesbian community."[15] The homosexual political movement in the United States thus remains in the romantic and hence somewhat militant stages, that is, homosexuality remains viable as a social posture. The requisite things having been said, now that high schools have gay clubs, one wonders how much longer it will be until homosexuality is viewed as a simply normal human variation, no more significant than hair color, and Buchan's prediction will be fulfilled. Homosexuality matters, but so does nationalism in the Balkans, and both concerns are at odds with the progressive narrative that defines the City of Gold, the effort to replace as much of life as possible with the dialectic between money and property. Gay bashing is not just evil, it is anachronistic, and so quite rightly looked down upon by progressives. Presumably, the homosexual movement will, like the labor movement and the civil rights movement before it, succeed in the only way possible in a monetary society, by becoming a form of political capital, and therefore both treated absolutely fairly and unworthy of strong allegiance, despite the considerable efforts of the club's leaders to keep the members enthusiastic. [16]

* * *

As a theoretical matter, it is not entirely clear why liberals whose own rights or interests are not at stake should take any interest whatsoever in politics, particularly the politics of "globalization." It is tempting to insist that proper liberals, who nurture meaning in private gardens, should have no real politics, no concern for the world outside their gardens.[17] Observation suggests this is not the case. Many people in our society are interested in politics, and especially the politics of globalization. The vast majority of such people appear to be liberal, in the broad sense the word has been used in this essay; our political aficionados all believe liberal things about individual rights, limited government, and so forth. So how do such liberals square their political commitments, their concern for the substance and texture of the world, with the privatization of meaning that contemporary liberalism has carried to such lengths? Is this mere sloppiness, a lack of rigor? Or, as suggested above, should partisan politics simply be understood as another form of entertainment, a kind of sport, in which the theory classes indulge, just as the working classes in America race cars and shoot deer? Or should political concern be regarded as an anachronistic passion, either nostalgic or passé, akin to the nationalism the City of Gold was intended to neuter?

While the rhetoric of the protests against globalization is liberal in a broad sense, the protests are difficult to understand in any coherent way, that is, the protests are not easily recapitulated as policy argument, as, for example, the protests against the siting of the Pershing II missiles in Europe during the mid-1980s could be recapitulated as a fairly sophisticated argument over security. With regard to globalization, in some contrast, a wide range of discontent but mutually inconsistent things have been shouted. Certain protesters claim that globalization is undemocratic and hurts developing countries (over the objections of developing countries). Certain protesters claim that globalization makes people poor (in the midst of an economic expansion that, while far from perfect and which does not include most of Africa, is sufficiently sustained and widespread to have allayed the Malthusian anxieties of several generations in other places). Certain protesters claim that globalization leads to oppression, in spite of the fact that trade liberalization, the Internet, and so forth are widely believed to defuse military activity, end colonialism, and topple dictatorships. Certain protesters claim that the Bretton Woods Institutions have too much power, and almost as often that trade and financial organizations should also address labor, environmental, and other welfare concerns, which would drastically increase the competence of those same institutions. What is one to make of this?

Lacking a political myth adequate for their circumstances, contemporary critics of globalization tend to fall back upon the traditional language of liberalism. This is a mistake. Critics of globalization are not, at bottom, dismayed by some contemporary failure to achieve the liberal virtues of liberty, equality, and the fraternity of the bourgeoisie militant. There simply is no such failure; the bourgeoisie militant has never and nowhere been so successful. Liberalism is the personification of money, the restatement of economics in political language. The liberal values that the protesters use to condemn globalization are no more than the values of the City of Gold, the norms of a polity that finance has only now largely realized, with the end of the Cold War. Criticisms made in terms of what are ultimately monetary virtues lack purchase because the City of Gold has done so much to instantiate just these virtues. As a result, the common critiques of globalization seem at best confused suggestions that supranational capitalism should be more . . . monetary.[18] We aspired to the condition of money, and money we have become.

The City of Gold thus uses the Enlightenment against itself. Claims for rights, even political rights such as the freedom of assembly, are satisfied, even as the City subverts the possibility of republican politics. Consequently liberal protest at globalization, which can hardly issue in anything other than rights talk, is always already answered on its own (superficial) terms. This Byzantine structure is both fortuitous and perhaps to be expected from the mandarin founders: bureaucrats have little interest in direct confrontation, which is often risky and a waste of political capital. So at the founding of the City, those enlightened institutions, legal rights, were not only untouched, they were multiplied, so that we began to speak of social rights and civil rights, human rights, procedural rights—rights everywhere. At the same time, and more fundamentally, the conceptual basis of politics was switched away from the nation state to the market, from reason to desire, from light to darkness. To redirect a slogan familiar from feminist thought, one way to understand our politics is that the personal has indeed become the political: that which had been private (desire, self-interest) is now understood to be the mechanism of political life, most vitally, the construction of a global context. At the same time, the old enlightened political discourse, with its talk of democracy, reason, and the like, has been demoted to the status of accompaniment, something of a sideshow.

Some of the anger among liberals at globalization springs from this demotion, which insults a sentiment which is genuinely liberal, albeit liberal in a sense more capacious than this essay has employed so far. The liberal virtues of liberty, equality, and fraternity were political ends grand enough to inspire a revolutionary idea of government itself. After the French Revolution, government could, in its more expansive moments, argue that it was responsible for life. The individual's experience of the self was informed by the context in which individual life was lived, that is, the liberty allowed the individual by the state. The status of such life would be determined by the state, which declared that its citizens were equal (or degraded them through the criminal law, or elevated them, if sub rosa, through office). The ability of individuals to form associations, that is, allegiances and even polities that might conceivably compete with the state, was controlled by the state. In return, the state promised, albeit somewhat airily, that the mere condition of citizenship was sufficiently fraternal to allay the loneliness of being human. (Fortunately, there was always foreign combat to strengthen the bonds among the citizenry.) In short, after the French Revolution, the state claimed exclusive responsibility for the human condition. In logic and in France, government became literally totalitarian, recognizing no competing authority, and soon enough, totalitarian in what has become the now ordinary sense of a system of governance through pervasive terror.[19]

As Hegel so well understood, the state's expansive claims required the state to address that aspect of being human whose institutions we call religious, that is, the state was required to become a religion.[20] This requirement was explicitly recognized during both the French Revolution and the Russian Revolution, in which the regimes decreed that worship of gods other than the state was illegal. To put the point more institutionally, leaders of both revolutions saw the church as a rival and enemy, and forcefully argued that the state, or the state as comprised by the party, was the proper font of transcendent meaning. After the first excitement had passed, such claims were muted somewhat, but our political tradition has never entirely recovered. Many of our best and brightest still look to the state with great hope. Although naive in light of the evidence, this is unsurprising: any religion based upon the modern state, that is, upon the effort of the mind to shape history, is sure to appeal to the bright, articulate, well educated and privileged.

Despite its material benefits to the mandarin class, at bottom supranational capitalism renders politics literally incredible, that is, unworthy of strong assent, the blind obedience of the good soldier or other true believer. The partial exsanguination of various bodies politic, especially Germany, was not only the original purpose of the Bretton Woods Institutions that now draw such protests, but more broadly, the reason to found the City of Gold. We have had enough of blood and iron. But at the same time, to say that politics is not fit to believe in (die for) is also to say that it cannot serve as much of a religion. And that is what offends many liberals about the City of Gold: its very existence is a denial of their faith. The protests in Seattle and Washington and Prague were, among other things and in often inchoate ways, religious protests, rearguard efforts to defend the faith in politics, and the identities of the protestors as believers.[21]

The religion of the present, or at least the religion of a group of people currently important, the liberal ruling class, continues to be politics, the mind's control over history, what used to be called statesmanship. But statesmanship, in its wisdom, has in founding the City so diffused itself as to lose its force as a religion. We are losing the ability to believe that the mind of man gives shape to a worshipful history; the constitutional myth is running out. Runnymede and Philadelphia are places for meetings, no more interesting than Yalta or Dayton. All of which is to say that liberalism, as a creed, has accomplished its own undoing. The politics of consent has shaded off into the politics of collective action: the Philadelphia Convention eventually gave rise to the Bretton Woods Conference, which set the stage for a network of institutionally autonomous but culturally homogenous traders in the financial markets. Although many people evidently would prefer a viable religion to a successful politics, it is unclear that the failure of politics to maintain its religious status is any more disastrous than the not unconnected failures of economics to discover truth or markets to generate justice.

*   *   *

A traditional sort of novel is centered on the clever young man from the provinces who struggles to justify the dazzling world into which he has so recently been inducted, but where he feels like a child, or a bumpkin, or both. This justification is not altogether disinterested: the young man still feels lucky, honored, by his success, and will endure quite a lot before he criticizes the world that he feels has treated him so well, and more importantly, has made him the upstanding fellow he has become. His feelings of alienation present themselves to the young man as failure: he hopes that he looks like he belongs, but in his heart he feels alone and suspects he is an imposter who will soon be caught. Part of the drama in such stories is the tension between individual and social critique, the young man's sometimes fatal inability to decide whether he is a healthy mind in a sick world, or a sick mind in a healthy world. If the young man ultimately believes in himself and cannot be reconciled, he may condemn society and become a poet or a social critic, or even an anarchist, a drug addict, or a criminal. But this is melodrama or madness. In most literature and most real life the young man's attempt at reconciliation is successful; we persuade ourselves both that the society we have worked to join is salvageable and that our sense of alienation is a passing thing.

One of the strategies for justifying our world in the face of our alienation from it is participation in liberal democracy. The strategy works as follows: society is not alienating because it is liberal, that is, it is structured by the consent of the people. Even atomistic individuals may sign the social contract, and so belong in their commonwealth. Consent, not just to the idea of society itself, but to the contours of this society as it moves forward in time, is periodically secured through democratic processes, or what matters more, the opportunity to participate in democratic processes. Rather than consider himself a foreigner in his own land, the young citizen may tell himself that society is constructed by people just like him. He himself can help construct society if he wishes. How can such a society be unhealthy, and why should he feel alienated from it? Perhaps a given election comes out differently than he had hoped, but tomorrow is another day, that's how the game is played . . . and so forth and so on. In short, liberal democracy assuages the alienation endemic to market societies by providing opportunities for participation.

What is generally left less than clear is why—aside from its therapeutic value—liberal democracy should be supported. One might think that democratic processes, allowing for free and open debate, provide the best approximation of the truth available to political affairs. Or one might think that the will of the people speaks through democratic processes, although this idea seems implausible in an age of lying political advertisements and the legal gymnastics that have recently been necessary to elect the president of the United States. Even if true, the idea that democracy represents the will of the people quickly becomes quasi-religious and, in light of Nuremberg rallies, Cold War witch hunts, and other enthusiasms, not unproblematic. Or one might be skeptical of alternative forms of government, under some version of the motto, democracy is the worst system except for all the others. This may be at bottom an argument from the therapeutic value of democratic participation—a perception of democracy keeps yon Cassius from going for his knife, or young Timothy from loading his van with fertilizer.

But while "why should we be liberal democrats?" is a provocative question, lots of fun, the question is not very important for practical politics: the beauty of liberal democracy is that in the hurly burly of actual political campaigns the question may be endlessly deferred, conflated and destroyed, and need never finally be resolved. Flippancy aside, and however dark its roots may be, liberal democracy allows us to understand ourselves to be complicit in our governance, one and all, and therefore to believe that we have some semblance of solidarity, however shallow, with the masses, our peers. This, at any rate, is one way of understanding liberal democracy, and perhaps more to the point, one way of providing some foundation for the reflexive and strangely durable belief of all our young women and men from the provinces that political life ought to make sense, that political questions ought to yield to their minds.

But whatever solace participation may offer to the alienated citizen of the putatively democratic nation state, it is unclear how liberal democracy can reassure the alienated citizen of the City of Gold. The institutions of the City of Gold—the Bretton Woods Institutions and the European institutions in particular—have persistently and largely correctly been criticized for a lack of democratic accountability. Policy is generally set by autonomous bureaucrats placed in power by member states with more pressing things to do. Individuals have no chance to vote for individual representatives or even parties that might represent them at the European or global level. The European Parliament is something of an exception, because it allows Europeans to vote for representatives who do something at the European level. The importance of the "something" has grown from negligible to more than that in recent years, and remains a matter of contention, but the fundamental point remains: the WTO, the IMF, the World Bank, the European institutions, and for that matter the entrenched national bureaucracies that shape the City's politics (to say nothing of corporations or even nongovernmental organizations) are not even formally bodies in which individuals consent to their representation. To make matters worse, from a democratic perspective, most such institutions conduct their business with little or no concern for transparency. Our would-be democrat would have to work hard to have a basis for an opinion on the affairs such bureaucracies manage, and so perhaps should not miss the opportunity to vote too much.

It has been argued that market societies are "consumer democracies," that markets are themselves a form of liberal democracy. From this vantage point, it might be tempting to argue that participating in markets, rather than in political institutions, ameliorates the alienation of life in the City of Gold. We should not miss voting so long as we can shop. Such loose thinking has been supported by liberal democrats, and the United States government in particular, who have traditionally understood liberty in fairly undiscriminating fashion: freedom of speech is like owning a small business is like voting for governor. Such things are not very alike in any theoretical sense, but they are all part of the ball of wax implied by "the land of the free." As Americans we have understood our freedoms to imply one another, and of course they do—that is what it means to be an American. But this ball of wax is history and culture, not logical necessity or nature, despite the American ideology that all freedoms are created equal.

Turning from marketplace "democracy" considered as expression of the will to marketplace "democracy" considered as an engine for the people's truth, similarly sloppy thinking has prevailed. Democracies—open societies, built on the free flow of information and with the possibility of dissent—draw their strength from their collective use of information. And what institution is better at processing information than the capital markets? Where do people have better incentives to find out the truth? From here it is a short step to understanding democracy and capitalism to be virtually synonymous modes of social choice; free markets may come to seem equivalent to fair elections. Or so it was widely said in the new economy after the end of the Cold War, when global capitalism, and particularly the bond markets, were offered as a plebiscite on the governments of individual countries. If one is fortunate enough to believe that the market is essentially democratic, then the City of Gold can be embraced as a playground constructed by the collective mind for our individual use. Rather than alienated by markets, one might instead be enthusiastic. One might even come to see capitalism as an adventure. No time to be lonely, I've got a deal to close and some windsurfing to do. *Vamonos a la playa.*[22]

As with most follies, there is truth here. Ideas of liberty expressed through market activity and democratic participation are not entirely distinct; economic and political liberalism are hard to consider apart from one another. For practical and recently popular example, capital markets often punish despotisms, which tend to have violent enemies and succession problems and so present credit risks greater than those of more democratic countries. That said, bond markets cannot seriously be taken as a surrogate for democracy in developing countries, and more broadly, the criticism that the City of Gold is no democracy cannot be answered by bland reference to the functioning of markets. Democracy may not be a very good way of articulating the truth, the objective world of pure reason, but money—by its structure—cannot be a way to articulate such truth at all. Money simply does not have that representational capacity. Similarly, democracy may not reflect our individual will, or even our religious feelings about the collective will, or even the autonomous good will of liberal morality, but the market, again for structural reasons, reflects the current state of disagreement among selfish wills to exclude, nothing more. As has been suggested, democracy may serve as a social instrument for collective judgment, the conflation of truth and will through the exercise of what Kant calls "common sense." The aggregation of the market, however, is an aggregation of rights, less than true, and desires, less than autonomous, in the absence of any sense of commonality. Whatever hope we may have for democracy as the political realization of our mind's desire cannot be maintained for market activity.

Participation in neither liberal democracy nor capitalism can relieve the alienation of life in the City of Gold. One nonetheless might propose that the City's institutions be made more democratic, and in the nature of our entertainment society, it is expected that such institutions can be made to look somewhat more democratic. Not-for-profit institutions could play various roles; still more documents could be posted to the Internet and otherwise made publicly available; elections could be held for certain positions. But the political barriers to any real change along these lines are enormous, and in any case, change is practically unimaginable at the present time. Democratic representation is hollow unless the representatives wield real power. Few people want a world government, even assuming they could vote for their representatives. Even were there more enthusiasm for vesting international institutions with the usual mechanisms of democratic legitimacy, it is unclear how institutions so large could be accountable in a way that would be satisfying. Certainly the United States, where dollars raised are counted and often decisive long before the tiresome formality of the election, is hardly a model in this regard. But the bitterness of this last line rests on an idealistic distinction between a dollar and a vote, an insistence that desire is different from thought. Whatever hopes may remain to us for democracy in the nation state, the City of Gold was intentionally constituted by dollars rather than votes.

And so it will remain for the foreseeable future. As discussed in part 1, the City of Gold is constituted with respect to different parts of the soul than is democracy. The City is built upon satisfaction of the appetites, where democracy appeals to the mind.[23] Our bright young man from the provinces cannot be at ease with the City insofar as he cares about wisdom, or God, or beauty, or truth, or any other noble end, that is, anything which cannot be made the object of property law and so traded. One can, of course, imagine polities different in kind, even read about them or visit their remnants in distant parts. As part 1 attempted to show, however, the City of Gold presents a literally compelling vision of life, so compelling that we view its adoption and perfection as development or progress, and failure to join as dangerous in the manner of the old politics of mind (and sometimes insanity) that in important ways seemed to end, at least in the developed world, with the Cold War. Serious criticism of the monetary institutions that alienate us from our world is idle, at best philosophical, playful and irrelevant and done for love, rather than normative, moral, or otherwise earnest, because we have no other history available to us. We need to get used to our awareness of the distance from our better selves that our participation in supranational capitalism entails.

PART 4

Toward a Metropolitan Political Economy

These essays have gestured toward answers in the course of their critique. We cannot speak of our inability to communicate the truth without a notion of truth, of injustice without some idea of justice, of citizenship without a sense of the community that we feel we lack. Criticism of our own thinking thus incessantly leads us back to what we have just denied. The genre constructed around this sort of tension is the essay. And so, in these last essays, we ask the same questions once again: what sort of truth may we share in the City of Gold? How may we think about justice? And if the politics of the City of Gold is necessarily partial, impoverished, may we ever feel content, at home?

Paul Delvaux, *La gare forestière* (1960)

CHAPTER **XII**
True Markets

Review of structure of apology. Toward a political economy. Market regulation in a skeptical time. Information as practical rather than objective concept. Teleology, myth, and aesthetics in U.S. securities law. Political economy as circular pursuit. Appropriate response humor instead of contempt.

The first three parts of this apology have endeavored to delineate and criticize what it means to do politics through supranational capitalism rigorously understood; they have argued that our current thinking about markets is no longer sufficient. The first three parts have attempted to set forth the *ideas* that informed the City of Gold, and pursued those ideas to their logical, often bitter, conclusions. But life is arranged by much more than logic. In this fourth and final part, therefore, we relax the assumption that the logic of markets completely determines life in the City, and attempt to discern promising possibilities for political thought in current practice, with all its ambiguities, ironies, and outright contradictions, in the belief that political philosophy may renew itself by moving toward social criticism.

To be more specific, while this chapter XII admits that markets cannot be true, the essay nonetheless wonders about markets that are as true as possible, at least not experienced as thickets of lies, and more positively stated, conform to our notions of what history and imagination conspire to suggest our markets can be. Similarly, chapter XIII discusses order within markets even while despairing of the idea that markets can themselves generate justice. Here again history plays a role in steering us toward ideals of markets, ideals that can be used to orient, if not determine, policy. The approach in chapter XIV is similar: although the private is a psychologically necessary response to an inherently partial public order (chapter VIII), and though such order cannot (and should not) fulfill the religious function that the Enlightenment suggested for the state (chapter XI), we might ask one last time if the City of Gold is necessarily the City of Pigs, to be made bearable only through the solace of private life and the recognition of history's awful alternatives.

This part's more realistic, if less rigorous, understanding of our situation reveals that the City of Gold is not constituted solely as a matrix of private interests. Chapters XII and XIII suggest that markets are themselves structured by laws, in the way that games are structured by rules. In particular, chapter XII discusses truth, especially the question of adequate information in the securities markets, and chapter XIII discusses the sublimation of war into monetary policy. In both cases political minds, bureaucrats, set the stage on which market interests play. Thus, even at the heart of the market, we see ideas at work, a politics of the head rather than the gut. Similarly, turning one last time to authority and identity, chapter XIV discusses, if only briefly, the public role of the intellectual in the City of Gold, how principled minds might confront a world that valorizes private interests, and discerns the possibility of sympathy—the traces of our ancient hope that we are political animals, not entirely alone.

*   *   *

If we are to remain committed to markets as a method of organizing a wide range of social relations—and it appears that we are—we must at least implicitly believe that markets do a pretty fair job at governance. Despite circumstances once thought to be ripe for, even to cause, violent political action, as of this writing there is little revolution in the air. There does not even seem to be much desire to try and switch away from markets to some other political mechanism for deciding things like where we work, live, the way we structure most of culture, much of education and health care and so forth and so on. To many, probably to most, citizens, markets are the obvious, even sole, political mechanism with which to undertake such tasks. There are reasons for this tendency to rely on markets, such as many other modes of social organization have been more or less discredited in recent years, many other modes of social organization are now understood to be markets in disguise, and many other modes of social organization are not really suitable to the large scale and yet detailed work that modern societies require.

And yet it is difficult to believe that we are well governed by markets. We have compelling reasons to be skeptical of the proposition that markets communicate the truth, including recognition of the epistemological limitations of the price mechanism; the testimony of many of civilization's better minds to their alienation; and even the need for economics, an account of what markets mean (to say nothing of the discipline's disappointments). We thus appear to have a polity in which governmental decisions are based on and expressed in communications that we do not believe to be true.[1] How are we supposed to feel about this?

A practical, albeit inelegant, place to start thinking about politics through markets under conditions of doubt is to deny that the bifurcation between truth and untruth is very useful for understanding governance.[2] "True" is a capacious word, and "untrue" is another. There are huge differences between failure to state the entire truth, which is inevitable, and various partial, and often mutually exclusive, truths. Partial truths must be judged on their merits. Statements may be fraudulent and yet largely true, or statements may be fair, in the sense of true to the best of the speaker's belief, but prove to be untrue in fact. And this, of course, is only the beginning. Language games are a bitch, as Wittgenstein discovered even without having to teach his children to distinguish among a mistake, a joke, and a lie, not to mention God. Statements present a bewildering array of ways to be meaningful, almost all left unaddressed by the simple bifurcation between "true" and "untrue." So in what way do we hope for truth in political economy?

We are ordinarily unaware of the dizzying possibilities because we unself-consciously situate statements. We understand statements in light of what we know about a host of other questions: What exactly was said? Who said it? To whom did he speak? What were the prior understandings of the audience? What were the speaker's intentions? and so forth. Most importantly, we judge a communication's success in light of our understanding of its purpose, that is, we judge whether a statement is true or false to its (presumably sincere) intentions. Insofar as a communication is used for governance, then we should evaluate the quality of the communication in terms of its contribution to the activity of governance, that is, a society's effort to confront its future in the best way available to it. Rather than the abstract and binomial correspondences suggested by the bifurcation between "true" and "untrue," it is more useful to ask whether the communication in question informs appropriate decisions. The task of governance organizes the questions posed by the multiplicities of truths in narrative terms: for purposes of governance, we are interested in communication as it informs good decisions about the collective future. Information is a practical and prospective subset of truths, what the security community and some lawyers call intelligence. The political question, then, is not whether governance through markets is based on truth, but whether marketplace decisions are well-informed, that is, whether market actors have sufficient quantities of good information to make good decisions. Or, to put it the same point in terms of securities law, the truthfulness of a company's disclosure is evaluated in terms of what a reasonably prudent investor might want to know prior to making an investment decision.[3]

A constitutive metropolitan myth is that the aggregation of private interests in a well-informed market is, or should be, the public interest. (As discussed in chapter V, we must still believe in the invisible hand.) This myth has numerous expressions. Market regulators, such as the Securities and Exchange Commission (SEC), attempt to ensure that markets are in fact so well-informed. Scholars ask what "well-informed" might mean, and whether our markets are sufficiently well-informed ("efficient") or if government action to improve the quality of information would, despite its costs, be desirable. For example, in the wake of Enron and other accounting scandals, the federal government passed the Sarbanes-Oxley Act of 2002, which, among other things, sought to reform the practice of financial accounting, and hence the quality of information available to the financial markets. Such efforts are, by all accounts, expensive. Scholarship on, lobbying about, reporting as required by, negotiation and litigation under, and enforcement of the securities laws employ myriad academics, lawyers, accountants, bureaucrats, and general support staff. And the reward for all of this? Insofar as we believe that metropolitan political economy is successful—that the markets get it right enough—then we may be somewhat content with our system of government. We may even be slightly less alienated.

By way of extended example and demonstration of how this myth informs the governance of an important class of markets, let us consider in some detail the laws governing the market for corporate equity in the United States. Securities laws require many market participants to make vast amounts of information publicly available, and moreover impose severe penalties for fraud. Every offering of shares to the public must be preceded by filing a registration statement with the SEC, describing in great detail the business and its prospects. The SEC in turn makes the information available to the public. Under the securities laws, it is not enough for the disclosures a company makes in its registration statement (and elsewhere) simply to be true. Disclosures must not be misleading. Similarly, disclosures must be full—registrants must disclose information that a reasonable investor might think "material" to an investment decision. The securities laws thus endeavor to ensure that market participants have the ability to reach their decisions on a sound basis, and by extension, that the societal decisions made by the equity markets are also sound.

In light of the continued political importance of the corporate equity markets, the federal government's expensive effort to ensure that such markets are well-informed seems to be worthwhile. As discussed in chapter III, finance in general and corporate equity markets in particular are ways to collectivize progress, that is, finance is one way in which society confronts the future, and therefore our governmental concerns may be expected to be at a height in the financial markets. The stakes are high, and so great prudence is warranted.[4]

At this juncture it may be useful to sketch how the equity markets affect social life—how the political mechanism works—even at the risk of a certain degree of repetition of discussion in various passages of part 1. The corporate equity markets use a collective pricing mechanism (an auction) to provide liquidity to economic actors. For example, start-up companies, which by definition have few marketable assets and thus are unable to secure debt, tend to be established through the use of equity. Not just venture capitalists and later-stage private financing, but managers, scientists, even law firms and support staff are compensated with equity. Without equity markets, there would be no cash flow with which to realize many good ideas, and many of the companies that make up the new economy would not now exist.[5] While we trust the primary (offering) markets to ensure that good ideas receive enough liquidity to be tried, we rely on the secondary (trading) markets for much of the governance of existing corporations, including, if indirectly, their business decisions. Managers are often compensated with stock and options, and evaluated by boards of directors who represent shareholders, who in turn care about the price at which their shares are trading. Managers who do not secure adequate share prices may be forced out. Share prices influence a company's cost of capital both directly and indirectly, by setting the return on shares issued or sold by the company, and by setting the terms on which debt financing can be secured. By governing the cost of capital, the secondary markets constrain or facilitate a company's efforts to expand, renovate, and otherwise compete. Publicly traded companies with low share prices are vulnerable to takeover. Conversely, a company with a strong position in the secondary markets is better able to bid—often using its own stock as partial or full payment—for another company. As discussed in chapter V, the mechanisms of classical liberal economics have been shifted, to great degree, onto the markets for corporate equity and hence control. So, what companies are established, how they conduct themselves, whether they flourish or even survive, in short, the landscape of commercial life and that which it produces, is governed largely by the market in corporate securities.[6]

As much as this is, this is far from the full extent of the importance of the market for corporate equities to the construction of the United States today. (While the U.S. economy has long been dominated by its securities markets, it is worth noting that numerous economies worldwide are increasingly adopting an equity-driven approach to finance.) Traditionally, the *rentier* class has claimed that what was good for those who trade in capital is synonymous with the good of the nation. That need not be true. Those who trade in, or consume, real goods may have interests different from the *rentier* class. That said, the distance between Wall Street and Main Street has diminished. Even apart from ownership, the democratization of finance in the late twentieth century has meant that an unprecedented number of Americans—over half—hold positions in the stock market, either directly or indirectly, mostly through mutual funds. Such positions directly affect the individual welfare of most Americans in many ways. Stock pays for education, and hence social position in a meritocracy based on institutional validation; insures us against adversity, so that we need not rely on a social net that might not hold; ameliorates old age in a society segregated by generation; and provides inheritance—civil continuity—in an economy divorced from land. Nor are these matters of concern solely to members of the *rentier* class. The institutions that provide human services, at all levels of society, from hospitals to universities to movie production houses, tend to be themselves publicly traded or endowed, and in either case, deeply involved in the capital markets. In short, we are all capitalists now, and should profoundly hope that the decisions of the market are well-founded. No wonder that securities law is obsessed with information.

But after incidents like the currency crises of the late '90s, the collapse of Long Term Capital Management, the bursting of the silicon valley and telecom bubbles, the less dramatic but very substantial decline in the value of shares held in core indices, the wave of accounting scandals discussed under the rubric of Enron, trying to ensure that our financial markets are in any sense truthful seems like a formidable challenge. Moreover, as part 1 of this book was at pains to establish and as even Adam Smith acknowledged, price is not equal to value, and so financial communication bears scant relationship to truth. In such circumstances, the question is not yet what may be done, but instead what may we hope. Perhaps, at least, we can try to ensure that our markets do not lie, even if they cannot be true.

* * *

In light of the thinking that informs securities law, one might expect that all economic law would be obsessed with information. After all, many markets—consider housing, labor, or education—are socially dispositive, and hence politically important. But the law imposes vastly different requirements on different markets. Most markets are not like securities markets. In most markets, the law does not require sellers to disclose much information to buyers or the public generally. In some consumer markets, buyers are held responsible to inform themselves about what they are buying, under the ancient doctrine of caveat emptor, buyer beware. In regulated consumer markets, such as aviation or food and drugs, the law limits what is made available to buyers, but generally does so as a matter of bureaucratic fiat (the jobs of the Federal Aviation Administration, a part of the Department of Transportation, and the Food and Drug Administration, respectively), often with little or no reliance on consumer's ability to judge information. In commercial transactions, lawyers use contracts in order to secure their client's access to adequate information. In short, the law governing information in different markets is different.

Is the law wrong to set forth different regimes for the provision of information in different markets? If caveat emptor is the basic rule, why does it not apply to all markets, including securities markets? If, on the other hand, the legally required provision of information is so beneficial to the U.S. securities markets, why is this regime not extended to other markets? Or perhaps the market for prescription drugs, in which the government requires and evaluates information, is correct? Or is the law right, at least in not attempting to make one size fit all?

As a matter of common sense, it seems clear that law should not attempt to require buyers to provide the same level of information to buyers in all markets. Nobody wants to be given, much less read, a document with the depth of an offering prospectus prior to buying an apple. Gathering, evaluating, analyzing, communicating, and absorbing information is expensive. Laws that require information thus tend to raise the cost of products, and price is of course relevant to market activity. So the law should not require information to be provided when it is not necessary. In many situations, an adequate amount of information is likely to be available in the marketplace without legal requirement. Some sorts of things are easily understandable. If the fruit looks good and smells good, for example, it is a fair bet that it also tastes good—but we may still want to regulate what pesticides can be used to grow the fruit. Similarly, a business dependent on repeat customers or a professional bound in various ways to meet certain standards of conduct may be trusted, to considerable extent, to provide good information. At least in the abstract, the idea that law should require different levels of information in different markets seems sensible.

Even within securities law, the general legal requirement that information be made available to the market is riddled with exceptions. So, as mentioned above, every public offering of shares must be preceded by filing a registration statement with the SEC, which makes the information contained therein available to the public. However, this requirement does not apply to offerings that are not public, that is, so-called private placements. An enormous body of law has grown up around the distinction between a public offering and a private placement, between a situation in which a company must make information available to the public and one in which it need not do so. The chestnut *SEC v. Ralston Purina* is instructive.[7] The feed company, Ralston Purina, had a benefits program pursuant to which its employees were issued stock in the company. The SEC maintained that this constituted a public offering within the meaning of the Securities Act of 1933, and therefore Ralston Purina needed to go through the expense of a formal filing with the SEC. For its part, Ralston Purina maintained that there was nothing public at issue. The company, a private entity, was issuing stock to its own employees, who were part of the entity, not the general public. In agreeing with the agency, the Supreme Court reasoned that the purpose of the securities law was to protect the public investor by making sure he had access to information. Rather than some abstract understanding of who simply was a member of the public, the Supreme Court asked instead who might be presumed to be well-informed. In a small and closely held corporation, the founder's friends and perhaps his family members and even employees could be presumed to be well-informed. In a large corporation such as Ralston Purina, the senior management could be presumed to be well-informed about the health and prospects of the company. But the ordinary employees of such a large corporation could not be expected to know what an investment in the company might mean, simply because they could not be expected to know how the company was situated in the marketplace. The Supreme Court thus held that the point of the Securities Act of 1933 was to require the provision of information to the investing public, and the public, circularly enough, was defined as those investors who needed to be protected by the law.

Conversely, it is unnecessary, and unnecessarily costly, to require as a matter of law that well-informed participants in the marketplace be further informed. So, for example, the venture capitalists who finance start-up companies in exchange for a substantial share of the equity, and usually a seat on the board, have little need for the information provided pursuant to the securities laws. They have the cash the venture needs to survive, and therefore are in a position to demand whatever information they deem relevant. Moreover, as well as being powerful insiders, they are wealthy enough to hire people, investment advisers, lawyers, accountants, and so forth, to help them make sound business decisions. They can buy information and other counsel. Although securities law requires information be provided gratis to retail investors, the proverbial little guys, venture capitalists are not little guys. They are capable of protecting themselves, and so do not need the protection of the securities laws. Again circularly enough, such actors must not be "the public" that the laws regulating publicly offered investments were designed to protect. Different markets, with different players, have different needs for laws requiring information.

Private placements are not the only exceptions to the rules designed to protect the public, nor are they the only exceptions to the general requirement that participants in the equity markets must make public disclosure of information relevant to investment. For example, the resale of certain restricted securities (which have not done filings, and about which information is generally not available) is prohibited, except to a "Qualified Institutional Buyer" (QIB) as defined by Rule 144A under the Securities Act of 1933. For another example, the rules of the National Association of Securities Dealers that govern the conduct of brokerage activities require brokers to "know your customer," and not to sell inappropriate securities, such as certain derivative products, to certain sorts of customer. If, however, the customer in question is an "Institutional Customer," then the broker-dealer has much wider latitude to sell. For a third example, a mutual fund is subject to a host of regulations, mostly under the Investment Adviser's Act of 1940 and the Investment Company Act of 1940. But a hedge fund, which at a certain level of abstraction serves the same economic function as a mutual fund (in both, an agent uses a pooling arrangement to make investments in accordance with a loosely agreed upon strategy for a minimum period of time), is generally exempt from the provisions of the laws and regulations governing mutual funds.[8]

One could multiply examples, but a pattern has emerged: through a web of laws designed to protect "the public," and exemptions from those laws for those economic actors who may be presumed to be able to protect themselves, the United States has created a market for securities that is in important respects two tiered. On what might be called the public tier, retail investors rely on publicly available information, that is, information is made available to the market as a matter of law. More broadly, the law regulates the context in which investments are made. On the other, what might be called the private, tier, accredited investors and other "sophisticated" (a disturbing euphemism for rich) actors rely on private information—on a market in information—to tell them what they need to know in order to invest, and they may invest across a broader range of products, under a broader array of conditions. Thus, on either tier, the market may be well-informed, but different political mechanisms (bureaucratic regulation on the one hand, and a market on the other) see to the provision of information.

In light of the success of the private tier, it is not entirely obvious why the law requires even publicly traded firms to register, that is, to provide the market with information. If information is property, then why should information not be distributed, like other forms of property, by a market? One might think that a market would distribute information more efficiently—with better incentives and less waste—than a government bureaucracy could ever mandate. Legal scholars have argued that people who need to know information should be willing to pay for it, thereby ensuring that the market remains sufficiently well-informed. That is, the supply of information available to investors should rise to meet the demand of investors. Who, better than investors, knows what information they need to make a sound investment decision? From this perspective, it is wasteful to have the government require that companies provide information to people who do not want it, generally in a relatively useless form, all those unread prospectuses, all those arcane filings. The securities laws already allow a market in information for sophisticated players, so why not abolish the public tier, and let ordinary investors participate in the market for information, and make their investments on that basis?

There are customary answers to this argument, voiced in various ways. For example, it has been argued that without requiring firms (that wish to raise money on the public equity markets) to provide information to the public, retail investors would have little access to such information, and little opportunity to verify it. Prudent investors might stay out of the market, lessening the depth and liquidity of the public securities markets. Those that did participate in the market would often be forced to operate on the basis of unverifiable statements, resulting in a (rational) lack of confidence, and associated volatility. As a result, the process of capital formation might be impeded. Another answer is that there are considerable transaction costs associated with establishing a market in information. Particularly in light of the fact that modern communications technology allows nearly costless reproduction of data, it may be less costly societally to impose the costs of providing information on firms (that wish to access the public equity markets) rather than disparate individuals, whose efforts would be duplicative and hence inefficient, or who might be deterred from investing at all, thereby restricting the liquidity of the market.

One could go on listing such arguments on either side of the debate over how law should require that information be provided to the securities market (there is a large professional "literature" on the topic), but for our purposes there is no need. The point here is not to determine why, when, how, or to what extent disclosure of privately held information would be a good idea, but to suggest the deeper structure of the arguments over disclosure. In order to do so, let us reexamine the differences between the public and private capital markets with a more appreciative eye.

Securities law requires a firm to disclose information only if the firm decides to raise capital by offering securities to the public. Firms that are content to raise capital on the private equity markets need not go through the considerable bother, delay, and expense of preparing and filing a registration statement. A firm's decision to go public reflects the fact that certain financings require the public markets. Otherwise, they would be done for less money on the private markets.[9] In back of the disjunction between public offering and private placement lie differences between the public and the private equity markets. The public market is deeper. The private market is more flexible. Certain sorts of financing are appropriately done on one tier; other financings are appropriately done on another tier.[10] The purpose of the two-tiered structure is to allow these two markets, which are far from completely discrete, to coexist.

The underlying reason to require disclosure—to make information on the public markets largely independent of the market for information—and the other measures through which securities law seeks to protect the investing public, is the learned belief that failure to require disclosure and take such measures would make the public equity markets like the private markets, that is, the exclusive and rather volatile realm of industry insiders, where retail investors journeyed at their peril. Wall Street circa 1928, in short. In addition to the legal expressions of this belief mentioned above, the SEC explicitly insists on the need to protect investor confidence, that transparency is vital to ensuring investor confidence, and that disclosure should be easily understandable. The SEC further believes that, at least in the public markets, every investor should have access to the same, public, information. So insider trading should be punished, because it undermines the idea that every market participant has a fair chance.[11] For the same reason, broker-dealers must be held to strict professional standards, so that any divergence of interest between the retail investor and the broker-dealer not be exploited by the broker-dealer. The commission has even discussed the idea of a "National Market System," a sort of massive real-time convergence of trading, in which each market participant has access to the best price for a given security available anywhere at that instant.[12] With these and similar positions, the SEC has cultivated an ideal of the public equity markets that are fair, in the legal (and sporting) sense of giving equal opportunity to each participant.

The ideal embodied by the private markets, in contrast, is different. Without cumbersome legal requirements for the provision and dissemination of information, opportunities can be exploited quickly and, at times importantly, discretely. This allows those with superior information to profit from their knowledge. More generally, a market in information—like that found in the private equity markets and sometimes urged for the public markets—necessarily puts investors in unequal positions.

Securities law thus turns on judgments of what the markets for stocks should be like. In its effort to foster one or another sort of market, securities policy turns on imagination of what sort of market is possible. There is certainly nothing natural about the two tiered structure of the U.S. equities markets—they result from a series of technical efforts to satisfy quite distinct goals, to realize quite distinct images of possible securities markets, and to channel actors toward the market believed to be appropriate for them. The same point has an explicitly political aspect. If the equity markets are a governance mechanism, it is reasonable to ask in what sort of government do we wish to participate. Securities law—considered as a practical species of political economy—asks not only what kind of society do we wish to achieve through markets, but also in what kind of government do we want to take part? We appear to have decided that we believe in broad-based participation in the market for corporate equities, fostered not only by disclosure, but by making disclosures in plain English, by making information available over the Internet, by allowing investment through mutual funds, by deferring and so in effect forgiving taxes on profits from retirement investments, and so forth. We also believe in limiting access to more volatile, but rewarding, investment markets. Such decisions are exercises in political aesthetics.[13]

Is the SEC, are any of the regulators active in the capital markets, right about their aspirations for the markets they are charged to regulate? Answering that question in responsible fashion is an undertaking beyond the scope of this chapter. A sound answer would require a nuanced understanding of the policy that a given regulator was trying to achieve, in a given context, with all the constraints imposed thereby. Even if undertaken with great care, such analysis would be questionable. If government, such as the legal structure of the capital markets, were different, presumably the decisions of such markets, and hence society, would be different as well. Reasoning about the likely consequences of this or that regulatory possibility is necessarily speculative, a sequence of ifs followed by guesses at thens. In part because we do not wholly comprehend our own regime and would not understand another either, the truth at issue here—the only truth that could be at issue—is whether or not the markets we have comports with the image of the markets that we believe we should have, whether we believe we have done a fair job of realizing our visions. For the purposes of this chapter, it suffices to demonstrate that the capital markets are regulated in an effort to realize a fundamentally aesthetic vision of how we are to govern ourselves through markets, and that this vision is supported by collective fictions, myths.

This essay, then, has come full circle. The effort to make government through markets true—to discipline markets by an external standard that comports with our own sense of truth, thereby relieving the sense of alienation—has led us back toward whatever truth may be possible through market participation. To recapitulate: we began by noting that government through markets cannot be true, that participation in markets is alienated, most fundamentally because the translation of language into price and the world into property is a reduction that destroys much of what it is to be human. The human response to being condemned to live in such a society is to experience life as an exile from her true home, that is, she is alienated. The response of political economy to such alienation—once the pretensions of classical economics are abandoned—is to ask practical, teleological, questions about what is possible. In our example, even while conceding that Olympian truth is not possible, the securities laws nonetheless insist that we need not tolerate fraud and prescribe fairly onerous requirements for the provision of information. Certain actors, however, are exempted from certain requirements. In deciding what information needs to be provided, under what circumstances, and by whom, regulators—perforce political economists—transform the market, treating it as an objective, rather than an assumption, of politics. Political economy thus becomes constitutional, not only in trying to shape society through markets, but in deciding what sort of market participation will be made available, that is, what a good government through markets might be, a government that one might naively hope would be so popular, even loved, that its inhabitants would not be alienated.

*   *   *

Political economy—public-minded reasoning about the interaction of private interests—is a circular and so self-contradictory pursuit, the principled intention to make principled intention unnecessary, the considered effort to achieve a politics that relies on the self-interest of individual economic actors in lieu of the thoughtful political consensus of citizens. This contradiction is most acute in the jurisprudence of economic law. On the one hand, markets are informed by enormous amounts of highly self-conscious articulations—law. The inchoate aggregations of the market are comprised of rights in contexts constituted by the highly articulated processes of the law. And yet such actors are responding to law that, as discussed in the last section, is not independent of the market, but instead embodies some image of the market. Of course, to begin circling again, that image does not arise in a vacuum, but instead necessarily owes its debts to experience in markets, a government's view of economic history.

Until quite recently, this tension between law and market, mind and interest, principle and desire, was understood to be manageable by institutional division of labor, by the distance that separated the public sector, the province of government bureaucrats, from the private sector, the terrain of businessfolk. In the City of Gold, however, the distinction between public and private has become very blurry. If we understand markets to be a form of government, as we do, then we understand markets as public mechanisms. If, on the other hand, we understand the purpose of much of government to be the shaping of markets, as we do, then the conduct of politics turns on our collective imagination of what is appropriate for private life. The distinction between public and private may seem to be no longer useful, hopelessly old-fashioned, destroyed by the circularity required in order to do political economy.

Yet some notion of public and private seems indispensable to political economy. Without any such notion, how could one discuss the relative merits of one policy—one sort of market—vis-à-vis another policy, another market, and so another, slightly different, world? Any such discussion presumes the possibility of principled argument, argument that may be compelling even when it is against one's own self-interest. And yet the object of a discussion in political economy is a market, whose participants are presumably governed by their perceptions of their own self-interest. As with the idea of "truth," we who live in a market society seem unable to dispense with or entirely believe in the bifurcation between public and private.

Public and private are still useful categories for thought, but they must be used with more care than public discourse generally does. The left has often tried to argue that the personal, especially domestic and social, aspects of life are matters for political disputation, and so public. For its part, the right has often tried to define issues, such as concern for the environment or the welfare of others, in terms of the aggregation of private interests, and so in some important way private. One might therefore think that both left and right have sought to abolish the distinction between public and private. This would be too easy. The left has also often insisted on privacy, that is, insisted on the inviolability of certain liberties, private spaces in which the state does not tread. Similarly, the right has often declared that certain ideas, such as property rights and the opinions of like-minded economists, should be adopted by the public and written into law. Thus left and right tend speak as if a given area of human intercourse can objectively be described as either public or private, as if "a woman's right to choose," or "a man's right to bear arms" *just is* private, or public, as the case may be.

The spatial imagery of public and private obfuscates by implying that spheres of human activity are so recognizable, that is, inherently are one sort of social arrangement (governed in one sort of way) and not the other sort (governed in the other sort of way). If one insists on a map of human activity, one might think about the border between Germany and France, political conclusions regarding the appropriate label for certain pieces of land. Such conclusions often change in the course of history. Nothing about the soil makes the political category of German or French automatic; there is nothing magic in the way Karl der Grosse/Charlemagne's empire was divided. Similarly, the spatial imagery with which we discuss public and private should not be allowed to obscure the fact that "public" and "private" are labels used to describe how certain people regard certain activities, that is, they are political conclusions about the governance of activities, not objective descriptions of the activities themselves, upon which one might premise a political argument.[14]

Which is not to say, as many in the legal academy do, that the distinction between public and private is dispensable.[15] At this juncture, and insofar as we remain committed to any form of liberalism, it would be really strange (totalitarian or anarchistic) to believe that politics should resolve the tension between public and private by abolishing one or the other. Public and private entail one another. There is no way that private can somehow be redefined as public, any more than down (the gut or the groin) can be redefined as up (the brain). Conversely, it does no good to deny that the public exists, that private interest can be understood—or even discussed—without regard to the public. Rather than denominating preexisting spaces in which this or that activity naturally occurs, public and private should instead be understood in opposition to one another, as directions for politics broadly construed. A given political action may bring some area of life under the aegis of certain institutions that feel more public, or a different set of institutions that feel more private: the question is the direction of politics.

So understood, the conceptions of public and private can help us argue over political questions: should a given activity be considered more or less public, and therefore governed by certain mechanisms? "Political questions" is here meant rather narrowly, questions to be determined collectively and with regard to particular things in the course of time, that is, through history (not to be answered by abstract appeal to some principle). Resolving such questions from among countless possibilities, finding a modus vivendi among mechanisms that aspire to mind and mechanisms that apportion individual satisfaction, is one of the vital processes through which a culture comes to be what it is. And so the ruling class of the City of Gold must perpetually confront, as ongoing political and hence legal tasks, the question of what activities should be governed by markets, and what should be governed by some other mechanism, and the requisite details . . .

Political economy thus understood is hardly intellectually elegant, no more than an incessant and self-consciously ignorant effort to imagine what might be done, and to do something that can be imagined in light of what has been done already. In place of achieved categories such as Aristotle might have used, we have teleology only in the sense implied by the word's roots in foot races, a movement toward, a process of becoming. But we are free, indeed required, to reset the stakes every morning, altering the course of the day's races. Instead of public and private mechanisms, we speak of more public or more private mechanisms, just as we should speak of true enough for good government, as we presently imagine it . . . all too aware of the circularities. Political economy so imagined does not understand markets simply as objects to be studied, about which true things may be said. No such pure truth is available. Nor does it understand markets as objects of the will, which may be handled in moral ways. No such pure liberty is available, either. Instead, life as constrained and enabled by markets is a constant renegotiation between assumption and objective. Such renegotiation aims to ensure that price reflects if not true value, at least not fraud, and so property is disposed of tolerably well.

Nothing in this essay has refuted the fundamental objections to politics through markets raised earlier, that property and money simply do not have resources to say much about the human condition. What markets do say about the human condition is rather base, necessary and sometimes pleasurable, but base nonetheless. Markets are unlikely to be true in any satisfactory sense for the same reason that the higher faculties of mind never convince the lower that principled thought does not erase self-interest, that democracy fails, and that love does not cure lust. If the criterion by which we judge our politics is truth, and the failure to achieve a public truth engenders that species of unhappiness known as alienation, then political economy has no cure for markets, and the inhabitants of market societies are doomed to be alienated.

Yet there is an immodesty about this insistence on truth. At least in self-consciously epistemological discourse, we no longer require (if we ever did) that even good writing simply be true. As has been clear at least since Plato, truth is glimpsed, not possessed, and almost impossible to state. Nor can we seriously have hoped that law, particularly something as arcane as securities law, can structure political mechanisms in such a way as to provide relief from our sense of alienation. After all, nothing is more alienating than the law—Kafka's law is perhaps our most important image of alienation. So we cannot honestly be surprised when the institutions of supranational capitalism, like any communicative speech of such broad reach, only fleetingly if ever are felt to be true, felt to be home. Our alienation is here to stay, and political economy should not be expected to somehow rejigger markets in order to solve that unease.

If our expectation to know were more modest, we might regard even contemporary political economy as true enough, in its way and such as it is. And so, even though we have only the haziest idea of what such actions might mean, we might watch with equanimity, maybe even a degree of bemusement, as economic policy is executed. We might appreciate the moment when the Chairman of the Federal Reserve moves interest rates one way or another, when regulators require truthful but unread disclosures, or when financial institutions spin apart and merge. Instead of a failure to cure alienation by convincing us of their objective rightness, we might find these and similar examples of the conflicted state of political economy— self-consciously obsessed with its partial truths—to be a most sympathetic reflection of our own state of alienation. We might find thinking about political economy to be a strangely dualistic and unsettling enterprise: the (necessarily general and somewhat abstract) problems of politics—how to imagine people happily living together—are impelled by the desire to solve the (necessarily intimate and hence ill-focused) problems of one's own life in community, of finding oneself at home. We would then regard political economy as true, albeit only in a contingent and critical sense, not altogether unlike the sense in which the experience of alienation is true. Rather than contempt, perhaps we can regard the City with gentle irony.

If we lower our expectation that we are somehow owed truth by markets, and hence are less disappointed when markets fail to deliver on the truth, we might be able to position ourselves a certain critical distance from markets, some distance between servitude to market sovereignty and the exile that is alienation. This is not an ideologically comfortable stance. Positions drawn on such middle ground—the no-man's land between conflicting camps—are difficult to define or defend on their own terms, without reference to the certitudes of the opposing camps. Proselytizers for the truth of markets will continue to urge a sort of servility, while critics of markets will continue to point out that markets are untrue and hence illegitimate. But from the middle ground we may be able to draw distinctions, and perhaps even philosophize.

The middle ground is also the terrain of political jokes. After all, a regime that does not speak the truth—as the City of Gold cannot—risks delegitimation, even if no practical alternative to the regime exists. This can be denied (as the right does), or treated solemnly and unpleasantly, as alienation (the preferred stance of the left). But a bit of delegitimation may render that regime light, something of a joke. As Milan Kundera has lived through and worked out twice, first in communist Eastern Europe, then again in France, one need not be so earnest about bad government. We too may come to find funny—if perhaps sometimes darkly so—our efforts at governance. Financial regulation, the efforts to structure capital markets so that a healthy postnational polity arises of its own accord will continue to produce a wealth of hilarious incongruities, and we should try to laugh, for example at Jeffrey Skilling, CEO of Enron, who claimed shortly before the then biggest bankruptcy in U.S. history that the company was "laser focused on earnings."[16]

So, now that we have solved the problem of truth, it is time to turn to the problem of how to think about political order—that which is disturbed by and renewed through comedy—in a society constructed by markets.

CHAPTER XIII

Orderly Markets

Synchronic order in markets and the image of the bargaining table. U.S. policy regarding foreign exchange markets. Diachronic order in markets and the image of the house of cards. Monetary policy. Impossibility of money. Monetary policy as sublimation of war.

Unless we define justice to be synonymous with success in the marketplace, there is no reason to think that markets will produce outcomes consistent with whatever set of propositions we believe constitute justice, except partially, on happy days. But we cannot give up on justice altogether. Political thought, including a concern for justice, is required even for this society, which is constructed on markets and therefore doomed to a degree of inauthenticity. But how are we to think about justice without succumbing to the currently popular delusion that the outcome of the markets are, ipso facto, just, and that we therefore have neither problem nor responsibility?

The last chapter argued that though it is foolish to rely on markets for truth, one might nonetheless attempt to avoid lies. In order to reach a modest truthfulness in market affairs, that essay suggested the employment of a sequence of pragmatic and loosely teleological distinctions, organized by an aesthetic sense of what a particular market ought to be. The essay concluded that this enterprise was bound to indefinite failures, that we would continue to be surrounded by untruths, lies, and other infelicities, to which the best response, if we can manage it, is bemusement and another try. It is this bemusement—gentle irony—that is the starting point for this essay's consideration of justice. Humor rests on incongruity, a disjunction between our idealized picture of how the world should be and our actual experience (which is why even outright injustice is often funny, even if often desperately so). To suggest, as the last chapter did, that we find life in the City bemusing is to assume, even if implicitly, a vision of social order. This essay seeks to make these implicit ideas of order a bit more explicit, to examine the order of marketplace relations, synchronically and diachronically, using the familiar imagery of the bargaining table and the house of cards. Although it may be too much to hope that markets will generate the just society, this chapter proposes that we may understand markets in terms of their own order. Insofar as we understand markets on their own terms, markets may appear genuine to us, if still limited.

The image of the bargaining table elegantly expresses some very fundamental ideas, yet the familiarity of the image can make those ideas hard to discern. To reconsider the metaphor literally, bargaining tables are pieces of furniture over which negotiations happen. In such negotiations, each side gives something to the other side, in exchange for something else, a what for what, quid pro quo, across the table. After a bit of reflection, this may seem to be an awkward metaphor for markets, at least for some important markets. Unless one has a certain rather specialized job, such as a diplomat, a commercial lawyer, or a labor mediator, one rarely enters into formal negotiations over a table. Instead of negotiated bargains, one might tend to imagine markets in terms of consumer transactions, in which one party exchanges cash or a close equivalent, such as a check, in return for a consumer good. And yet the absence of explicit negotiations does not mean that buyers and sellers do not need to reach agreement about what each will surrender in exchange for what the other surrenders. We understand buying and selling to be voluntary acts, at least in the sense that nobody orders one to buy or sell. We also understand markets to be competitive, that is, to offer alternatives.[1] The "negotiation" between a grocery store and its shoppers may be understood as an argument, made by the store in question, that it offers better value (however value may be defined) than the grocery store's competition. If the store is successful, the customer buys, contributing to the grocery store's survival. If the grocery store is unsuccessful, the customer goes elsewhere. This process of reaching agreement, even without explicit negotiation, is also evident in the financial markets, where buyers and sellers unknown to one another bid and ask through intermediary institutions until agreement is reached. To understand markets on the metaphor of the bargaining table, then, is to understand markets as the effort to reach agreement among interests that compete within a context or frame, or, in language often used by lawyers, arguments over the disposition of what is "on the table," conducted in terms that are themselves "off the table."

To continue being simpleminded, what is on the table, always and by definition, is the property of the parties, that which one party has control of and can convey in exchange for that something else, also property, to be conveyed by the other party. In the case of grocery shopping, the consumer has the right to control cash, which is exchanged at the register for the right to carry the celery outside the store. The property on the table may be rights in various instruments that we may more usually understand as money. So, for example, one can imagine a stock plus cash acquisition of a company, in which the owners of the acquired company surrender their voting stock in exchange for a new issue of stock in the acquiring company, plus a certain amount of cash, perhaps raised through a separate bond offering, or better still, raised via a commercial loan syndicated among a consortium of foreign banks, each adequately hedged against currency fluctuations. While there is no theoretical limit on the contractual complexity of a financing, the nuances with which the properties exchanged are understood does nothing to affect the fundamental point that in any market transaction, one set of rights (collectively, property) is exchanged for another set of rights (also property), pursuant to an agreement.[2] If one party is forced or chooses to convey a property unilaterally, such as under a court order or by gift or via a will, the conveyance may be legal but it is not a market transaction.

If specific properties are always at issue in a transaction, property itself—the legal institution—generally is *not* on the table. Proponents of using market mechanisms to address social issues without exception argue that government should establish and protect the institution of private property. Expropriation is bad because it dissuades people from acting in the marketplace. Parties who know what they own can strike deals; it is far harder for parties who are uncertain about what each owns to reach agreement. Consequently, argue market enthusiasts, the institution of property should be held above the fray of politics. Once expectations about the nature of property are established, they should be fulfilled. Even at this level of analysis (which is as deep as such enthusiasts generally are inclined to go), property has two quite distinct meanings: first, property is a concrete instantiation of a legal institution, the legal rights to some thing (on the table), and second, property is an institutional context that is presumed by market participants (and therefore off the table).

Lest there be confusion, it is worth reiterating that the bargaining table under discussion here is a metaphorical image. Obviously and as discussed, transactions occur without explicit negotiations, much less over tables. Nor is there any logically a priori reason that any particular aspect of a transaction be "on the table," that is, contested between the parties, and others be "off the table," that is, assumed by both parties. What the image of the table concretizes is a different and a bit elusive (hence the need for metaphor) aspect of trade. Every transaction entails some interplay between context and action, ground and table, between the rules and the game, between what is off the table and what is on. Without such an interplay, there can be no market transaction.

Like property, "contract" has a dual meaning, and is both on and off the table. On the one hand, the contract is the collectivity of everything on the table. In a sale of moveable property for cash, for example, the parties must reach agreement on the price of an item. Other aspects of the transaction—method and time of payment, method and time of delivery, condition of the item at delivery, penalties for default, the list is potentially endless—may also be negotiated. If such negotiations lead to a contract, then the resolution of such negotiations becomes binding, and those aspects of the deal may be understood in terms of rights conveyed between the parties. Achieved contracts therefore may be expressed as transfers of property rights, and property rights are what is haggled over—on the table—in a market transaction.[3]

At the same time, a regime of contract law—like a regime of property law—is a prerequisite for functioning markets, and hence off the table. Markets presume contract law in ways that parallel the presumption of property law, and with similar normative implications. Only if contracts are believed to be legally enforceable will parties obligate themselves; the parties' willingness to participate in a given transaction depends on their confidence in the system of contract law. Markets are collections of transactions, and without transactions there can be no market. Therefore, in order to foster the development of healthy markets, governments need to secure the existence of a stable regime of contract law. Common practical proposals for achieving such a regime include the establishment of an independent and highly professionalized judiciary; a prejudice in favor of the enforcement of contracts as written, as opposed to legislative efforts to specify the terms on which parties may contract; and the enforcement or even wholesale importation of sophisticated contract law and resolution procedures (often by express reference to London or New York). In short, the establishment of markets requires a state to take the institution of contract out of the hands of the parties, off the table.

The distinction between a negotiation's assumptions, which are off the table, and its objectives, which are on the table, not only reiterates but requires the abstract distinction between public and private, and between state and civil society.[4] To understand the state as necessitated by market interaction, however, amounts to no more than an excavation of the social contract imagery that stands at the beginning of modern political thought. The state is necessary to secure entitlements, to prevent the stronger from robbing the weaker and the weaker from killing the stronger in their sleep, that is, to prevent chaos. Individuals enter the social contract (grant rights to and thereby create a sovereign) in exchange for peace. In the language used above, by granting the sovereign a near monopoly on the use of force, individuals take certain tasks "off the table." Private individuals in civil society do not expect to secure their possession of their property, nor are private individuals expected to enforce contracts. Such matters are the concern of the state, leaving private individuals at peace and liberty to make more sophisticated contracts, to secure ever more elaborate social arrangements, and collectively, to erect civil society.[5]

In understanding law as the formal articulation of the society's assumptions, leaving markets to negotiate in the context established by law, we understand law and the market to be synchronous rather than sequential aspects of social life. In this view, markets are not an alternative to law, because there is no negotiation without a context. Thus it is nonsensical to argue, as financial market enthusiasts are wont to do, that government action is a last resort, to be used only in important instances of market failure. Law—which in the absence of a publicly available tradition or religion, strongly implies the institutions of the state—is always already present in markets. To be fair, what proselytizers for "the market" (as if there were one, like the Holy Grail) usually really mean is that they would like matters to be decided by competitive bidding rather than bureaucratic or forensic or other processes, that is, through pricing property interests rather than through other political mechanisms. But such arguments employ radical simplifications of a much more complex reality. Actual markets—for example, for corporate equities in a manufacturing company in the United States—take place with due regard for a host of nonmarket processes, including the fiduciary duties of directors and management imposed by state law, perhaps backed by the litigious processes of the Delaware Chancellor; the regulations of the SEC, OSHA, the EPA, and other federal and state agencies; customary law of accounting, particularly as it may be incorporated into the law of the foregoing agencies; the structures of highly regulated financial institutions; markets in the supplies, labor, capital, and products of such a company, each of which presumes its own property law regime and a web of legally enforceable contracts . . . the market in such shares cannot be understood except in a context that includes a host of institutions, processes, and laws we associate with the convenient but rather imprecise term "government."

Which is not to say that the choice of political mechanism does not matter. Society may and indeed should decide that certain matters should be governed by markets, that is, through the aggregation of individual interests rather than by reference to either a publicly available truth (the idealized outcome of democratic debate imagined in most enlightened terms) or even the will of the sovereign (whether or not democratically legitimated) less rationally understood.[6] But the question should not be stated so simply: the issue is what precisely is to be on the table, negotiated, and what is to be off the table, assumed, and ultimately, law? While the image of the bargaining table can provide some understanding of the symbiotic relationship between market and nonmarket mechanisms, and even some inkling that the state is what the market is not, the imagery does not specify the division between the market and the state. Rephrased, the imagery helps us understand the difference between public and private, and even why such distinctions are continually drawn, but does not tell us what should be considered public and what private.

So, for example, property may be defined in countless ways. The endless academic efforts to provide a doctrinally satisfying and somehow final law of takings presumes it is possible to discern, or at least argue for, "the" necessary division between state and civil society, between regulation and private property. Since no single such division exists, academics are free to continue proposing divisions, and courts must continue declaring, with each judgment, where the division is with respect to the case before it. Although a fairly stable tradition may be discerned, such divisions may be redrawn as new circumstances present themselves. Similarly, the scope in which contracts may be made is continually reconfigured, not just through the renewal of contract law, but also through shifts in regulation. And, as discussed in the previous chapter, there is no logically necessary reason that the law requires certain sorts of information to be provided in certain sorts of situations and not in others. Different sorts of property, or contract, or information, and conversely, what a given market trades, constitute the market in question, give it a particular shape and not another.

Different sorts of markets produce different sorts of outcomes, and over time, influence their societies in different ways. So it matters, for example, that corporate finance in Germany has traditionally been done through large banks, which often have seats on the boards of companies to which they lend, and that such finance has traditionally been done through the securities markets in the United States, with their quarterly reporting requirements. German and American business differ in character in part because of the cultural and regulatory structures that inform their financing, and thus their governance, their corporate culture, and their respective commercial societies, in each of which business plays a large role. To understand the politics of a market society, whether the United States, Germany, or the City of Gold as a whole, it is important but quite preliminary—completely insufficient—to note that social arrangements are governed through market mechanisms. The obvious line of inquiry is to ask for specifics: What kinds of markets govern what, and how?

The continually available possibility of a different configuration of a society's markets, a different set of items on or off the table, means that the markets are an occasion for, rather than an answer to, the political question of whether a given market should be structured in some other way.

Phrased institutionally, should regulation change the character of property entitlements or transactions in order to generate somewhat different outcomes? Moreover, as also discussed in the preceding chapter, markets are constitutional mechanisms in another, very literal sense: markets entail procedures that constitute their societies, thus participation in such markets is a form of political participation. We may reasonably ask ourselves in what sort of markets do we wish to do business, wish to become men and women in gray flannel suits, wish to be citizens? Understanding how particular markets function leads to social criticism, that is, leads us to ask in what regard the City is not well governed, and how improvement might be possible. Markets are not authorities, they are tasks.

∗   ∗   ∗

The foreign exchange markets, especially during crises such as those of the late 1990s, demonstrate just how difficult it is to think about markets as political mechanisms, as opposed to thinking of markets as an alternative to politics. The question appears simple: Should the value of money be considered the context for economic transaction, that is, be off the table, like the institutions of property and contract? Or should the value of money be on the table, that is, should parties to transactions trade in the value of currency?

The U.S. government implicitly takes both positions on this issue. Domestically, the United States maintains that the dollar should be stable, that is, that microeconomic decisions should be made with little regard for fluctuations in the exchange value of the dollar. The reasoning for this position is simple enough: economic transactions ought to take place, or not, on the basis of the fundamental values at issue in the transaction, not on the basis of speculation about the value of the currency used to facilitate the transaction. From this perspective, economic well-being is best served by price stability, or, phrased more negatively, inflation (and deflation not attributable to technological improvement or other benign causes) can inhibit growth by making it difficult for economic actors to plan.[7] Internationally, however, the United States has for some years—and with great energy in the '90s—maintained that currency should be freely tradable, that is, the value of currency should be on the table in a transnational transaction, an issue to be negotiated among the participants to a transaction. This represents a major, if unacknowledged, shift in U. S. foreign policy. During its participation in the gold standard, and explicitly through the construction of the Bretton Woods currency arrangement, the United States, along with other participants, subscribed to the view that cross-border transactions were best conducted with little regard to currency risk. At some point after the breakdown of the Bretton Woods system, however, U.S. foreign policy on this not unimportant question directly and almost completely reversed itself. Despite several decades of considerable success with the Bretton Woods regime, U.S. foreign policy began to encourage other governments to allow trade in their currencies. The United States went from advocating free trade in goods and services, in the context of relatively stable exchange rates, to advocating free trade, including free trade in currency. Indeed, free trade in currency was understood to be just like free trade in other commodities.

It is not clear that the United States took this decision in any particularly thoughtful, or even conscious, fashion. This is somewhat surprising. The United States in particular had been arguing for decades that healthy markets were the appropriate way to organize free societies, and that healthy markets required stable property, contract, and monetary regimes. Somehow, with hardly a murmur, the United States reversed its position on money and thereby reversed its position on what a market ought to be. Instead of belonging off the table, with property and contract law, the value of currency was suddenly held to belong on the table. So encouraged, the currency markets quickly became the largest—measured by value of trades—of all markets in the world.

Once the relative value of currencies was on the table, ordinary cross-border transactions became more complicated. Consider a shipment of French wine sold to the United States and paid for in dollars. In a stable monetary regime, the parties must consider how much the wine is worth vis-à-vis the supply in France and the demand in the United States, competition from California and other wine growing regions, to say nothing of the usual difficulties with transport and storage and distribution and marketing and so forth, that is, the circumstances of the business. Without a stable monetary regime, however, parties must also consider how much the dollars in which payment is made are likely to be worth vis-à-vis the francs (and now Euro) required by the producer. Currency risk means every real world transaction, here a sale of wine, is accompanied by a financial world transaction. (This is made explicit by the modern practice of buying currency hedges in the financial markets.) There is no reason, however, to expect people in the wine industry to know, good though they may be at their business, how to gauge currency risk. Or consider a shipment of U.S. goods to Mexico, Russia, Indonesia, Brazil, Korea, or Japan, and paid for in local currency. To what extent is such a transaction dependent on reaching agreement about the fundamental value of the goods, and to what extent is it dependent on agreement over the tendency of the currencies during the course of the deal? At the very least, currency fluctuations complicate real-world transactions.

At a certain level of abstraction, the value of money was not a new problem that arose in the 1970s, once it became clear that the Bretton Woods arrangement had collapsed and would not be restored. As was discussed at length in part 1, dollars, even under the Bretton Woods arrangement, even under the gold standard, never had a fundamental value extrinsic to the community in which they were acceptable. Any money, even gold, is a political expression, the meaning and function of which depends on a community that values such expressions. In this abstract sense, we might say that some degree of currency risk writ large, that is, the chance that the currency fails to perform as expected, or even altogether, is simply a concomitant of money payment. Such abstraction, however, misses at least three important reasons that currency risk is particularly important in the City.

First, as a practical matter, businessfolk are forced to consider the salient features of a deal. Bandwidth is limited, and many aspects of a deal must be assumed. There is a big difference between assuming the quality of the currency and simply negotiating its quantity, on the one hand, and negotiating both its quantity and quality, on the other. By way of analogy, property, like money, is defined politically, and therefore, as progressives have never tired of reminding us, contestable. Very few transactions in common law jurisdictions, however, hinge on reaching agreement over the meaning of fee simple estate in land. We may not be certain we *know*, as a matter of jurisprudence, what a fee simple estate is, but we are quite comfortable buying and selling such estates.[8] Similarly, no contract is certain until it is litigated, but that does not put the institution of contract on the table for most transactions. So while it is true that, as a theoretical matter, every transaction involving property, contracts, and money is subject to a degree of mystery and hence uncertainty, as a practical matter, such uncertainties are largely ignored in the ordinary course of doing business. In a world of volatile exchange rates, however, currency risk cannot be ignored—it may become a deal breaker. The abandonment of stable exchange rates has thus injected an enormous amount of practical uncertainty into doing business across borders.

Second, currency fluctuations undermine the political efficacy of markets. Consider the account orthodox liberal economics gives of how markets function: competition serves to reward good companies and punish bad companies, resulting, over time, in improvement of the breed. A currency crisis, however, can punish companies without regard to microeconomic fundamentals, that is, can slaughter both the sheep and the goats. A well-managed company in a country whose currency is devalued may well go out of business. In a globalized capital market, the virtuous actor can be swamped, and price discovery may be rendered impossible, by fluctuation of the currency.

Third, within the Western political tradition, and particularly in the United States, we have tended to see government power in the terms suggested by Lord Acton's famous dictum that power corrupts, and absolute power corrupts absolutely. Corruption, it has seemed too obvious to belabor, means that power seeks to aggrandize itself, that the powerful seek more power, moving forward like sharks until they die. The practical problem for political thought, then, has been to design institutional barriers to such aggrandizement. But now we see governments abdicating one of their traditional roles, the control over the value of money. The present danger appears to be government's abdication of responsibility, rather than aggrandizement. The rhetoric about the awesome power of markets is exculpatory; what blame can accrue to a mere government? The internationalization of the culture of financial regulation and the hope that, with proper transparency, markets can police themselves, imply that nobody is responsible. There is no reason to believe the buck stops anywhere. Currency markets thus may provide a convenient excuse for bad government.[9]

It is possible that the extreme volatility of the '90s—at least in the foreign exchange markets—will ameliorate. More and more governments are abandoning monetary policy altogether, either through dollarization, currency boards, or through creating larger currencies, most notably the Euro. More fundamentally still, in a world of nearly frictionless trade, nearly perfect and perfectly uniform and instantaneous information, and widely available hedging, the opportunity for arbitrage (at least among established currencies) ought to be vanishingly small. Depressingly, however, this Friedmanesque vision of equilibrium in the sweet by and by has been the theory for some time. Although this comforting vision serves, albeit incongruously, to structure remarks at conferences devoted to volatility, actual volatility (particularly intraday volatility) of both currency and equities has been increasing for some time. Bets among currencies remain important, and so long as that is the case, the argument that global financial markets do a good job of regulating the real economy will be difficult to sustain in any fine-grained sense.

At least for now, currency risk creates uncertainty, interferes with the market's regulation of the real economy, and provides an excuse for the irresponsibility of some states. History resolves and sometimes even teaches, but the solutions may be unpleasant and there is no guarantee that the lessons will be learned in time or at all. Maybe one of those lessons is that the current regime for the trade in money is less than ideal.

* * *

Having abandoned the hopes that market society be authentic (chapter VII), or that markets produce just results, that is, some stable relationship between price and a vision of justice (chapter X), this essay has tried to suggest how we could nonetheless understand markets as orderly environments, true at least to their own natures, and where we might pursue our interests. Nothing in this essay has refuted the charge with which we began, that market society, founded as it is on jealousy over the right to exclude, misses much of human life, and particularly the longing for justice. Instead of addressing this charge directly, this essay has lowered the sights, and used the imagery of the bargaining table to understand markets in terms of negotiations, bargains, contracts. From this perspective, one might regard markets as contexts in which much is inherited or assumed, but also as contexts in which much can be done. That is, we may come to regard markets as scientists sometimes urge to us to regard the natural world, a matrix of indifferent and objective forces, neither pitiless nor generous, but on its very limited terms, authentic.[10]

And yet even this limited appreciation of market order is troubling. Markets require construction in a way that nature does not. While the extent to which it makes sense to understand nature in objective or determinable terms is perhaps not entirely clear, it is quite clear that markets cannot be understood without vast human complicity. Even at the heart of the market, the decision of how to construct the market appears unjustified, open to challenge, although it is always already answered by history. We always find the bargaining table, but can answer neither why we should assume what we have been taught to assume nor what is to be negotiated. So we cannot really appreciate markets as we do nature. Nature is made by God, or nobody, but in either case there is little to be criticized. Markets, in contrast, are constructions all too human.[11]

The political objection to the order of the marketplace can neither be silenced—markets are in fact human constructions, for which humans are responsible—nor be satisfied—we must cope with history, we cannot choose it. And so this essay's rather long pursuit of the possibility of a joke has led us to an impasse: markets make sense, but only on their own very limited terms. If we adopt the ironic perspective of the critic, however, the market presents itself as ridiculous rather than authoritative: the *Wall Street Journal* makes for very, very funny reading. We may contemplate life in the marketplace with an ironic smile at what might have been otherwise. We know better. The railroad track could have been placed elsewhere in the forest. History does in fact constrain us, but at least as an intellectual matter, we know that our situation has always been a matter of doubt and mischance rather than logical necessity.

It is difficult to see, however, how the realization that "things could have been otherwise," the predicate for ironic jokes, helps us to formulate an idea of how society should be, a normative ideal that could inform our thinking about justice in the marketplace. If we want to think about justice, we need a more regulative ideal of order. Perhaps day to day life—common sense—can provide such a baseline. In the daily work life of the City, contexts are inherited successfully, that is, we do find the table. Most people have to work, and therefore take their environment seriously and at face value. Few citizens are often at leisure to indulge an ironic attitude to their environments. Intentional humor in the financial press is limited to the human interest stories. Markets continually represent themselves as given. This is promising: perhaps thinking about how common life (habit, and in that sense, history) bequeaths us markets, which in our turn we must simultaneously accept and reform, can help us to find an attitude toward markets a bit more nourishing than irony. Perhaps thinking historically can help us forge an idea of justice useful for judging the politics generated by markets, and so help us think about the construction of markets. And so we turn from the bargaining table to the house of cards, from synchronic to diachronic imagery of the order of market societies.

* * *

Justice has long been understood diachronically. Justice, one remembers from Babylon, is an eye for an eye . . . an effort to restore the world. Although we may quarrel with the ancient arithmetic, we still often consider justice as a restoration, a correction, putting things back in their proper place. So, for example, criminal law traditionally is said to serve four purposes, each of which illustrate our not very deeply buried temporal approach to the problem of justice. The purposes are retribution, rehabilitation, and restitution, that is, three of the purposes of criminal law explicitly refer to the order that the criminal act has disturbed. (The fourth purpose is deterrence, that is, protection of the current order from further disruption.) Does the fact that we experience both markets and justice in terms of a prior order suggest some way that we can experience markets as just? Our ideas about justice, and our understanding of property, both reflect our fondness for our inherited world, quite literally, our prejudice. Why, then, do we not understand the distribution of property to be just? Why does the past not serve the markets as a justification and ideal, as it appears to serve the criminal law?

One reason is that the temporality of the law that configures our markets is not the simple past implied in the foregoing caricature of the purposes of criminal justice.

As discussed in chapter III, financial markets are about creating or surviving tomorrow's world, not restoring the order of yesterday or even maintaining the situation we find ourselves in today. Market activity is intended to change things. A financing is an effort to make deals with time, to exchange money now for more money (or less risk, in the case of insurance) later, to come out ahead in the passage of time. The vital assumption of any financing is that the future can be better than it would be in the absence of the financing. In this situation money is a tool—or a weapon—with which we bend the future to our will. This is explicit in areas of the law (antitrust, intellectual property, and the effort to ensure free trade spring to mind) that justify their existence by explicit reference to an ideal of progress.[12]

Understanding financial markets simultaneously in terms of the future of finance and in terms of the inherited assumptions with which we began, in terms, that is, of both hope and constraint, is only a beginning. We give little serious thought—almost no jurisprudential thought—to the temporal narratives that organize our political arguments, and hence our laws, and hence our markets. So, for examples, progress is served by competition among firms (if one is an antitrust aficionado), or progress (the same progress?) is served by the right to exclude others from making, using or selling one's ideas (if one believes in intellectual property), or progress (?) leads to environmental degradation (if one believes in the competing and antiprogressive ideal of nature) and so forth and so on. Temporal notions structure political argument, but little attention is paid to the temporal claims that are implicitly made.

The great practical example of self-consciously using markets to regulate the making of history is monetary policy. If the economy appears to be rushing along too quickly, "shows signs of overheating," then central banks tighten the money supply, thereby exorcising the successively more fearsome demons of inflation, correction, and crash. Conversely, in recessionary or simply boring times, there are calls (often by those interested in the welfare of the less fortunate) for a looser monetary policy, that is, an effort to speed the pace at which financings flow, and as a result, material progress happens. Central banks are thus the bureaucracies whose portfolio is how fast we progress, and in that sense, history in the making.

Monetary policy relies on control over the money supply, which might seem to require an answer to the antecedent question, what is money? As should by now be clear, the money supply simply cannot be defined with any precision. A partial, and for some time workable, solution to the problem has been to raise the price of holding money, at least some forms of money, by manipulating certain interbank interest rates, and by open market interventions (the buying and selling of currency). Central banks thereby adjust the ease with which money can be borrowed, and limit—or encourage—bank financings at the margin, as well as economic confidence more generally. So, if inflation appears to be the problem, that is, money looks to be getting cheaper vis-à-vis other goods, central banks can cause commercial banks to raise the rates at which they lend money out, thereby making money more expensive and bringing prices back into line. ("Cause" is a bit strong; the mechanisms at the disposal of central banks, including the U.S. Federal Reserve, are more modest than this account suggests.) If, on the other hand, money looks to be getting too expensive, central banks can cause the price of bank money to be lowered. Although perhaps theoretically inelegant, this practice has maintained a considerable degree of price stability in the United States and much of Europe for well over twenty years.[13]

As already suggested, it is not clear that the techniques of central banks can continue to be so efficacious. The Asian currency crisis of 1997 and 1998 saw a number of unsuccessful interventions by central banks. The recent difficulties of the Euro suggest that even a large and powerful central bank may have difficulty intervening to support the price of its currency in the face of any substantial doubt in the marketplace. More generally, the proliferation of financial products and the increasing ease with which asset classes are exchanged for one another may mean that the bank debt of a given country will no longer be, or already is no longer, as central as it once was to the formation or management of capital in that country. Even at the retail level, larger and larger shares of individual wealth are held in instruments that have little to do with bank debt. Moreover, a host of new financial products, including payment vehicles, presaged by abortive efforts at e-money, may come to serve monetary functions with little or no interface with the central bank. Recent activity in the equity markets has seemed somewhat oblivious to central bank signaling. Most notably, the Fed's efforts through the late '90s to coax the prices for U.S. equities into some semblance of conformity with traditional measures of valuation were unavailing. After the market peak of March 2000, and the ensuing worries about a recession, the economy has appeared quite resistant to repeated loosenings of monetary policy. Such recent developments pose the more general question: How do we begin to think about monetary policy in a world in which the money supply—even the cost of holding money—is not clearly defined? More profoundly, how do we begin to think about our society's confrontation with the future, at least as instantiated by central banking?

*   *   *

Return to how central banks realize monetary policy: they manipulate interest rates and thereby change the cost of borrowing, of renting money. They also intervene directly in the money markets, thereby changing the supply of a given currency. Central banking explicitly regulates the conditions, and hence the supply, of credit, and hence the likelihood of borrowing, and more deeply still, of promising. Central banking, in short, is the arm of government responsible for encouraging or discouraging promises in the private sector. This is usually expressed in terms of worries of inflation, which causes the central bank to tighten the conditions of credit, implicitly arguing that we have too many promises and need fewer. Or, in the other direction, central banks may worry about recession, which causes central banks to make credit available, to encourage promises.

There is no theoretical limit to promises; webs of credit can be extended indefinitely. Credit builds on top of itself, the house of cards goes up. To state the matter practically: suppose we use shares in a company to compensate people, pay for retirement, acquire other companies, and collateralize loans for the purchase of houses. Suppose such shares are priced based on estimates of the future prospects of the company, and prospects are widely believed to be good. Suppose such companies sign contracts promising payment to various suppliers, partners, builders, and so forth. Suppose such contracts are understood to be assets of the firms who receive such promises. One could go on, but the point is clear: the functioning of the market tends to build more and more elaborate webs of obligation, complexity. The citizens of capitalist societies manufacture their own money so long as they have the confidence to lend and invest, to place another card upon the top of the tower.

The danger of a long peace is hope, the extension of credit on top of credit, the construction of the house of cards. The longer disaster is averted, the more hope people have, the higher the house of cards and the farther they have to fall, the more vulnerable they are. Markets may correct, break, or crash—hopes may be dashed by collective repricing. The purpose of central banking is to sustain the health of market societies by measured frustration of the market's efforts infinitely to extend credit.[14] The anticipatory tight monetary policy of Germany's Bundesbank, now the European Central Bank, and to a lesser extent the U.S. Federal Reserve is ultimately justified, not by real growth (about which too little is known), but by fear of volatility and particularly inflation. Specifically, if expectations are not absolutely grounded, indeed tested by adverse conditions (if necessary, difficulty borrowing), then expectations will mount, will be eventually corrected, and the ensuing volatility might not be contained. This Nietzschean anxiety about history—how much complexity is possible, before violence begins to look inevitable, perhaps even attractive—pervades central banking. The tight money policy of central banks seems a rather civilized alternative.

We now see the impossibility of money, the contradiction at its heart. On the one hand, money is a present token of faith in the collective future, and the supply of such faith is unlimited. Yet money cannot function, and so does not exist as money, unless it is a commodity, believed to be limited in supply, even if the exact quantity is unknown. Money is not a thing, but a dialectical process which unfolds, like all dialectics, in time, specifically in the perpetual renegotiation between hope and disappointment. In endeavoring to limit the money supply, to engineer soft landings and such, central banks side with the finite, commodity aspect of money, over against the market's tendency to extend the communicative, infinite aspect of money. Central banking is not merely an alternative to the violent repricing associated with war. Central banking is instead the sublimation of war, and so remains an expression of the thanatotic urges of developed societies. The anxieties which led to the founding of the City of Gold—the suspicion that culture had its limits, which, once transgressed, led to frenzy—are ultimately recapitulated in the urbane hearts of central bankers.

Capital makes and unmakes itself, and so progress is at least a mirage. Marx was right that culture tends to replace nature through history, but did not see how right he was, that the necessities of culture, an individual's work, a government's accommodations, would replace the necessities of nature, that liberty gained through the conquest of nature would be forfeit to the goddess of culture, progress. And Marx does not seem to have imagined that we would sicken of the goddess of progress, or history as he styled her, or even culture. Instead of Marx our world is described by late Freud, a world in which eros and thanatos whirl about one another, making and destroying without going anywhere much. If our busy-ness is our eros, nowhere is thanatos more evident than in central banking, and behind that, the widespread turn to a simple version of economics, the desire to have done, to escape from a culture of which we are not proud to where it is clear and cold and hard. Rigor, the professors call it. The City of Gold has never escaped from this struggle, the same struggle that gave fascism birth, and so occasioned the founding of the City.

In this narrow regard, the City of Gold is authentic. As this book has suggested since its beginning, a sense of history can help us appreciate the politics of markets, even if such politics cannot respond to the richness of being human. We have the markets we have because that is the way our history has unfolded. We may have done with irony, wipe the smile off our lips and earnestly appreciate our markets, if we wish to dwell on the constraints that have been imposed in the passage of time, that is, if we wish to approach life as historians and dwell on our limitations.

But the historical imagination is not the only imagination. Political thought—and certainly any hope for justification—requires more than history, it requires an imagination of possibilities, hope. The fact that all history constrains, that tracks are laid here and not there, makes past decisions consequential, but does not abolish the present responsibility to make decisions. The dance of eros and thanatos may move in many ways, and it would be fatalistic—and wrong—to insist that the dance we observe is the only dance possible. Thus, to phrase matters academically, our consideration of social order—of justice—takes place in the no-man's-land between history, understood as the study of constraint, and social criticism, understood as political fantasy.

Insofar as we insist on understanding markets in political as well as historical terms, a somewhat ironic stance—simultaneous acknowledgements of both our possibilities unrealized and the constraints upon us—appears to be unavoidable. We are constantly impelled to recognize at least the broad outlines of our political order and to deny that such order has much by way of ultimate justification, and is therefore risible in light of what might have been. And with the wry comfort of ironic humor, we turn once more to the problems of authority, loyalty, and the possibilities for metropolitan identity.

CHAPTER XIV

Beyond the Market
Authority and Identity

Political idea of markets. License. Bureaucracy necessary in order to legitimate markets. Bureaucracy central to intellectual life in market societies. Success of modern university, and the decline of republican forms of discourse. Social criticism between history and philosophy. Tragic disposition of social criticism; reality of comedy. Identity redux: the possibility of autonomy of judgment. The possibility of sympathy, and a politics of imagination. The need for language and the problem of lies.

Chapter VIII discussed the private not in spatial terms, as an area of life somehow distinct from public life, but instead in psychological terms, as the self's rejection of a polity that, however lush in appearance, ultimately is defined in the austere dialectic between property and money. Chapter XI argued that traditional liberalism, the intellectual effort to construct a polity as a matrix of private interests, is no longer sufficient, is in fact bankrupt. The liberal vision of political life is uncompelling; the self cannot be satisfyingly understood as the liberal rights holder. Liberal understandings of political life, and hence citizenship, merely recapitulate the inadequacies of capitalism.

The first two chapters of part 4 offered a different way in which the self may be at home in the City, thereby lessening the need to reject the City in favor of a private garden. These chapters discussed ways in which markets are structured by laws, just as games are structured by rules. In particular, chapter XII discussed truth, especially the question of adequate information in the securities markets, and chapter XIII discussed an ideal social order, specifically the effort to curb the destructive enthusiasms of markets through monetary policy. In both cases, bureaucrats structured markets. Thus, even at the core of the market, we see ideas at work, a politics of the head rather than the gut. In response, this essay seeks to develop an idea of authority implicit in such an understanding of bureaucracy, in the hopes that the individual could acknowledge such authority rather than merely endure the force of officialdom. Perhaps the private realm need not be so hostile to the realities of our lives together—this essay concludes with a preliminary discussion of the possibilities for political thought that such engagement may offer.

*   *   *

Even at the heart of markets, the rational self-interest of indisputably private actors is not the exclusive frame of discourse. So, for example, the securities markets are not "private" mechanisms, with which the "public" organs of the "government" may choose to interfere. Securities markets are themselves always and already also public mechanisms, and so from time to time require public-minded responses. The question posed by, for example, the role taken by the New York branch of the U.S. Federal Reserve in the affairs of Long Term Capital Management is not simply whether "the government" should intervene in the capital markets to bail out a loser, but what role the New York Fed—a unique institution—should take in defusing a situation that had arisen among several sorts of institutions, constituted in a variety of ways, that appeared to threaten the very public financial system. Once our idea of government has been expanded to include markets, we cannot understand markets in exclusively private ways.

Examples of social markets, that is, markets intentionally established in order to achieve public goods, are ubiquitous. State run pension plans are being replaced by private retirement systems, perhaps most extensively in Chile, but also in the United States. Environmental entitlements (rights to pollute) are traded in a number of regimes, notably the carbon dioxide system established by the Kyoto treaty. Public education in the United States may soon be provided by a voucher system, which would allow schools to compete for public money controlled by the parents of school children. A multimillion dollar market has emerged for the management of prisons. In short, the last few decades have seen an explosive growth in the deployment of market mechanisms to achieve social ends that traditionally had been addressed by other political mechanisms, or had been left unaddressed. Markets, in short, can be the rational answer to questions of public policy.

Markets remain, however, different from other institutions, such as administrative agencies, courts, and legislatures, that we commonly call government. We still distinguish between public service and the private sector, and think we mean something.[1] Market decisions announce themselves as motivated by self-interest, appetites, while government gestures towards principle, mind. In order to be comfortable with markets, we must believe that the aggregation of private interest, through competitive mechanisms, redounds to some public good, that is, we have to believe that some public good will be achieved through the pursuit of private interest. Which is not to say that there is no morality within the marketplace; it bears repeating that markets have their own morality. A moment's reflection should remind us that markets are often inhabited by moral people, people we know. Nor is the appearance of moral people in the marketplace accidental. Markets require virtues, especially trust, and market societies have ways of encouraging virtues and punishing error. Those things said, the morality of markets is quite limited, for reasons discussed in chapters VIII and XI. Many virtues cannot be articulated as intrinsic to economic life. Instances of virtue in the marketplace tend to be denigrated as mere preferences, or, when necessary, as in the case of trust, are often justified as means to the overarching end of self-aggrandizement. Most importantly, markets require people to be treated as things. In short, markets are morally impoverished, and we attempt to protect those we love and ourselves from the marketplace—we construct the private realm.

Therefore, when we approve of arranging social affairs through markets, we implicitly approve of the self-interested behavior of actors in that marketplace. We grant license. The terms of that license, however, are limited. The very idea of a competitive market assumes rules, a context. Competition within markets is bounded by law and regulation. One function of government (in the traditional sense) is to provide the context in which market transactions take place, most obviously, to define and enforce the property, contract, and monetary regimes on which the market is founded. As discussed in chapter XIII, the need for nonmarket governance is endogenous to the structure of governance through markets. Another function of government—more specifically, of bureaucracy—is to ensure that the license is limited in such a way that the aggregation of private interests does in fact redound to some public good, and that we are therefore well governed, and that we therefore forgive actors in the market for their greed, their tendency to treat people like property. That is, as discussed in the present essay, the need for nonmarket governance is also exogenous to the structure of governance through markets.

Even actors in the marketplace—traditionally conceived as self-interested ("rational")—may rely on the fact that the terms of their licenses (and those of their competitors) are limited. Just as states often desire legality, that is, comply with international law, and are embarrassed about or even deny outright their failures to do so, private actors often want to know that the realization of their desires is legitimate rather than shameful.[2] Economic actors may be self-interested—who is not?—but we need not believe that people are malevolent. Insofar as we think about the indirect consequences of our actions, we have no desire to believe that our choices will lead to harm. We worry, and should worry, about pollution, the health of workers recently unemployed, the collapse of currencies, wars, and countless other harms that may flow from the operation of the market, that is, from our collective pursuit of our private interests. If we are conscientious, we need to know that our participation in the market, the fulfillment of our desires, necessarily somewhat private, is bounded. We thus rely on governance, which here means the conscious articulation of norms through law, to bound and so legitimate desires.[3]

In regulating, bureaucracy articulates the bounds of the license granted private interest, and hence the shape of the market, and hence the goods we as a society try achieve through markets. Thus, although the City of Gold, like all liberal polities, denies that it embodies a substantive good, and loudly claims instead to be structured around the move from substance to process, the City—like any government must—does in fact have substantive notions of the good, and exercises power in order to achieve them. So bureaucracies are fora where substantive public discourse on the nature of the good takes place.[4] Indeed, as a legal matter, bureaucracies are structured explicitly by a substantive good, generally provided by the legislature in the organic statute that establishes the bureaucracy. Legislation typically grants "The Administrator" or other high official numerous powers and sends her out in pursuit of some general objective, sound financial markets, safe commercial aviation, clean water . . . what emerges over time is a set of expectations, bounds, about what the market for corporate equity, air travel, or water should look like, and the market for such things is legally, and often in fact, informed by such normative parameters. Just as the creation of a global polity requires the creation of a private realm of meaning, our consciousness of ourselves as venal actors, would-be slaveholders, requires us to hope for government.

* * *

Thus bureaucracy has become a central mode of political life, the revenge, as it were, of the mind on a society that glorifies the gut (or perhaps the loins). Although we have hardly scratched the surface of what bureaucracy might mean for markets and thus politics, what does bureaucracy mean for the activity of thinking about politics? Unsurprisingly, perhaps, bureaucracy has become a central mode of intellectual life. We have come to understand even the university to be a bureaucratic enterprise, informed by the virtues as understood by university administration (evidenced by alumni donations, prizes won, that sort of thing) and collectively referred to as "excellence." Perhaps as late as the early 1980s, it seemed as if Humboldt's project, to use the institutional capacity of the university to map the world, had been nothing but a success.[5] As work on the map progressed, however, it became so large and so detailed that it demanded a lifetime of study, so much effort that knowing anything considerable about the map generally precluded knowing much of anything about the world. The map of the world became itself a world—the world of academe—with its own rules, fiefdoms, even small wars. It became clear that professors were responding to their universities, not to the world the university was designed to describe, and for which the university was charged with educating students. Academics began to understand that peculiar reality known as academic life as self-sufficient, true unto itself, in effect giving up on the culture outside the university. As a result, it became increasingly difficult to claim that university faculties were structured around a division of knowledge that reflected the world rather than expressed political currents within the university. The distinction between academic culture and national culture became a gulf.

During the same period of time, however, the university also became central to success in what has come to be called, flatteringly enough, the knowledge economy. Although education had always been important, since the technology-driven boom of the 1980s, education has come to be seen as the mainspring of the economy. Higher education appeared to be America's comparative advantage, and years of worrying about Japanese planning and German labor sharing gave way to frank celebration of brilliant entrepreneurs who moved in the orbit of university life, even when they did not bother to take a degree. University towns became centers for economic growth. Corporate life began to model itself on the culture of the university; a corporation's headquarters is now often called a campus. In short, the university became economically and politically vital just as fast as it lost intellectual coherence. This is the sort of controversy that bureaucracy was invented to paper over, and so administrators have replaced faculty as the central figures of the university.[6]

Bureaucracy authorizes intellectuals to establish authoritative conceptual categories. This development has not been entirely unwelcome to the mandarin class. In a world in which government consists largely of the bureaucratic manipulation and actualization of authoritative concepts, the intellectual, that is, the person who articulates such concepts, can have immense impact. A saying once and perhaps still current in the European Commission captures the point: it does not matter what revisions the

Member States make to the Commission's legislative proposals, because while they (the Member States) have the red pen, we (the Commission) have the blue pen. Drafting thus sets the terms of debate. Editors amend. They rarely, if ever, write. Bureaucracy thus works a miracle: the life of the mind becomes the life of action; philosophy denies its nature and becomes politics; speculation becomes practical.[7]

Participation in bureaucracy is hardly the only way that intellectuals could engage, or even have engaged, in politics. Republican government has always provided a stage for the intellectual, whose ideas may persuade the electorate, and even inform the culture more generally. The feuilleton of many European papers proceeds on the assumption that ideas have importance in the lives of the populace, and therefore deserve careful, but not professional, discussion. In the United States, contributors to politically engaged magazines such as *Partisan Review* might have imagined themselves addressing the thoughtful urban voter. At the end of the '60s, Hannah Arendt's discussion of Nazi evil as banal was first published in *The New Yorker*. If we allow for faction and some stylistic changes, such magazines addressed roughly the same audience that eighteenth-century editors presumed would read the *Federalist Papers*. Insofar as this was politics, the political theory must have been that the reader was important enough to require convincing, that is, writers once presumed that, in a representative democracy, their readers chose the government. The job of the republican intellectual, then, was to think through and articulate solutions to political problems in ways that the republic's leaders and voters and so leaders would espouse.

But little politics is done in that fashion any more. Far more often, the important political question is setting the agenda at a given bureaucracy. The public press has a role to play in this enterprise, but it is hardly convincing voters. Demographically few voters read *The New York Times*, *The Wall Street Journal*, or *The Washington Post*—or *Le Monde*, *The Frankfurter Allgemeine*, or *The London Times*—but an inordinate number of politically significant people do. The few remaining papers of note are not used for argument to the people writ large, or even what remains of the middle class, but instead as a context for public posturing. Although delivered in the traditional form, as substantive points, such interventions are not intended to inform or persuade. They are instead primarily commitments by important people, commitments that cannot costlessly be denied and so must be reckoned with by other important people as they make their own various commitments. The construction of a policy consensus unfolds in the usual venues with a tentative progression disturbingly reminiscent of the path of a butterfly across a flowered meadow, until it becomes obvious that the decision is inevitable, not because some argument has overwhelmed all others, but because nobody in the game is in a position (and so not inclined) to disagree.

Intellectuals continue to play a role in our politics, but their audience has shifted. Substantive political thinking is directed not to the people who elect government, but instead to the organs of government itself, to bureaucracy and related personnel. Unsurprisingly, this shift in the mode of political persuasion has institutional and formal consequences. The shift in our writing makes newspapers less important, and countless newspapers have folded, merged, or survive by printing items of very local interest and reprinting material from the wire services. While a few papers (including those just mentioned by name) survive as fora for public posturing—they may be more important than ever, because they have so little competition—the argument published in a newspaper of general circulation is no longer the paradigmatic form for political discourse. If the republican tradition of public intellectual activity is best exemplified by the *Federalist Papers*, intellectual work in our polity is informed by the idea of the white paper, generated by a bureaucracy (either governmental, academic, corporate, or most interestingly, a not-for-profit, particularly a think tank) to be consumed by other bureaucracies. Done properly, a white paper synthesizes substantive conception and political commitment in such a manner as to inform and constrain subsequent political discourse.

The university has adapted to this new political and intellectual environment with unseemly ease. The bureaucratization of intellectual life has been paced by the intellectualization of bureaucratic life in government, in business, everywhere. (Not least of the farcical elements of the Clinton administration was its faith in graduate degrees.) Consequently, demand for the university's tangible product, students, appropriately graded and priced, has soared. Moreover, the new authority granted the university has caused the institution to return to its roots in state-sponsored theology. The university is once again an institution devoted to the profession of moral accreditation and politically authorized belief. These developments have, after the fashion of production schedules and orthodoxies, tended to inhibit thought. (But it was probably naive to suppose that philosophy, to say nothing of art, could be cultivated in a greenhouse.) Whether or not the life of the mind has suffered from recent changes in the university, it is clear that as a matter of social prestige the university as an institution has not so flourished in centuries, if ever.

There are plenty of worse things than mandarin politics. The City of Gold's claim to democracy is fairly thin, even in the United States, where such claims are made most heatedly and probably most (if not very) plausibly. Nor is political engagement likely to be the way to think really clearly: mandarins tend to subtlety rather than clarity. But whatever the democratic or intellectual problems one may have with mandarin politics, one cannot live in the City of Gold and honestly believe that politics, even here, is a matter of the appetites to the exclusion of the mind. The North Atlantic mandarins who founded the City redefined their political context; they did not commit mass suicide. The mandarins are with us still, and, in its way, that is a comfort.

The City of Gold is a commercial polity, but it does provide some space for the exercise of the mind. Contemporary politics is not merely the aggregation of appetites, but requires the sorts of considered exercises of power that we happily might regard as governance, to constitute markets and for much else. Conversely, we may regard our complicity in the City of Gold with some respect. There are worse things than siding with the mandarins, viewing life from the perspective of petty officials in a vast organization.[8] Even relatively powerful bureaucrats must admit that in the nature of things the scope of their authority tends to be limited by their office. For the vast majority of us who are lesser mandarins, or who have no jobs within the castle at all, we must be content with enthusiasm, with deluding ourselves that proximity to, or at least sympathy with, power is the basis for our individual identities. We fight for bigger cubicles, if we are lucky, over corner offices.

* * *

Living in the world seems to require things of which we are not proud. For relevant example, participation in capitalism involves treating people like property. Dwelling on such matters, however, might be considered bad manners. We have all been to the moneychangers; some of our best friends are moneychangers. What else is to be done? The sustained effort to criticize vital aspects of a culture could be expected to provoke defensive responses, and does.

Money, its defenders argue, is hardly the acultural, dehumanizing force its critics would maintain. Money facilitates the construction of meaning; money has its own meanings; business has its virtues. Another defense: although fungible in theory, in point of fact the money that people spend on entertainment is different from that they use to pay their monthly expenses, which is different from the money they use for retirement. People's lives organize their money, not the other way around. Still another: money liberates people—especially women—from the oppression that they have traditionally had to endure. And yet another defense: in 1863, at the unsurprising age of thirty-five, Jules Verne wrote *Paris in the Twentieth Century*.[9] The manuscript was rejected by Verne's publisher and then mislaid, and rediscovered in 1989. The book is a dystopia about Paris in the 1960s, based on the idea that money, and its lackey, industry, had rendered Paris a miserable place to be, and in particular, a place where art and humane letters were completely useless. Paris became rich, but art and romance died. At least from the viewpoint of many now senior academics, Paris in the 1960s was the most romantic time and place imaginable—and so something is wrong with Verne's narrative, and by extension, with critiques of commodification. One could go on, but the point is the similarity, not the variety, of such claims. Criticism of money, and the defenses against such criticism, share an underlying structure. The criticisms are all arguments that money dehumanizes. To which the defensive responses have the structure: I have used money. I am human. Money therefore does not dehumanize. You are wrong.

As a matter of intellectual style if nothing else, inhabitants of the City should confront the possibility that the monetization on which their social life is constructed has in fact created a polity unworthy of respect, and moreover, that monetization has left them spiritually impoverished. As discussed in chapter VII, however, the charge of spiritual impoverishment is not unproblematic. After all, if this is a monetary society, and if money truly destroys the possibility of meaning, how is social criticism—this argument—possible? Social criticism is possible, even here, chapter VII maintained, because commodification is necessarily partial. Human experience always affords ground from which the property regime can be criticized. Nor is this accidental. As this part 4 has demonstrated, markets—what is on the table—presume contexts, even law, that are not themselves subject to market transactions. At the very least, from the perspective of such contexts, markets may be criticized. In fact, such criticism is intrinsic to market regulation, such as the regulation of commerce in securities, or of the money supply.

Let us attempt to restate the foregoing argument in somewhat more down to earth terms. Consider the claim that I am not dehumanized—it is less of an answer than it initially appears. On the one hand, the claim is technically true: presumably if one is capable of engaging the argument against monetization one is still a human. But if "dehumanization" is understood to mean the degradation of some preferred state, then the critical argument would not be affected. To take a specific and pointed example, prostitution is often said to be dehumanizing. This statement is not literally true—prostitutes are obviously human—but it is instead a way of expressing the widespread belief that it is wrong to understand physical intimacy in explicitly monetary terms. To put the point in somewhat incoherent contemporary terms, a woman (or a man, especially a boy) who exchanges sex for money is said to lack self-esteem, to have no self-respect.[10] The point is not that the woman is not a woman, human all too human, but that we may have hoped that she would lead a different, better, sort of life.[11] So testifying to the trace of humanity that we undoubtedly possess hardly answers the criticism of monetization, and we are left responding to the charge that the inhabitants of the City of Gold lead lives that are spiritually bankrupt—the question is not whether or not we have become machines, but whether we are admirable humans.

So stated, the argument may sound elitist and brutal, and perhaps it is, but milder versions of the argument have become so commonplace as to be normative, even orthodox.[12] Most inhabitants of the City believe that life in most quarters of the City is not worth living. In America, a nasty joke runs, as you move away from the coasts, people grow stupider. Until you get to Kansas (and begin approaching the opposite coast). To put the same point a bit more nicely: many well-educated people find the idea of the suburb itself somewhat disturbing, perhaps pleasant or convenient but somehow less intellectually defensible than living "in the city." The point here is not that life in Kansas or elsewhere is meaningless. (Life in fact may be more meaningful in less fashionable places.) The point is that the meanings of lives lived out in such places are increasingly unspeakable within the City, and are therefore denigrated. Within the logic of the City, if one is not at the center of desire (prestige), one must admit one's peripheral status. This social geography is often understood in terms of the simple geometry of the hub and spoke. Within the logic of the City, it means nothing to be in or especially of a particular place, with its own personality, incommensurate and somewhat independent of other, neighboring places. To use more unkind language, one may live in Manhattan, or resign oneself to being a bridge-and-tunnel person, in from the steppes. Similar things are said about Paris and Hong Kong. We have thus created a polity that admits to discounting the lives of most of its inhabitants. For we happy few, who live in the metropole, all the world is Provence. But when the inhabitants of Provence begin to believe that they live in the middle of nowhere, then they lead impoverished lives. From this perspective, can one really argue that the creation of a global communicative space—in this aspect the City of Gold usually is thought of as a culture of celebrity—does not dehumanize the lives that it engulfs? (Is this not, at bottom, an egalitarian critique?)

Turning the table, however, critics of monetization must somehow take account of the fact that talk about the decline of gemeinschaft is an invitation to all sorts of sloppiness. As the story of *Paris in the Twentieth Century* illustrates, the world has always been en route to hell, but never quite arrives. Verne's manuscript was rediscovered in 1989, by which point Verne had expected literature to be dead. In fact, however, his book is not only read, but celebrated.[13] Such stories make it tempting for the historically minded to dismiss the critiques of monetization as golden age stories, not only because we may testify to our own humanity, but also because we may testify to the venerable practice of social criticism. Social criticism focuses on the particular evils that seem most worthy of attention right now; an inevitable lesson of historical study is that similar difficulties arose in other times and places. Moreover, if we turn our attention to other moments in history, we may find various sources of unhappiness, and it is very difficult to argue that the present period is particularly unhappy, or that the particular evil that concerns us, monetization, plays a particularly large role in what unhappiness does exist. So, it might seem, criticism of monetization simply does not fit the historical facts.

The relationship between history and social criticism, however, is considerably more complex than such a counterargument allows. Social criticism, political thought, tends to look like history because it tends to rely on narratives, stories, myths (generally, an account of how things are getting worse). But political thought is not history. These stories are not understood to be true in any naive sense; social criticism as such does not aspire to the sort of truth that academic history once claimed and has yet to replace, *wie es eigentlich gewesen ist.*[14] Because it is social criticism, contemporary anxiety over monetization is somewhat independent of the academic discipline of history, and it is to that extent somewhat beside the point to argue that we are not now alienated, or that other periods of history were more alienated, or that processes outside markets may cause alienation. The question posed by the narrative of monetary dehumanization is not historical (were other times more venal, are we losing ground?), but whether we should understand a particular aspect of our lives in monetary terms, and what the consequences for doing so are, that is, how we will have to reconfigure our understanding of our existence to account for the change. Narrative myths help us do that.[15]

While narrative social criticism is not history, it can never be completely independent of history, either. The enterprise, criticizing society, requires abstraction from an actual social life, that is, thinking conceptually about what it means to lead a certain sort of life, a life inescapably located in time. So while it is wrong to assume that a narrative argument is a historical claim, it is not a claim that is entirely outside the reach of academic history. For example, Marx's cry, "all that is solid melts into air," is social criticism that expressed something important about the contemporary (for Marx) translation of various sorts of relationships into the grammar of property law. That is, the criticism had an occasion, a factual predicate, and was therefore constrained, although not determined, by that occasion. To update the example, in our own time it seems that even property, in the old sense of fee simple interests in land and movables, is far too solid, too heavy, and we are witnessing the melting of property into the ephemera of financial interests. This is not the full historical truth, nor absolutely unique in the course of human events (there is, always and inevitably, much more to say), but it is not inappropriate to ask what such changes to an important aspect of our lives together means. And so the course of events occasions social criticism, philosophy in which the effort is to understand what this moment has come to mean.

Ironies arise. As a result of its focus on the problems presented by this moment, social criticism ultimately may be more historically sensitive than it initially appears to be. In contrast, academic history, for all the discipline's emphasis on the particularities of a particular time and place (the necessity for primary research, etc.), often implicitly suggests the opposite stance, and may be less historically sensitive than it appears to be. In responding to social criticism as Arcadian grousing, yet another golden age narrative, the historical perspective may find itself suggesting transhistorical truths. So contemporary worries about globalization are discussed with reminders of the extent of international economic integration prior to World War One. Worries about the excesses of the WTO are dismissed along with Marx and Verne, Carlyle and the Luddites, St. Francis and Christ, Aristotle and whoever first told the story of Midas: there has always been money, and there has always been worry about it. Carried to its logical conclusion (which it rarely is, at least not explicitly), the historical response to social criticism would seem to teach, bizarrely enough, that there have always been critics, and that times are fundamentally alike.

Much the same objection can be made with regard to the treatment of evidence: in order to understand social criticism as the usual grousing, Arcadian and so irrelevant, the testimony of individual social critics is often discounted. So, although the world may not have fallen apart, it matters that, in the two and one-quarter centuries since *Wealth of Nations* was published, we have seen so many rebellions, by so many intelligent people, against the monetary understanding of life, and against social transformations which required such understanding. Despite the beauties of comparative advantage, it matters that so many people protest the Bretton Woods Institutions. Such complaints are evidence of *something*, and therefore, even from a historical perspective, we must take seriously the possibility that people have grown more alienated, or, constitutionally, that the City of Gold is an unworthy polity.

Which is to say only that the possibility needs to be taken seriously, not to argue that a given social critic has it right, not that we must view the City of Gold with the horror that some critics of globalization recommend. Even though the center does not hold, things rarely fall completely apart. Europe went to hell in the twentieth century, and is still a pleasant place to

live. The United States, fresh from threatening the world with nuclear an-
nihilation, is doing some marvelous things—as well as being the first hy-
perpower. The Russians have enormous difficulties, but they have boldly
given up an empire and a system of terror, in civilized fashion. It is not
enough to remark, with Adam Smith, that there is a great deal of ruin in a
nation, as true as that is.[16] One must also ask why there is so much ruin in
social criticism, why philosophy—not just worldly philosophy, economics—tends to be dismal.

And here we come to a weakness that seems entailed in the doing of social criticism, and that therefore infects the criticism of monetization, and
so this apology. Social critics depict ruin in part because they are social
critics. As already suggested, social criticism attacks developments that are
seen to be contrary to life as we have come to understand it, not so much
our actual life as our current ideals. Social criticism tells stories, always already begun, which if continued will destroy the meanings we have constructed. A coming must also be a going—to say that a situation has come
to mean something is also to say that the same situation no longer means
what it once did. Another word for what was once meant is home, and
most people are fond of their homes—it is much of who they are. Insofar
as we are fond of the way of life in which we grew up—and because it made
us who we are, we have to have a certain respect for it, whatever might be
said against it from the outside—then we will tend to view such change as a
bad thing, and we may even speak of dehumanization. Social criticism thus
tends to rest, if only implicitly, on a sense of dislocation, a sense of losing a
pattern of meaning, along with the past in which such meaning was
formed. Social criticism is always, at bottom, a charge of impiety, betrayal,
leaving home.

Money (like technologies and wars) dehumanizes because it changes
patterns, destroys meanings, that human life has built up so far. Capitalism, in its relentless commitment to the future, remakes homes, for better
and worse. And yet there are reasons that capital is attractive, that people
choose to treat themselves and others as slaves. Any successful impiety has
its attractions, which ideology presumes to state in general terms. Money
provides, if in the abstract, the realization of our will, which most of us
conceive to be happiness, and what could be more tempting? The dramatic
expression of destructive conflicts between goods, such as old meanings
and new temptations, is tragedy.[17]

It is also important to remember, however, that humans are resilient.
People make meaning all the time. Culture reconstitutes itself. While people
leave and die, they also find one another and babies are born. As an intellectual matter, however, it is much harder to say much about things which have
not yet come together, about meanings as yet unconceived. So the narrative

structure of social criticism—the effort to understand this moment inevitably in terms of a past that we suspect we are losing (indeed, that is a condition of our mortality)—fosters the sense that things are falling apart, and that one ought to be alienated. Social criticism tends to spring from a partial vision, a formal, analytical, and ultimately tragic perspective, as opposed to an intimate, synthetic, and comic perspective. Knowing when one or the other perspective is appropriate would be wisdom.

* * *

We are now in a position to describe the sense in which a thoughtful inhabitant may hope to feel at home in the City. Our inhabitant understands that truth is neither available nor dispensable. That while he cannot be truly at home in his world, he is no more lost than anyone else, and all should be presumed to deserve sympathy. That while our marketplace institutions will not produce justice, they are not truly acceptable until they do so—and yet, of course, they must be accepted. The thoughtful inhabitant of the City is nothing if not comfortable with such contradiction; he is worldly.

The City is what it is up to this point: a great deal of track has been laid, for better and worse. The inhabitant cannot change the larger situation in which he finds himself. For an inhabitant who is not powerful, his central choice is in what stance to take toward his situation. There are a few options. The inhabitant might appreciate only the opportunity the City affords, that is, he might be a philistine who cannot imagine how things might have been otherwise, and who does not understand how much is inevitably lost. Or the citizen might wallow in the limitations of the situation, thereby running the risk of being practically irresponsible while annoyingly moral. We may hope, however, for citizens who understand that success in the marketplace (like occurrence in history) in itself implies neither justification nor condemnation. Good things happen, even in markets, and so do bad things, even in markets. The citizen appreciates; he is a critic.

In this regard Hollywood, of all places, has been exemplary. Participants in the movie industry, more broadly speaking the entertainment industries, speak of themselves as if they were making cars, shaving cream, or any other consumer product. It is an industry, after all, and the success or failure of a given undertaking is sensibly enough reported in frankly monetary terms. At the same time, film is an art form, and movies, even Hollywood movies, can be works of art. The fact that a film was made in Hollywood, and was successful, means only . . . that a film was made in Hollywood and made money. Many good films make money; many good films do not. And the same is true of bad films. No intelligent person, particularly in Hollywood, would claim that a film was good merely because its opening week had been lucrative. Hollywood thus teaches that although we may live within markets, we can and should reserve judgment. There is no reason to believe that this is the best of all possible worlds; believing that it is suggests a lack of imagination. We all know how to make better movies, and on good days, we do.

In understanding marketplace politics, and so history, as a critic understands drama, the citizen can achieve a kind of autonomy. This is not, however, the autonomy familiar from liberal discourse, and expressed most completely by the Kant of the moral works. The necessity, benefit, and sadness of treating people like property is not liberating. Treating people like property destroys their particularity; the commonly heard talk of diversity is mostly a lie told to keep the peace and an index of our public dishonesty. Rights are necessary in a society of strangers, but whenever possible the critic should eschew the superficial formalism of rights talk in favor of attention to happenstance and beautiful possibility. The citizen may turn from understanding autonomy as liberty to understanding autonomy as the possibility of exercising judgment, from the will to the aesthetic.

Aesthetics implies a certain emotional distance, and perhaps some of that is psychologically necessary. The world is still vast, and suffering deep, and our hearts cool in order that we may cope with the images of big-eyed children, the tales of brutality and pettiness, the waste of humans. At the same time, however, the inhabitant should try—as a matter of political morality—to remember that images, whether televised or legal, are drawn from life. Pictures are made of people; rights are held by others worth sympathy. But there is more than philanthropy at stake—imaginative projection, sympathy, is necessary if we are to understand what we do, and so to have a chance at justification. And so we see the turn to aesthetics accompanied by a somewhat contradictory effort to sympathize.

Sympathy is hardly a complete cure for the distance at which we must conduct politics—for the fact that we cannot know the people behind the images suffering on our screens, that we have no principled way to organize, much less respond to, the agonies reported on a provisional basis. Insofar as we still dare to have a political imagination, we cannot be uncritical, even in our sympathies—it is often in our sympathies that we are most complicitous, and so must be particularly self-critical.

This need to find the right moment for distance or commitment, this ceaseless oscillation between without and within, makes social criticism tiring. When, as now, both true anomie and zealotry are so easily available, when we may change the channel or become fanatics in vans, when we have so little sense of decorum, it is difficult to maintain an appropriate attitude toward politics. It is difficult to navigate between complacency and bitterness. Ongoing social criticism, trying to make nice judgments about how we live among one another, becomes rather groundless work for the mind, the effort to create and yet be critical, to be both author and editor of a political aesthetic that must stand forth with little other foundation.

Our sympathy may or may not be adult. The media tends to offer a childlike view of the soul, captured by advertising and expressed most movingly by the Olympics, in which we regard all humanity as like ourselves. This vision lacks focus, and is imperious in the way of children, but it can also be a form of love, and we are increasingly charitable with it. Such a vision, however, is not without its own dangers. It tends to be self-serving, and hence intellectually (and sometimes practically) irresponsible. It is to be hoped, therefore, that the inhabitant will begin to replace the relatively easy moral task of acknowledging difference as if it were respected, celebrating diversity, with the far harder challenge of sympathizing, even while understanding that we are not equal in fact, that decisions will be made, power will be exercised, and lives will be lived—or not—accordingly. Rephrased, it may be hoped that the inhabitant will learn to sympathize, understand, even love after a fashion, in the absence of personal affirmation or even solidarity. And so, at the distances at which we operate, we must hope for political feeling based on imagination rather than experience. Sympathy is the best that we—whose leaders command smart bombs and credit—can hope for in order to justify the repressions which we cannot escape.

It is difficult to live long or well with others—and it certainly is difficult to sympathize—in the absence of solidarity. And so we chat. But in our chat, our very social use of language, there is more danger. The need to use language in order to stitch the culture, with all its contradictions, together threatens to overwhelm language's somehow antecedent function of helping us cope with reality. Once reality is no longer available to ensure that our separate speeches are trued to a common world, we may cease communing with each other and doubt ourselves, and thus, despite our efforts to maintain consensus, end up being truly isolated. We may begin hearing and presumably speaking as if we were courtiers, whose words are no more meaningful than the burble of a stream, so that nobody is entirely certain what they or anybody else intends. Perhaps we already have. Any morning's tour through the media provides ample reason to believe that our language has already slipped its moorings. Consider almost any example of that institutionalized practice of lying called advertising: What truth is being conveyed? Philosophers have long wondered what it meant to understand a lie, but that problem seems to have become political, even in the narrow sense. Consider any political speech—surely the managers of the candidates know that the audience understands the rudiments of media presentation, and we recipients understand that they understand, in an infinite regress of thoughtful deployment of language that never commits anyone to actual speech, sincerity, some statement of here I stand. There is a short distance from the worldliness implicit in understanding such things (and the comfort with contradiction that such dramatic understanding requires) to public hypocrisy and private irony, and from there it is not far to untrustworthiness and a self-conscious loss of perspective, doubt.[18] We in the City of Gold seem to communicate through a set of half-guessed codes. At some point we may come to suspect that we have lost the thread, that our guesses are wrong and our errors are compounding, and not even our therapists, listen as they might, can keep us from babbling to ourselves. Life may become surreal, and madness and exile, even brutality, threaten.

Here again, social criticism must be kept in perspective. Language has never fulfilled its promise. The tendency of our reality to bifurcate into the seen, felt, sensed—what we have lived—and the described—what we know how to say—is a danger for all societies. The lies of Edwardian Europe were never forgiven by the men who survived the trenches of World War I, a loss of credibility that later facilitated the telling of much bigger lies. Numerous communist regimes seemed to be constructed entirely out of lies; at some point it became impossible to proceed any further into the hall of mirrors. In order to escape such regimes, artists became dissidents, exiles of one or another sort, and viewed their work as the relation of truth in a time of lies.

But again, and on the other hand, history's comfort is limited. Although it may well have roots in the human condition, there is little reason to believe that this propensity of language to become untrue is constant. National glory and solidarity through history were explicitly political efforts that were shown to be lies, not because such things do not exist (lies always relay some truth), but because at particular times and places such lies obscured far more important truths, like the sanctity of life. Language does not always fail in the same way and to the same extent, and so the way in which language fails—the way in which language succeeds—is one way to judge the success of a polity. Thus the relationship between language and truth is also if not only a question of politics, and we may hope for a political regime that is relatively successful in ameliorating the problem.

Due to the nature of politics conducted through money, the City of Gold has special problems with lies, which is why consciousness in our time so often involves a feeling of alienation, a condemnation of our society as inauthentic, and a construction of the self as a rejection of politics, or, at best, a worldly acceptance of the necessity of politics. One might hope that literature could—as it did in communist Europe, and is attempting to do in China—speak the truth. This appears to be difficult for us. Perhaps the brazen quality of authoritarian lies makes the truth artistically available, if often physically dangerous to speak. Where the dissidents found it dangerous to speak but easy to speak truly, at least more truly than the official lies, we find it easy to speak and almost impossible to speak truly.[19] Many of our writers have abandoned the idea that language can reclaim reality by force. What realism we have tends to be magical or ironic, aware that whatever presents itself as reality cannot be more than an intimation. Indeed, some writers have gone so far as to undertake the chilling project of demonstrating how we can create lives, policy, even military policy, out of the fundamentally vacuous discourses that modernity apparently requires.

Toqueville remarked that there was an abstract quality about American speech, which he ascribed to democratic life—by which he meant political life that had no foundation more important than the abstraction of political enfranchisement.[20] Americans, even in the first half of the nineteenth century, shared relatively little among themselves by comparison to European peoples, whose lives were governed by authoritative webs of politics, religion, language, tradition, history, and so forth. And is not all the world indeed en route to America, albeit by inverting Locke's vision of a land without money?[21] Inhabitants of the City of Gold share so little beyond legal abstractions, most notably property rights. And in light of that fact, can we expect more from speech in the City than polite vacuity, the language of business, bureaucracy, therapy, and the occasional war? And is such language capable of preserving more than a semblance of sanity? Time will tell.

Until then, however, on good mornings we are able to confront our nightmares as tasks. We may hope that our inhabitant refuses to allow "worldly" to mean dishonest; that she has the energy to sustain the contradictions that contemporary language requires; that she still somewhere finds the emotional strength to forget herself and sympathize. But such things are unlikely without considerable work, and from a quarter that now seems to be devoting its energies to more private pursuits, the intelligentsia. There is no more important task for political thought in these times than the maintenance of language, so that our reality is articulable, so that we may construct a polity where it is possible to live, if never yet in truth, then at least in good faith.

Conclusion
The Possibility of Affection

One of the things that is new about our time is that the primary object of political thought has changed. A web of market relations, coordinated and most perfectly expressed by the capital markets, has come to structure the way most all of the powerful individuals and many of the rest of the people on the planet live together. Contemporary political thought should therefore confront what it means to organize affairs through markets, as political thought in other times concerned itself with the problems of bureaucratic states, republics, monarchies more or less absolute, feudal orders, empires, city states, and so forth. This is one of those times when the grammar of human association has changed, and such changes have consequences. For the honor of thinking as well as the hope of better politics, we should consider the consequences of living in a City of Gold.

The North Atlantic mandarins were probably justified in attempting to restructure international politics in the wake of World War Two. Contemporary arguments over the nature and benefits or harms of globalization tend to forget that the alternative to such integration may well be the violence that seems to characterize international politics conducted by autonomous nation states. That, at any rate, was the view in the mid-1940s. Since then, we have had several decades of superpower nuclear confrontation, followed more recently by a resurgence of bloody, but nonetheless ridiculous, nationalisms—and the postwar notion that the impassioned commitments of heart and head could be replaced by the *bürgerlich* satisfactions of metropolitan life appear understandable, perhaps even brilliant.

Regardless of whether the choice was justified then, the choice was made, and human life and commitments have sprung up accordingly. In particular, institutional and technological structures that we take for granted, such as supplies of food, textiles, energy, and especially capital, have been built up on the assumption that national boundaries do not organize economic, and hence broadly speaking political, activity. History is not contingent, not once it has become history. No doubt things might have turned out otherwise after World War Two, but they did not. We have inherited not only the horrors of that war, but also the responses to those horrors. The reconstruction of Germany and Japan, the isolation of the Soviet Union, the capabilities of nuclear weapons are realities that continue to operate in contemporary politics. Which is not to argue that the way things did turn out—the conception and slow maturation of the City of Gold—need not be understood in countless ways. It is to maintain that so much history cannot be unwound without a cataclysm.

Metropolitan life constitutes a culture, that is, metropolitan life entails (or requires or imposes) certain understandings of the individual, communication, human association, governance, the structure of time, and the hope of progress. At the same time, metropolitan life is unsurprisingly susceptible to the deep criticisms that have long been directed at money. This apology has attempted to organize such criticisms around three classic problems. First, what can be known, more particularly, to what extent are political mechanisms likely to be true? Generations of critics have thought that real truth cannot be spoken in market societies, that life in society alienated them from their true selves. I have conceded this point and argued that this is a result of the nature of money and property. Second, how do we live together? Again, it is traditional to argue that market societies are inauthentic. I have conceded this criticism as well; inauthenticity is nothing more than the fabric comprised by the lies that led to the feeling of alienation, including lies about the individual's ability to exercise the will, impress himself upon the world, that money seems to satisfy, yet betrays. Third, what kind of citizen does such a polity produce? What is it like to call such a place home? Again, it is rather traditional—and I agreed and extended this argument—that such a place cannot be a good home, that we end up choosing alienation from the public realm, constructing a private life, because solidarity is impossible, and because we cannot abide ourselves as we are constructed through the market. In short, alienation, inauthenticity, and the unfulfilled longing for a public self are interrelated problems entailed in market societies. This is bad, but unavoidable. Living in, perhaps finding a way to love, a polity we are inclined to despise is one of our tasks.

Despite this critique of the City of Gold, I have not argued that much of political life should be conducted through institutions other than markets, that the City of Gold should be abolished. There are several reasons for this. First, the thought that informed the founding of the City of Gold, that markets are political solutions to the problems posed by World War Two, seems correct. Second, markets have many benefits. In light of the plethora of contemporary paeans to the markets, there seems no need to devote more than passing attention to such benefits. Third, just over ten years after the fall of the Berlin Wall, it simply seems unavailable to suggest that markets are a stage in history to be overcome. But that we will, and even, on balance, should, have markets does not mean that the criticism of them was wrong, that we have no conflict and hence no need to make peace with our polity—hence the need for an apology.

Perhaps surprisingly, I have not supported the City's reliance on markets on the basis of some argument from growth. Despite the contention of economists since Smith and Ricardo that free trade leads to domestic growth, and the strong evidence that the liberal economic policies central to the construction of the City have on balance contributed to growth as conventionally measured, I have paid almost no attention to the idea of growth. There are several reasons for this, the most basic being that economists have no well-received theory of what causes growth (lots of things seem to contribute), and neither do I. More deeply, no notion of growth can make sense without a convincing idea of progress, and we do not seem very close to such an idea. More practically, this book is written, and most of its readers will live, in a milieu of physical comfort almost unimaginable to most people. At some point, and many in the intended audience for this book should have reached that point, one is unlikely to be convinced by a claim that a given course of action may make an incremental addition to aggregate wealth, from which one might individually benefit. Finally, material comfort is at best a distraction from, not really an answer to, the constitutional charges that the City of Gold has no truth, no justice, and no admirable sons and daughters.

For various reasons, I have not relied on orthodox political virtues such as utility, social justice, or liberty, and I have hardly bothered to discuss democracy or equality at all. These ways of thinking about politics, traditional since the Enlightenment, are instructive—good thought is always instructive—but are not very useful, in the sense of directly applicable, because our circumstances have changed so profoundly. There is therefore a lack of fit between our intellectual apparatus and our political longings. So the political language of economics fails to quell the suspicion that metropolitan politics obscures human truth. Similarly, the traditional expectations of social justice come to seem ridiculous, a category mistake, in a polity constructed by price mechanisms. And because liberalism approaches perfection in the City of Gold, it is foolish to attempt to address any discontent we now may feel in terms of liberalism. There are, of course, plenty of people who still believe in economics, social justice, or liberalism. I have made no serious effort to convince any believer that economics is not a science, that workers are not blessed, and that conventional liberalism is merely the political expression of capital. This is a series of essays, not ninety-five theses. That said, even a believer should be willing to concede that it is hardly too soon to ask how we are to think about our politics if such faiths no longer command widespread assent, and if we therefore cannot rely on the presumptions of such faiths to structure our political thinking. But if the Enlightenment faiths are no longer politically efficacious, what is left to form the substance of an apology for the way we live now?

A tough-minded apology would assail the disappointment with political life in the City that this book entertains and develops. At its most forceful, such an apology would depend on the radical split between the public—the world of the market, relentless competition, and the substitution of money for violence—and the private, the world of meaning, the world in which we may speak of the life well lived and of love. From this perspective, this apology's discontent is wrongheaded because it looks to the public, the society constructed by the supranational markets, particularly capital markets, to satisfy essentially private desires for personal identity, for a sense of being at home. Such hopes for political life are simply unrealistic. Politics cannot be satisfying: alienation and inauthenticity are part and parcel of public life in the City of Gold. The individual, conversely, cannot hope to form a public identity and must instead rely on the possibility of a private world. In sum, we distinguish between public and private, official and unofficial, because we must, if we are to preserve our own sense of humanity in a world that is constructed on the principle of exclusion.

In those terms, if one is willing to be sufficiently tough-minded, one may declare the City of Gold a success, and we may simply enjoy that success, while tending to our own gardens. From this perspective, the bourgeois intellectual discontent with the City of Gold (part 2) is shortsighted, insufficiently aware of just how horrible history generally is. Any government that can deliver peace, keep us from burying our children, and leave us to make meaningful lives elsewhere, has done a great deal. The long peace in Europe, even though broken by outbreaks of violence such as the Prague Spring and the demise of Yugoslavia, has been an enormous accomplishment. The inhabitants of the City of Gold are safe, much safer than their ancestors in the days of rampant nationalism. Is not satisfaction of that very basic private interest, all by itself, enough?

But there is more. Private life, not least in the North Atlantic democracies among the intelligentsia, can be very comfortable. What, exactly, is wrong with a commodious life? The City of Gold has fulfilled all that

Hobbes ever hoped for from politics. How many readers of this book truly believe that they do not, personally, live well? I would bet that few readers believe that their own lives are without depth or meaning, gray, monetized. If the private benefits of life in the City are insufficiently appreciated, turning to the cost side of the ledger, we see that the difficulties that attend metropolitan life are exaggerated. Participation in markets may be unpleasant indeed, but need not be as important as Marx and subsequent critics have implied. To be simpleminded about it, we have time for other things. And most of us spend little time thinking about politics. We can afford to let the public realm recede (to be tended by bureaucrats and bond traders), thereby alleviating whatever anxiety we might feel if we were to spend too much time thinking about a civilization we do not understand.

From this tough-minded perspective, the characteristic discontent of critics of market societies, the sense that we are alienated from our true selves, can be annoying, whining. The critics of monetary society take their alienation—guilt, romance, and other obsessions discovered in the leisure of the theory class—and by extension themselves, far too seriously. On the contrary, there is something liberating, to use an old-fashioned word, about the alienation and inauthenticity entailed in living behind formalism. Owning securities is so much less of a bother than running a company. Property does not mediate our experience in ways the young Marx worried about, because property has become too abstract to be experienced at all. We are not alienated by our relation to property because we do not know what we own. Participation in the economy to which we have claims is impossible, and the self forms itself in regard to other pursuits. In short, we have achieved the very utopia of which Marx dreamed (in *The German Ideology*), where one could do many things in a day, without ever becoming defined and so limited by one's occupation of the moment. (That most of us are obsessed with our careers is our own fault.)

Turning to public affairs, is the City well governed? Yes. We have lots of goods and services, and so markets seem to work well for us. We want markets to be the mechanism through which most goods and services are distributed. From this perspective, much of the earlier critique of metropolitan life is, well, soft. We are, or should be, willing to let markets be markets. We should expect market competitors to compete with one another, struggle to destroy one another, and we should not be surprised when most competitors do not enjoy the struggle. That is life in the big city. We do not choose modes of governance based on how pleasant the activity is, or else we could never pursue wars, careers, or financial services reform. The market works because it is all business. It is just beside the point to say that there is more to life than business—of course there is, which is why we have private lives.

For similar reasons, we should not expect the City to feel like a village, any more than a jet is a horse. We may travel the world, but our selves cannot identify with the people so encountered or be identified by them. So we must be represented, portrayed, symbolized, which is what property and so liberalism is about, the substitution of rights for facts. Rousseau's political ideal, the self-government of free individuals in small republics, remains attractive, but simply is not open to us—it was not even open to Rousseau or the Unabomber. Societies grow, and anomie grows apace. Technology, which makes it possible to exercise such power at such distances, precludes the possibility of small, intimate societies, at least without revolution. And alienation is better than slaughter.

There it is: an apology for global capitalism.

* * *

But this is not much of an apology, and much of this book has been an effort to do better. I would like to say that we live in a good world, not merely a world that can be endured, especially if one is wealthy. Is more possible for us? What may we hope from political life?

In order to approach this question, I have in various ways employed a number of very traditional distinctions, such as between the faculties of the mind and the appetites, between disinterested principle and self-interest, and most obviously, between public and private. Each of these distinctions has been "discredited" in recent years. Strong versions of each distinction will quickly generate contradictions, that is, each may be thought logically impossible to maintain. Particularly in a skeptical age, however, imperfect logic cannot be allowed to mean dispensable logic. More importantly, once we have turned from rigor to aesthetics, a certain amount of contradiction, tension between competing objectives, is expected. From an aesthetic perspective, the question is how the tensions that inhere in the traditional distinctions (and in life) are managed. I have employed such distinctions in ways that seemed to me appropriate, albeit unjustified by any systematic defense. For example, the legal distinction between public and private is a jurisprudential mess, but is psychologically necessary, even for jurisprudes. Similarly, while eschewing any effort to derive a detailed political theory from a Kantian understanding of the life of the mind, I often employ just such an understanding while discussing politics, and in particular my dissatisfaction with utilitarian thought. After philosophy comes philosophy—we must use ideas playfully, in ways we cannot defend, if we are to think at all. Nor should we be ashamed of this: thinking itself is not to be defended; it is indeed indefensible.

Apart from the preceding paragraph, I have made few postmodern noises about the ineffability of truth. At the same time, however, these essays clearly reflect a postmodern epistemological sensibility, an awareness of limitation, ambiguity, historical and other contingency, indeterminacy. It would be wrong, however, to understand this book as an antifoundational enterprise. Especially in part 2's concern for the experience of alienation, the recognition of inauthenticity, and the sense that the self confronts community as a lover and a task, this book has presumed that humans live vis-à-vis certain truths, and that the City of Gold must be respected, or not, to the extent to which it can deliver on such truths.

It is difficult to discuss truths of most any sort (certain pieties aside) in a time of what might be called epistemological paranoia, at least in the academy. This difficulty is aggravated by an awareness that the institutional framework within which such conversations are held, the university, makes little sense, and in the present instantiation is not even very interesting. We do not quite want to ask whether philosophers (to say nothing of writers) should be professors, because we know the answer, yet we see no viable alternative. This situation might seem to require a certain playful immodesty (in the sense of nakedness), coupled with a deep intellectual honesty. But it is difficult to be playful, naked, or honest in such a competitive society as the academy. Instead of playfulness we tend to pointless or partisan critique; nakedness is usually an opportunity for self-indulgence; disciplines make honesty superfluous. We live in a time of bad style, if not worse, in academe.

The decline of the university's authority, however, presents new opportunities. Now that the university is in ruins, it has become more clear that intellectual journeys need not remain within the disciplined boundaries of academic thought. Consequently, I have taken idiosyncratic paths, if they seemed to lead in the right direction. So, for examples, I have explored explicitly teleological approaches; taken aesthetic steps to reach conceptual categories; and proceeded with a pragmatic concern for the feel of thought, particularly for the emotion with which a line of thinking is experienced. All this, in order to reach the City of Gold—a myth of our own politics that may prove serviceable.

The myth of the City emerges from conflict with the skeptical claim that the supranational capital markets are merely that, markets, which simply do not constitute a polity. In this view, we may live in the ruins of old polities, or we may construct local communities within the broader framework of supranational capitalism, but the City itself is no polity, and therefore cannot satisfy the traditional political yearnings. More specifically, the argument that the City is no polity is threefold. First, the City is not founded on the desire for solidarity, amity, but instead on exclusion, envy. The City is not based on a desire for political connection. Second, the City does not have the institutional capacity to account for all that is appropriate to being human. It is difficult even to think about truth, justice, or identity from a metropolitan perspective. Third, the City inverts the relationship between head and gut, making the appetites the ruler of the mind, indeed banishing the mind. From this classical perspective, politics should be an institutional articulation of the human condition, but the City is only a macrocosmic shopping mall.

A modern response to this charge would be simple enough to offer and defend. From a modern perspective, the charge is based upon an overly ambitious conception of what is possible for politics. Political thought is a more limited enterprise than the charge presumes; political thought should satisfy itself with what is possible for actual people in actual societies. If the charge sets the standard for what it means to be a polity, then the modern nation state, as understood since Hobbes, is not a polity, either. After all, most modern political thought is founded on rather base emotions, like fear. And yet we have had several centuries of modern political thought.

My trouble with this response, however, is that this apology is hardly modern. Indeed, both substantively (especially in part 3) and methodologically, throughout, I have argued as if modern political thinking is in important ways at an end. More particularly, I have argued that the City represents an inversion of modern approaches to politics, that the City is in important respects not enlightened. More fundamentally still, I am sympathetic to the neoclassical charge that the City is an inadequate polity. Modern political thought has tended to leave out too much of what it was to be human, and so the question—to what extent can we think about politics, in this our world, in a way that responds to these deep human desires—is a very real question. Being superficially tough minded about our situation, limiting our aspirations for politics in order to make our achievements, such as they are, appear to be successes, does not solve much.

A more fruitful approach is to ask whether the classical idea of a polity ought to be understood seriously or playfully. I think it should be playful. It might be argued that the Greeks, paradigmatically Plato, put forth a complete vision of politics, and some version of this vision is entailed in the charge that the City is no polity. But Plato is explicit that his vision is unrealizable. The *Republic* is a thing of beauty, an exercise in thought, instructive in countless ways, but it is not a map of this or any possible world. Nor is it meant to be: the dialogue resists scientific and certainly instrumental readings. Plato employs myths, and myths are nothing until later adopted. The *Republic* is not just about education, it is itself educational, intended to be used later, by someone else. And surely it is the beginning of wisdom (a teacher's or a father's wisdom) that no matter how good the education, we cannot know the life that will flow from it. From this perspective, not even the *Republic* is a complete vision of politics—it is rather the effort to articulate such a vision and justify it logically. More generally, philosophy finds itself challenged (and perpetually failing) to overcome its limited resources. That is the fun of doing philosophy; games are not to be perfected. But Plato knows this too. One reason why the philosopher is always frustrated at the artist and bans him (from the middle of an artwork!) is because the artist, like the child, always means something that the mind cannot yet know. If we understand philosophy to be incapable of reaching its horizon, then the classical idea of a polity put forth above is a critical device that we can use to think about our politics, not some sort of cultural object that we do, or do not, possess. So the question should be reasked: To what extent do we, in the City, satisfy these yearnings? How far have we come in our journey toward an achieved political life?

This apology has put forth two groups of answers. Each group is loosely organized by traditional—if ultimately intertwined—concerns for how the polity handles truth, justice, and individual identity. The first set of answers flows directly from the logic of markets. The founding mandarins founded a society on markets—what does it mean to restrict political life within market interactions? So, throughout part 1, we amassed true things that could be said about living in this market society. We sketched the City as a historical phenomenon, with a particular sort of communicative space, with certain ideas about time, with its own erotics, and its own mode of governance. Although the intentions of the essays in parts 2 and 3 were primarily critical, even in those essays the social order entailed by the logic of the City seemed both true and justified in its way. Moreover, the structure of the market, and the human unwillingness to be treated badly, required the construction of the private individual who both participates in and rejects the market. But though private life is by definition limited, it offers its consolations. Private life affords not only the possibility for meaning, but even philosophy. In short, life in markets offers some truth, some sense of social order and hence justice, and some ways in which to feel at home.

The second group of answers, in part 4, flows from a broader and more social understanding of markets, in which markets themselves must be situated. What does a market require? How do we respond to our doing politics through markets? Whereas the first group of answers results from a rigorous effort to follow the founding logic to its conclusions, the second group of answers results from a more evaluative set of judgments about how the founding logic has been possible, and what it has meant since the founding. The first set of answers took the claims of market ideologues seriously, and pursued the logic of markets from within. The second set of analyses is literally more responsible. The same questions are asked from the perspective of one who has chosen a market (rather than inherited it), and is therefore responsible for the emergence of a market society. Such analysis presumes it is possible to stand outside markets, to do political economy.

In this second analysis, we saw that markets require government. In order for markets to function, their parameters must be established, that is, society must have an enforceable consensus on certain goods, most obviously the goods necessary to property, contract, and monetary regimes, but also health, environment, labor, and whatever else is required to ensure participation in a market society of that sophistication. Markets thus require truths, a politics of the head, and a set of responsible institutions to formulate and administer such truths. The City is not, and cannot be, a complete turning away from the politics of the mind.

Nor is the idea of truth restricted to the immediate questions of the marketplace—answers to the question of where to put the table, or what sort of marketplace do we wish to have. In deciding to do politics through markets, as we have, we grant license to market actors to act in their own self-interest, that is, immorally. In order that we may live with ourselves, we seek to bound the terms of such licenses. We desire rules, in order that we may be at liberty within the spaces delimited by the rules. Realization that life in markets is in many ways immoral is simultaneously a realization of the need for government. As a result, the commitment to governance through markets need not be an abdication of the responsibility for justice.

The most difficult of the elements of political life for the City to achieve, due to its vast extent, is a positive political feeling, solidarity, amity, the social glue that binds humans one to another. Even here, however, there are possibilities. We understood our distinction between public and private to be plausible if imperfect (and some such distinction appears to be necessary), and even to afford the possibility of aesthetic autonomy. That is, the City may give us the space in which to reflect and to understand. From this perspective, we may realize that although we publicly encounter economic actors as strangers—as other rights holders—behind those rights are people in many ways like us. In order to understand such people, we must attempt to imagine their situation as they confront it, we must try and sympathize. Thus the City holds the promise of an amity, not based on the shared experience of the polis, but based instead on imagination. In lieu of community or solidarity, we have sympathy. And so we return to myth— our effort to imagine our community.

There may even be practical implications of such a myth. Understanding the necessities and limitations that surround supranational capitalism may loosen its hold on our imaginations. The right wrongly has believed that we could avoid politics, that the proper construction of markets would relieve us of our obligations. But once we understand markets as modes of governance, rather than as oracles of truth, machines for processing "information" in order to determine that dictatorial species of truth known as "value," it should be easier to think about what a worthwhile civilization, our culture, should have. The left has wrongly believed that salvation lay in a sufficiently righteous approach to politics other than that of markets. But once we understand that we must make do with markets, those who think about politics in terms of eighteenth-century principle and nineteenth-century romance should be able to devote more attention to how we live now. Thus intellectually liberated, it is not too much to hope that at least the mandarin class will understand that beauty realized is more important than the potential satisfaction of money. If so, we may yet have the possibility of building a civilization we admire, that we are proud to call home.

Such sentiments need to be kept in perspective. For at least the two hundred and ten years since the French Revolution, intellectuals have sought religion in politics, including the politics of markets, and have failed to find it. Although we can and should hope to build a better polity, the City of Gold is not, and never can be, the City of God.

Afterword on Method
Apology, Essay, Myth

Why do I essay an apology for supranational capitalism? Why not sound the trumpets in the triumphal procession? There are plenty of trumpet players, who believe an apology for supranational capitalism in light of recent history is, to put it mildly, unnecessary. Or why not bang the drum slowly, as we mourn beauty lost and lives destroyed by markets? There are plenty of drummers, too, who gather to protest major meetings of the Bretton Woods Institutions, and who believe a convincing apology for supranational capitalism, responsible for so much misery, is impossible. I call the first group the right, the second the left, and count myself among neither.

What have I come to believe? I believe supranational capitalism is not only inevitable, it is morally right. But I also believe marketplace arrangements pose enormous difficulties for living well today. I want both trumpets and drums, playing different tunes. The dissonance of our times calls for the ambivalence of the apology. An apology has the structure of a legal justification, that is, the facts, upon which the charges are founded, are admitted, but the condemnation of those facts is contested. To mention two famous apologies by way of example: Plato was not ashamed of Socrates, and Sir Philip Sidney did not regret his poetry. At the same time, both Plato and Sidney admitted that the charges were grounded in fact, and serious. Socrates' teaching was impious, and poetry is founded on nothing more factual than the fancy of the poet. These are not trivial charges, even if they are not the whole truth. In our case, it matters that we live under a regime that is essentially base, alienating, and inclined to a certain tyranny.

Nonetheless, I maintain that the metropolitan constitution may be justified, even, with reservation, admired. Hence I apologize for our situation, and for the politics that brought us here. To make some peace, however provisional, with the conflicts that characterize the metropolitan consciousness (the mind that thinks in terms of supranational capitalism, as opposed to, for example, in terms of the nation state) is one of two vital aspirations for this apology. The second aspiration is to contribute to the revival of an unfashionable intellectual tradition and think politically about the economy.

My apology is couched in the form of a series of essays. Since the essay is not such a professional form as the article or the treatise, my use of the essay may raise a few eyebrows, and so merits a few words. Musil describes the essay as the "form assumed by a man's inner life in a decisive thought." Such thinking has an essentially narrative character: the essay reflects the process of learning what something has come to mean, and is in that sense an intellectual tale or account, a journey. This book of essays, then, is the story of my thinking about how to regard certain ways in which we now live together, and what a polity so constituted may hope to accomplish, or at least permit.

As a form, the essay is quite different from the Aristotelian discourse, or its descendents, the article or treatise traditional in academe. Aristotle felt the human condition to be available to perceptive minds, and therefore he could write in order to demonstrate truth, the unavoidable consequence of first principles, that is, he could write (or lecture) didactically. Today this attitude would seem pompous, or perhaps just ridiculous in a sophomoric way. We seem to have lost the sense that the human condition writ large, even our own condition, can be communicated or even thought with enough surety to make didactic writing plausible for oneself and for other adults, outside the covers of self-help books. Although we still manage to write didactically, we do so by allowing professional consensus, or sometimes advocacy, to serve in the role of truth. But what if we have also lost our faith in whatever professional training we have? If we are honest with ourselves, how much faith do we have in the institutions that reared us? And how much trust do we put in advocacy? More generally, what if we admit that we do not know what the significance of recent history will be? Although we may continue to write professional articles for professional purposes, and we may enjoy arguments by way of middlebrow relaxation, our serious efforts to make judgments—locate our lives within a meaningful frame—are unlikely to be expressed as articles. The essay has become necessary because neither the article nor its more argumentative derivatives, the editorial, the op-ed piece, the *plaidoyer*, are completely serious any longer.

Thoughtful writing need not stop just because we find ourselves to be "men on an adventure who have gone astray," for whom particular meanings are obscured by the lack of a general framework. Big questions should still be asked, and the essay remains a viable way to interrogate our situation. The essayist endeavors to secure both particular judgments—what to think—and the situation that makes such judgments possible, how we and our worlds are comprised. Without indulging in confession, for now it suffices to say that I have had adventures, and for that matter gone astray, and am probably as ready as I will ever be to try and articulate, even justify, the way we now live. The turn from the academic article to the essay mirrors a turn from knowledge to experience, from truth to belief, and from logic to telling. The authority of the essay—which, I hope, can support philosophy—lies in its kinship to the novel, or even the tale. This is how I came to be where I am; this is why I think as I do.

Essays, walks, presume geography, the terrain they traverse. In living thoughtfully here and now, we have ways to think about the place, myths. The word "myth" is not meant pejoratively, as an untrue story, some sort of deception. Myths may be very true. Just as Chief Justice Marshall famously admonished that we must not forget that it is a Constitution we cannot escape interpreting, we must remember that it is our world that we are constructing.[1] We are surrounded by collective fictions so deep as to constitute political discourse and so relations. Consider, for instances, money, the market, the nation, democracy, and the self—by "myth" I mean nothing more or less than the cultural apparatus with which our world is constructed and so apprehensible. So myths of supranational capitalism are inevitable, are arising even now, with talk of globalization and the ensuing stories. Such myths are psychological necessities, understandings in the most subjective sense, which cannot wait for truth (the play is too short for truth to arrive).

Myths are of constitutional consequence; they make the culture in which they are believed. To use a recent example, the amazing success of the neoconservatives is largely due to the fact that they have made their myth, in essence a retelling of the Hobbesian state of nature story, central to contemporary political discourse. (One could of course tell a similar story about myths told around leftist campfires.) On the basis of such myths, more rationalistic structures, theories, can be erected. But it is the foundation, the myth, that is at issue here. The neoconservatives offered a perspective, and though a great deal of research has been done, the success of that perspective is not at all dependent on any particular fact, reading, insight, or truth. The perspective works, that is, the myth explains a world, which might plausibly be our world, at least until a better myth comes along. Until then, however, the neoconservative myth presents and so creates a world with a certain appeal. The myth describes the rather atomistic life indeed found in competitive markets, particularly spot markets; provides elegant ideological arguments (hence the tendency to convert doctrinaire minds of the left); is oddly comforting in its machismo ("rigor"); plays to the alienation of affluent white males, who feel beleaguered in the academy and elsewhere; and generally relieves guilt. It would be childish to ask whether such a myth is true. The point is, for a great number of people, the myth has been true enough to inform political life.

The neoconservative myth, however, is no longer serviceable. Our markets have become so central to how we live that they should be understood in deeper fashion. We need an alternative account, a new mythology, that responds to more of the human condition, and in particular, that accounts for the many, and true, criticisms of a narrowly economic understanding of life. As mentioned above, this book is an effort to articulate such a mythology.

Serious mythological thinking does not come easily in the United States, which has a long and deep tradition of realism—by which I here mean the tendency to confuse the denial of some set of myths with thinking. In this tradition, Roosevelt could say that he and Stalin understood each other so well because both were "realists."[2] Such realists went on to organize the planet around ideological distinctions drawn from dimly or indirectly remembered Enlightenment thinkers. Millions of lives were lost in the name of ideas held by men who, throughout, insisted on the necessity of their actions. My point is not that unawareness of our myths is immoral, dangerous, and bad form, though it is all of these things. I argue more simply that myths are inevitable, and it is one job, perhaps the most important job, of the political thinker to make our myths conscious, available to our minds.

The issue, then, is not something like the correct theory of globalization (references to enough reading for several lifetimes attached), but rather how a thoughtful citizen should envisage the situation formed by supranational capitalism. How do we imagine where we are? What is our constitutive myth—for this constitution? Each of us is always and already prepared to write some sort of apology, more or less sophisticated, more or less accurate (and verisimilitude does matter) for this our world.

With that, let me welcome you home to the City of Gold.

Notes

Front Matter

1. Wilkins & Pike trans/ed., 273

Introduction

1. To establish the moment: during the period this text was drafted, in the Delphic language of Wall Street indices, the Dow Jones Industrial Average closed at 11,722.98 points (on January 14, 2000), and the NASDAQ reached 5,132.52 points (on March 10, 2000), closing at 5048.61 points. The scores had never been better—with numbers like those, we must have been happy. Things changed in the equity markets during the revision and editing, of course, but the fact remains that most readers of a book such as this are materially wealthy by almost any standard.
2. This book uses "Marxian" to denote thinking indebted to Marx, even if only indirectly, as in "Marxian tradition." In a most un-Marxian distinction between thought and ideology, speculation and *praxis*, the term "Marxist" is used to denote an ideology, political affiliation, or a government.
3. Whether or not this is the result of objective historical forces, such as economic laws or technological progress, or the successful execution of a conspiracy, seems to depend on one's political prejudices. Amusingly enough, the political right now tends to argue from historical necessity, while those on the left, now again calling themselves "progressives," argue from the corruption of power.
4. There are, of course, other ways to approach globalization, or one may speak of globalizations, of technology, of professional standards, of bureaucracy, of knowledge, of culture, and so on. Money is hardly the only place to start. That said, money occupies a central place in contemporary political life, the concern of this book. A far more total, indeed encyclopedic, account of recent changes is provided by Manuel Castells in his imposing and impressive trilogy (which he calls a book), *The Information Age: Economy, Society, and Culture* (Cambridge, Mass.: Blackwell, 1996, 1997, and 1998). My assessment of our situation and my understanding of how to think and especially write under contemporary circumstances are quite different from those of Castells. *The Information Age* is explicitly a book written from an enlightened standpoint. The present book argues, in a variety of ways, that the age of the *philosophes* is past, and no longer available or even really attractive to us. Even Castells, in his conclusion, is a bit wary of the presumptions entailed in his book, presumptions of a scale that in less genial hands have led to horror, and so he quite frankly eschews policy.
5. The argument that improved technology would make geography irrelevant has been around for some time. See, e.g. John Naisbitt, *Megatrends: Ten New Directions for Transforming Our Lives* (New York: Warner, 1982). This argument may easily be overstated—global culture seems increasingly an urban phenomenon, with specific locations that matter.

6.   In the wake of recent terrorism, the continued necessity of the state cannot reasonably be denied, but even those who acknowledge the state's ongoing vitality are likely to acknowledge that the state no longer holds the exclusive position it once did.

7.   Westbrook, David A., "Law Through War," 48 *Buff. L. Rev.* 299 (2000). See also id, "Islamic International Law and Public International Law: Separate Expressions of World Order," 33 *Va. J. Int'l L.* 819 (1993).

8.   See Joseph P. Quinlan, *Global Engagement: How American Companies Really Compete in the Global Economy* (McGraw Hill/Contemporary Books, 2000).

9.   It is not clear how to begin thinking about national competitiveness (and associated balance of payments and hence currency problems) if trade in goods and services is no longer the primary form of commercial intercourse. As a purely intellectual matter, the question is somewhat misstated. Quite apart from foreign direct investment, economies need not be organized along the lines of a nation. This is hardly news to economic historians. See e.g. Gavin Wright, *Old South, New South* (New York: Basic Books, 1986): vii: "Nations are not necessarily economies and vice versa," writes Wright (crediting William Parker). An abstract understanding of the economy—including the political understanding that is this book's concern—simply has little to do with national boundary lines.

10.   An analogy to competition law (antitrust in the United States) may be helpful. In order to determine whether a competitive market exists, competition law looks not just at actual competition, but for barriers that prevent potential competitors from entering into a given market. Where barriers to entry are low or nonexistent, one would expect prices to be disciplined by the threat of competition. Market participants that attempt to extract great profits (in the jargon, exercise market power to extract rents) tend to attract competitors. Similarly, the mere threats of arbitrage (selling the same item in different markets) and of foreign direct investment act to unify markets, even in the absence of actual economic activity.

11.   For example, in his deservedly widely read book *The Lexus and the Olive Tree*, Thomas Friedman writes "that I feel about globalization a lot like I feel about the dawn. Generally speaking I think it is a good thing that the sun comes up every morning. . . . But even if I didn't much care for the dawn there isn't much I could do about it." Thomas L. Friedman, *The Lexus and the Olive Tree: Understanding Globalization*, updated edition (New York: Anchor, 2000): xxi–xxii. And who could disagree?

Part 1

1.   "Since the start of the peace negotiations, which by then had been in progress for almost three years, the road from Osnabrueck via Telgte to Muenster had been much traveled in both directions, from the Protestant to the Catholic camp and contrariwise, by couriers in carriages and on horseback, bearing an archive-glutting mass of petitions, memoranda, scheming missives, invitations to festivities, and agents' reports on the latest military movements, which had been going on undeterred by the peace negotiations." Günther Grass, *The Meeting at Telgte*, trans. Ralph Mannheim (New York: Harcourt, 1981): 9. The book was originally published in 1979. Grass writes of culture at the end of the Thirty Years' War as a way to understand culture after World War Two. "Our stories of today need not have taken place in the present. This one began more than three hundred years ago. So did many other stories. Every story set in Germany goes back that far." Id., 3.

Chapter I

1.   The end of World War Two witnessed the emergence of a great number of other international institutions, and a great deal of law, much of which promoted economic development, and all of which matters in some sense. One might, for example, also mention the United Nations Educational, Scientific, and Cultural Organization (UNESCO), or the Organization for Economic Cooperation and Development (OECD), or the International Organization for Standards (ISO). In particular, the OECD grew out of the Organization for European Economic Cooperation (OECC), which had grown out of the Marshall Plan. By the same token, one might note that quite a few people besides Madison attended the Constitutional Convention, or were otherwise active in U.S. politics in its formative moments, and that too is important as a matter of historical study. Foundational myths, however, are both less and more than academic history.

2. Modern political thought purports to be useful. Both Machiavelli and Hobbes thought they were doing, not just reflecting on, politics, and most political thinkers since have been explicitly practical. Whether modern political thought has in fact been useful is not quite so obvious as it might first seem. Though we tend to regard the familiar arrangements of modern liberalism as a practical success, the incidence of tyranny is sobering—it is difficult to believe that twentieth-century history, even in the United States, will be taken as evidence for the power of our political thought. No doubt it was not our fault, but its Madisonian liberalism did not prevent the United States from engaging in numerous wars, and even nuclear confrontation, with the fate of humanity on the line. Such drama may make for good reading, but it is bad politics, even bad at securing the life, liberty, and pursuit of happiness that we Americans have traditionally claimed as our goal. But whatever the practical insufficiencies of the modern political tradition, the tradition has been an enormous success as philosophy and ideology—we have difficulty thinking in other terms.

3. At this level, history's lessons tend to be rather simple and abstract. Consider a familiar example relevant to this book: the crash of the United States stock markets in 1929 was caused by widespread buying on margin and on insufficient, even fraudulent, information. The crash caused a series of bank failures, which were inadequately addressed by the Federal Reserve. The collapse of the securities and banking industries in turn caused the Great Depression. This story may or may not be true, and is certainly the sort of radical simplification that makes academic historians cringe. It is not clear how fraud and margin buying contributed to the crash, nor is it at all clear that the crash, with or without an effective Fed, caused the depression. But whether or not this is a fair simplification of the truth, it is more or less the simplification that informs U.S. securities and banking policy and law.

4. "Victory in this war is the first and greatest good before us. Victory in the peace is the next." Franklin D. Roosevelt, 7 January 1943. Quoted in Georg Schild, *Bretton Woods and Dumbarton Oaks* (Basingstoke: Macmillan, 1995): ix. Variations on the theme of winning the peace were widespread, and were used by both White and Keynes in their proposals for the Bretton Woods institutions. See Rosa Lastra, "The Bretton Woods Institutions in the XXIst Century," in *The Reform of the International Financial Architecture*, Rosa Lastra, ed. (Boston: Kluwer, 2001): 69.

5. It could well be argued that continental war had been tried before, notably during the Thirty Years' War, but the depth of World War One nonetheless appears to have been a shock to all involved. And it is worth recalling that the Thirty Years' War also marked the end of an epoch, and the birth of another. Grotius wrote in response to the Thirty Years' War; the Peace of Westphalia is taken to be the founding of modern international law; it is the Thirty Years' War that gives legal form to the nominalist idea of the nation state. The point here is that the World Wars, and particularly World War Two, bring to its end the political era inaugurated by the Thirty Years' War.

6. For a discussion and copious bibliography of the contemporary and subsequent objections of the economics profession to the Smoot-Hawley Act, see Michael A. Bernstein, *A Perilous Progress: Economics and Public Purpose in Twentieth-Century America* (Princeton, N.J.: Princeton, 2001): 1–2.

7. Competitive devaluation is the practice of devaluing one's own currency, making exports cheap and imports expensive, thereby benefiting domestic producers.

8. In the United States, the federal government's response to the depression, the New Deal, was both a package of economic reform and a restructuring of the nation's constitutional order, comparable to the Civil War years and to the founding itself.

9. See Federalist No. 10 (Madison). *The Federalist Papers*, Willmore Kendall and George W. Carey, eds., (New Rochelle, N.Y.: Arlington House, 1966). This is not to deny that Madison understood faction to be a source of great danger to the polity as well. The genius of his argument, however, is that Madison saw the political opportunity in faction, which had traditionally been regarded solely as a threat.

10. Atlantic Charter Conference (held at sea); Casablanca; Moscow; Cairo; Teheran; Quebec; Washington (several, most importantly Dumbarton Oaks); Yalta; Potsdam.

11. The informal but very successful gold standard, in which the Bank of England had functioned as liquidity provider to a worldwide network of similar currency regimes, had collapsed in 1914, with the beginning of World War One. Efforts to recreate the system after 1918 were less than successful, and England went off gold, again, in 1931.

12. Jean Monnet, Memoirs (trans. Richard Mayne) (New York: Doubleday, 1978) at 296. On Schuman's actual announcement of the proposal, Monnet said "I am not at all sure that

Schuman's dull, hesitant voice immediately convinced them that they were witnessing a profound transformation of international politics . . . " id. at 304.

13. This is not to imply that there exist only two configurations of property rights, communist collectivization or liberal privatization, or, as is still heard from unreconstructed economists, that there is a single natural ("optimal") configuration of such rights. Property may be configured in endless ways. Consider: takings law; different requirements for owning real estate or taxable income in various countries; socialism, democratic and otherwise; or contemporary regulatory theory, which proposes the construction of markets. If property were simply private or public, these would not be conceptually difficult and contested areas of law.

14. The text reflects my concern with how community may be achieved. Minds of a more technocratic bent, such as corporation law scholar and F.D.R. braintruster Adolf Berle, stressed the convergence of Soviet and U.S. economic organization until at least the end of the Second World War. See Jordan A. Schwarz, *Liberal: Adolf A. Berle and the Vision of an American Era* (New York: Free Press, 1987): 75. The idea that the Soviet and U.S. economic systems were fundamentally alike is also compatible with a belief that economic truth transcended politics. See Bernstein, supra n. 6 187–88.

15. A youthful effort to consider this question in terms of Rousseau is available in David A. Westbrook, "One Among Millions: An American Perspective on Citizenship in Large Polities," *Annales de Droit de Louvain*, 333 (1993).

16. Old visions of judgment day and more recent millenarian suggestions of nuclear apocalypse or the obsolence of humanity would involve the end of markets and are almost imaginable, but are not visions of a political history.

17. Dean Acheson, *Present at the Creation: My Years in the State Department* (New York: Norton, 1969).

18. Four slightly more detailed examples should suffice to demonstrate the continued vitality of the distinction between economics and politics:

    1. The Bretton Woods Institutions routinely claim that their policy prescriptions are required by sound economics, and have no political, i.e., self-interested, motivation. Many critics of the Bretton Woods Institutions rely on the same distinction by arguing for "economic" aid of various sorts to developing nations without "political" interference.

    2. Social critics rely on the distinction between politics and economics when they view the market as a malign or benign influence on formal political processes, e.g., bemoan the corrupting influence of money on elections, or argue that economic liberalism will require political liberalism in China.

    3. For economists, the professional requirement of methodological individualism prohibits thinking in political (i.e., group) categories. Economists often do think in terms of groups, e.g., corporations, states, or the market, formally forbidden them by the tenets of their faith, but their fidelity to the idea of the autonomous rational market actor, even in the breach, is shown by the widespread tendency to treat such forbidden entities as if they were individuals.

    4. Finally and most obviously, both triumphal and alarmist attitudes toward globalization tend to require a distinction between those institutions we think of as "the market" and those institutions we think of as "the government."

19. Keyne's thought here has direct antecedents. George Eliot's Felix Holt says: "I would never choose to withdraw myself from the labour and common burthen of the world; but I do choose to withdraw myself from the push and the scramble for money and position. Any man is at liberty to call me a fool, and say that mankind are benefited by the push and the scramble in the long-run. But I care for the people who live now and will not be living when the long-run comes. As it is, I prefer going shares with the unlucky." George Eliot, *Felix Holt: The Radical* (New York: Harper & Brothers, 1866). Keynes did not withdraw from the pursuit of money—he was preternaturally good at it, in fact—and could not be considered unlucky. Keyne's remark thus illustrates doubt and reconsideration at the heart of the polity.

20. Robert Musil, *The Man Without Qualities*, trans. Sophie Wilkins. (New York: Knopf, 1995): 648.

21. The quotations from both Wilson and Roosevelt are available in Daniel Patrick Moynihan, *On the Law of Nations* (Cambridge, Mass: Harvard Univ., 1990) 52–53, 74, respectively.

22. The phrase nation of shopkeepers arose in the context of Adam Smith's discussion of colonial empire:

> To found a great empire for the sole purpose of raising up a people of customers may at first sight appear a project fit only for a nation of shopkeepers. It is, however, a project altogether unfit for a nation of shopkeepers; but extremely fit for a nation whose government is influenced by shopkeepers. Such statesmen, and such statesmen only, are capable of fancying that they will find some advantage in employing the blood and treasure of their fellow-citizens to found and maintain such an empire.

    Adam Smith, *An Inquiry into the Nature and Causes of the Wealth of Nations* (New York: Random House/Modern Library, 1937): 579.

23. Plato, *The Republic*, ed. G.R.F. Ferrari, trans. Tom Griffith, (Cambridge: Cambridge Univ., 2000): 55. Socrates has just sketched a very prosaic understanding of the *polis*, a city with simple handicrafts and rudimentary trade. Objecting particularly to a description of meals in such a city, Glaucon characterizes the city envisioned by Socrates as "a City of Pigs," and asks for civilization, "If they are going to eat in comfort, they should lie on couches, eat off tables, and have the cooked dishes and desserts which people today have." Socrates immediately deflates Glaucon's request, calling it a desire for "luxury," and noting that such luxury requires wealth, and the pursuit of wealth is likely to lead to war. But Socrates' heart remains with Glaucon, and the rest of *The Republic* is devoted to a vision of the possibilities available to civilized—the Republic will soon say "spirited"—politics. The City of Gold may be understood as an effort to achieve the polity Socrates initially suggests, rather than Glaucon's countersuggestion, precisely for the reason Socrates suggests, the avoidance of war. The difference, of course, is that the City is premised on the idea that war can be avoided through satiety, rather than the material modesty Socrates suggests. In light of contemporary violence, the City's premise is by no means conclusively demonstrated.

24. As already suggested in the discussion of international law, other developments have been immensely important, e.g., decolonialization, the emergence of human rights, and the idea that the state is responsible for social conditions, but each of these may be seen as a logical if perhaps not inevitable outgrowth of enlightened liberalism, carried out within the context of the nation state, or the community of nation states. Economic integration, in contrast, was epochal, in large part because it has required the reconception of the state, and so politics.

25. Erwin Panofsky defined the "Renaissance proper" as the time during which the belief that art could be both true to nature (scientific, taught, rule-bound) coexisted with the belief that art could be true to the genius of the artist and to ideals of beauty that were not mere images of observed realities. See Erwin Panofsky, *Idea*, trans. Joseph J.S. Peake (Columbia: Univ. South Carolina, 1968): especially 67–68. The book was originally published in 1924.

26. Churchill said, "No one pretends that democracy is perfect or all-wise. Indeed it has been said that democracy is the worst form of Government except all those other forms that have been tried from time to time." Speech, *Hansard* 11 November 1947, co. 206.

27. Which may go far to explain why Western intellectuals, alienated yet with faith in thought, tended to support communist regimes long after they should have known better.

Chapter II

1. It must be acknowledged that the market was never only a specific place at a specific time. Behind the corner grocer's bag of flour has always stood the dispersed situation of farmers, factors, government, consumers, and other actors in the broader market for wheat. Even a highly localized market in an agrarian society, such as one might imagine in medieval Europe or in the developing world today, reflects a span of weather, labor, peace or war, and itinerant traders, i.e., signifies far more than its immediate particulars. That said, our experience of markets is more ethereal than formerly.

2. And yet, even though we trade no place, we continue to imagine, and perhaps must imagine, marketplace activity in spatial terms. We speak of entering and leaving the market. Markets themselves rise and fall, sometimes in cyclical ways. We graph everything. Despite the dematerialization of markets, we still think in spatial, even geometrical, ways.

3. "Economics" comes from *oikonomikos*, the management of the household.

4. Talking Heads, liner notes for the album *Stop Making Sense* (New York: Sire Records, 1984).

5. Which is not to say that markets (or sex or dominion) are perfectly represented by their institutional reifications. One can certainly imagine markets based on barter, sex without institutionalization of its negotiation or consequences, and raw physical dominion, but just barely, and only in a place so primitive as to approximate the mythical and in some influential quarters longed-for state of nature.

6. Aristotle, *Politics*, Book I, sec. IX, trans. Ernest Barker (London: Oxford U. Press, 1958).

7. Fortunately, many participants in our dispensation have a sophisticated if perhaps somewhat inchoate understanding of the nature as opposed to the mere appearance of money. For those who do not, this book leaves the task of denaturalizing money to any competent historian of the topic, and especially the elegant novelist and essayist James Buchan. See James Buchan, *Frozen Desire: The Meaning of Money* (New York: Farrar, Straus & Giroux, 1997).

8. See, for example, Alan Greenspan, "New challenges for monetary policy," before a symposium sponsored by the Federal Reserve Bank of Kansas City in Jackson Hole, Wyoming, August 27, 1999, available at www.federalreserve.gov/boarddocs/speeches/1999/19990827.htm

9. Perhaps price discovery is a good thing, like being told the outcome of an election, but it is the telling that is at issue here.

10. Quoted in Thomas A. Bass, "The Future of Money," *Wired* Issue 4.10 (October 1996): 202. Information about states to which one has extended enormous amounts of credit is pretty important, too.

11. Miserliness, the refusal to participate, is abhorrent both because it indicates a lack of sympathy for others (selfishness), and because, more generally, it indicates withdrawal from the community (abandonment).

12. Derrida insists that such difference is at the root of language.

13. As discussed below, money is not an internally consistent institution. As the numbers involved get truly large—the market capitalization of certain firms, or the amounts needed to buy a corporation—amounts may be only notionally reckoned in dollars. The supply of cash, even though dematerialized, limits the size of acquisition that can be done as a "cash"—meaning wire transfer, i.e., communication between banks—deal. In such situations, stock is used in lieu of cash. (There are, of course, other reasons to use stock in lieu of cash for certain deals, e.g., tax considerations and a rising stock market.) Thus the functionality of the dollar as a medium of exchange is restricted by its character as a commodity of limited supply. The functionality of the dollar as a unit of account, however, is unaffected by the actual supply of dollars (at least in the short term, i.e., holding to one side the affects of such transactions on monetary psychology).

14. The collapse of the sucre was eerily foretold in the Vonnegut novel *Galapagos*. See Kurt Vonnegut, *Galapagos* (New York: Dell, 1985): 30.

15. Nor was this a new sensibility. The father of Gothic architecture, Abbot Suger of St. Denis, contemplating the gold and jewels that ornamented the Abbey, wrote "Thus, when—out of my delight in the beauty of the house of God—the loveliness of the many-colored gems has called me away from external cares, and worthy meditation has induced me to reflect, transferring that which is material to that which is immaterial, on the diversity of the sacred virtues . . . that, by the grace of God, I can be transported from this inferior to that higher world in an anagogical manner." Abbot Suger: On the Abbey Church of St.-Denis and its Art Treasures, trans. Erwin Panofsky, 2d ed., ed. by Gerda Panofsky-Soergel (Princeton, N.J.: Princeton University Press, 1979): 63–64. Erwin Panofsky edited and translated the first edition in 1946.

16. The City of Gold is founded on a rejection of gold.

17. In the first sale, one asset account, X, is debited, but another asset, cash, is credited an amount equal to the value of X, viz., 1000. Similarly, in the second transaction, the purchase, one asset, cash, is debited 1000 (A spent 1000), but another asset, Y, is also booked at value 1000. Liabilities and equity, the right side of the balance sheet, remain unchanged.

18. In order to minimize the problem that even relatively stable currencies have fluctuating, rather than fixed, values, accountants generally specify the value of the currency as of a specific date, i.e., remove the temporal aspect of the problem. The more difficult epistemological difficulties are simply ignored, i.e., money and value tend to be equated.

19. Joseph H. Sommer, "A Law of Financial Accounts: Modern Payment and Securities Transfer Law," *The Business Lawyer* 53 (1998): 1181; "Where is a Bank Account?" *MD. L. Rev.* 59 (1998): 1.

20. In a provocative and wide-ranging book, *Money in an Unequal World*, Keith Hart correctly seizes on the analogy between money and language, and—as does this book—tries to use

that analogy to fashion a political theory. Hart is progressive: he argues that information technology should allow us to reinvent markets, so that money becomes much more like language, so that we eventually would come to feel at home with our monetary transactions, kind to our fellows, and so forth. Hart, in short, attempts to imagine a capitalism that would be progressive in a very old-fashioned sense. Without quibbling, I think Hart has identified the problem correctly (and in that, his book is far more advanced than most), and I'm sympathetic to his attempt. In practice and in theory, however, money will never be language, and our capitalism will never be as warm as Hart wishes. See Keith Hart, *Money in an Unequal World: Keith Hart and His Memory Bank* (New York: Texere, 2000).

21. The SEC's worthy plain English initiatives pass for thinking about communication.

22. A certain sort of reader may wish to read *City* as an application of postmodern thought to the phenomena known as globalization. By this point in the text, however, such a reader may well have noticed that although *City* seems very sensitive to the thrust of postmodern critique, this book eschews standard postmodern approaches. *City* may seem to be aware of, yet to have suppressed, its postmodernity, and so a bit of explanation about this book's stance may be helpful.

First, *City* is a postmodern book in that it explicitly takes "the turn to interpretation." I have not felt it necessary, however, to recapitulate the epistemological realization implied by the turn. This point is significant only because the entire discipline of economics has not taken this turn. For a large segment of the hoped for readership, taking economics seriously as cultural production will be profoundly problematic. The mainstream of economics has been the effort to establish a scientific, objective, and hence precultural social science. As *City* will demonstrate at great length, I do not believe this is a worthwhile enterprise, but I have not attempted to make this argument directly. The important bridge between the oft-mocked physics envy of so much economics and a more serious political economy is not rational argument but the undeniable ubiquity of law. The financial markets are constructed by law, law, and more law—and a more artificial, in that sense cultured, process cannot be imagined.

Second, *City* eschews the postmodern historical approach. An entire raft of books understands the present predicament by retelling intellectual history. I saw no way that such an approach would make *City* a better book, so I have not constructed, and then criticized, some enlightened idea of certainty (although sometimes I have been tempted by economists to do so). In general, I have serious problems with the "genealogy of postmodernity" approach, which typically implies that contemporary predicaments are the logical, even necessary, outgrowths of intellectual mistakes made in the past (usually mistakes that one has just learned about, in the tendentious history provided to support the author's critique of the status quo). Criticism through recounting the thoughts (or errors) of major thinkers thus prompts the classic error of intellectual historians, which is to overemphasize how important thinkers are to a society, and how responsive societies are to fine thoughts. This is flattering, but generally untrue.

Moreover, these "historical" arguments participate in two discourses that I find intensely problematic, for reasons both embodied and protested by Nietzsche: understanding through history and understanding through the university. Postmodern books are, in countless ways, university books. The modern university, first embodied in Humboldt's Berlin and understood as a certain engagement with history, is precisely what Heidegger dishonors. We may have poetry after Auschwitz, but for our crowd the tougher question is how to take the University—and with it, the thinking through history taught us by the Germans—completely seriously after Heidegger. I strongly suspect we cannot, and have said as much. See David A. Westbrook, "Pierre Schlag and the Temple of Boredom," *Miami L. Rev.* (2002). As Lyotard and others have pointed out, it is the university that the move out of modernity calls into question. See, e.g., Jean-François Lyotard, *The Postmodern Condition* (St. Paul: U. Minn. Press, 1984). In its antagonism to the University, *City* is almost a radical book, that is, the book nips the hand that feeds its author so well.

Third, *City*'s critique tends to be internal. As an article of faith, postmodern critique explicitly denies the possibility of an outside perspective, an Olympian point, but then goes on to carry on critique, and to prescribe, as if the author were not involved in politics, were, in fact, standing on some Olympus (presumably high up in the humanities building). So, for example, capital is almost always somewhere else, deployed by someone else. "The law" not incidentally occupies an analogous position in much legal scholarship. Implicitly, the scholar is just an honest critic, trying to make the world a better place through the production of articles, i.e., scholarly *praxis* as the path to liberation. More seriously, great swaths of the academy have not abandoned the position of the *philosophes*—we are legitimated by the illegitimacy of the regime we oppose (and will invent if necessary). Modernity is harder to leave than it looks (as Habermas has pointed out for decades now), even by those who identify themselves as postmodern.

In contrast to such postmodern critique, *City* candidly adopts an internal critique (I am a capitalist, and so are you), and asks what the psychic costs of such a position are. It turns out the costs are considerable, and so we need to find a way to make peace with our complicity, i.e., we need an apology. Therefore *City* examines the practices that comprise our capitalism, and asks, over and over again, what is logically entailed in that set of practices. So, for example, a certain obsession with the future is entailed in borrowing money—and so finance is inherently progressive in the literal sense of discontent with the present, premised on the future . . . and anxieties flow from that. This is not a new idea of critique: Kant did this all the time. In a different way, so do lawyers.

Fourth, *City,* and especially chapter II, examines structures on the assumption that structures are meaningful. Social practices are abstracted, and their relationships are discussed as if they were logical. For many theorists the problem (apart from lack of experience and laziness) with such a neo-structural approach seems to be that entering the world won't work in theory. It seems impossible to describe a given set of social practices without imposing a logical order, and such an order is, well, logocentric. Horrors. It turns out that the exercise of power may be inescapable, even in intellectual life. Further horrors.

The epistemological argument for the neostructuralist project undertaken here, and the effort to forestall poststructuralist critique, is based on history, and is in the last part of the book. The recognition that our situations are historically contingent is not a purely negative recognition, to be deployed when one senses a foundationalist argument and an associated assertion of dominance. To be historically situated is to be limited, to recognize that not all thoughts are available to us, and that what we actually do (and we inescapably do something) can serve as an object for thoughts worth discussing, even if they never completely determine themselves.

Fifth, and turning away from recognition of our historical situation, *City* is a self-consciously mythological project. *City* is truly after-modern in that it rejects the claim of political science/philosophy since Machiavelli, that thought is justified insofar as it results in better politics. That is the kind of thing said by people with axes to grind, or who don't really understand much about how politics is made in this or any other time, or who (most commonly and often in good faith) simply delude themselves about the fate of thinking in the world. *City* has rather modest *practical* aspirations for thought. This, too, may reflect my experience of the law. Soberly considered, the usual role for political thought is to figure out what it means to be living in a certain way. Adopting a given social practice entails a certain set of consequences for who we are and how we judge our own lives; adopting another practice entails a different set of consequences for the same existential questions. So, for example, organizing things through markets means that we do not take substantive equality very seriously.

Insofar as philosophers make politics, they do so by making myths—and that is how I understand the political success of Hobbes, Marx, Rousseau, Kant, and especially Adam Smith—except for scholarship, we do not really care what they said, we have forgotten most of what we have read, but it is not reading that is important. Few convinced capitalists have read Adam Smith. What is politically significant about such thinkers is how they have populated our minds. In this vein, the point of *City* is to see if we can create a myth out of the end of WWII and the rejection of Hitler . . . a myth of integration, alienation, and perhaps chilly sympathy, rather than the warmer pleasures of nationalism.

23. That this has not happened yet may reflect a fundamental problem in the sociology of knowledge: on those rare occasions when humanities types consider markets, they tend to recite egalitarian pieties rather than thinking hard about what markets might mean.

24. Limited monies that restrict the scope of payment, and so the purposes for which such money may be spent, have been proposed and even issued, e.g., company scrip, campus cash, or latterly, electronic money embedded in smart cards that can only be spent at certain venues. Turning to corporate finance, there are many forms of what might broadly be considered money—lines of credit, or equity, or options to buy equity, in a company. Such instruments fuel corporate operations, executive hiring, and acquisitions, and are restricted

by law or contract in ways that the fiat money the federal government issues through the banking system are not restricted. That said, such media of exchange suffer in comparison with money, or do not fully realize the idea of money, precisely insofar as the scope of their use is restricted by their particular legal situation. Such money is more or less illiquid, i.e., not convertible into cash understood as the unrestricted token of a desire not yet decided or even envisioned.

25. Similarly, it must be admitted that in practice, dollars are not perfectly fungible. The existence of markets in government obligations and foreign exchange reflects not only uncertainty regarding the worth of dollars, but also the different values different actors place upon cash flow as opposed to net worth considerations. For example, a pension fund that has relatively well-defined and predictable monthly outlays for benefits will sacrifice a considerable amount of value in order to ensure the ability to service that outlay, hence the market in, instruments that offer a high degree of predictability. More generally, corporations and individuals tend to allocate cash or its equivalents to different uses, and held in different accounts. Within the system of accounting, however, monies may be separated but they remain fundamentally equal.

26. See "Politics and the English Language," in George Orwell, *Shooting an Elephant* (New York: Harcourt, 1984).

27. For years the sovereign has been understood in terms of the nation state, either headed by a monarch, or, latterly, by the liberal institutions of republican democracy. Even then, however, so long as positivism did not hold absolute sway over the legal imagination, the ability to conduct all sorts of relations across national borders was taken to reflect the law of nations, that is, the law common among civilized peoples, "nations." The term international law was coined by Bentham to account for the law created by states on the analogy of contract, i.e., in an effort to discuss international law without necessarily nebulous reference to the shared law of nations. Regardless of the extent to which one deems Bentham's effort to have been successful in its day, once the details of political life organized without regard to national borders bulk sufficiently large, then the term "international law" seems somewhat outmoded, and one hears talk of globalization, and even world law. See Harold J. Berman, "World Law," 18 *Fordham Int'l L.J.* (1995): 1617.

Chapter III

1. The attentive reader may note a shift from "money" in the last essay to "finance" in the present essay, and wonder if the claim that the City is built upon money is equivalent to the claim that the City is built upon finance. It is, because money is itself understood in temporal terms. Rephrased, there is no essential distinction between money and credit. Both money and credit consist of promises. Indeed, the U.S. Federal Reserve has traditionally counted bank loans as money. Credit, then, indicates a hierarchy of promises, a metaordering, but no difference in essence.

2. Finance is usually discussed in terms of various categories, ultimately derived from various sorts of obligations to repay. The actors within such categories have various names, such as shareholder/company, bank/borrower, creditor/debtor, mortgagor/mortgagee, etc. As the text emphasizes, however, the structure of finance remains the same, regardless of legal detail. This book uses "enterprise" and "investor" because those words best suggest the psychological stances at issue.

3. Leverage is an ambivalent term. He who has borrowed money, and is therefore leveraged, is also vulnerable—and leverage has taken on that negative connotation as well.

4. *Contra* the Marxian tradition, the *haute bourgeoisie*, providers of capital, are the facilitators of change. Whether such change proves good for the proletariat, however "good" and "proletariat" may be defined, is a local matter, but quite possible.

5. A certain skepticism about the concept of progress may be unavoidable, but is necessarily suppressed in development organizations.

6. Modern development policy appears, perhaps correctly, to consider governance to be like farming.

7. At one level, of course, we have no choice but to live here, and it is a waste of time—unless you incline to philosophy—to worry about such matters. We are who we are, when we are, and it boots little to reflect on a world very different from our own. And yet, for those of us

who lack a certain mental discipline, there is something truly marvelous about how a financing nestles in its world, a single thread in a tapestry of collective fiction.

8. Even chthonically so—finance enables change often both dimly imagined and rooted in deep desires. In this light, the mandarin class of the City of Gold did not experience life as radicals, breaking with the past in any fundamental way, but instead found their actions to be quite natural or sensible, which we may now understand as very late expression of the North Atlantic bourgeois psyche. Keynes might have asked Huxley why his *Brave New World* would not feel like Cambridge. The French wine merchant Monnet may have remarked to Woodruff, the businessman who assured Roosevelt that every U.S. serviceman would have access to Coca-Cola, that gentlemen have always traded wine futures over lunch—what more is there?

9. This asymmetrical financial structure is the fundamental justification for most modern bank regulation, including both national schemes for deposit insurance and the lender of last resort function shouldered by most central banks.

10. This point may be too obvious for anyone who thinks candidly about actual business practice, but it is important in the academy and for policy purposes. The discipline of law and economics, with its insistence on the prevalence of rationality, is radically disconnected from what I at least saw in the business world. I had thought about this disconnect for several years when I was disappointed (again!) to learn that the point had been brilliantly made generations earlier by Frank Knight. See generally Frank Knight, *Risk, Uncertainty and Profit* (Cambridge, M.A.: Houghton Mifflin/Riverside 1921, 2d ed. 1935).

11. So long as investors are risk averse, the size of the investment matters: uncertainty becomes more significant as the size of the investment increases. Lots of investors will make fairly uncertain small bets, but few people will willingly hazard their houses, and few managers their corporations, in circumstances that are perceived as more than minimally uncertain.

12. Kenneth Arrow noted that our knowledge came "trailing clouds of ignorance," and Fisher Black remarked that many things which seemed quite certain in Cambridge seemed less so in New York, with real money on the line. Recounted in Peter Bernstein, *Against the Gods: The Remarkable Story of Risk* (New York: John Wiley, 1996).

13. Even U.S. Treasury notes, the paradigmatic "riskless" investment, are technically not without risks, notably those of inflation and reinvestment.

14. This is a considerable simplification. Money never sleeps; investors must invest. Investors therefore confront reinvestment risk, and are not as constrained as the text implies. The text, however, is focused on the enterprise seeking finance, and more generally, on the impact of finance for development in the real economy.

15. Indeed, corporate law is classically understood to be our society's response to the problems posed by an entity, the modern publicly held corporation with limited liability, in which ownership and management are in different hands, those of the shareholders and of the executives of the company. The locus classicus of this view is Adolf A. Berle and Gardiner Means, *The Modern Corporation and Private Property* (New York: Hein, 1932).

16. More recently, and turning from the American to the world stage, it was the failure of a detailed theory of history, the collapse of the argument that institutions were merely the expression of underlying economic law, that led to the fall of the Wall and hence the debate over the third way. At this late date, it is difficult to muster enthusiasm for the sort of detailed theory of history a belief in one capitalism would require, even if sometimes we think we discern a direction to the course of events.

17. 328 U.S. 293, 298–99 (1946).

18. The true value of a security is not at issue here. Whatever the true value of a security may be, it must be to come. Value, like the horizon and Godot, awaits our arrival. Finance asks after the appropriate price of the security in currency, that is, whether the price paid is reasonable vis-à-vis other risks on offer. As I once heard finance theorist Bruce Lehmann put it, "finance, unlike economics, is agnostic about value."

19. Imagery is interesting here. If we understand time as a journey and the future as a destination, then investment awaits arrival at the destination. If we personify the future, as we commonly do with death, then the future awaits us, and we may say reality awaits investment, as the lady and the tiger wait behind the door in the story. See Frank Richard Stockton, "The Lady, or the Tiger?" (1884). In *The Lady, or the Tiger? and other Stories* (New York: Scribners, 1920).

20. As discussed in chapter V, the financial economy in many ways controls the real economy.

21. Although legal instruments formally recognizable as securities appear in various Italian cities during the late Middle Ages (like much else that we think of as modern), widespread

buying and selling of securities, the first securities markets, appear in Amsterdam and London in the seventeenth century. (Almost immediately thereafter, the first bubbles burst.) The security market's early modern, and not medieval, appearance is not accidental. The three aspects that we, following the *Howey* Court (more or less), have taken to define a security, i.e., expectation, fungibility, and collectivization, are all deeply at odds with the medieval worldview. Briefly, the expectation entailed in securities, the idea that time changes things and that we should exert ourselves to make money off the change by attending to the near future, was foreign to the medieval mind, with its emphasis on continuity in this world and immortality in the next. Similarly, the security is in form a contract, but the parties to the contract are not personally bound. Securities are issued by institutions, not persons, and the holder of a security is permitted to sell the security without a thought. Securities are fungible in order to enable such sales. Medieval society, in contrast, was largely constituted by personal obligation, legally formalized by institutions such as the system of vassalage, feudal landholding, and the master/apprentice structure of the guild system, and glorified by the tradition of chivalry as well as Christianity generally. Collectivization is not, in and of itself, at odds with the medieval mindset. To the contrary, Europeans in the age we came to call medieval were constantly organizing themselves in groups: cities, religious orders, guilds, orders of knights, and so forth, and more importantly for present purposes, the very idea of the corporation as a legal construct is largely medieval in origin. But the idea that self-interested market activity could be used to socialize activity—in a world of just prices!—was alien to the medieval mind. Indeed, a defense of the proposition that markets served the common good, regardless of the venality of market participants, required a legitimation of greed, and an understanding of the state as arbiter among antagonistic interests, that was only achieved at the end of the eighteenth century, with the high tide of the Enlightenment.

22. Lloyd's coffee house was a thriving establishment in the late seventeenth century; the South Seas bubble was in 1720.

23. This chronology is by no means strict, but reflects instead the general course of retail. Wealthy individuals have long invested in shares of financial enterprises, whether banks or pools of risk.

24. We are doing this so often, we had to convert the noun, "security," into a verb, "securitize."

25. Such debt is pooled according to criteria such as rate and default risk, rather than lender or geography, so that the market in SPV shares is better able to assess the return on the pool. Although somewhat obscure, SPVs (also known as SPEs) are anything but rare: modern banking and many other forms of financial management would not be imaginable without it. One of the problems revealed by the collapse of Enron—which used SPVs to create misleading financial statements—is that the policy community had hardly begun to think what the widespread use of "vehicles" and "entities" might mean. In fact, there was at the time of Enron little accounting for, much less regulation of, SPV interests.

26. Futures markets, of course, are quite old. Indeed, what is traditionally regarded as the first securities market crash, the Dutch tulip mania, was the crash of a futures market.

27. Actually using such instruments to insure against risk requires an appropriate counterparty, but if the price is right . . .

28. Karl Marx and Frederick Engels, *The Communist Manifesto* (1848), reprinted in *Karl Marx: Selected Writings*, ed. David McEllean (Oxford: Oxford Univ., 1977, 1988): 221, 223–24. Marx and Engels thought this was a good thing, necessary to the revolutionary course of history:
    The bourgeoisie, historically, has played a most revolutionary part.
    The bourgeoisie, wherever it has got the upper hand, has put an end to all feudal, patriarchal, idyllic relations. It has pitilessly torn asunder the motley feudal ties that bound man to his 'natural superiors', and has left remaining no other nexus between man and man than naked self-interest, than callous 'cash payment'. It has drowned the most heavenly ecstasies of religious fervor, of chivalrous enthusiasm, of philistine sentimentalism, in the icy water of egotistical calculation. It has resolved personal worth into exchange value, and in place of the numberless indefeasible chartered freedoms, has set up that single, unconscionable freedom—Free Trade. In one word, for exploitation, veiled by religious and political illusions, it has substituted naked, shameless, direct, brutal exploitation.
    As both intellectuals and politicians, Marx and Engels thought this was honesty, and was an advance. For the communist movement, formalization was seen to reveal the truer meanings of history and power. This idea seems hopelessly naïve, dependent as it does on under-

standing history and power. Formalization is far more likely to be the destruction of meaning rather than a revelation—hence my recasting of *The Manifesto*'s image.

29. Somewhat ironically, ownership of a derivative instrument does not provide any rights to the underlying. Even a futures contract for the delivery of a commodity may, by its terms, be cashed out, i.e., the owner of the contract has no enforceable right to the commodity in question, even if she for some reason wanted to take delivery. The contract is founded on the underlying only in some notional sense.

30. A great deal of history is reflected by different meanings of "security." Consider the instrument with which we began, the increasingly faint token of ownership in, or debt of, a business; the recourse in the event of an enterprise's failure to pay the investor, the sense in which a transaction is spoken of as "secured" by collateral; the psychological sense of assurance to the parties to a transaction; and most generally of all, the idea that our collective transactions, our markets themselves, our houses of cards, are built on solid ground. It is precisely this last sensation of collective security, usually called "confidence," that Enron and similar accounting scandals have brought into question.

31. Recall the Senate confirmation hearings of U.S. Supreme Court Justice Breyer, at which the question of the responsibility of then Judge Breyer's involvement with Lloyds was asked.

Chapter IV

1. What would constitute new or old (wired or tired) economies would require a theory of history beyond the scope of this book.

2. The aesthetics of technology entailed in such a sentence might be a place to start an inquiry into a responsible theory of history. For present purposes, suffice it to say that the City has no such theory politically available to it.

3. Somebody who gives researchers with an idea a million dollars gets a substantial chunk of the company in return. A more established start-up that has absorbed fifteen million dollars in venture capital and that has several patents, over a dozen employees, and that may be bought any day by a potential competitor, is worth a lot more, and so a million dollars buys a much smaller share of the company.

4. In the lingo of Wall Street, a "bear" is a market observer who believes that prices will fall. A "bull" believes that prices will rise.

5. As a matter of financial theory, it is common to understand the value of stock as the right to receive a share of the profits of the company. Historically, and by way of example, imagine a joint stock company, founded to raise money for a voyage. If we imagine a company that engages in an enterprise on an ongoing basis, then the share may be thought of as the right to receive profits on some regular basis, stretching into the future. The value of a share, then, might be thought of in the same terms as the value of an annuity. However, there is no legal or otherwise necessary relationship between a company's earnings and its dividends. A corporation's board of directors decides, on the basis of its collective business judgment, whether to declare a dividend, i.e. make a cash payment to shareholders out of earnings, and what the size of any such payment should be. If the corporation does not declare a dividend and retains the money, then the corporation—and hence its shares—are in theory that much more valuable. To exaggerate for emphasis, and ignoring things like cash flow considerations, currency risk, tax considerations, agency risk, reinvestment risk, transaction costs and opportunity costs, a shareholder should be indifferent as to whether or not a dividend is paid. Therefore, earnings are often treated, and not completely without reason, as if they represented actual payments to shareholders. For tax and other reasons, a policy of not paying dividends may even be preferred by shareholders, and many very successful modern companies—both Microsoft and Warren Buffet's Berkshire Hathaway spring to mind—generally do not issue dividends. Nonetheless, the basic point of the text remains the same: without dividends, the cash value of the share is only realized at its sale.

6. The number y represented by x/0, where x is some number not equal to 0, is undefined. Let $y = x/0$, then $y(0) = x$, then $0 = x$. But, by hypothesis, 0 is not equal to X. The notation generates absurdities, dealt with by simply declaring x/0 *verboten*.

7. Even more technically, the index is not the same over substantial periods of time. Unsuccessful companies are delisted, replaced by reasonably successful ones. Indices are consequently skewed upward. Conversely, the market's losses during a major downturn are larger than suggested by the indices.

8. As evidenced by the continued relevance of the oft-reissued classic from 1978, Charles Poor Kindleberger's *Manias, Panics and Crashes: A History of Financial Crises* 4th ed. (New York: Wiley 2000). See also the even older Charles MacKay, *Extraordinary Popular Delusions and the Madness of Crowds*, ed. Bernard Baruch (New York: Metro, 2002). The book was originally published in 1841.

9. As discussed in chapter III, and generally speaking, a shareholder has: a right to dividends if declared for the class of stock in question; a right to vote equal to the voting rights of the class of stock in question; in the event of the dissolution of the company, a residual claim to any assets remaining after the claims of debtholders and others have been satisfied; and the right to sell the share to a third party. There is more. For example, the shareholder is owed fiduciary duties by directors, officers, and sometimes majority shareholders. The shareholder may sue—in a so-called shareholder derivative suit—on behalf of the corporation to enforce a right of the corporation against an officer or director. Except in very limited situations, the shareholder is not liable for the acts of the corporation beyond the value of the original contribution made by the shareholder.

10. Technically speaking, not the same thing as make more money—"never sell IBM."

11. A centrally important idea in academic finance theory is that the form of finance is fundamentally irrelevant. The classic citations are Merton Miller & Franco Modigliani, "The Costs of Capital, Corporate Finance, and the Theory of Investment," 48 *Am. Econ. Review* (1958) 261; id., "Corporate Income Taxes and the Cost of Capital: A Correction," 53 *Am. Econ. Rev.* (1963) 433. As with much of academic finance, many in the business world disagree.

12. Analysts often discuss a company's earnings on a "pro forma" basis, under which various costs are understood to be occasional and therefore not relevant to the true earnings potential of the company. Whether or not pro forma numbers provide a better picture of a company's prospects than the GAAP figures, the pro forma numbers make a company look better.

13. State is used here in the philosophical sense. In most countries, both company law and monetary policy are functions of the national state. In the United States, however, most corporate and contract law is state law, while securities law is largely but not exclusively federal, and currency is exclusively federal.

14. Wilderness has no return on capital because it has no status within the marketplace. Insofar as land is understood to be property, alienable and hence at least somewhat liquid, it is not wilderness. In the United States, parks used to be called reserves—that is, certain lands were to be reserved from the mechanisms of the market, particularly the market in frontier land fostered by federal policy.

15. Formerly, in the common law system, a lawyer had to be very careful to make a complaint in the right form, to plead the correct cause of action. Although all common law jurisdictions have relaxed this requirement in the last two centuries, lawyers still speak of legal claims as "sounding" in one or another area of the law. So a claim that is conceptually based on a breach of contract "sounds" in contract, and implies the intellectual structure of contract law, which has a different feel from the intellectual structure of, for example, tort law. Similarly, money and property are different, subtly antithetical, ways of thinking.

16. The tolls are likely to show up in earnings—the traffic among these conventions is heavy! The most obvious example of such gatekeeping is intellectual property law, which in effect grants a limited monopoly. Also, it is possible that, on account of network efficiencies, the new economy is comprised of monopolies, as has been suggested by then Assistant Secretary of the Treasury Lawrence Summers and others. See "Knowledge is Power: Do we need a new competition policy for the new economy?" *The Economist* (September 23, 2000): 30. If so, this reinforces my point.

17. Repeating the point is hardly accidental. The preceding essay was about the City's attitudes towards the future. The present essay is about the not unrelated topic of how the City reproduces itself.

18. A Belgian friend assures me that this neologism of mine "sounds French but is not . . . " which seems right on several levels.

19. The fact that much of our property is so abstract as to be unreal probably helps keep the have-nots from resenting the haves overly much; there seems to be more resentment when property is visible as land or even personal luxury in economically integrated cities, i.e., the nineteenth and parts of the twentieth centuries. Rephrased, the striking absence of class conflict in our time, despite enormous inequality, probably has something to do with the character of contemporary property. That said, an egalitarian ideology, the successful destruction of

any powerful notion of class, and the real if rare chance at great success, are probably more important in preventing inequality in the United States from breaking out into open hostility, and so they, rather than religion, must be deemed the real opiates of the working classes.

20. It is difficult, although perhaps not impossible, to acquire status by appreciation alone. Consider the figure of the dandy in eighteenth- and nineteenth-century London, or the people without visible roles who seem associated with the entertainment industries, and hence most often found in contemporary Los Angeles.

21. Denigrating the desire for status, the joy of hierarchy, is not actually required in order to become a professor, just very fashionable.

22. Without the state's guarantee of the security of property, property owners would become robbers, and would have to endure robbery in their turn, instead of offering or demanding their price.

23. Although highly problematic, particularly in the American context, the traditional connections between property holding and responsible voting, and between inheritance and education, are hardly accidental.

24. The text is concerned with money and property as reciprocal ideas. The ability to make an actual purchase is also dependent on other factors, most notably the possession of a sum of money equal to the price of the item in question. A very sound dollar will not buy a Ferrari.

25. Miller and Modigliani, supra n. 11, took this idea for other ends.

26. The relational conception of wealth is important for any sense of community to which we may aspire (despite living in the City). The fact that poor Americans may enjoy material goods unavailable in an earlier age—better televisions, for example—does not make them less poor contemporary Americans. Our poor do not live in an earlier age, or another land; they are poor relative to others, here, not relative to some abstraction. Such ideas of capital can only be discussed in the context of a given polity.

27. It should be clear that I am speaking of neither the economists' notion of "growth" nor the Marxian (or any prior) idea of the labor theory of value, though both of these other notions have related intentions.

28. "These fragments I have shored against my ruins" T.S. Eliot, "The Waste Land," line 431, reprinted in T.S. Eliot, *Collected Poems 1909–1962* (New York: Harcourt, Brace, 1963).

29. Inflation has its uses, too, particularly for certain classes.

30. Particularly if we believe that earnings are relevant to valuation—and who doesn't?

31. At the same time, rapid economic growth is generally accompanied by inflation, and policy debate continues over the degree of inflation a polity should tolerate in pursuit of growth.

32. Understanding mere complexity as wealth is not unproblematic, and is discussed in later chapters.

33. It is worth noting that professional money managers do far more of this than individual investors, who, at least at the present time, exhibit great stomach for volatility.

34. From 1993–95, Nick Leeson, a so-called "rogue trader," engaged in a series of bets which ultimately resulted in the collapse of Barings Bank. From a family of German wool traders, John Baring moved to England in 1717, married and otherwise did well. His sons prospered in London, and the family was a significant bank by the late eighteenth century. In 1803 the bank financed the United States in its purchase, from Napoleon, of what is now the central section of the United States, the Lousiana Purchase. See Nick Leeson with Edward Whitley, *Rogue Trader: How I Brought Down Barings Bank and Shook the Financial World* (Boston: Little, Brown, 1996). For material on the history of Barings Bank, and for that matter money in general, see the magisterial Glynn Davies, *A History of Money: From Ancient Times to the Present Day* (Cardiff: University of Wales Press, 1994).

Chapter V

1. When Washington, D.C. sank into a miasma of corruption, violence, and social disarray especially shameful for the capital of a rich country, the U.S. Congress took virtually all political power away from the local government, and the license plates read "Celebrate and Discover."

2. For Hardt and Negri the mere existence of a global logic is enough to recommend labeling our political order as an empire. Michael Hardt and Antonio Negri, *Empire* (Cambridge, Mass.: Harvard University Press, 2000). I agree with Hardt and Negri's idea that globalization should be understood as a logical order; *City* also is an effort to articulate that logic. Emperors, however, are not known for their logic—establishing and ruling an empire is a

matter of something quite antithetical to logic, call it vision, or will, or destiny. Moreover, understanding our situation in imperial terms facilitates, if only at the level of rhetoric, Hardt and Negri's effort to take a stance against the empire, which evidently appeals to their imagination of both progressive politics and themselves. *City*, in contrast, is more interested in exploring the ramifications of a complicity that I believe is both justified and, perhaps more importantly, unavoidable. Those things said, it is extremely unlikely that the United States will reinvent the idea of empire in the old fashioned sense. See infra notes 7–9 and accompanying text.

3.   A point made at least since Kennedy: "Freedom has many difficulties and democracy is not perfect, but we have never had to put a wall up to keep our people in, to prevent them from leaving us." Remarks in the Rudolph Wilde Platz, West Berlin, June 26, 1963 (the "*Ich bin ein Berliner*" speech) available at http://www.cs.umb.edu/jfklibrary/j062663.htm.

4.   Remarks at the Brandenburg Gate by President Ronald Reagan, Berlin, June 12, 1987, available at http://www.usembassy.de/usa/etexts/ga5–870612.htm.

5.   Most Europeans of my acquaintance do not understand that, or how, Americans can hold such a belief. They therefore tend to see American disavowals of nationalism (beyond sports) and ideology and certainly imperialism along a spectrum ranging from idiocy to bad faith. When I was very young, I found myself arguing, in a quasi-official, quasi-academic gathering (*volkspolitische Bildung*) of German Socialist Party members, that America was not ideological. Needless to say, I lost that argument. I went on to spend much time articulating and criticizing American ideology, by which I here mean the effort to realize political belief, the debasement of philosophy (and why the philosopher does not want to be king). From this vantage, America is among the most ideological of all countries—we even understand philosophy as normative practical discourse, vide legal academe. Therefore it has been difficult for me to recover what I meant so long ago, but the basic idea is that, in its transcendental mood, American political thought understands itself as divorced from history altogether, as somehow above argument and hence nonideological. Mathematics, for example, is an intellectual discourse that is generally considered non-ideological. The Soviet perspective, due to its intellectual heritage, saw the world in ideological terms. But one might imagine an intellectual in a Marxist utopia who would know the laws of history, and hence would understand his political speech to be merely true, more or less, objective rather than ideological. The structure of traditional American belief is not so different.

6.   William Pfaff, *Barbarian Sentiments: How the American Century Ends* (New York: Hill and Wang, 1989): 186.

7.   In discussing American politics, I have used imperial imagery at length. See *Law Through War*. supra Introduction n. 7.

8.   This proposition seemed far more secure prior to September 11th, 2001. As this text is being revised, the United States is openly contemplating the forcible and, if need be, unilateral disarmament of Iraq. Nonetheless, I do not think the United States is capable of reviving the idea of empire, for reasons I discuss herein and elsewhere. But I must admit to being shaken by recent events, and worry that my objections to describing our governance as imperial may end up being semantic quibbles.

9.   Frankly imperial aspirations in modern governments are ridiculous, risible, even when they risk killing a lot of people. Consider Beijing's blustering over Taiwan, or the Indian and Pakistani nuclear tests. Imagine the puffery of the bureaucrats, the generals, the scientists— as *Dr. Strangelove* taught, naked lust for power is funny even when the technology is new and so bids fair to be astonishing, and the governments in question have real prominence. Stanley Kubrick, director, *Dr. Strangelove or How I Learned to Stop Worrying and Love the Bomb* (Columbia, 1964). The imperial efforts of lesser powers, however, are merely ridiculous. And yet there is also something pathetic—something that would be worthy of sympathy were it not so dangerous—in nations struggling to prove their modernity and succeeding in proving only how little they understand of what it now means to be modern.

10. The text exaggerates. Many businessfolk have a real sense of, and a concern for, a well-ordered market. "Business culture" may not suffice, but it is not an oxymoron.

11. My insistence on a political articulation of the City is in this sense a republican longing, anachronistic but I believe not impossible—the point of this apology is to suggest how political thought remains possible, and that even normative political thought is not an entirely lost cause. Part four and the conclusion will suggest how the City's intentionally impoverished foundations can support a politics worthy of some affection.

12. *United States v. Curtiss-Wright Export Corp.*, 299 U.S. 304, 316 (1936).

13. This problem is not new. Commercial interaction has formed recognizable cultures—consider the Hellenic world, or the Hanseatic League, and perhaps the Italian city states—without a capital.

14. The political vacuum never existed outside the jurisprudential mind, but the idea long held sway over such minds. At this juncture, however, the idea has, as it were, imploded. See Abram Chayes and Antonia Handler Chayes, *The New Sovereignty: Compliance with International Regulatory Agreements* (Cambridge, Mass.: Harvard University Press, 1995).

15. Friedrich Nietzsche, *Die Frohliche Wissenschaft (La Gaya Scienza)* para. 203 in *Nietzshe: Werke in vier Bänden* (Salzburg: Das Bergland-Buch, 1980), vol. 4, p. 85.

16. This is a radical simplification of the thought of both men. Smith held a chair in moral philosophy; Madison believed in republican virtue. But both men's influence stems from their explorations of political construction in the relative absence of virtue.

17. Or suppose a privately held medium-size business, a leader in a small city, with perhaps five stores and twenty million dollars in annual gross revenue. Suppose a national, publicly traded operation announces to the owner of this business that it would like to enter his market, and would like to do so by offering shares in the national enterprise worth several times the annual earnings of the privately held business. Because the owner knows the local market so well, the national company would like him to continue running the stores pursuant to a contract; he would become an assistant regional manager of operations for the national company. Representatives of the national company also say that, while they will be disappointed if the owner chooses not to sell and join their team, they are determined to enter the market in his city.

This is a sketch of a form of market consolidation known as a roll-up, from the perspective of one of the rolled-up companies. Roll-ups are interesting from the perspective of the acquiring company as well. Acquirers may be founded for the purpose. They tended to use a form of accounting until recently available (it has been abolished for most purposes) to certain stock transactions known as "pooling," that allowed the acquirer to count revenue of the acquired company as its own, and which did not require the acquirer to depreciate accounting goodwill. Both counting revenue of companies bought, and not depreciating accounting goodwill associated with such purchases, were widely alleged to strengthen the stock market valuation of the acquirer. This allegation was contested in the academic literature—the market should be able to look through accounting methods. What is uncontested is that roll-ups are dependent on strong stock market valuations in order to pay for their acquisitions.

Further suppose, plausibly enough, that the owner decides to sell to the national operation. Why not? At least so long as the secondary market in the acquiring company's shares remain strong, or he can cash out, he will have made money. By moving from real estate to common stock, he will have traded illiquid for liquid assets—he can spend some of the equity he has built up, without finding a buyer for all five stores, or refinancing. Moreover, it is an offer you can't refuse, as the saying goes. Aside from the carrots tempting the owner to make the decision, the national company displayed a stick to help to make sure he made up his mind in the right way. Had he refused to sell and the national company moved in (perhaps by buying out his competitor), he might not have been able to compete, even in his home city, with the economies of scale and brand recognition that the national franchise could bring to bear. By that point, the sale of his company might have become impossible—it might be very difficult to find a third-party buyer who enjoyed the owner's advantages, and who relished competition with what would by then be the locally well-established national company. So, in order to avoid riding his company down, the owner was wise to decide to sell. As a bonus, the owner even was allowed to control the day-to-day operations of the business, for which he was paid and which he presumably enjoyed (or else he would have sold earlier and retired).

Although much seems the same, the medium-size local business has been transformed by the sale. What had been a proprietary operation, owned and managed by the same people, is now part of a publicly traded corporation. As an employee and shareholder, the man who had been the owner has lost a great deal of control over the business. He may be fired, or his contract may not be renewed. While he does hold some shares, this is a relatively diluted form of ownership. The man who had owned the place is transformed into a shareholder trading in the stock market, who could be anywhere. Our manager is now in finance, in addition to whatever his old business had been. Due to the fact that it is publicly traded, the acquiring company itself may be acquired without his complicity. In short, finance transforms the levers of control over enterprises, and hence the nature of business, and so the economy.

18. This is slightly overstated for emphasis. The disclosure requirements for participation in the public securities markets do require some acknowledgment and even discussion of the world.

19. The bursting of the internet bubble in U.S. equities and the wave of accounting scandals should cause the same anxiety.

20. Friederich Nietzsche, *Thus Spake Zarathustra*, ed. Oscar Levey (Oxford: Oxford University, 1964), Third Part, LVI, "Old and New Tables."

21. See Letter of Thomas Jefferson to John Adams (July 5, 1814). Reprinted in Bernard Mayo, *Jefferson Himself*, "The whimsies and jargon of Plato," (Charlottesville: University Press of Virginia, 1942): pp. 300–301. Jefferson, for whom "[t]he doctrines which flowed from the lips of Jesus himself are within the comprehension of a child . . ." It is difficult to know how to respond to such impatience.

22. Now that United States (the nation that alleges affairs of state are independent of religion) seems to have avoided meeting, on the plains of Armaggedon, the Soviet Union (the nation that purported to be the triumph of history over God) (is there a greater irony in our time? in any time?), we may fairly ask after the religion of a polity, even a polity, like Jefferson's Virginia or the City of Gold, that denies it has a religion.

23. Inequality generated by markets can be justified, of course. Rich people may be more talented, or may work harder, or may otherwise be more virtuous. (Or not, as the case may be.) Such justification, however, is at bottom a claim that the market is a natural aristocracy, in which merit is rewarded. The argument that the rich deserve both their money and, by extension, their political power is merely a restatement of the aristocratic idea of government: governance is best done by the virtuous few who are skilled at this task. This is not a democratic argument.

24. This argument is usually made as a theoretical limitation on the efficiency of markets. The argument runs as follows: in an absolutely efficient market, in which all relevant information is available to all participants, there would be no trading, so the existence of trading proves disagreement over the worth of assets. Similarly, if market participants truly believed that markets were efficient, i.e., price changed only in response to news, then there would be no need to analyze companies. So the existence of market analysts indicates a belief, within the financial industries, in the inefficiency of the market.

25. If one were desperate to justify the market on democratic grounds, one might attempt the following: while price discovery is a result of disagreement between actual buyers and sellers, the vast majority of potential actors, who do not invest, must believe that the market price is roughly speaking correct. If one believes the price is too low, one can profit by buying, and if one believes the price is too high, one can profit by selling short. Thus, while price discovery represents a failure of local consensus, the price thereby discovered receives the tacit approval of the host of potential investors who do not in fact invest. By extension, outcomes in the marketplace are tacitly justified by the people, or at least the set of potential investors. It would be tedious to mount a counterargument to such piffle, beyond noting that any system of governance that did not provoke widespread violent rebellion could be justified in this manner.

26. The object of any engrossing enterprise is authoritative for those engrossed. Climbers often speak of mountains, particularly large and dangerous mountains, in personal terms. Mountains can be angry, even vengeful. More beautifully, Tenzig Norgay spoke of his first ascent of Everest (with Edmund Hillary) as a child, repeatedly trying to climb up into the lap of his mother, and finally being allowed to do so.

27. See Warren Buffet, *Essays of Warren Buffet: Lessons for Corporate America*, ed. Lawrence Cunningham (New York: The Cunningham Group, 2001) esp. p. 64.

28. See St. Augustine, *City of God* (New York: Doubleday, 1958) Book II, ch. 21 (reading Cicero).

Chapter VI

1. Like money, electronic communication bridges distances. Moreover, the communications revolution of the 1990s—computer to computer linkages—means that, again like money, communication is flexible in time. Consider, in this regard, both program trading and the shift from face to face or telephone communication to e-mail. Electronic communication has given natural language messages more of the capabilities of money.

2. Of course, money was never the only way to buy leisure. One might work little, and be poor, like Socrates.

3. To some extent such posturing is merely risible expression of a still widespread, if aging, stance, modernism: the modern mind defines itself critically, rejecting its world, so that creative efforts are understood as proposals, by definition current and hence modern. The world opposed is comprised largely by money, and modern art's rejection of its world amounts to a critique of monetary society.

 If one takes art as argument seriously (the way we have understood so much of what is important in modern art), then one must take such critique seriously. However, for the vast majority of artists, and so for our understanding of the role art plays in our society, the fact of this oppositional stance is more important than the substance of the argument. There is no reason to assume that artists are likely to be political thinkers of consequence.

4. Women writers perhaps used to have a more positive view of money. Consider Jane Austen's concern with prosperity, or Virginia Woolf's high hopes for a secure income. Traditionally, women have had a tendency to see money rather simply as an index of security or perhaps as an instrument of liberation from their status. Men knew better then. Now women do too. Any number of contemporary women write with extreme diffidence about money, perhaps none more brilliantly than Joan Didion.

5. Fisher Black, the theorist who, along with Myron Scholes, is largely credited with the theoretical work that made modern derivative markets possible (the "Black-Scholes theorem") was trained as a mathematician and not as an economist.

6. Keynes, Law, and Ricardo are notable exceptions.

7. Buchan maintains that Smith's thought is profoundly conflicted, and that this conflict is resolved by a series of sleights of hand, notably his equation of the division of labor with the institution of money. See, inter alia, Buchan, supra ch. II, n. 7, 175–78. From this perspective, and as I've suggested, replacing money with labor is the technical aspect of Smith's effort to forgive the world. The invisible hand not only solves the problem of morality (how should we act), it solves the problem of affection, specifically, it excuses the world for its continual frustration of the "moral sentiments" that had concerned Smith in his early intellectual life. I recognize that Smith was by all accounts kindly and gentlemanly to a fault, and indeed Robert L. Heilbronner, in the deservedly ubiquitous text *The Worldly Philosophers*, entitles a chapter "The Wonderful World of Adam Smith." Robert L. Heilbronner, *The Worldly Philosophers*, 5th ed. (New York: Simon & Schuster, 1980). But perhaps Smith's inner life was more conflicted and isolated than the received sunny view has it. He argued against restraints on trade, but was a customs official. *The Wealth of Nations* articulates a businessman's moral vision, but Smith did not engage in business. Apart from being a customs official, he was a university professor and a tutor to the aristocracy (an elevated form of servant). He had no wife or children, and while he moved in society, he had few colleagues— he abandoned the University in which he began his intellectual life in order to work on his own. And tellingly, Smith's writing has flashes of brutality, even gruesomeness, for example in his discussion of drowning Chinese babies, see Smith, Ch. I n. 21 supra, at: 72–73, or the horrors of life in the Highlands of Scotland. In light of all this, it is worth considering the possibility that *The Wealth of Nations* was not merely a compendium of the thought of early market societies, but a bulwark erected, however decorously, against a mind's fear.

 Keynes was more explicit about his problems with money. He wrote:

> The moral problem of our day is concerned with the love of money, with the habitual appeal to the money motive in nine-tenths of the activities of life, with the universal striving after individual economic security as the prime objects of endeavor, with the social approbation of money as the measure of constructive success, and with the social appeal of the hoarding instinct as the foundation of the necessary provision for the family and for the future.

 J.M. Keynes, *The General Theory of Employment, Interest, and Money* (London: Macmillan & Co., 1947): 135–37.

8. See Aristotle, *Nicomachean Ethics*, 1133a, 1133b.

9. The word alienation has become difficult to hear, after a few centuries of varied Romantic usage (including that of the young Marx reading Shakespeare's *Timon of Athens*) and the later Marxist usage derived from the mature, "scientific" Marx. For the Romantics, money is an especially soulless aspect of society: the desire for money is antithetical to the passions that make life worthwhile, in particular, the self's intense sense of being. As a Romantic, the young Marx focused on money as a mechanism for alienation, an institution that fractures

the identity. Later in life, in his "scientific" phase, Marx shifted his focus to property and the phenomenon of alienated labor. During this later period, Marx came to understand money in Smith's terms, as the facilitator of the division of labor, and more specifically, as the mechanism by which owners could pay laborers a wage less than the value of the labor, alienating a portion of their work to themselves. The fundamental human problem, for the later Marx and much political economy since, was the perversion of labor relations—solve that, and money would take care of itself.

10. From this perspective, *intellectual property* might seem to be an oxymoron. At least in intention, however, the term is more properly regarded as a misnomer. The idea embodied by a patent is, through the patent if nothing else, made public and is therefore not property. The patent holder's property rights are embodiments of the patent. A similar structure exists in copyright: ideas cannot be protected, but specific expressions can be. Intellectual property law has thus sought to distinguish property from truth, the private from the public, the market from the world of ideas. Those things said, the enthusiasm over linux, and open source computing generally, is based on the conviction that intellectual property law is being used to thwart the pursuit of truth and the establishment of communities based on such pursuit.

11. In different ways, the Romantics, Marx, and Weber all thought that money destroyed social bonds by destroying meaning. Although this is probably true, the criticism here is more modest, and perhaps political in a somewhat narrower sense: capitalism cannot recognize, acknowledge, or articulate what it is to be human, and therefore a politics constructed on markets must be recognized as partial. It is not just that *Gesellschaft* (society, implicitly modern and industrialized) is not equal to *Gemeinschaft* (community, implicitly traditional), or even in Marxian or Weberian fashion, that the construction of *Gesellschaft* requires the destruction of *Gemeinschaft*, according to some historical process of oppression or rationalization. These things may be true, but for present purposes its suffices to insist that *Gesellschaft* simply cannot express *Gemeinschaft*.

12. The need for recognition might seem to be a distant echo of the classical understanding of humans as social creatures, political animals. Perhaps, but the echo is very distant. The fact that the individuals can only transact within the context of a given market, that is, can only be recognized, within a given society (one with a property regime and a currency), does not make the individual thereby defined any less singular. Many deals can only be done in London, but the proximity of so many people does not make the deal makers any less alone, any less defined by the right to exclude or the right to choose.

13. The exile from traditional politics, embodied for us by Solzhenitsyn in the Gulag, or Mandela on Robbin Island, retains some sense of community—indeed loneliness and hence community lost is presumed by understanding exile to be punishment. The exile entailed in market politics is deeper, however, because transactions themselves are based on alienation, and so within the terms of the market there can be no name for community, and hence no name for loneliness.

14. Joseph Conrad, *Heart of Darkness & The Secret Sharer* (New York: Signet Classic, 1983): pp. 69–70.

Chapter VII

1. The etymology of prestige is fortuitous for this argument: the word once meant a conjurer's trick, and, further back, to strain or draw tight, suggesting precisely the sense of constraint, of being trapped, engendered by life in society.

2. This argument can be overstated. The trophy wife is, after all, a trophy, as is an exotic car—there is status associated with the toys acquired during the crisis. So while some costs of a midlife crisis (especially costs of divorce) are mere losses, the conspicuous use of cars and boats and women and so forth may enhance local prestige, at least so long as the toys remain glossy.

3. Lionel Trilling, *Sincerity and Authenticity: The Charles Eliot Norton Lectures, 1969–1970* (Cambridge, Mass.: Harvard Univ., 1971): 124, quoting Marx from the *Economic and Philosophical Manuscripts* (1844), quoting Shakespeare, "Timon of Athens."

4. Trilling's argument has a diachronic element on which the argument of this book does not depend, though it may well be true: authenticity has, over the last few centuries, displaced sincerity.

5. Trilling discusses the counsel Polonius gives to Hamlet as an exhortation to sincerity—the idea of the self is understood to be politically defined. The phrase "to thine own self be true," taken by itself (and with little regard for Shakespeare's time), could be understood as an exhortation to authenticity. But the entire verse reads: This above all: to thine own self be true//and it doth follow, as the night the day,//Thou canst not then be false to any man." Shakespeare, *Hamlet*, Act I, scene iii, line 58. The correspondence between self as it is, and self as it appears to be, is immediately put in the service of honest relations.

6. Trilling notes that, prior to the sixteenth century, "sincere" meant pure, unadulterated, and could be used to describe things that had not been tampered with, and were not passed off as something other than what they in fact were.

7. "Das Geld ist die menschliche Glückseligkeit (in abstracto); daher, wer nicht mehr fähig ist, sie <in concreto> zu genießen, sein ganzes Herz an dasselbe hängt." Arthur Schopenhauer, *Vereinzelte, jedoch systematische geordnete Gedanken uber vielerlei Gegenstande*, in *Samtliche Werke*, 10–320 (Zurich, Diogenes Verlag, 1977), p. 641. Quoted in Buchan, ch. II n. 7 supra, at p. 30 n. 27.

8. One might argue that Lancelot's consummation of the romantic idea, thereby violating his feudal and chivalric obligations to Arthur, explored similar conflicting commitments in late medieval imagination.

9. Although the privileged classes are as alienated by the structure of money as are marginal people, this realization may not be very disturbing from the comfort of the first class seats, from where we may flatter ourselves that our truths are successful, astride the world, and so we are at home. One may, in the vernacular, sell out and therefore rest easy.

10. In a nice twist, the term "Philosopher King" entered American constitutional jurisprudence erroneously, to suggest the idea that people could be rulers and philosophers at the same time—an understandable error, considering the nature of law, so close and yet so far from philosophy, and considering how comforting it is to think of our politics as the result of how smart we are.

11. This attitude is common across large stretches of the university, and tends to produce two strategies for academic argument: the first is an incessant demonstration of the nonfoundational nature of some putatively foundational claim, a claim allegedly heard somewhere. The second strategy is an easy relativism, lazy pomo, whose practitioners bow in the direction of the nonfoundational nature of truth and get on with whatever matter is at hand. Neither antifoundationalism nor lazy pomo requires much thought about the problem of authenticity.

12. The desire to locate ourselves in the sea of finance, to orient ourselves in the world, explains the sometimes obsessive use of personal finance software. While such software purports to give individuals some sense of their own economic situation, that is, their "net worth," this sense is illusory. Even if such software succeeds in collecting the prices of the assets and liabilities of a given individual, that is, even if a person is very diligent in keeping track of and inputting their affairs, the software can only produce an accounting, a report of prices, in some currency such as U.S. dollars. While the dollar, like other monies, presents itself as stable, it is not: the price of goods, and of a given currency, are in constant fluctuation. We can know prices, but we do not know value; we may know the financial situation, but we must guess at the economic situation. As any stock market correction makes clear, the best that personal financial software can hope to do is situate its users in the markets. This is helpful as far as it goes, but it cannot relieve the sense of dislocation caused by participation in the markets. Knowledge of finance does nothing to situate one in the world that markets obscure.

13. It may be possible to be authentic in the future tense, e.g., the will of the people, but it is difficult. Much of what is prized for its authenticity is explicitly not modern, even when relied upon by the quintessentially modern. Consider Picasso's African masks, or the fondness that the financial classes have for the hunt clothing of the English landed gentry. Organic food, even if flown to Berlin, is authentic, but genetically modified organisms are not.

14. Surrealism is interesting to us for reasons in addition to the traditional ones, such as (i) surrealism's critical insights into the nature of language, representation, and our understanding of reality, or (ii) its depiction of Freudian anxieties, although both of these preoccupations remain more than interesting enough.

   A surrealist sensibility (such as displayed by this apology) does not require or even indicate sloppy relativism. Indeed, it is at least as likely that such a sensibility may be conjoined with a playful "rationalism," as the Delvaux paintings that introduce each part of this book (and perhaps the structuralist arguments of part 1) illustrate. In light of the polyphonic character of this book's "argument," I was pleased to find that the catalogue of the centenary exhibition of Paul Delvaux mounted by the Belgian government was written by none other than longtime Delvaux admirer Claude Lévi Strauss. See *Paul Delvaux 1897–1994* (Wommelgem, Belgium: Editions Blondé, 1997): 10.

15. A word of clarification: there are any number of prosaic ways in which politics could be made better: we may support the local school board, oppose certain tax breaks, encourage people to vote, speak up at rezoning hearings . . . the list is endless, and such political activity can be very important. Such activity does not, however, constitute the sort of grand political truth looked for when we talk of globalization or democracy. One cannot understand the world in terms of zoning hearings, full stop.

16. Trilling goes so far as to claim that the deepest root of authenticity is suicide, but his etymology is disputed. See William M. Chase, *Lionel Trilling: Criticism and Politics* (Palo Alto, Calif.: Stanford, 1980:161–62). Whether or not Trilling's Greek is correct—and it is difficult to know what associations were available to ancient Greeks—matters little to his deeper point.

17. For Hegel, the self only becomes aware of itself (literally, self-conscious) in being recognized by another self. We consider how we look, that is, divide ourselves against ourselves. This hall of mirrors leads to profound doubt about the existence of the self, doubt which is resolved through violence. Through attempting to establish lordship, we establish not only our freedom, but demonstrate our own existence to ourselves. See G. F. W. Hegel, *Phenomenology of Mind*, trans. J. B. Baillie, (London, George Allen 2d ed. 1949, 7th impression 1966), IV. A. Independence and Dependence of Self Consciousness, p. 228–240; Walter Kaufmann, *Hegel: A Reinterpretation* (Notre Dame, Indiana: Notre Dame Press, 1978):136–42.

18. See Augustine, *City of God*, book XIX, ch. 13.

19. Quite apart from the important question of creating a marketplace for art, the idea of the alienated self engendered in market societies (discussed in chapter VI) is kin to the idea of the artistic genius, who distances himself from his audience, often attacks his audience's beliefs, and in so doing, remakes their ways of understanding. The idea of the genius is not the only way to understand the artist, but the point here is that art is a source of authority in competition with the political regime. Not incidentally, neither the fascists nor the communists were willing to cede much political power to the poet, and official art suffered as result (unofficial art was suppressed, and some benefited therefrom). Plato suggested that the completely just republic would ban poets; a serious political order has little patience for art. The City of Gold is not so serious, however, and continues to allow art. In light of his own efforts, I suspect Plato was not that serious, either.

Chapter VIII

1. This question is a particular concern of my friend Jack Schlegel. It certainly appears that relative inequality has grown since the 1950s. Insofar as that economy remains normative for these United States, in the literal sense of establishing what relationships we consider to be normal, then inequality is growing. If, however, we broaden the time horizon to include earlier phases of industrialization, or even slavery, then present inequality may not appear so striking. At a deeper level, as such comparisons are extended across time, the underlying assumption of commensurability becomes increasingly problematic. It is difficult to say whether a contemporary resident of Buffalo is more or less well off, either relatively or absolutely, than the Seneca Indian who may have hunted across his land two hundred years ago, during the frontier settlement, or that hunter's great grandfather. Everyone has their life to lead.

But while market societies like the United States should expect the market to do its job of creating winners and losers, magnifying inequality, such societies cannot allow inequality to increase indefinitely. The political problem with inequality is that it leads to resentment, which, in the right circumstances, can lead to civil disorder. Partially in order to protect the United States from such division, a variety of redistributive mechanisms, particularly federal income and inheritance taxes, limit the ability of individuals to secure the wealth of their progeny, and so endeavor to blunt the market's—particularly the financial markets'—tendency to create and entrench inequality. Nonetheless, inequality in the United States is widening, or at any rate and more importantly, is strongly believed to be widening. At the same time, people in the

United States vehemently believe that equality is the natural order of things, and so could be expected to view the economic polarization of the nation with considerable dismay. One might even believe the United States to be ripe for civil unrest. Despite the economic distress of many inhabitants and the corruption of many corporate boardrooms, the republic appears calm.

2. The decline in the importance of ideas of class is part of a larger devaluation of the past. Consumers are defined not so much by their situation within a class (or, more broadly, history), but by desire, by materialistic pleasures and perhaps hopes for the future. The United States, of course, has always lived forward, and defined itself in opposition to history. Sometimes the American denial of history reaches sublime heights: in a nation where an inordinate percentage of young men are jailed, a catalogue for prisoners has arisen, allowing felons to shop in spite of their inability to travel. Just because a young American has a bad past and therefore few civil rights does not mean he cannot exercise consumer choice. Even in jail, the future lies ahead, unless, of course, he is so unfortunate as to be executed, but that rarely happens and always takes years. Other nations have moved away from history for other reasons. In Germany and Japan, events in living memory are so horrid that history has been ignored to the point of denial by the Japanese and, though endlessly discussed, abolished for practical purposes by the Germans, who have declared 1945 *die Stunde null,* the hour zero. In Russia and other communist countries, the former regime was substantively and totally discredited. So for various reasons in various countries, the past is compromised, which might make it easier to adopt the relentless future imperfect of the City of Gold. Thinking more globally, one might analogize the devaluation of history to the conquest of space brought about by technology and discussed in passing in the Introduction.

3. For Locke—and much of early modern Europe—America stood forth as the canvas on which culture might be begun, written, anew. As wilderness, America had no history, in large part because she had no money:

> Sec. 48. What would a Man value Ten Thousand, or an Hundred Thousand Acres of excellent *Land,* ready cultivated, and well stocked too with Cattle, in the middle of the in-land Parts of *America,* where he had no hopes of Commerce with other Parts of the World, to draw him *Money* by the Sale of the Product? It would not be worth the inclosing, and we should see him give up again to the wild Common of Nature, whatever was more than would supply the Conveniences of Life . . .
> Sec. 49. Thus in the beginning all the World was *America,* and more so than that is now; for no such thing as *Money* was any where known.

See John Locke, *Two Treatises on Government, Second Treatise,* sections 48 & 49 (1690). It is a bit precious to use the neuter pronoun, "it," to refer to consumers, but it makes a point.

4. Of course the traffic between concepts such as art and advertising can be complicated. If we hang a ski poster from the thirties, it is art, or at any rate no longer advertisement—that which it was made to sell no longer exists.

5. Two personal stories. I once showed a Peruvian woman, a mountain climber of notable experience in the Andes, around Atlanta. I figured that she might be interested in seeing the big buildings, particularly the very influential open atrium convention hotels built by John Portman (a strong contender for the distinctive architectural achievement of the City of Gold). Overwhelmed, she suddenly felt a long way from home, and began to cry. Some years later, very shortly before the dissolution of the Soviet Union, I found myself taking a group of Soviet law students to Boston's Quincy Market, which like many historical areas in America, has been remodeled as an upscale shopping venue. Somewhere between the boutique candy shop and the electronics store, one of the students began to cry.

6. Plato's *Crito,* Socrates refuses Crito's entreaties to escape, and makes the filial argument explicit:

> "Tell us [the laws] what complaint you have to make against us which justifies you in attempting to destroy us and the State? In the first place did we not bring you into existence? Your father married your mother by our aid and begat you. Say whether you have any objection to urge against those of us who regulate marriage?" None, I should reply. "Or against those of us who regulate the system of nurture and education of children in which you were trained? Were not the laws, who have the charge of this, right in commanding your father to train you in music and gymnastic?" Right, I should reply. "Well, then, since you were brought into the world and nur-

tured and educated by us, can you deny in the first place that you are our child and slave, as your fathers were before you?"
Plato, *Crito* trans. Benjamin Jowett (New York: Walter J. Black, 1942): 74.

7. Of course, it is somewhat overheated to understand modernity to require a choice between alienated servility and whoredom. Such thoughts present themselves to people with a certain predilection for abstraction—philosophers, social critics, and the like—who seek to understand experience conceptually, and to draw links between conceptions, and who thereby risk losing sight of concrete realities, specific experiences. In jeremiads against money, words like whore (or slave or pig) are mostly used for dramatic effect, to make abstract formulations concrete and aggressive, but do so at the cost of a certain amount of confusion. "Whore" means a great deal more than one who understands her own body as a leasehold; even after the sexual revolution the word "whore" still has a whole bundle of specific associations. So, for example, Buchan, following Dostoyevsky, exaggerates for emphasis when he understands monetary culture, that is, utilitarians (economists!) as engendering a society of whores (and when things go badly, murderers). As a practical matter, we have little trouble distinguishing whores from models, to say nothing of murderers.

8. Of course politicians are quite interesting as objects of social criticism or even cultural anthropology, but that is another matter altogether.

9. The great Hegelian Kojeve, whose intellectual influence is still being untangled, vanished into the bureaucracies of the nascent European Community.

10. Konrad Heiden, *Der Fuehrer: Hitler's Rise to Power* (New York: Howard Fertig 1968): 774. The book was originally published in 1944.

> The real degradation began when people realized that they were in league with the Devil, but felt that even the Devil was preferable to the emptiness of an existence which lacked a larger significance.
>
> The problem today is to give that larger significance and dignity to a life that has been dwarfed by the world of material things. Until that problem is solved, the annihilation of Naziism will be no more than the removal of one symptom of the world's unrest.

11. Maybe even Viennese. We should lighten up; the modern situation is better, and certainly more pleasantly, approached through minds like Kafka, Musil, and Kundera (and still Nietzsche, but read less earnestly).

12. Such imagery of the good life is even strikingly prevalent among inner city youth, who after all receive advertising, go to malls, and often wear clothing originally designed for yachting or bird hunting. Veblen would be delighted.

13. Indeed, they should be excluded—that is the central political purpose of wealth, the ability to exclude, and hence to generate envy, and thereby to keep society together.

14. It bears repeating that alienation is not a phenomenon restricted to market societies. While both Kafka and Camus lived in societies that had markets, their works are hardly set in the marketplace. Certainly the bureaucracies of Marxist governments could be alienating in the way that has come to be called Kafkaesque, requiring their inhabitants to lose their souls or become subversive in one way or another, as the literary tradition that has come to be called dissident teaches. But while capitalism has no monopoly on alienation, alienation is a result of capitalism. Kafka reads well here, today, in the City of Gold, not because we are living as minorities in the labyrinths of a decrepit empire, but because we experience life with similar sensations of dislocation, longing, and mystery—even though the social and political institutions that produce such sensations have changed.

Although true, it is far too easy—is indeed the sort of existential lite reading that comes so naturally to Americans—to say that these thinkers are concerned with the radical isolation of the individual in modern society. The habitual American focus on individuals (literally, those without community, idiots) tends to obscure the profoundly social cast of Kafka and Camus. Their characters experience their alienation not as an indifferent dearth of people but as exile in the sense of legal punishment, the condemnation of a community. For both Kafka and Camus the life led alone is understood vis-à-vis a life led in community, even if that community is imaginary and altogether impossible, so that the only practical possibility is the life of a criminal or other outcast, condemned by his community but at least recognized. Kafka's K is offered the opportunity to kill himself and thereby become part of the apparatus of his own trial, as well as its victim. He refuses, however, claiming a lack of strength, and thereby dies "like a dog," perhaps innocent but certainly without respect. And yet even here K worries that the shame of his behavior—a bad reputation in the community that has killed him—will survive him. Similarly, Camus' Merseault even comes to welcome his punishment: his execution becomes theater, a political spectacle, and he thereby becomes somebody. (Camus was a sunnier author.) See Albert Camus, *The Stranger*, trans. Stuart Gilbert (New York: Knopf, 1946), 154.

15. See David A. Westbrook, "Law Through War," Introduction n. 7 supra.
16. It may also be the case that terrorists such as al Qaeda are best understood in terms of modernity, not as an alien civilization. See David A. Westbrook, "Triptych: Three Meditations on How Law Rules after Globalization," 12 *Minn. J. Global Trade* 337 (2003).
17. A perception which the United States Government, for historical and mostly bad reasons of its own, has an unfortunate tendency to foster. After Ruby Ridge and Waco and unspeakable things done by the Department of Energy, a large part of the population, especially black people, believe that almost any heinous act is possible, and probably occurred (O.J. was framed). Which may be to suggest that the United States never completely recovered from World War Two. As the essayist DeVoto wrote in *Harpers* in October 1939, the war would transform America into a place less free. See Louis Lapham, *Waiting for the Barbarians* (New York: Verso, 1998): 158–60.
18. Which is not to say that, as a general rule, a loser's rantings should be taken at face value: These people are crazy. Nonetheless, while the availability of firepower and the unavailability of adequate daycare and other such quotidian "factors" undoubtedly play roles in contemporary violence, we also should have the intellectual courage to confront such violence on its own, explicitly political, terms, as at the very least a failing of our polity to ensure security, not to say happiness.
19. See ch. VII n. 17 supra.
20. Historians will no doubt draw links between anarchy in the late nineteenth century, and the violence discussed here.

Chapter IX

1. One might hope that political desire could be segregated from natural laws, so that the laws would not be tainted with subjectivity and could be known. After all, the desire to build bridges or fire cannon did not vitiate Newton's work. But key economic concepts, like utility, efficiency, and self-interest, cannot be described without recourse to teleology.
2. In 1887 the economist William S. Jevons wrote a rather classic work, *The Theory of Political Economy* (New York: Kelley & Millman, 1957). Jevons, however, had no interest in politics, spent his time trying to establish an apolitical economics, and confessed himself to be "in a fog" about matters political. See Robert L. Heilbronner, *The Worldly Philosophers*, ch. VI n. 7: 181. In 1890 Alfred Marshall published an even more authoritative text entitled *Principles of Economics* (London: Macmillan, 1961).
3. A story well told with regard to the economics profession in the United States by Michael A. Bernstein, *A Perilous Progress: Economists and Public Purpose in Twentieth-Century America*, ch I n. 6 supra. I am professionally familiar with this progression in the strange—and staggeringly influential—career of law and economics.
4. For an interesting multidisciplinary and multinational consideration of this question, see Rosa Lastra, *Central Banking and Banking Regulation* (London: Financial Markets Group, 1996).
5. "Physics" is here understood as the paragon of the sciences. As of this writing, there is considerable excitement about "behavioral economics," which has done much to complicate, and perhaps improve, our thinking about the economy, in the process making it look less like physics. Behavioral economics springs from Daniel Kahneman and Amos Tversky's pioneering psychological work to insist that people (who make economic decisions) do not think in the ways presumed and modelled (and glorified as rational) by conventional economics. Kahneman received the 2002 Nobel Prize in economics (Tversky had died, and so was ineligible) for these insights. Kahneman and Tversky's work was championed by economist Richard Thaler (credited with beginning the field of behavioral economics). In finance, Robert Schiller has insisted on examining the psychology of actors in the financial markets, work that tends to undermine claims that the market is an efficient processor of information. In that part of the American legal academy devoted to corporations and finance, Henry Hu and Donald Langevoort are

among many who are attempting to rethink some of the insights of law and economics with a more sophisticated psychology. Although I welcome these developments, they do not affect the basic argument of the text. First, as suggested, the economists' turn to psychology is a turn to the authority of another science, and so economics remains a scientific enterprise, within the realm of Queen Physics. That said, there is some question whether psychology, as soft a science as it is, can save economics, at least as traditionally understood. From the perspective of ortho-dox economics, the turn to psychology must be a sign of desperation. Second, psychology is unlikely to replace the rationalist caricature of contemporary economics. As Kahneman him-self recently said, "But it's not as if this [our work] has swept economics. It hasn't, and for very deep structural reasons, it's not going to. The rational model has a hold on economics, and it's going to stay that way. Behavioral economists fiddle with it, improving the assumptions and making them psychologically sensible. But it's not a completely different way of doing eco-nomic theory." Erica Goode, "On Profit, Loss, and the Mysteries of the Mind," New York Times (November 5, 2002) sec. F, p. 1. In short, economists will continue to be as rational as they need to be.

In 2002, as this text is drafted, it seems historically appropriate that we moderate our claims to rationality. The largest bull market in American history has come to an end, and NASDAQ lost some 80 percent of its value in dollars (in light of the skew inherent in in-dices, it is hard to know exactly how much was lost). Enron, WorldCom, and a host of other accounting scandals make the financial markets look less than careful, to put the matter kindly. The market break of 1987, Long Term Capital Management and various currency crises involved sudden losses borne by the most sophisticated of investors, casting doubt on who, if anyone, was all that rational. Academic and policy circles were dominated in the 1980s and 1990s by neoliberal rationalists, and the stance was so well rehearsed as to have become rather boring, and, as the conventional wisdom, neoliberal nostrums seemed inef-fectual when new crises arose, e.g., in Argentina. In short, it has come time for a change of fashion. Finally, while economics as a discipline has been dominated by a tendency to ratio-nalism, a significant countertradition exists, represented by names like, in reverse chrono-logical order, Galbraith, Kindleberger, Keynes, Knight, and Veblen.

6.   There is a debate over whether the theses were actually nailed, or merely posted, or whether, in view of the widespread practice of posting such notices, it was likely that they were in fact posted, albeit perhaps not by Luther himself . . .

7.   The interplay between faith, the terms of argument, and knowledge, the product of dispu-tation, is endlessly fascinating. See Alfred L. Malabre, Jr., *Lost Prophets: An Insider's History of the Modern Economists* (Cambridge, Mass.: Harvard Business School, 1994), for a mor-dant view of theory from the perspective of financial journalism. Robert H. Nelson has written a more academically economic, and simultaneously explicitly theological, interro-gation of the economic faiths that inform discourse in Washington, and which, it should be evident, is an underlying preoccupation of not only this chapter but indeed this apology. Robert H. Nelson, *Economics as Religion: From Samuelson to Chicago and Beyond* (Univer-sity Park, Pa.: Pennsylvania State Univ., 2001).

8.   See, e.g., "The future of economics: In the long run, is this subject dead?" *The Economist*, March 4, 2000:112.

9.   This passage owes debts to Kuhn and Koyre. See Thomas Kuhn, *The Structure of Scientific Revolutions*, 3d ed. (Chicago: Univ. Chicago, 1996); Alexander Koyre, *From the Closed World to the Infinite Universe* reprint (Baltimore: Johns Hopkins Univ., 1994). However, the ques-tion here is somewhat different: at what point does a mythology, recognized as a mythol-ogy, fail to satisfy a portion of the population?

10. At a conference sponsored by the United Nations, I once heard a Russian economist com-plain publicly and at length about being placed on the panel dealing with human aspects of environmental problems, i.e., in the company of social scientists. Economics, he kept insist-ing, was a science. After all, there was a Nobel Prize in economics, just like physics or chem-istry. And like literature, I thought.

11. Quoted in Richard Rhodes, *The Making of the Atom Bomb* (New York: Simon & Schuster, 1987): 77.

12. The ECMH goes so far as to maintain that the market aggregates and evaluates informa-tion, one is tempted to say understands, that is, ECMH treats the market as a subjective en-tity, a vast cybernetic device. Not only is the market intelligent, it is smarter than the humans who comprise it: the market's decisions can be understood by humans only halt-

ingly and after the fact. For adherents of the ECMH, the market is not just a collective noun, it is an almost all knowing and yet almost unknowable being, a god if not the one true God. (The market cannot be the God of the Jews, Christians, or Muslims, because trading ceases under conditions of perfect knowledge.) I do not know why this radical violation of methodological individualism has not received more attention.

13. So, for famous example, Ronald Coase speaks of the theory of the firm, without feeling any need to distinguish among a limited liability corporation, a GmbH, a S.A., or any of the other names that different communities have assigned to different business entities. See Ronald Coase, "The Nature of the Firm," 4 *Economica* 386 (1937). This example is somewhat misleading, because Coase tends to be quite sensitive to the particulars of specific economies (transaction costs, which are ubiquitous, arise precisely in the circumstances of actual, as opposed to theoretical, markets).

14. Science and Lutheran thought are often identified as nominalist enterprises. But despite Bacon's enthusiasm for induction, physics after Galileo is in many ways Platonic. Similarly, Luther identified himself as a nominalist, but Plato through Augustine runs deep in his thinking.

15. The util has been trading well against the yen as the Japanese refuse to make much needed banking reforms. It is hard not to joke about utils, about the desire to simplify the world and so solve everything. Jack Schlegel suggests I should have employed the more graphic phrase "joy units." Similarly, "Edgeworth saw no particular obstacle to devising a Unit of Pleasure (presumably to be named the Pound Sterling)." Buchan, ch. II n. 7 supra, 179–80.

16. Conversely, any critique based on alienation presumes a better (often "more natural") relationship between the self and the world, and so holds forth the possibility that the self may be reformed. Critiques of alienation thus suggest discontent not just with the world, but also with the self. As a result, ostensibly political criticism may be an expression of self-loathing . . . a different problem.

17. There is a fairly widespread sense that painting, understood in terms of a fairly specific set of traditions (or argumentative narratives) came to some sort of terminus, perhaps even an end, in the 1960s. See Arthur Danto, *After the End of Art: Contemporary Art and the Pale of History* (Princeton, N.J.: Princeton Univ., 1997). While I agree with this historical account, Danto goes on to argue that this presents an opportunity, indeed a liberation, for the contemporary artist, who is free to borrow from any tradition. In this view, for the postmodern artist (especially with an Internet connection), all the world is a museum, a quarry for ideas and images. I think Danto is far too hopeful here, and seriously minimizes the social and spiritual requirements for artistic production. In lieu of argument at this juncture, I offer two observations. First, I certainly have not felt that access to libraries, real or electronic, has made it easier to know what is worth writing. Second, Danto himself stopped painting in the '60s, that is, at the point in time when the tradition to which he had devoted himself ran out.

18. That may not be quite right. The qualities of mind on which much poetry turns sometimes read well in translation, and some poems are evocations of just the sort of loss with which Frost charges the act of translation.

19. Jean-Francois Lyotard, Foreword, Joseph Kosuth, *Art after Philosophy and After: Collected Writings, 1966–1990,* (Cambridge, Mass.: MIT Press, 1993).

Chapter X

1. In the interest of clarity, it should be noted that this apology has no problem with the idea that government may choose futures different from those created by a price mechanism.

2. Conversely, the observed absence of any such correlation implies that we live in an unjust society, in which meaningful work is not well paid, and great incentives are provided for work that is bad. Moralists on the left even expect that a perverse labor market, in which incentives are not correlated with morality, ultimately degrades the moral life—hence the expected corruption of the financially successful individual (who has "sold out"), and the presumed virtue of the poor.

3. In the seventieth anniversary edition of *Fortune Magazine,* published weeks before the internet bubble burst, James Wood argued that work was simultaneously being homogenized and becoming specialized. Homogenization—everybody staring at computer screens, or engaged in "sales"—made work rather uninteresting. At the same time, the professional specialization that many modern jobs require made the substantive details of work rather

inscrutable to all but colleagues. The changing nature of work has created serious difficulties for novels set in the workplace, but is less troubling for film. See James Wood, "Sister Carrie Is Gone for Good," *Fortune* F-29 (March 6, 2000).

4. In the late 1990s, in the United States, the Non-Accelerating Inflation Rate of Unemployment (NAIRU), the rate of unemployment below which demand for jobs leads to inflationary wage pressures (wage-earners getting raises because they are in demand), appears to have fallen. The extent of and reasons for the fall are unclear. Job insecurity has been widely understood to be one of the reasons, though probably not the only reason. For example, low commodity prices and failure to measure promotions as wage increases may have masked the extent of wage pressure. See, e.g., "The Great American Jobs Machine," *The Economist* (Jan. 5, 2000):25.

5. Cameron Crowe, director, *Jerry Maguire* (Columbia/Tristar, 1996). "Show me the money!" is the slogan of Cuba Gooding, Jr.'s character, Rod Tidwell.

6. Thorstein Veblen, *Theory of the Leisure Class* (New Brunswick, New Jersey: Transaction, 1992) (originally published 1899): especially 33–40.

7. A friend, evidently unwilling to give up on the idea of economic justice entirely, has remarked "a certain cavalier arrogance" in the text's emphasis on such people. The arrogance is inescapable: the subject is the politics of markets, and so we must be prepared to stomach the attitudes of those who would be oligarchs. It would be soft-minded to argue that labor markets reward a sort of gentle sincerity. So the text is concerned with people who take care of business—themselves—and attempt to live their lives as best they can. Rephrased, part of the point here is that markets are terrible things, and until we understand that deeply, we will not be able to have a worthy political economy.

8. Academics in particular have traditionally identified with labor, despite the fact that universities are funded by tax dollars or endowment or contributions and to limited extent by tuition paid in exchange for credentialing—academics cannot seriously be considered labor, either.

9. Although, as Veblen points out, it is difficult to become convinced of this point. In order to understand it, one must adopt the Marxian view more or less in toto:

> Except as a whole and except in the light of its postulates and aims, the Marxian system is not only not tenable, but it is not even intelligible. A discussion of a given isolated feature of the system (such as the theory of value) from the point of view of classical economics (such as that offered by Bohm-Bawerk) is as futile as a discussion of solids in terms of two dimensions.

Thorstein Veblen, "The Socialist Economics of Karl Marx and His Followers," *The Quarterly Journal of Economics*, volume 20 (1906) (Veblen's lectures on Marx at Harvard), available online at http://www.socsci.mcmaster.ca/~econ/ugcm/3II3/veblen/marx1.txt.

10. For those of us who are skeptical of knights errant, Marx argues that the peasants will win, and it is good to be on their side, come the revolution.

11. The modern mind is still not entirely comfortable with interest. Most states still have laws prohibiting usury; businesses that lend money are everywhere highly regulated; loan sharks are widely assumed to be violent criminals.

12. This phrase is traditionally ascribed to the Benedictine order, but is not part of the Holy Rule of the order. The idea that work, especially manual labor, was itself a spiritual practice, is well-established. See, e.g., Claude J. Peifer, O.S.B., *Monastic Spirituality* (New York: Sheed and Ward, 1966): 308–13.

13. Legally, the institution of mortmain, the practice of bequeathing wealth in perpetuity to the church, removed land from the cycle of purchase and sale or conveyance, from the tax base of the sovereign, and thus from the flux of politics. The monastery and its possessions were legally eternal, at least until a political convulsion of sufficient violence, such as the nationalization of God's property by England's King Henry the VIII.

14. In his introduction, translator Michael Hamburger wrote that "Speaking about poetry, Celan quoted this definition by Malebranche: Attention is the natural prayer of the soul." Paul Celan, *Poems of Paul Celan* trans., with an introduction by Michael Hamburger (New York: Persea Books, 1998): 31.

15. Thomas Carlyle, *Past and Present* (New York: New York Univ., 1965). Note that *Past and Present* was written in 1843, virtually the same time as Marx's *Economic and Philosophical Manuscripts of 1844.*

16. Max Weber, *The Protestant Ethnic and the Spirit of Capitalism*, trans. Talcott Parsons, foreword R.H. Tawney (New York: Scribner, 1958).

17. See Karl Marx, "On the Jewish Question," (written in 1843) and "Economic and Philosophic Manuscripts of 1844," both in Robert C. Tucker, ed., *The Marx-Engels Reader* (New York: Norton, 2d ed. 1978).

18. The phrase "unremunerated labor" is from Gottfried Benn, quoted in Buchan ch. II n. 7 supra, at 207.

19. Although, as suggested above, what Marx said and probably thought he was doing, and what he actually was doing, appear to be quite different things. Hegel was explicit that his theory of history was intended to recapitulate Christianity. Marx, for all his materialism and atheism, appears to have ended up with a similar recapitulation.

20. Enemies may be admired for other virtues, such as courage or endurance, and the excellence of enemies reflects well on one's own prowess, but the truth remains that mortal enemies frequently praise one another for doing a job well, admire one another, and have since Troy.

21. The watch is from Alasdair MacIntyre, *After Virtue: A Study in Moral Theory* (Notre Dame, Ind.: Univ. Notre Dame, 1997):57–59; the knife is from Aristotle, *Politics*, ch. II, n. 6, at ch. II, §1. Aristotle speaks of the Delphic Knife, which has many purposes, and is therefore unnatural.

22. Simply handing out checks may have unintended but beneficial effects. For example, the economic downturns in Great Britain, combined with the generosity of the dole, led to an explosion of British achievements in all aspects of mountaineering.

23. Indeed, American doggedness has often been recast as bravery when questions of justice are irrelevant or ignored, and all that is left is the style with which existential crises, preferably violent, are confronted. The dust blows and the farm is lost, or the Sioux come over the ridge and struggle is futile. Consider much of Earnest Hemingway or Dashiel Hammett.

24. Misplaced happiness is particularly upsetting for the left, which believes happiness to be a function of a just, i.e., egalitarian, social order. Since the social order is manifestly unjust, i.e., hierarchical, leftist intellectuals confronted with the spectacle of happiness are compelled to tell patronizing (and so compromised) stories about false consciousness.

25. The ultimate impossibility of class in a mercantile society is a subject for comedy. Old money has looked down upon new money for as long as there have been social climbers, not because new money does not have sufficient wealth (by definition, it does), but because new money is not traditionally educated, knows nothing of the folkways of old money. The *nouveau riche* thus precipitate a special kind of conflict, even crisis, of the following form. The parvenu possesses enough money to buy entry into society. The fact that he is ignorant is finally irrelevant, because money is money, regardless of who owns it. From the perspective of old money, this means two things. The first, which everybody realizes, is that new money is tacky, unfinished. The second, more sobering, fact is that despite tackiness, the holder of the new money will be admitted eventually to all the best circles. This precipitates a crisis of the old guard, who must confront the fact that everything they take seriously is superficial: what really matters is the money. Thus, while capital creates substantive inequalities, it simultaneously upsets the narrative expectations, traditions, on which class is built. Sometimes this is funny.

26. This paragraph is a reduction of several conversations with Jack Schlegel regarding the United States in the fifties.

27. We might talk about the fit between our experience of the market and our ideal market, that is, talk about "efficiency," a matter considerably different from justice.

28. The Marxian edifice was a monumental effort to establish a scientific basis for social concern, in effect to undue the immorality wrought by Adam Smith, who established a scientific basis for guiltless aggrandizement, and the devil take the weak. Marx, like Smith before him, believed that economics could be used to found the good society in the perdurable world of scientific law, could use concrete economic reality to secure ephemeral human hopes. To put the matter polemically, Smith thought the market could be understood to provide absolution, and hence freedom from the guilt that stalked moral philosophy. Smith, in essence, attempted to justify the economy and therefore abolish the problem of social justice. The efficient market was already just. In contrast, Marx thought a reformed economics could provide social justice, and hence community. Both men sought to cure alienation as they understood it.

Chapter XI

1. Thus stated, this is a strange claim indeed. In the context of seventeenth-century thought, however, it makes considerably more sense. After the religious wars, the philosophical prob-

lem was to show that a political order could be made intellectually available, that one could sensibly think about politics in light of its tendency to veer off into madness. In what remained a market society, for that matter a Christian society with a functioning system of property rights, a judiciary, and so forth, the tradition of contract must have appeared to be durable in ways that certain matters of religious doctrine (and hence cosmology, political theory, and so forth) were not. Apart from such context (which is not entirely dissimilar from our own context) it is hard to see why ideas like freedom and contract, confidently asserted in Hobbes, and more recently, by economists, have a particularly secure ontological status. Viewed from the perspective of legal doctrine, as opposed to liberal political thought, the paragraph in which this note appears is impossibly difficult. A brief effort should suffice to demonstrate how hard it is to define what could be meant by "the essence" of a contract, or the "freedom" that a contract by nature somehow requires but then extinguishes. This problem is not too distressing, however, because in real life, even real intellectual life, context is in fact available, if not always acknowledged. Political and economic theory are sufficiently abstract that they may restate context—here, seventeenth-century Western Europe—as first principle without raising too many eyebrows. Along similar lines, for these purposes property can be treated as natural despite what lawyers who actually quarrel over property may say. In short, liberalism has been an enormously powerful philosophical response to a historical situation, what we might call the political nominalism that attended the Reformation.

2. Liberalism may be—and often is among American legal academics—loosely understood as a political instantiation of the Kant of the moral works, especially Immanuel Kant, *Critique of Practical Reason*, trans. Lewis Beck (Indianapolis, IN: Bobbs-Merrill 1956) (originally published 1788). American political thought can be understood without reference to Kant, and yet Kant is very convenient. Somewhat like Toqueville, Kant said things that Americans would come to find well said, but in an intellectual idiom that Americans did not themselves command. Unlike Toqueville, Kant's work is sufficiently opaque to require an American restatement in the form of Rawls' *Theory of Justice*, which recounts Kantian morality in political terms. The imagery of political choice made without regard to the position of the parties, i.e., "behind the veil of ignorance," resonated deeply with traditional American beliefs in equality, and especially with the contemporaneous civil rights movement, the effort to achieve a "colorblind" society. But while judging has long been conceived to be blind, the imagery is even less apt for politics writ large. Hannah Arendt was not wrong to point out that Kant never developed a political theory, that is, never located a theory of interaction within a polity that had a culture, a history. Hannah Arendt, *Lectures on Kant's Political Philosophy*, ed. Ronald Beiner (Chicago: Univ. Chicago, 1989:7). The autonomous individual of the moral works is free, rational, good-willed, but has no history, no connections or entanglements, no culture. From an American perspective, however, Arendt's point has not been very important, because the citizen imagined by American political discourse is constructed similarly to Kant's moral actor. American political discourse since Rawls has, as it were, enthusiastically recognized itself among, rather than influenced by, Kant's moral writings.

Kant came to understand his critique of moral thinking to be insufficient, in part because it could not relate itself to the world of ideas (concepts, understanding) without a theory of judgment. The problem of making morality operational, oddly enough, seemed to hinge on questions of judgment more familiar from aesthetics. Immanuel Kant, *Critique of Judgment*, trans. Werner Pluhar (Indianapolis, Indiana: Hackett, 1987) (originally published in 1790): 35. But judgment, it quickly emerged, is enormously difficult to think about in the systematic and atemporal terms with which Kant approached the other faculties of the mind. The not-so-secret agenda of this section of this apology is to suggest that the liberalism of the second critique cannot be sustained, and that political thought must become self-consciously aesthetic. One way to do so may be the essay, i.e., the form in which we explore the roots of our judgments.

3. It is unclear what tense this last clause should be in, but the pose will be maintained for the sake of decorum.

4. See *First Nat. Bank of Boston v. Belloti*, 435 U.S. 765 (1978). The Supreme Court believes that corporations are people too; we are very superstitious about economics in the United States.

5. Liberalism thus stands in marked contrast to both Marxism and consumerism, each of which imagine an end-state, a utopia, that would make its processes obsolete. In a world of oceanic solidarity or aesthetic perfection, there is no need for the class struggle or acquisition, respectively. Liberalism, however, cannot even imagine such an end-state.

6. In the *Metaphysics of Morals* Kant attempted to specify a theory of law from principles of autonomy. Immanuel Kant, *The Metaphysics of Morals*, trans. Mary Gregor (New York: Cambridge University Press 1991).

7. Koenigsburg was Kant's hometown, now the Russian city of Kaliningrad.

8. John Rawls, *A Theory of Justice* (Cambridge, MA: Harvard, 1971): ch III, sec. 24, 136 et seq.

9. Advertising campaign of the all-volunteer U.S. Army. In its recruiting efforts, the military has presented itself as a way of becoming a certain kind of person, that is, the surrender of certain sorts of autonomy is justified by the creation of a disciplined self, presumably more autonomous in the long run. Although easy enough to lampoon, this may be the best way to present military obligations in a society without a non-liberal mode of political discourse.

10. As Louis Lapham phrased it a couple of presidential elections back, "It is this government ["a secular oligarchy"] that hires the country's politicians and sets the terms and conditions under which the country's citizens can exercise their right—God-given but increasingly expensive—to life, liberty, and the pursuit of happiness." Lewis Lapham, ch. VIII, n. 17 supra, ct 104.

11. While politics may come to be understood as economics, as a matter of logic the reverse is equally true: a strictly liberal understanding of political life requires a conception of markets. If we understand humans in Hobbesian political terms, as atomistic and dependent, then they require contract (as in "social contract") to create an order. But what are the objects of contract, if not those institutions we regard as property or as money?

12. As the history of affirmative action in the United States amply demonstrates, there are conflicts between identity politics and liberalism other than those addressed in the text.

13. Buchan, ch. II n. 7 supra, at 174.

14. There is an implicit natural law argument here. Any number of jurisdictions have laws against sodomy. In such jurisdictions, one cannot speak of a (legal) right to the proscribed practice. The right referred to, then, is the right as imagined in a more just polity, or at least one with similar sexual mores.

15. It is as impossible as asking seriously after the relationship between the words "native" and "American." That is, we live in a profoundly anti-intellectual milieu, but history teaches that things have often been worse, much worse, so no complaints here.

16. At the point that homosexuality becomes nearly irrelevant, it might be possible to pursue rather basic but perhaps not unimportant questions without being called homophobic. (The widespread adoption of this part of the Freudian apparatus is one of the little ironies of our time.) For example: what do we members of the theory class, who tend to be environmentalists, and who tend to rely on birth control if we are not gay, understand to be "natural" in sexual relations? If the answer is nothing—anything is permissible in a caring relationship ("caring" evidently remains special), and that any caring relationship must be accorded the respect accorded other, roughly analogous, relationships—does it follow that we should abandon the environment as a lodestar for politics? If the concept of nature is inapplicable to human relations, must we think about our most intimate relations—mothers, fathers, daughters, sons, wives, husbands, lovers of various sorts, in terms that would just as well describe the relationships among members of a joint venture, e.g., empowerment, trust, choice, obligation, respect, and the like? There are plausible and humane answers to such questions, I think, but they cannot be found by thinking within the bounds of liberalism as it is now constructed.

17. Indeed, as Arendt pointed out, Kant had no political philosophy. *Lectures on Kant's Political Philosophy.* Arendt, supra n. 2. Hobbes suggested that the citizen should not be allowed to have much concern for politics (which only led to faction and hence trouble). Locke and Madison, bourgeois gentlemen, do not seem to have been too concerned with the problem, but instead seem relatively confident that political involvement would track private interest (including personal ambition) fairly closely. More recently, Richard Rorty has urged that liberal interests—often expressed in terms of "equality"—in fact spring from a sympathy which has nothing much to do with liberalism as formally constructed (or legally instituted). See, e.g., Richard Rorty, *Contingency, Irony and Solidarity* (Cambridge: Cambridge Univ., 1989). Although Rorty is correct to suggest that the doctrinaire liberalism at issue here is an inadequate theory of political psychology, the protests against globalization suggest an additional, and more complicated, relationship between liberal ideology and the concern for politics.

18. In a partisan atmosphere, it is tempting to exploit such confusion by offering an oh-so-well-intentioned description of certain errors, coupled with a suggestion that correction of these errors will not only clear up the confusion (unlikely), but also will reveal—voila!—

the speaker's position. So the liberal proponents of free trade, big business, the financial industries, and others have addressed the protests against globalization as if they were rooted in misunderstandings, nostalgia for the sixties, and a bit of hooliganism. Nor is this diagnosis entirely incorrect. But it is ungenerous and wrong to think that all liberal discontent with globalization is a matter of confusion over first principles.

19. For an account of the French Revolution as a the prototype of future totalitarianisms, see Simon Schama, *Citizens: A Chronicle of the French Revolution* (New York: Knopf, 1989). It has been argued that the strong ideals of democracy and community in much Continental thought (exemplified by Rousseau, Hegel, and Marx) is ultimately antagonistic to the idea of individual liberty protected by rights, and is hence illiberal. From this perspective, the fetishization of the state discussed in the text is perhaps Western, but not specifically liberal. This argument often has had nationalistic underpinnings, viz., constituted a claim that the Anglo-American political tradition was better than the Continental political tradition because the latter tended to totalitarianism. But, first, even if we accept *arguendo* the idea of importantly distinct traditions within Western political thought, the fetishization of the state—and hence the argument in the text—is dependent on the opposition between the individual and the state, an opposition central to modern Western political thought, whether Anglo-American or Continental. Once politics was understood to be the individual's confrontation with the polity writ large, represented by the state, the tensions implicit in that confrontation can be, have been, logically resolved in totalitarian fashion. Second, the putatively genteel liberalism sometimes fondly ascribed to the Anglo-American political tradition has a stern lineage. Hobbes quite consistently and powerfully argued for Leviathan, as the only way to prevent the horrors of civil war. While subsequent thinkers such as Locke and Madison assessed the dangers of political life differently, the Hobbesian logic has always been available, and used in the right circumstances. Lincoln suspended a host of constitutional rights—there was a civil war on, after all, and a similar steeliness underlies American jurisprudence, particularly as expressed and influenced by Holmes. For striking example, during World War Two, the Supreme Court found itself able to justify the internment of thousands of Americans of Japanese extraction. See *Korematsu v. United States*, 323 U.S. 214 (1944). Third, the existence of formal rights in liberal societies does not mean that tyranny is impossible. Rights need not be granted (U.S. and Australian history is instructive), and rights granted in form may be taken away in substance through legal process (the Nazis found the Weimar legal machinery quite serviceable). Insofar as rights do not restrain the state, liberal theory offers little else. The understanding of the state is not limited on its own terms, and could not be, without being defined as something more definite than the will of the people.

20. The text implies a rather un-Hegelian linearity. In Hegelian terms it would be more precise to say that the development of the state and the development of religion were complementary aspects of the same unfolding of spirit in history, an unfolding which transforms the institutions of both state and church as it proceeds. See, e.g., the conclusion to *The Philosophy of Right*, paragraphs 341–360. *Hegel's Philosophy of Right*, trans. T.M. Knox, (Oxford: 1967) (first published Clarendon: 1952).

21. Such irrational defenses of the true faith, the State, are not new. In earlier generations, many otherwise worthy souls were constitutionally unable to believe in the possibility of Soviet atrocities (or spies), or that the United States could do evil things on the basis of almost no knowledge.

22. "Let's go to the beach!"

23. "In general I feel that we never do justice to the value of our vulgar qualities: if they were not so dependable, no history would be made at all, because our purely intellectual efforts are incurably controversial and shift with every breeze." Robert Musil, ch. I n. 19, or Front Matter, n. 1 supra, 446–47.

Chapter XII

1. It bears explicit mention that important strands of liberal thinking, and particularly the thinking associated with freedom of speech, staked a claim on precisely the ability of liberal society, including markets, to process information and provide true answers. Consider J.S. Mill, Louis Brandeis, and Isaiah Berlin, each of whom argued that the individual's freedom of speech was necessary for public reasons—so that through open argument, society could come

to the most true possible answer. In recent years, this strand of thought has been enthusiastically updated by proselytizers for the wonders of communications technology and capitalism. Consider, in this regard, any edition of *Wired* or the *Wall Street Journal*. Although politically necessary as a response to totalitarianism, on its own terms the argument is a bit bumptious, requiring great faith in argument, little attention to language or history, and low standards for truth.

2. Another practical response is political nihilism. To say that market communication is necessarily untrue does not, in and of itself, recommend a switch to another mechanism of public choice. All communications are untrue in some respect; partiality is endemic to communication. Once intellectually satisfying truth is understood to be unavailable, then switching from one mechanism, e.g., a market, to another mechanism, e.g. a bureaucracy, may seem to be merely substituting one sort of lie for another. Viewed from a sufficient altitude, all politics are the same, and the mode of social choice does not matter. In light of bloodbaths, however, such thinking borders on the blasphemous.

3. For a discussion of truth, uncertainty, and the obligations on the issuing corporation, see *Basic v. Levinson*, 485 U.S. 224 (1988).

4. There is some anachronism here. The securities laws were passed out of concern with fraud in large part because fraud was wrong, not just because fraud degraded the quality of information available to the markets, and hence their political legitimacy.

5. I am aware that this account contradicts the orthodoxy begun by Miller and Modigliani, supra ch IV, n. 11, according to which an efficient market should price various financial structures appropriately, making the choice of structure (absent tax or other exogenous consideration) irrelevant. For discussion of the importance of structure to even identifying what constitutes a securities exchange, much less evaluating its operation, see Ruben Lee, *What is an Exchange? The Automation, Management, and Regulation of Financial Markets* (Oxford: Oxford University Press, 1998).

6. It is worth recalling that the merger wave of the 1980s and the emergence of leveraged buyouts was funded largely by debt rather than equity. At the level of abstraction of the text at this point, however, distinctions between debt and equity are unimportant.

7. *Securities & Exchange Commission v. Ralston Purina Co.*, 346 U.S. 119 (1953).

8. Hedge funds are not even defined by the securities laws, but may instead be understood as an investment vehicle (a fund organized as a limited partnership among wealthy parties) that exists in the locus of exceptions from the securities laws that might, in the absence of the exception, be expected to apply. So, for example, under section 4(2) of the Securities Act of 1933, the interests in the private limited partnership, the fund itself, must be registered as securities, if the partnership has more than thirty-five such limited partners. From the perspective of hedge funds, at least, this would be bad because it would limit the number of investors and so the ability of hedge funds to pool large amounts of money. Almost as importantly, registration would require updating and would hinder the ability of the fund to move quickly and anonymously. Fortunately (from the fund's perspective, at least), being wealthy enough to invest in a hedge fund is wealthy enough to be an "accredited investor," as defined by Regulation D. Because "accredited investors" are not counted in Section 4(2)'s limit of thirty-five partners, hedge funds can have more than thirty-five participants. In addition to the fact that interests in the fund are not registered as securities under the Securities Act or the Securities Exchange Act, the fund itself is not registered as an investment company under the Investment Company Act of 1940. Moreover, the general partner of such a fund need not be registered as an investment adviser under the Investment Adviser Act of 1940.

9. In general, however, the antifraud provisions of the securities law would apply even to such "private" transactions, i.e., nonregistered offerings are not completely unregulated.

10. For example, start-up companies generally seek several rounds of private financing before attempting the cost of an initial public offering.

11. There is a substantial legal literature arguing that insider trading is efficient, and therefore should not be illegal. Henry Manne is generally considered the most influential voice of this position.

12. The National Market System (NMS) is obviously in tension with the two-tiered structure of the equity markets. The NMS may be understood as the idealization, or perfection, of the virtues of the public equity markets as understood by the Depression-era securities laws.

13. We are all capitalists now (or we are truly marginal), and so we wish to be treated, if not like citizens, at least as participants. To exaggerate for emphasis, we expect the aggregation of the

market to suggest, if not mirror, the representation of the institutions of republican government. This point is made unapologetically by those, generally on the right, who understand the free market and democracy to be synonymous, or the market to be a replacement for governance. The point is also made by the SEC, with its incessant talk of the retail investor, the little guy with money in the stock markets, and worse still, widows and orphans. The point is, of course, an exaggeration—whatever the capital markets may be, they are not fora for republican self-government—but the fact that Wall Street will never be Rousseau's Geneva does not mean that society has no interest in fostering broad based access to the capital markets.

14. This problem is central to analyzing whether a government action took property, and therefore, under the Fifth Amendment to the U.S. Constitution, owes compensation to the owner of the property.

> The question of whether private property is at issue would seem to be logically antecedent to any takings decision. But from a realist perspective, property ultimately is defined as a bundle of enforceable rights, that is, in terms of how an organ of government, a court, will act. Thus, in reviewing the actions of coordinate branches of government, courts may, to the frustration of academics, jump the metaphysical question: what is property? Instead, courts may review government action directly: should the government compensate the claimant? If the answer is yes, then it must be said, in the course of granting relief under the Takings Clause, that the government took a property interest. Successful takings claims define property rights as much as the other way around. The circularity is complete.

David A. Westbrook, "Administrative Takings: A Realist Perspective on the Practice and Theory of Regulatory Takings Cases," 74 *Notre Dame L. Rev.* (1999): 717, 757–58 (citation omitted).

15. At present, however, it is difficult to talk unself-consciously about the distinction between public and private, between laws and the markets laws would inform. There are a number of not very consistent reasons for this state of intellectual affairs. Economists have increasingly insisted that so-called "public" matters should be understood in terms of microeconomic ("rational") drives first used to characterize market behavior. Progressives of all stripes have long insisted on the legal (and in that sense public and politically contestable) character of "private" systems of ordering. More practically, the economic importance of government action—ranging from trade law to intellectual property protection to outright business—bulks so large in our consciousness of how politics is actually done, rivaled only by our awareness of the influence of money on the institutions of republican government, that the idea of a public realm, distinct from oligarchical interests, or a private realm, whence government does not tread, seems hopelessly naive. Perhaps more importantly still, the private is widely understood to have overwhelmed the public. Markets have triumphed; governments are increasingly irrelevant. So it is said by globalization enthusiasts. More specifically, the despatialization of electronic capital means that governments—now relatively local entities—have difficulty regulating the financial markets. The asymmetry between global money and national regulation might even be taken to mean that political economy is a purely theoretical enterprise, that no practical policy, no law, is possible.

16. "The Amazing Disintegrating Firm—Enron," *The Economist* (U.K.) (Dec. 18, 2001): 77.

Chapter XIII

1. This essay seeks to explore the structure of sound decisions to organize some aspect of society through markets. For purposes of this discussion, therefore, markets are assumed to be relatively healthy, that is, fairly competitive markets. Markets need not be competitive, of course, but insofar as they are not, they become difficult to justify as a mode of social arrangement. In recognition of the fact that many of our markets are not very competitive, considerable effort has been devoted to explaining why market power (might) is more or less right, or at least not all that bad. So, for example, some people manage to believe that market power might be disciplined without competition, perhaps by fear that other firms may enter the market, or fear of new technologies that are likely to transform the market. We all have to make our peace.

2. However, modern financial theory—after Fischer Black, Myron Scholes, and Robert Merton—analyzes complex transactions by conceiving them as a combinations of assets, liabilities, and put and call options, which can then be priced.

3.   Economists tend to use the word "contract" for any voluntary and reciprocal transaction, a usage that would constitute malpractice for lawyers, for whom "contract" means a legally enforceable agreement. The distinction is important, because the concept of enforceability links contract and property. Contract rights are property rights because the plaintiff in a successful case founded on a contract has a right to dominion, good against the world and enforceable by the polity. Enforceability of the agreement, its existence as a legally binding contract as opposed to talk, publicly legitimates, and so politicizes, the relationship.

4.   The proposition that the distinction between a transaction's assumptions and its objectives requires, as opposed to merely reiterates, the distinction between government and market, public and private, may be politically contingent. One can imagine, and there is reason to believe, that societies have existed in which property is secured by force and status within a clan or tribe; obligation is guaranteed by religious sanction and fear of retaliation; and law is understood as a suprapolitical order. While anthropologists suggest that even such a society is likely to have a sense of light and dark in human affairs, of decorum and so public and private, the distinction between public and private need not inform conceptions of private property and private legal ordering through contract, on the one hand, and a sovereign state, on the other, which resolves disputes in the private sphere. In a society more civilized than Homer's, however, it appears that sovereignty's requirements engender opposing orders (noble, clerical, or private) with some authority of their own, and hence the jurisdictional fights that moderns experience as the bifurcation between public and private. That, in fact, is one of the problems in the *Iliad*—Achilles is outraged at Agamemnon's repossession of his prize, the slave girl Briseis. But it is not entirely clear whether Achilles is angry because he contests the right of Agamemnon to repossess the slave (contests the political authority of the King), or because Achilles is insulted by Agamemnon's decision to take the girl (contests the dominance of the man). Nestor's speech suggests that both are at issue—here as elsewhere the *Iliad* stands at the dawn of what we might regard as Western civilization.

5.   Although state of nature stories generally make little sense as historical accounts, it is worth noting that one of the earliest of the common law writs was that of *novel diseisin*, through which property was restored to its prior holder while questions of title were resolved.

6.   Indeed, the present period is remarkable for the spectacle of government officials declaring that the task at hand is simply beyond the competence of government officials such as themselves. Instead of attempting to do the impossible, one hears that governments should recognize the superior force (and, fortunately, superior if often inscrutable wisdom) of markets. This attitude reaches a fever pitch, oddly enough, among the civil servants entrusted with the regulation of financial markets, and the participants in such highly regulated markets. Markets are not to be led, and human innovation cannot be predicted, so governance is the . . . well, it is unclear what governance is for, but usually the punishment of outright fraud. What used to be called the ship of state—implying a pilot—is now understood to be more of a raft, or perhaps flotsam, borne along on the tide of opinion and desire and fantasy and hard work and so forth and so on called markets, as if we were not somehow responsible for both river and raft.

7.   After the appointment of Paul Volcker to the chairmanship of the Federal Reserve Board in 1979, the Fed followed Germany's Bundesbank in treating price stability as the most important macroeconomic objective, i.e., unemployment and growth rates would, if necessary, be sacrificed on the altar of price stability.

8.   It is true that certain deals carry political risk insurance, because there is a nonnegligible chance that a government could expropriate property central to the deal, that is, the institution of property might itself be on the table. One might understand the use of political risk insurance to demonstrate that transactions can go forward, regardless of what is on the table. But it would be more accurate to say that the necessity for such insurance means that otherwise deals do not go forward. Political risk insurance may be excessively expensive or unavailable, thereby precluding the transaction. Moreover, political risk insurance is often provided at below-market rates by governments or international institutions such as the World Bank Group's Multilateral Investment Guarantee Agency (MIGA), expressing a political decision, taken at national or multilateral level, to support transactions in the name of development.

9.   On the other hand, currency controls—particularly at the national level—provide tempting opportunities for corruption.

10. As a matter of intellectual history, biologists seem to have conceived nature much as industrial capitalism was contemporaneously conceived. This was certainly true in the nine-

teenth century, and is probably true today, i.e., the resurgence of interest in disequilibrium and creative destruction in economics may well be related to the move to discontinuous models of evolution.

11. This discomfort with the markets we inherit is conventionally and earnestly discussed among legal scholars in terms of the injustice of distribution, i.e., marketplace games are unfair because they are skewed to benefit those already in privileged positions. The argument from fairness masks a deeper anxiety: no set of rules can be justified. The game cannot be played until it is played out, at which point there will be winners—and losers. Distributional arguments are thus commonly expressions of guilt, liberal or otherwise. However, such arguments need not be expressions of guilt: some people actually do care about equality, solidarity, and the like, quite apart from any feelings of guilt they may or may not have.

12. Sometimes *Fortuna* is strong and bad, and brings inconveniences, disasters, eventually death. In such cases, wealth (money and its twin, property) serves as a shield against misfortune, rather than the sword with which new horizons are threatened. Wealth, particularly in the form of contingent contractual rights to payments, i.e., insurance, helps people to live without untoward fear of various forms of misfortune. Wealth also allows parents to provide for their children, and do something to secure their happiness, or at least their safety. Wealth grants the gentleman his leisure, freedom from banal importunities. And, as Madison was so concerned to ensure, wealth even can secure the individual against his own society, so long as the society remains committed to property rights. Many areas of the law, including labor, environment, health and safety regulation, tort, and the effort to ensure fair trade, justify themselves by defending a privileged status quo ante against the onslaught of misfortune, one might say, ally themselves with the party of insurance. One could go on, but the point is that markets, particularly financial markets, are the terrain on which we confront the future.

13. Price stability does not require a theory of value—the question is the change in price, not whether price reflects, in some profound sense, value.

14. Central bankers incessantly talk about their faith in markets, but it is difficult to imagine a less market-oriented activity than monetary policy.

Chapter XIV

1. Similar things may be said about the impossible distinction between law and politics. Realist theories of international relations focus on a world of national self-interest, while legalistic efforts toward articulating international law concentrate on a principled context in which international affairs may be conducted.

2. The United States and Great Britain officially maintained that Operation Iraqi Freedom (the toppling of Saddam Hussein's regime in 2003) was legal, as a matter of technical international law (and quite apart from questions of what obedience is due to such law). Although this view was widely criticized, and a range of concerns from philosophy to history to morality to politics are immediately implicated, as a technical legal argument, the Coalition's view was not implausible. International law is, to put the matter gently, ill determined, even for law. The point here, however, is only that the governments of the United States and Great Britain made legal arguments, rather than claiming that international law did not apply.

3. Moreover, we rely on government to legitimate the desire to be rid of society itself, including its government, that is, we rely on government to preserve the semblance of nature. I consider this point at more depth in the essay "Island on the Horizon of Desire," published as the second "meditation" in David A. Westbrook, "Triptych: Three Meditations on How Law Rules after Globalization," ch. VIII n. 16 supra.

4. The moral/intellectual problem posed by the rhetoric of liberalism—how to have a discussion of the good when such discussion is incompatible with the terms of political discourse—is thus solved by the creation of bureaucracies, which are liberally legitimated but fundamentally illiberal institutions.

5. There is a perhaps dramatic tendency to understand the student revolts in 1968 as the watershed moment when the university transformed itself. In consequence, to my mind undue attention has been paid to the intellectual importance of the late 60s, and in particular to the student revolts at Paris and Columbia. It is also worth noting, in this regard, that Belgian regionalism is often dated from the strife between Flemish and French faculty at

Leuven/Louvain. The problem with this tendency is that all the participants presume the spiritual centrality of the university, and understood such centrality rather traditionally, as connected with the culture's quest for transcendent truth. The fact that the '60s were in so many ways excessive—politically, chemically, sexually, and so forth—does not mean that such excesses were not undertaken and understood to be part of a time of awakening, discovery, new truths, great liberation, and other nonsense, and the university was the place where such truths were to be found. My sense is that at some point considerably later, that sense of the centrality of the university died among better minds—once the university was understood in terms of employment, excellence, administration, and similar concepts, it became difficult to take the university any more seriously than other banalities. I have written about these matters elsewhere at some length. See David A. Westbrook, "Pierre Schlag and the Temple of Boredom," ch. II, n. 22, supra.

6. There have been instances, e.g., Paris in the time of Abelard, when the university may be understood to have been centered on students.

7. As Marx knew and the Chicago school of law and economics has rather recently demonstrated, there is nothing so practical as a good "theory," i.e., a good discrediting of the other side combined with an intellectually tidy defense of one's own proposals.

8. In Kafka's *The Trial*, K was invited to become an official of sorts, when he was asked to carry out his death sentence upon himself, i.e., to become an agent of the state that was killing him. K maintains that he lacked the strength, but we are the richer for the fact that Kafka was unwilling or unable to comply with the strictures of his world, to find his success within the structure of an insurance company. Kafka, however, was an artist, a genius in the pejorative sense, and lived a heavy life—his example is demographically irrelevant, and his actions can hardly be regarded on political grounds.

9. Jules Verne, *Paris in the Twentieth Century*, trans. Richard Howard (New York: Random House, 1996).

10. On its own terms, the language is incoherent because a prostitute may gain self-respect in the same way a business owner or a manager gains self-respect, by being well paid—the real objection, difficult to express in polite liberal language, is to understanding oneself as a slut.

11. Consider another example: What do we mean when we say that the guard of a concentration camp is "dehumanized" by his job?

12. It behooves us to confront such an argument, even if we do not like it.

13. Jules Verne's scientists provided recurring images in the work of Paul Delvaux, whose paintings introduce and strangely illustrate the parts of this book.

14. "How it actually has been" was what the great German historian Ranke asserted that the historian ought to write. The status of truth in history and in the social sciences more generally, and hence the right conduct of these enterprises, indeed, the status of truth in Ranke's slogan, have all been the subject of endless debates that this note will not resolve. Without resolving such problems in any fine grained manner, however, it still seems reasonable to demand that history (or social science) understood as such, i.e., as an enterprise that purports or at least intends to be objective (*wissenschaftlich*), should understand itself as different from social criticism understood as such, and vice versa.

15. For a perhaps familiar analogy, state of nature stories take place in some context that does not exist for anthropologists. Anthropologists have repeatedly pointed out that there never was a state of nature in which individuals came together and agreed to form a state. Anthropologists tell other stories about how they think human societies were formed. In so doing, anthropologists miss the point that nobody, certainly not Hobbes or today's economists, is talking about primitive people in the dawn of time. State of nature stories structure the way we imagine the contemporary relationship between state and citizen, and so our ability to conduct constitutional politics. Similarly, the idea of liberal decision making that takes place behind the veil of ignorance is not a way that a decision is actually reached. Nobody lives behind a veil; we all live in a context. The metaphor of the veil is a way that we think about, and perhaps aspire to reach, just decisions. The way in which social criticism is true is difficult to express, but its truths certainly are not falsifiable in the sense that the right citation from the historical record could be dispositive.

16. This was reported to be Adam's Smith's response to Sinclair's worry that, after its defeat in the battle of Saratoga, Great Britain was ruined. See John Rae, *Life of Adam Smith* (New York: Macmillan, 1895): xxii.

17. Socrates may have laughed at Aristophanes' *Clouds*, but it is also said that, in his youth, Plato aspired to write tragedy, and in some way, he succeeded.
18. These are the anxieties aroused by theater; resolving the conflicts within the metropolitan situation by cultivating a dramatic understanding among the citizenry is problematic.
19. Milosz remarked:
    > Western audiences confronted with poems or novels written in Poland, Czechoslovakia or Hungary, or with films produced there, possibly intuit a similarly sharpened consciousness, in a constant struggle against limitations imposed by censorship. Memory thus is our force, it protects us against a speech entwining upon itself like the ivy when it does not find a support on a tree or a wall.

    Czeslaw Milosz, "Nobel Lecture" (8 December 1980), in *Beginning with My Streets: Essays and Recollections* (New York: Farrar Straus, and Giroux, 1991): 273.
20. "Debating clubs are to a certain extent a substitute for theatrical entertainments: an American cannot converse, but he can discuss; and when he attempts to talk he falls into a dissertation. He speaks to you as if he was addressing a meeting; and if he should warm in the course of the discussion, he will infallibly say 'Gentlemen,' to the person with whom he is conversing." Alexis de Toqueville, *Democracy in America* (Birmingham, Alabama: American Classics Library, 1990 (facsimile of first American edition, Adlard and Saunders, New York, 1838): 231.
21. Locke said that all the world was America, a space unencumbered by history and especially money, ch VIII, n. 3, supra. Rather than wilderness, the City (and the United States) are societies that suppress the particular and local, i.e., history and identity, in favor of the commensurable and mobile.

Afterword

1. *M'Culloch v. State of Maryland*, 17 U.S. 316, 408 (1819), ("In considering this question, then, we must never forge that it is a *constitution* we are expounding.") (emphasis in original).
2. Robert E. Sherwood, *Roosevelt and Hopkins: An Intimate History* (New York: Harper, 1948): 9: "He [Roosevelt] liked to fancy himself as a practical, down-to-earth, horse sense realist— he often used to say 'Winston and Uncle Joe and I get along together because we're all *realists*'—and yet his idealism was actually no less empyrean than Woodrow Wilson's."

Index

Abelard, Peter, 342n.6
Acheson, Dean, 23, 32–33
Acton, John Emerich, (Lord Acton) 264
Adams, John, 323n. 21
advertising, 154–155
Agreement on Trade Related Aspects of Intellectual
    Property Rights (TRIPS), 10
Airbus S.A.S., 10
alienation, ch. VI
    relation to authenticity, 141–144
apology, 303
Arendt, Hannah, 278, 335n.2, 336n.17
Aristophanes, 343n.17
Aristotle, 31, 40, 49, 55, 88, 120, 149, 162, 251,
    284, 304, 334n.21
Arrow, Kenneth, 316n. 12
Augsburg, Peace or Treaty of, 20
Augustine, St. of Hippo, 111, 327n.18, 332n.14
Austen, Jane, 324n. 4
authenticity
    etymology, 145
    relation to alienation, 141–144

Bacon, Francis, 332n.14
Bank of England, 28, 72, 309n. 11
bargaining table. *See* markets, synchronous order
Baring, John, 320n. 34
Basic v. Levinson, 338n.3
Bass, Thomas A., 312n. 10
Benn, Gottfried, 201, 334n.18
Bentham, Jeremy, 315n. 27
Berle, Adolf, 310n. 14, 316n. 15
Berlin, Isaiah, 38, 217, 337n.1
Berman, Harold, 315n. 27
Bernstein, Michael A., 309n. 6, 330n.3
Bernstein, Peter, 316n. 12

Black, Fisher, 316n. 12, 324n. 5, 339n.2
Boeing Co., 10
Bohr, Niels, 178
Brandeis, Louis, 337n.1
Brecht, Berthold, 121
Bretton Woods Conference, 28–29, 229
Bretton Woods currency arrangement, 27, 28, 37,
    41, 57, 261, 263
Bretton Woods Institutions, 3, 12, 22, 26, 140, 167,
    171, 172, 180, 210, 228, 230–231, 310n. 18
Breyer, Stephen, 318n. 31
bubble theory of U.S. equity markets in 1990s,
    76–78. *See also* financial crises
Buchan, James, 225, 324n. 7, 329n.7, 332n.15,
    334n.18
Büchner, Georg, 121
Buffett, Warren, 110, 318n. 5
Bundesbank, 269, 340n.7
bureaucracy
    as mode of intellectual life, 276–279
    as response to alienation, 279–280
Burke, Edmund, 186

Caesar, Julius, 100
Calvin, John, 89
Camus, Albert, 164, 165, 329n.14
capital
    historically defined, 93–95
    politically defined, 92–93
capitalism
    as generally used, 3–5
    reconception and defense needed, 1–5
    as used in this text, 1, 5
Carlyle, Thomas, 284, 333n.15
Castells, Manuel, 307n. 4
Castro, Fidel, 30